Systematic Musicology: Empirical and Theoretical Studies

Hamburger Jahrbuch für Musikwissenschaft

Herausgegeben vom
Musikwissenschaftlichen Institut
der Universität Hamburg

Redaktion:
Arne von Ruschkowski

Vol. 28

PETER LANG
Frankfurt am Main · Berlin · Bern · Bruxelles · New York · Oxford · Wien

Albrecht Schneider
Arne von Ruschkowski
(eds.)

Systematic Musicology: Empirical and Theoretical Studies

PETER LANG
Internationaler Verlag der Wissenschaften

Bibliographic Information published by the Deutsche Nationalbibliothek
The Deutsche Nationalbibliothek lists this publication in the Deutsche Nationalbibliografie; detailed bibliographic data is available in the internet at http://dnb.d-nb.de.

Gratefully acknowledging financial
support by the University of Hamburg.

ISSN 0342-8303
ISBN 978-3-631-63553-7
© Peter Lang GmbH
Internationaler Verlag der Wissenschaften
Frankfurt am Main 2011
All rights reserved.

All parts of this publication are protected by copyright. Any utilisation outside the strict limits of the copyright law, without the permission of the publisher, is forbidden and liable to prosecution. This applies in particular to reproductions, translations, microfilming, and storage and processing in electronic retrieval systems.

www.peterlang.de

Table of Content

Albrecht Schneider, Arne von Ruschkowski
Introduction 7

Albrecht Schneider, Arne von Ruschkowski
Techno, Decibels, and Politics: an Empirical Study of Modern Dance Music
Productions, Sound Pressure Levels, and 'Loudness Perception' 11

Daniel Müllensiefen, Geraint Wiggins
Polynomial Functions as a Representation of Melodic Phrase Contour 63

Klaus Frieler, Frank Höger, Jörg Korries
Meloworks - An Integrated Retrieval, Analysis and E-learning Platform
for Melody Research 89

Albrecht Schneider, Valeri Tsatsishvili
Perception of Musical Intervals at Very Low Frequencies:
Some Experimental Findings 99

Robert Mores
Nasality in Musical Sounds – a few Intermediate Results 127

Florian Pfeifle
Air Modes in Stringed Lute-like Instruments from Africa and China 137

Tim Ziemer
Psychoacoustic Effects in Wave Field Synthesis Applications 153

Orie Takada
Sound Radiation Patterns in Classical Singing Styles 163

Andreas Beurmann, Albrecht Schneider
Some Observations on a Stein-Conrad Hammerflügel from 1793 175

Rolf Bader, Albrecht Schneider
Playing "Live" at the *Star-Club*: Reconstructing the Room Acoustics
of a Famous Music Hall 185

Till Strauf
"You Don´t See the Stitching" – Some Comments on Stylistic Diversity
in Rock Using the Example of Jethro Tull 211

Jan Clemens Moeller
Comments about Joni Mitchell´s Composing Techniques
and Guitar Style 233

Ulrich Morgenstern
Egalitarianism and Elitism in Ethnomusicology
and Folk Music Scholarship 249

Rolf Bader
Buddhism, Animism, and Entertainment in Cambodian Melismatic
Chanting *smot* – History and Tonal System 283

Rytis Ambrazevičius
Concerning the Question of "Loosely-Knit" Roughly Equidistant Scale
in Traditional Music 307

List of Contributors 317

Introduction: Systematic Musicology and Empirical Research

As is known from many sources, Greek and Hellenic philosophers and scientists directed much of their inquiry to a field covering fundamentals of music and mathematics (see, e.g. Szabo 1978, Barker 2007). Different from biased opinion according to which these approaches were based on mere 'speculation' (by the way, an approach relevant to heuristics), there is evidence that theoretical thought was accompanied by observation of nature as well as by some experimentation. In regard to music, at times also 'practical' issues were taken into account (as is obvious from the writings of Aristoxenus).

Music and music theory again played a central role within the framework of the scientific revolution that took place in Europe between, roughly, 1550 and 1750. It was during this period that basic discoveries relevant to acoustics and psychoacoustics were made (cf. Cannon & Dostrovsky 1981, Cohen 1984). Again, calculation and also 'speculation' were combined with by then much more extended and thorough observations and experiments, many of which had an impact on contemporary organology and instrument building as well as on other areas of musical practice. Also, music theory took up concepts developed in acoustics in order to maintain scientific foundations. In particular Rameau has been criticized for having introduced 'physicalism' into music theory (Handschin 1948), and Riemann has been blamed to have even conducted dubious 'moonshine experiments' to give his harmonic theory a semblance of rigour. Such criticism perhaps is not without reason. It seems inadequate though given the problems any attempt at establishing a 'scientific' music theory (demanding more than just a practical and propaedeutical orientation) had to face.

In fact, it can be shown that a certain amount of 'physicalism' in music theory was, and still is appropriate (or at least unavoidable) if music is considered first and foremost as consisting of sound organized in tonal, temporal, spectral and dynamic patterns (cf. Cogan & Pozzi 1976) that is produced by instruments (including the voice) and is perceived by listeners. Even though Rameau, Tartini, Riemann and other theorists perhaps did not succeed in solving some intricate problems in regard to defining the minor tonality, they rightly underpinned the necessity of including acoustics and psychoacoustics into music theory (cf. Schneider 2010/11). Giving music theory and music related research 'scientific' foundations implies that mathematical treatment of such matters to some degree is not only useful but indispensable (cf. Benson 2006).

From this context sketched in brief, it should be clear that Systematic Musicology as established in the 19th century by Helmholtz, Stumpf and other scientists (cf. Schneider 2008) in part must be considered as a continuation of fundamental research that was begun in antiquity and given new directions in the 16th, 17th, and 18th centuries, respectively. In particular experimental investigations and analytical studies in the field of vibration and sound paved the way for modern musical acoustics. This field, to be sure, was not restricted to theory but included various 'applications' (as is obvious from, for example, Chladni's work on developing new musical instruments; see Ullmann 1996).

Also in the course of the 19th century, areas of research now known as psychophysics and psychoacoustics were established. Empirical studies directed to basic mechanism of pitch perception did yield the now "classical" paradigms of frequency analysis (according to Fourier and Ohm) and periodicity detection (as proposed first by Seebeck and explored in the 20th century by Schouten and his students; see de Boer 1976). Also, models such as the "two-componential" helix for pitch developed by the mathematical psychologist Moritz W. Drobisch as early as 1855 made a lasting impact (cf. Schneider 2008). In 1860, Fechner published his *Elemente der Psychophysik*, in which he discussed, among many other issues, sensation and scaling of pitch and of loudness. In 1863, Helmholtz' seminal book on *Tonempfindungen* appeared, in which he established a framework ranging from acoustics and psychoacoustics to music theory. By 1890, two vols of Stumpf's *Tonpsychologie* had become available (as had the Phonograph and the Gramophone, two inventions that changed music production and distribution as well as reception of music substantially).

The field of research that emerged in the course of the 19th century, and that was labelled Systematic Musicology (Systematische Musikwissenschaft), included empirical orientation and experimental methodology from the very beginning. One could point to Helmholtz' experiments on the sensation of combination tones as well as on roughness and beats (Helmholtz 1870, 239-331), or to Stumpf's many experiments on *Verschmelzung* (Stumpf 1890, § 19), in which he acted as both "experimenter" and "subject". Stumpf gave meticulous descriptions of his observations, which were obtained in compliance with explicit rules. However, experiments where a researcher reports what he has perceived when listening to certain sound stimuli might be looked upon with suspicion by such 'empiricists' demanding "objective" measurement. Of course, Stumpf conducted also experiments with subjects having little musical training and competence, and he even gave some quantitative data in regard to perception of 'tonal fusion' (number of judgements for certain interval categories relative to percentages of correct judgements; see Stumpf 1890, 144-149). He considered such data illustrative, as they were mostly corroborating what he had already found for himself, yet not in any way decisive since the importance of a judgement for Stumpf was largely correlated with the musical competence of the experimenter acting as observer, and by no means dependent on the sample size (in Stumpf's view: a number of n "unmusical" subjects cannot "outweigh" one professional expert in music as their judgements are less solid and reliable, and more prone to error and circumstantial influences). It is perhaps not surprising that, after decades of experiments where researchers were often counting on observations obtained from 'random samples' comprising k subjects, Manfred Clynes (1995), a researcher also trained as a professional artist, stressed the role of the musical expert as someone who can do the most profound and valid judgements in experiments on music (his claim is that adequacy of judgements correlates significantly with musical proficiency).

Of course, data obtained from a single informant or subject in an experiment can constitute 'empirical evidence'. The term 'empirical' in this way should not be interpreted in the very narrow sense it was given in the context of behaviorism and operationalism in the 20th century. From a philosophical perspective, 'empirical' in Kant's epistemology (KdRV B74/75) means a mode of thinking that includes sensation and perception, and which leads to *Anschauung* (images and formation of concepts relating to objects that are 'real') as complementary to 'pure' reasoning based on abstract notions. Brentano (1874) in his philosophical psychology extended 'empirical' even to phenomena accessible by what he described as *innere Wahrnehmung* (not to be confused with 'introspection'), for example, objects stored in long-term memory (e.g., melodies) that can be 'perceived' internally.

Hume (1748/2006) had stressed the fundamental importance of experience against a priori thought and abstract reasoning (though he considered the latter legitimate in mathematics). Notwithstanding Hume's sceptical chapters on making inferences for the future from observations of past events, it was a methodology based on induction that guided much of 19th century science (along with some similarly strong concepts such as 'evolution' [natural, technical and social] and [technical and social] 'progress'). In opposition to idealist and 'mentalist' orientations, 19th century philosophy of science as developped by John Stuart Mill and Auguste Comte advanced arguments to focus research on what is 'real', 'observable', and 'positive'. Mill's (1843/1973, book III) justification of 'induction' was influential in many ways; even the concept of 'unconscious inferences' (which is an integral part of Helmholtz' theory of perception) can be identified as an offspring of 'inductivism'.

The works of Comte and Mill became well known also in Germany and Austria where 'empiricism' was further advocated by Ernst Mach whose writings on science and scientific method as well as on topics of psychology and psychophysiology where widely read around 1900-1920. At Vienna, in the 1920s and early 1930s, philosophers and scientists (coming from various disciplines ranging from mathematics and physics to linguistics and psychology) constituted a movement known as 'neopositivism' (cf. Haller 1993) that became quite influential in the United States, and in disciplines such as psychology (cf. Boring 1950). The first decades of the 20th century also saw the vast development of mathematical statistics (by Karl and Egon Pearson, Ronald Fisher, Jerzy Neyman, and others) that was a crucial condition for a new paradigm to emerge in psychology summed under the title of "The Inference Revolution" (Gigerenzer & Murray 1987, ch. I). It was during the years 1940-1955 that statistical concepts gained a prominent place in experimental design, and that testing of hypotheses as well as using inferential statistical methodology were regarded state of the art (if not mandatory) in psychological research. Researchers were expected to present "significant" results (by refuting a "null hypothesis" H_0) if they wanted to see their work published.

The scheme of formulating (in the most simple case) pairs of hypotheses (H_0, H_1) and then "test" $H_0 : H_1$ works perfectly well since it assumes (often implicitly) that two points X_i and X_j representing the [arithmetic] means for a random variable from two samples drawn at random from a population are sufficiently apart from each other ($X_i \neq X_j$) as well as from the mean of all means derived from samples (i.e., the 'population parameter', μ). It can be shown that for a random variable representing a property or feature that is normally distributed within a given population, the likelihood for the two cases $H_0: \mu - X_i = 0$ and $H_0: X_i = X_j$ to occur in a standard normal distribution is close to zero. That is, H_0 represents the two most unlikely cases, and hence can be typically "refuted" with ease while it is more demanding to "prove" H_1 (see Bortz 1984, ch. 5).

The "Inference Revolution" led almost directly to the "mind as computer" metaphor since some models of causal reasoning apparently treated the mind as calculating a Fisherian ANOVA including the F-test in making decisions (cf. Gigerenzer 2000, ch. 1). The "Inference Revolution" was followed by what has been labelled "The Cognitive Revolution" (see Gardner 1987), which includes several and quite diverse ingredients (from the rise of computer science and 'artificial intelligence' to developments in brain research and neurophysiology, not to forget a reactivation of Gestalt psychology within a new framework). One of the welcome effects of this 'revolution' was a to break the barriers of behavioristic 'empiricism' and to restitute 'the mind' as a meaningful area of research accessible to both theoretic reasoning and empirical investigations (see Botterill & Carruthers 1999, Metzinger 2003). The paradigm of cognitivism opened fresh perspectives for inter- and transdisciplinary research that soon included perception and cognition of music (see, e.g., Howell et al. 1985, Sloboda 1985, Dowling & Harwood 1986, Bregman 1990, Leman 1995, 1997, Godøy & Jørgensen 2001, Deliège & Wiggins 2006). In the context of cognitivism, modelling, simulation and also advanced statistical methodology have gained central roles (cf. Leman 2008, Müllensiefen 2010).

Two recent volumes (24, 2008 and 25, 2009) of the *Hamburger Jahrbuch für Musikwissenschaft* have been devoted to Systematic and Comparative Musicology (see Schneider 2008, Bader 2009). Both volumes offer a range of studies from musical acoustics, psychoacoustics, psychology of music and neurocognition but also include articles on 'systematic' music theory (as different from historical approaches) and on methodological issues. Further, both volumes contain ethnomusicological contributions as well as articles dealing with folk and popular music(s).

The volume at hand shows a similar pattern of content reflecting a broad spectrum of research as well as an inter- or transdisciplinary perspective (which was characteristic of Systematic and Comparative Musicology from the very beginning). Some of the articles include considerations and results that may be of use in 'applied' contexts such as public health or sound system design. After all, it has been argued that 'science' these days should take greater responsibility in regard to 'society' at large, meaning the days of small elitist circles working within 'peer groups' of experts secluded from 'the world' may be numbered, or at least that 'the public' may want to see even more benefits from science than it did already (cf. Nowotny et al. 2001). Though Systematic Musicology almost by definition has a focus on fundamental research covering musical acoustics and psychoacoustics, psychology of music and related areas (cf. Leman 1995, 1997, 2008, Schneider 2008, Bader 2005, 2009, Godøy & Leman 2010), this does neither preclude practical applications nor that sociocultural phenomena are duly considered. In this respect, the present volume offers articles on popular and folk music as well as a study of concepts and ideologies pertaining to "ethno" and folk music research in addition to those papers that take an approved or new 'empirical' direction in regard to method and content.

Hamburg, June 2011

Albrecht Schneider   Arne von Ruschkowski

References

Bader, Rolf 2005. *Computational Mechanics of the Classical Guitar*. Berlin: Springer.

Bader, Rolf (ed.) 2009. *Musical Acoustics, Neurocognition and Psychology of Music. Current Research in Systematic Musicology at the Institute of Musicology, University of Hamburg*. (=Hamburger Jahrbuch für Musikwissenschaft 25). Frankfurt/M. etc.: P. Lang.

Barker, Andrew 2007. *The Science of Harmonics in Classical Greece*. Cambridge: Univ. Pr.

Benson, Dave 2006. *Music: a mathematical Offering*. Cambridge: Cambridge Univ. Pr.

Boring, Edwin 1950. *A History of Experimental Psychology*. 2nd ed. Englewood Cliffs, N.J.: Prentice – Hall.

Bortz, Jürgen 1984. *Lehrbuch der empirischen Forschung*. Berlin (etc.): Springer.

Botterill, George, Peter Carruthers 1999. *The Philosophy of Psychology*. Cambridge: Univ. Pr.

Bregman, Albert 1990. *Auditory Scene Analysis. The Perceptual Organization of Sound*. Cambridge, MA: MIT Pr.

Brentano, Franz von 1874. *Psychologie vom empirischen Standpunkt*. Bd 1. Leipzig: Duncker & Humblot.

Cannon, John, Sigalia Dostrovsky 1981. *The Evolution of Dynamics: Vibration Theory from 1687 to 1742*. New York: Springer.

Clynes, Manfred 1995. Microstructural musical linguistics: composer's pulses are liked most by the best musicians. *Cognition* 55, 269-310.

Cogan, Robert, Pozzi Escot 1976. *Sonic Design: The Nature of Sound and Music*. Englewood Cliffs, N.J.: Prentice-Hall.

Cohen, H. Floris 1984. *Quantifying Music. The Science of Music at the First Stage of the Scientific Revolution, 1580-1650*. Dordrecht, Boston: Reidel.

De Boer, Egbert 1976. On the "Residue" and Auditory Pitch Perception. In W.D. Keidel & W.D. Neff (eds.). *Handbook of Sensory Physiology*. Vol. V,3. Berlin, New York: Springer, 479-583.

Deliège, Irène, Geraint Wiggins (eds.) 2006. *Musical Creativity. Multidisciplinary Research in Theory and Practice*. Hove, New York: Psychology Pr.

Dowling, John, Dane Harwood 1986. *Music Cognition*. New York: Academic Pr.

Gardner, Howard 1987. *The Mind's New Science. A History of the Cognitive Revolution*. New York: Basic Books.

Gigerenzer, Gerd, David Murray 1987. *Cognition as intuitive statistics*. Hillsdale, N.J.: Erlbaum.

Gigerenzer, Gerd 2000. *Adaptive Thinking*. New York: Oxford Univ. Pr.

Godøy, Rolf Inge, Harald Jørgensen (eds.) 2001. *Musical Imagery*. Lisse (etc.): Swets & Zeitlinger.

Godøy, Rolf Inge, Marc Leman (eds.). *Musical Gestures. Sound, Movement and Meaning*. New York: Routledge.

Haller, Rudolf 1993. *Neopositivismus. Eine historische Einführung in die Philosophie des Wiener Kreises*. Darmstadt: Wiss. Buchges.

Handschin, Jacques 1948. *Der Toncharakter. Eine Einführung in die Tonpsychologie*. Zürich: Atlantis-Verlag.

Helmholtz, Hermann von 1870. *Die Lehre von den Tonempfindungen als physiologische Grundlage für die Theorie der Musik*. 3. Aufl. Braunschweig: Vieweg.

Howell, Peter, Ian Cross, Robert West (eds) 1985. *Musical Structure and Cognition*. Orlando, Fl. (etc.): Academic Pr.

Hume, David (1748/2006). *An Enquiry concerning human Understanding*. Critical edition. Ed. by Tom Beauchamp. Oxford: Clarendon 2006.

Leman, Marc 1995. *Music and Schema Theory. Cognitive Foundations of Systematic Musicology*. Berlin: Springer.

Leman, Marc (ed.) 1997. *Music, Gestalt, and Computing. Studies in Cognitive and Systematic Musicology*, Berlin, New York: Springer.

Leman, Marc 2008. *Embodied Music Cognition and Mediation Technology*. Cambridge, MA.: MIT Pr.

Metzinger, T 2003. *Being No One. The Self-model theory of subjectivity*. Cambridge, MA: MIT Pr.

Mill, John Stuart 1843/1973. *A System of Logic: ratiocinctive and inductive* (London 1843), ed. by John Robson (et al.). Toronto: Univ. of Toronto Pr.

Müllensiefen, Daniel 2010. Statistical techniques in music psychology: an update. In R. Bader, Chr. Neuhaus, U. Morgenstern (eds.). *Concepts, Experiments, and Fieldwork: Studies in Systematic Musicology and Ethnomusicology*. Frankfurt/M. (etc.): P. Lang, 193-215.

Nowotny, Helga, Peter Scott, Michael Gibbons 2001. *Re-thinking Science: Knowledge and the Public in an Age of Uncertainty*. Cambridge: Polity Pr. (Repr.: Oxford: Polity Pr. 2002).

Schneider, Albrecht 2008. Foundations of Systematic Musicology: a study in history and theory. In A. Schneider (ed.). *Systematic and Comparative Musicology: Concepts, Methods, Findings*. (=Hamburger Jahrbuch für Musikwissenschaft, Bd 24). Frankfurt/M. etc.: P. Lang, 11-71.

Schneider, Albrecht 2010. Music Theory: Speculation, Reasoning, Experience. A Perspective from Systematic Musicology. In Ph. Sprick/T. Janz (Hrsg.). *Musiktheorie / Musikwissenschaft. Geschichte – Methoden – Perspektiven*. Hildesheim, New York: Olms 2011, 23-67 (also *Zeitschrift der Gesellschaft für Musiktheorie*, October 2010; http://www.gmth.de/zeitschrift/artikel/574.aspx).

Sloboda, John 1985. *The Musical Mind. The Cognitive Psychology of Music*. Oxford: Clarendon Pr.

Stumpf, Carl 1890. *Tonpsychologie*. Bd II. Leipzig: Hirzel.

Szabo, Arpád 1978. *The Beginnings of Greek Mathematics*. Dordrecht, Boston: Reidel.

Ullmann, Dieter 1996. *Chladni und die Entwicklung der Akustik von 1750-1860*. Basel: Birkhäuser.

Albrecht Schneider
Arne von Ruschkowski

Techno, Decibels, and Politics: an Empirical Study of Modern Dance Music Productions, Sound Pressure Levels, and 'Loudness Perception'

Summary

This paper focuses on possible hearing damage for mainly young people from exposure to excessively loud music in discotheques, clubs, live music venues or by using mp3-players. Current risk evaluating procedures do not take into account a number of factors in an appropriate way, especially when 'high energy' music like various styles of techno, trash metal, but even modern pop music, is listened to. In our investigation, we started out with the analysis of several pieces of music from various styles (Techno, Gabber, Pop, Trash Metal, etc.) regarding their level and spectral content. It could be shown that a high overall level combined with reduced dynamics, a high amount of energy in low frequency bands and pulse-like sounds are generally used as stylistic devices in modern popular music. Especially with pulse-like sounds, there is a great risk of hearing damage because high energy levels are reached in a very short time span. In addition, exaggerated overall levels with reduced dynamics lead to a maximum of energy consumption by the hearing system for most of the listening time. Then, in a second step the tracks were played back over a professional sound system in a club located in Hamburg, recorded via an artificial head and analyzed for their sound pressure level with several common temporal and frequency weightings afterwards. It could be demonstrated that because of the typically high levels in clubs and discotheques, combined with the characteristically exaggerated low frequency components of the music, the commonly used dB[A]-measurement is not a valid predictor for the energy that reaches the ears in such listening situations. The dB[A]-filter cuts the frequency components that are essential for popular music. Consequently, the results of measurement are much lower compared to dB[C]-measurements, which seem to be more suitable for listening situations with high levels and overemphasis of low frequency bands like in discotheques. SPL readings obtained in dB[A] and dB[C] differ by 10 dB and more which means more than a triplication of sound pressure. Therefore, severe hearing damages are possible, even if 100 dB[A], nowadays used as a guideline for the level in discotheques, are not exceeded.

In summary, measurements of loudness levels which should help to prevent young people from hearing damage need to incorporate the distinct features of the acoustic stimulus and the listening situation. They should not be based on a norm designed to measure low-level environmental and industrial noise. Moreover, measurements must take the pulse-like sound structure of modern popular music styles into account.

Zusammenfassung

Eine Reihe von Untersuchungen aus den vergangenen Jahrzehnten haben an Hand empirischer Daten (vorwiegend Messungen des Schalldruckpegels [SPL] in Diskotheken oder bei Live-Konzerten sowie audiologische Befunde von Patienten bzw. Patientinnen) auf die Risiken von Hörschäden durch die Wahrnehmung lauter bzw. zu lauter Musik aufmerksam gemacht. Dabei wurden Messungen des Schalldruckpegels fast immer in dB[A] durchgeführt und die Messwerte ebenfalls mit dieser Frequenzgewichtung dargestellt und meist so erörtert, als wären Pegelangaben in dB[A] ein zuverlässiger Indikator des Hörschadenrisikos. Dies ist jedoch, wie in dieser Studie ausführlich dargelegt und an Hand verschiedener Messungen demonstriert wird, keineswegs der Fall. Vielmehr zeigen sich dB[A]-Messwerte gerade bei moderner Pop- und Rockmusik als mit systematischen Fehlern behaftet, da der in solchen Musikstilen meist extreme Anteil tieffrequenter Signal- bzw. Schallanteile bei der A-Bewertung durch ebenso massive Filterung weitgehend unterdrückt wird. Hinzu kommt, dass bei etlichen Messungen der impulsartige Signalverlauf der Musik, der etwa bei Techno-Produktionen, aber auch bei anderen Genres geradezu typisch ist, durch zeitliche Mittelwertsbildung (etwa mit der Zeitkonstante ‚slow') eingeebnet werden kann. Durch A-Bewertung und zeitliche Mittelung entsteht so häufig ein stark verfälschtes Bild über den tatsächlichen Energieinhalt und Energiefluss bei solcher Musik.

Die vorliegende Untersuchung analysiert daher zunächst fünf Produktionen aus den Bereichen Techno, Electro Pop und Trash Metal, um die zeitliche und die spektrale Struktur solcher Musik deutlich zu machen. Die gewählten Beispiele sind nicht etwa Sonderfälle, sondern stehen exemplarisch für Gattungen gleichartiger Produktionen.

Längere Ausschnitte der fünf Musikbeispiele wurden sodann in einem Musikclub in Hamburg über das dort installierte P.A.-System in etwa mit dem Schallpegel abgespielt, der auch sonst bei Veranstaltungen in diesem Club üblich ist. Die über das P.A.-System abgespielte Musik wurde mit einem Kunstkopf (Head Acoustics) auf der Tanzfläche aufgezeichnet und anschließend mit einer Akustik/Psychoakustik-Software (Artemis 11) analysiert. Dabei wurden jeweils die Frequenzgewichtungen A und C sowie die Zeitbewertungen ‚slow', ‚fast' und ‚impulse' angewandt. Bei der auf das hier vorliegende, impulsartige und „basslastige" Musikmaterial und die in Diskotheken tatsächlich herrschenden Schalldrücke sachgerecht anzuwendenden Frequenzgewichtung dB[C] und den Zeitbewertungen ‚fast' oder ‚impulse' wurden Pegelwerte von deutlich über 110 dB[C], sogar bis zu 126 dB[C] gemessen.

In Anbetracht der zeitlichen und spektralen Merkmale moderner Pop- und Rockmusik sowie deren Darbietung in Diskotheken und Clubs über professionelle P.A.-Systeme mit Subwoofern sind die aus vornehmlich politischen Gründen immer noch angewandten dB[A]-Messungen für Diskotheken und Live-Konzerte faktisch irrelevant und zur Risikobewertung von Hörschäden allenfalls dann noch geeignet, wenn den in dB[A] gemessenen Pegelwerten sachgerecht ein Zuschlag von durchschnittlich 10-12 dB (entsprechend den tatsächlich akustisch realisierten Pegeln in dB[C]) hinzugefügt wird. Außerdem bedarf die Impulsstruktur moderner Popularmusik (ebenso wie andere impulshafte Schallarten) einer besonderen Gewichtung.

1. Introduction

Already several decades ago, sound pressure levels (SPL) as measured in discotheques and at rock concerts were reported to exceed, on average, 100 dB[A]; the geometric mean for a number of measurements published in scientific articles then was calculated as 103.4 dB[A] (Clark 1991, 176). From the data significant risks in regard to noise induced hearing loss (NIHL) were deemed likely. Exposure of (mostly) young people to very loud music in discotheques and rock music venues as well as at open-air concerts since long is common practice in many countries. In Germany, events like the so-called "Love Parade" (1989-2010), a huge techno party organized as a procession of professional sound systems mounted on trucks, playing techno music for hours and hours, attracted hundreds of thousands or even millions of participants dancing to the music. In addition to visiting discotheques and live music venues, the use of portable electronic devices suited to play back music from digital sound files is as widespread among young people as is the use of earphones along with such devices. According to actual data, 84% of young German people (age 12-19) possess a MP3-Player, besides other equipment (Media Perspektiven Basisdaten 2010, 67). There is evidence that many individuals listen to music via earphones for more than one hour per day, and that 10% of the population of 11-17 year old youngsters employ levels of 100 dB[A] or even more (see Plontke & Zenner 2004, 130). From a broad range of studies investigating exposure to music as technically (re)produced sound, on the one hand, and hearing loss phenomena already observed in young people (including children), on the other, experts predict that 10 to 20% of young people will suffer considerable hearing loss affecting their ability to communicate within the next ten years (summaries of relevant studies are given by Plontke & Zenner 2004, Streppel et al. 2006).

Given that exposure to loud or even very loud music is widespread among the younger generation (in the main, subjects of age 12 – 25), and that sound levels of 100 dB[A] and more are regularly experienced at rock and other live music concerts as well as in discotheques, the risks seem evident. Assessing such risks, there are a number of factors and issues that have not yet been taken into account in a reasonable and sufficient manner. One important factor that will be addressed in this article concerns the structure of various genres of modern electronic dance music in regard to the sound material that is employed in the production of, for example, techno tracks or so-called hard trance. Since many such tracks make use of pulse-type sounds and concentrate spectral energy in low frequency bands (see below), processing of such material by our hearing system for 'loudness perception' may be quite different from other types of sound. Concerning in particular sensation and perception of low frequencies (f < 100 Hz) there are some questions, which need to be discussed in regard to, among other issues, critical band concepts. Further, sound pressure level measurements in discotheques and rock music venues based on dB[A] weighting as well as traditional techniques of energy averaging need a critical examination with respect to scientific adequacy (vs. "political" and economic decision criteria).

The present article is organized into six chapters. Following this introduction, we outline in brief fundamentals of sound and the sound field in order to provide some technical background relevant also to measurements of sound pressure levels in discotheques or live music venues and to auditory processing of sound. In chapter 3, we present sonic analyses of some examples of techno, electronic dance music and heavy metal as recorded and published on CD. In chapter 4, we offer data from our measurements in a discotheque making use of the same music examples as well as a professional sound system installed in this club for playback of electronic dance music. We will relate to some concepts of auditory processing and loudness perception in chapter 5, and will also discuss the (questionable) adequacy of dB[A] weighting when applied to electronic music as a prevalent type of sound in discotheques. Finally, chapter 6 contains some conclusions as well as proposals with respect to current debates concerning critical values and limits for SPLs in discotheques and live music venues.

2. Fundamentals: Sound and Sound field

Sound can be described as a type of energy distributed within a medium (a solid, fluid, or gas). In the following, we are concerned, in the main, with sound propagation in air. Air can be considered as a gas (cf. Morse 1981, ch. 6) or as a fluid consisting of molecules, whereby a certain volume V is filled with n moles (see Morse & Ingard 1986, ch. 6). Air is an elastic medium that has a mass density, $\rho = m/V$ (kg/m^3) under normal atmospheric pressure $P = 101325$ Pa (= 1013,25 hPa) at a certain temperature T(°C). For a temperature of 20°C, density is $\rho = 1.2041$ kg/m^3, and the speed with which a plane wave travels in air is $c = 343,46$ m/s. Specific acoustic impedance ($Z = c \cdot \rho$), which is also called characteristic acoustic resistance in regard to compression of a volume of air under these conditions is $Z_F = 413,6$ Ns/m^3 = 415 Pa · s/m (Webers [1985, 58] gives 408 Ns/m^3 for normal pressure taken as 1 bar = 1,02 at). Wave speed increases considerably with temperature while density and impedance decrease correspondingly. If the temperature is raised to 30°C, wave speed in air is $c = 349,3$ m/s, density is $\rho = 1,1644$ kg/m^3, and the acoustic impedance is $Z_F = 406,7$ Ns/m^3.

For wave propagation in air under normal conditions it is assumed that the change in pressure and in local temperature are very fast, and that practically no exchange of heat between molecules takes place so that the process is regarded as adiabatic (see Recknagel 1986, 88ff., Gehrtsen/Vogel 1993, 152), and the wave speed in air can be calculated as

$$(1) \quad c = \sqrt{\gamma \frac{p_{\_}}{\rho_{\_}}},$$

where $\gamma = 1,4$ is the adiabatic exponent, $p_{\_}$ is the static air pressure, and $\rho_{\_}$ is the density of air in equilibrium state.

In regard to production and radiation of sound, typically one will distinguish between a generator and a resonator. For example, in a musical instrument like an oboe or clarinet, the reed (which, together with the mouthpiece, functions as a valve) forms the generator that is used to produce a pulse train of given frequency. The pulses then enter a tube of given length and diameter filled with a column of air that is the resonator (in which standing waves occur). If the tube does not have finger holes, sound is radiated only from the open end of the tube. A periodic change in pressure is observed at a given place x and time t so that

(2) $\quad p_\sim(x,t) = \hat{A} \cos(2\pi ft + \varphi)$,

where $p_\sim$ is the alternating quantity of the air pressure, and $\hat{A}$ is the peak amplitude of the periodic change that corresponds to a sine or cosine function.

In this model, a periodic vibration of the air column is the cause of a periodic change of pressure in the surrounding air. In general, it is assumed that the sound radiated with a certain power into a medium (e.g., from a loudspeaker into a room filled with air) is the cause that leads to (typically, periodic) changes in local air pressure and density as effect. In particular changes of local air pressure can be measured with instruments and are experienced by subjects in hearing. In fact, sound radiated from a source into a medium like air (viewed as a sound field of k dimensions that can be characterized by certain parameters and properties) leads to a 'disturbance' in that the molecules are set to motion causing local changes in pressure and density. Ideally, it is assumed that the sound field is homogeneous and unlimited so that reflection and refraction must not be considered; also Brownian motion of molecules is not taken into account. In order to affect changes to the equilibrium state of the medium (in most cases, a sound field of $k = 3$ dimensions: x, y, z), a certain amount of 'energy' is needed (see below). Regarding the sound as a 'force' that acts on the behaviour of molecules (viewed, in a general way, as particles), the variables and parameters that are of interest are

(a) the elongation of particles relative to their position at rest; the amplitude of the elongation ξ can be given as

(3) $\quad \vec{\xi} = \dfrac{v}{\omega} = \dfrac{p_\sim}{\omega \cdot Z}$

where v is the particle velocity, $p_\sim$ is the sound pressure, and Z the acoustic impedance $(c\rho)$.

Since the medium is elastic, a restoring force acts on the particle that undergoes periodic motion of the form

(4) $\quad \xi = \hat{A} \cos(2\pi \dfrac{x}{\lambda} - ft)$, or, since $\lambda = \dfrac{c}{f}$, $\xi = \hat{A} \sin 2\pi f (t - \dfrac{x}{c})$,

where $\hat{A}$ is the peak amplitude, λ is the wavelength of a plane wave and x is a space coordinate that indicates the distance from the source (on which elongation is dependent).

Stated in absolute values (ξ in mm), elongation is very small. For a loud conversation, where the intensity of sound would be close to $I = 10^{-6}$ W/m², the elongation can be calculated as approx. $11 \cdot 10^{-6}$ mm (see Recknagel 1986, 91).

(b) The velocity of particles that are set to motion by the sound considered as a force is the first derivative of the elongation with respect to time:

(5) $\vec{v} = \dfrac{d\vec{\xi}}{dt}$, which yields $v = 2\pi f\, \hat{A}\, \sin 2\pi f\left(t - \dfrac{x}{c}\right)$, or $2\pi f\, \hat{A}\, \cos\left(\dfrac{x}{\lambda} - ft\right)$.

Since the velocity (for a given elongation) increases in proportion to frequency of vibration, and $2\pi f = \omega$, the amplitude of the velocity is $v_{max} = 2\pi f \hat{\xi}_{max} = \omega \hat{A}$. However, because velocity is changing periodically between a minimum and a maximum value, one can use $v_{eff} = v_{max}/\sqrt{2}$ as well. Note that both elongation and velocity (m/s) are vectors. The usual point of reference for the velocity of sound in a plane wave propagating in air at a sound pressure level (SPL) of $p_0 = 2 \cdot 10^{-5}$ Pa is $v_0 = 5 \cdot 10^{-8}$ m/s (= 0.00000005 m/s), which is taken as equivalent to 0 dB.

(c) For practical reasons of measurability, the sound pressure $p_\sim$ is the most accessible parameter. The general view is that both elongation of particles and velocity are effected by a change of pressure, which acts as a force on the particles or molecules distributed in the sound field. This view implies that air is compressible to a certain degree in proportion to a bulk modulus κ, which can be given as κ = -V (dp/dV), where V denotes the volume of the gas, and dp and dV changes in pressure and in volume, respectively. (An approximate value for κ is 1,4 · $p_\_$, where 1,4 is the value of the adiabatic exponent, and $p_\_$ denotes normal pressure). Basically, a change of pressure from p_0 to p goes along with a change in density from ρ_0 to ρ so that

(6) $\dfrac{p}{p_0} = \left(\dfrac{\rho}{\rho_0}\right)^{\gamma}$

Change of pressure, of particle velocity and density are closely interrelated; according to Euler's law, we have:

(7) $-\dfrac{\partial p}{\partial x} = \rho_\_ \dfrac{\partial v}{\partial t}$

For a one-dimensional case like longitudinal waves in air, equation 8 can be used:

(8) $-\dfrac{\partial v}{\partial x} = \dfrac{1}{\kappa}\dfrac{\partial p}{\partial t}$

where κ denotes the bulk modulus (κ = 1,4 · $p_\_$).

Given that the density and the pressure in a medium consist of a normal component ($\rho_\_$, $p_\_$) plus an alternating component ($\rho\sim$, $p\sim$), we have

$$\rho = \rho_- + \rho_\sim \quad \text{and} \quad p = p_- + p_\sim$$

Accordingly, the velocity of air molecules is $v = v_- + v_\sim$ if the air is streaming at a certain speed v_-. Otherwise, velocity would be just $v_\sim$. Note that v is a vector; however, one can take velocity as a scalar for a plane longitudinal wave along one dimension x where the direction of wave propagation is clearly defined. Pressure p is a scalar. The movement of particles in the sound field (apart from molecular motion, see Morse & Ingard 1968, ch. 6) is dependent on time t and place r, thus $v(r, t)$ and $p(r, t)$. Looking at a very small element (dx, dy, dz) of the 3D sound field, for which constant density, pressure and velocity is assumed, any change in velocity can be described by the total differential of the function $v(r, t)$. According to Euler's basic equation for hydrodynamics, we have

(9) $\quad dv = \dfrac{\partial v}{\partial t} dt + (dr \, \text{grad}) v$

The acceleration a of the element (dx, dy, dz) is

(10) $\quad \dfrac{dv}{dt} = \dfrac{\partial v}{\partial t} + (v \, \text{grad}) v$

Since the element has a (very small) mass of (ρ dx dy dz), any acceleration with regard to Newton's 2nd law $\mathbf{F} = m \cdot a$ will bring about a force that, in this case, results in a change of pressure that acts on the element. The equation of motion then can be written as

(11) $\quad \rho \left[\dfrac{\partial v}{\partial t} + (v \, \text{grad}) v \right] = - \, \text{grad} \, p$

According to the law of maintenance of mass it is assumed that the portion of mass that will leave a space of volume V and a surface plane S within a small time span dt is equal to the reduction of (any) volume element (dx dy dz):

(12) $\quad \text{div}(\rho v) = - \dfrac{\partial \rho}{\partial t}$,

where div denotes the divergence (i.e., the difference between 'inflow' and 'outflow').

The modified Euler equation valid for gases now is

(13) $\quad \rho_- \dfrac{\partial v_\sim}{\partial t} = - \dfrac{\partial p_\sim}{\partial x}$

and the equation of continuity

(14) $\rho \dfrac{\partial v_{\sim}}{\partial x} = -\dfrac{\partial \rho_{\sim}}{\partial t} = \dfrac{1}{c^2} \cdot \dfrac{\partial p_{\sim}}{\partial t}$

from which the wave equation for plane waves propagating into one direction (along the x coordinate) can be easily derived:

(15) $\dfrac{\partial^2 p_{\sim}}{\partial x^2} = \dfrac{1}{c^2} \cdot \dfrac{\partial^2 p_{\sim}}{\partial t^2}$

In this equation, pressure (as a scalar) is the variable of the sound field that accounts for wave propagation in a homogeneous medium (like air). For the undamped case, we can write

(16) $\nabla p = \dfrac{1}{c^2} \cdot \dfrac{\partial^2 p}{\partial t^2}$, where $\nabla = \dfrac{\partial^2}{\partial x^2} + \dfrac{\partial^2}{\partial y^2} + \dfrac{\partial^2}{\partial z^2}$

denotes the Laplace operator for Cartesian coordinates (x, y, z). For periodic wave trains propagating along one dimension (x) only, solutions have the general form

(17) $p(x, t) = f(x \pm ct)$,

which means there two plane waves propagating from a point of excitation in two directions along the dimension x. For undamped harmonic plane waves, we have

(18) $A = \hat{A} \cos\left[2\pi\left(\dfrac{x}{\lambda} \pm ft\right) + \phi\right]$, where ϕ is the phase angle.

Such a wave would have a temporal period of $T = \dfrac{1}{f}$, and a wavelength $\lambda = \dfrac{c}{f}$.

(d) Sound intensity and energy transport

Concerning concentric propagation from a point source, pressure and velocity decrease with growing radius r according to

(19) $p, v \approx \dfrac{1}{r}$

Empirically, this relation known as the 6 dB rule is of importance because it implies that the intensity of sound decreases regularly with distance from the source. However,

strictly speaking the decrease sets in only from the border of the nearfield (cf. Ahnert & Steffen 1993, 33); for the nearfield the 6 dB rule doesn't hold (see below).
Intensity *I* of a sound can be calculated according to

$$(20) \quad I = \frac{1}{T}\int_0^T \hat{p}\cdot\hat{v}\cdot\sin^2\left[\omega\left(t-\frac{x}{c}\right)\right]dt = \frac{1}{2}\hat{p}\cdot\hat{v} = p_{eff}\cdot v_{eff} = \rho\cdot c\cdot v^2$$

Intensity of sound (I/m^2) represents the mean density of the energy transported in a (sound) wave. In any small particle or volume $V\Delta$ in a sound field, kinetic and potential (elastic) energy is contained (cf. Morse 1981, 223, Morse & Ingard 1986, ch. 6) according to

$$(21) \quad \frac{1}{2}\kappa p^2 = \text{potential energy density}$$

$$(22) \quad \frac{1}{2}\rho v^2 = \text{kinetic energy density}$$

The two energies add up to unity; written in a different form (Weinzierl 2008, 25), energy density *w* per unit volume $V\Delta$ containing a small amount of energy ΔW is

$$(23) \quad w = \frac{p^2}{2\cdot\rho_0 c^2} + \frac{\rho_0 v^2}{2}$$

Energy density *w* is a periodic function for both time and place. A (simple harmonic) wave of given wavelength λ travelling in one direction (in the most simple case, along x) with a frequency *f* at a phase velocity of *c* contains a certain amount of energy per period. If the wave is assumed to travel through a plane *S*, the energy that flows in a short time interval of Δt is

$$(24) \quad \Delta W = wSc\Delta t$$

The ratio $\Delta W/\Delta t = J$ is the power (or strength) of the energy flux (cf. Recknagel 1986, 85-91), and the ratio of $J/A = j$ is called the flux density, which again is a periodic function of time, implying that a wave travelling through a plane *S* carries in fact a sequence of energy pulses.

It is of interest to note that the frequency of these pulses is twice as high as the frequency of the (plane harmonic) wave and that energy density corresponds to the square of the unit of vibration (elongation ξ, velocity *v*) under consideration. Just as kinetic energy grows with v^2, and potential energy with ξ^2, growth of energy density must depend on a squared parameter like the amplitude of the wave and its frequency. The fact that one period of a harmonic wave carries two pulses of energy is relevant to music, and in particular to loudness perception (see below). The relation of a given waveshape to its energy is shown in Fig. 1 in a schematic way:

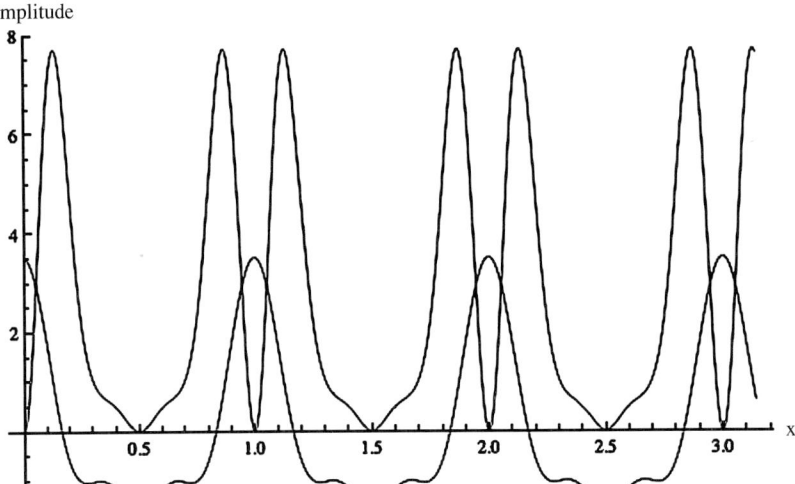

Figure 1: Harmonic wave of 3 components (lower trace), energy (upper trace)

Intensity of sound can be defined as mean density of the energy flux

(25) $\quad I = \dfrac{\rho}{2} c (2\pi f)^2 \hat{A}^2 \quad [\hat{A}^2 = \xi^2]$

The reference point for intensity usually is $I_0 = 10^{-12}$ W/m² taken as 0 dB intensity level. This is a very small intensity whereas 1 W/m² = 120 dB-SIL. Within certain limits, one can regard the sensory quality of sound level L as proportional to the logarithm of the physical property of sound intensity, I; the relation of L to I then is

(26) $\quad L = \text{const } \ln I$

The 6 dB-rule (see above) applies to plane waves propagating along one dimension normal to the wave front. In a plane wave pressure amplitude and velocity amplitude are in phase in the far field. In a real-world 3D sound field, sound often is radiated from a source that itself is three-dimensional (like a speaker cabinet containing several loud-speakers). In an idealized approach, one can consider monopole sources where sound is radiated omnidirectional. The radiated sound power P in this case is distributed over the surface of a sphere ($4\pi r^2$) with radius r so that for the intensity I we have

(27) $\quad I(r) = \dfrac{P}{4\pi r^2}$

and for energy density of sound in the nearfield (cf; see Ahnert & Steffen 1993, 33)

(28) $\quad w_{nf} = \dfrac{P}{c} \cdot \dfrac{1}{4\pi r^2}$

In case the sound radiation is spheric from a monopole, sound pressure p and velocity v are not in phase; impedance then consists of two parts (active and reactive power), which need to be considered also when calculating pressure and velocity (cf. Webers 1985, 55f.). Impedance for spherical waves is complex and dependent on frequency and on range (cf. Junger & Feit 1993, 27, 31, 64).
In the nearfield, intensity of sound decreases inversely proportional to the square of r like

(29) $\quad I \approx \dfrac{1}{r^2}$, or, taking I_0 as the intensity at the point of the source,

(30) $\quad I \approx \dfrac{I_0}{r^2}$

Though many sound phenomena stem from radiation somewhere in between spheric and plane waves, it is often sufficient to consider plane waves since, with increasing distance from the source, spheric waves at a receiver point (e.g., the ears of a subject listening to music) can be viewed as plane waves; sound pressure decreases according to $p \sim 1/r$.

Leaving aside damping, the relation of sound level to a growing distance from the source defined by r is

(31) $\quad \Delta L = 10 \lg \dfrac{I(r_1)}{I(r_2)} = 20 \lg \dfrac{r_2}{r_1}$

Taking into account that hearing in mammals (including humans) is based on sensing changes in pressure, it is useful to define intensity I as a function of pressure p (cf. Hartmann 1998, 31):

(32) $\quad I(t) = \dfrac{p^2(t)}{(\rho c)}$

Since the specific acoustical impedance is rather small at about 42 g/cm² sec (see also above), one can take the squared rms value of the pressure (p^2_{eff}) as proportional to the intensity of the sound. As indicated above, intensity represents the mean density of the sound energy flux (equ. 25) or, viewed instantaneously, the acoustical power per unit area. Sound intensity level (SIL) is defined as

(33) $\quad L_I = 10 \lg \dfrac{I}{I_0}$

where the reference point is $I_0 = 10^{-12}$ W/m^2 = 10^{-16} W/cm^2. Since the diameter of the ear channel is ca. 8 mm, and the acoustically relevant surface of the membrana tympani in humans ca. 55 mm^2 (Plattig 1975), it is obvious how small intensity at threshold is.

Table 1: sound level, sound pressure, intensity

dB-SPL	p(Pa)	I(W/m^2)
40	0.002	0.00000001
60	0.02	0.000001
80	0.2	0.0001
82	0.2518	0.0001585
84	0.3169	0.0002512
86	0.399	0.000398
88	0.5024	0.000631
90	0.6325	0.001
92	0.7962	0.001585
94	1.0024	0.002512
96	1.2619	0.00398
98	1.5886	0.00631
100	2	0.01
102	2.5178	0.01585
104	3.16978	0.02512
106	3.9905	0.0398
108	5.02377	0.0631
110	6.32455	0.1
112	7.96214	0.1585
114	10.0237	0.2512
116	12.619	0.39812
118	15.886	0.63096
120	20	1
130	63,246	10
140	200	100

Most relevant to hearing as well as to acoustical measurement is the sound pressure level (SPL)

(34) $\quad L_P = 20 \lg \dfrac{\tilde{p}}{p_0}, \qquad \tilde{p} = p_{\text{eff}}$

where p_0 denotes the point of reference $2 \cdot 10^{-5}$ Pa = 20μPa = $2 \cdot 10^{-5}$ N/m^2 = 0 dB, and p_{eff} is the rms value of the actual pressure level measured. Dealing with rms values implies integration over time and frequency bands. The range of SPL of interest in regard to music and hearing usually spans about 100 dB from very soft to very loud sounds. One has to remember that the range of pressure levels relevant to hearing indeed is extremely wide; at 0 dB-SPL we have 0.00002 Pa, at 40 dB 0.002 Pa, at 80 dB 0.2 Pa, and at 120 dB already 20 Pa. Increasing the SPL by 6 dB means doubling the pressure amplitude. At 126 dB, 40 Pa will be reached, and at about 132 dB SPL, even 80 Pa. The relation of sound level to sound pressure and intensity is summarized in table 1.

3. Sonic analysis of musical sound samples

For the present study, we have selected five pieces of music, of which four are available to the public on commercial CDs, and one has been produced as a demo especially to be included in a doctoral dissertation on techno (Volkwein 2001) by an artist formerly known as 'Beige' (Oliver Braun) then busy in a project called 'Antisept'. The pieces that represent different genres (electronic, trash metal) and styles (House, Gabber, Hard Trance, Electro-Pop) are:

1. *Fight for your right to party* (Disco Selection Mix), N.Y.C.C. (Control/Edel 1998), a cover version of the song of same title by the Beastie Boys (1986)
2. *Gabber-Track*, Beige, 2001, CD accompanying Volkwein 2001
3. *The Hype*, Special Force (Gang to Music, 1999)
4. *Pokerface*, Lady Gaga (Interscope, 2008)
5. *People = Shit*, Slipknot (Roadrunner Records, 2001)

From these tracks, portions were selected where musical structure indicates the use of electronic or natural (drums) pulse-type sounds, and of bass notes with significant low frequency content. Portions from all five examples were analyzed in regard to waveshapes, overall and local sound level (dB) as well as spectral characteristics (Cochleagram, excitation, LTAS). Several of the sound examples reveal recurrent patterns of temporal and spectral structure. Figure 2, which shows one second of *Fight for your right* by N.Y.C.C. (2'26" – 2'27"), indicates the pulse-type quality of the temporal organisation. Within one second of the sound, almost five short bursts will be noticed. The duration of each such burst is ca. 221 ms.

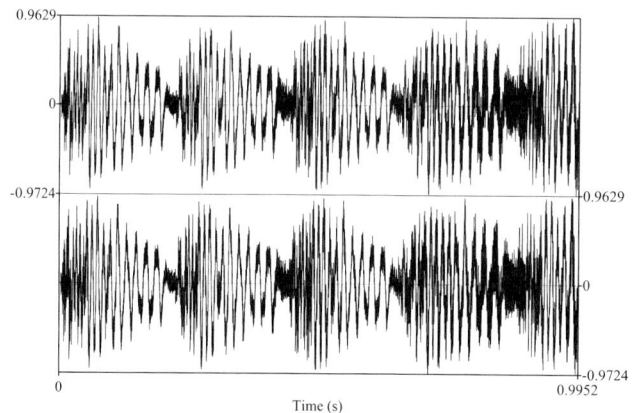

Figure 2: *Fight for your right*, N.Y.C.C., short segment of audio signal (2'26" – 2'27")

Sound level [dB-SIL] plotted against time for the same segment indicates the pulse-like structure (figure 3):

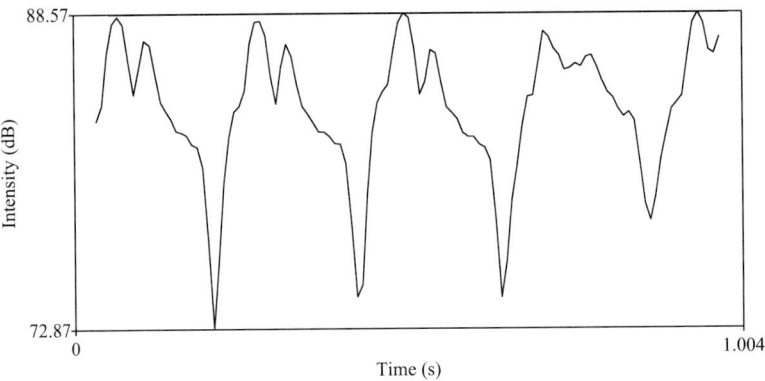

Figure 3: *Fight for your right*, N.Y.C.C., short segment of 1 second ≈ 5 pulses

Taking a somewhat longer phrase (2'26" – 2'31") of the track, the sound level of the CD recording yields a mean of 83.68 dB. For another segment of the audio file, mean level is 84.83 dB, and the rms energy (expressed as sound pressure) is 0.3489 Pa.

The cochleagram (figure 4) for one second of sound (corresponding to figure 3) clearly shows that spectral energy covers the full bandwidth (25.6 Bark), and that there is a concentration of spectral energy in the very low frequency bands (Bark [z] 1-2) plus a second not just as strong condensation at about Bark [z] 18-20 (which is, roughly, from 3.5 – 7 kHz).

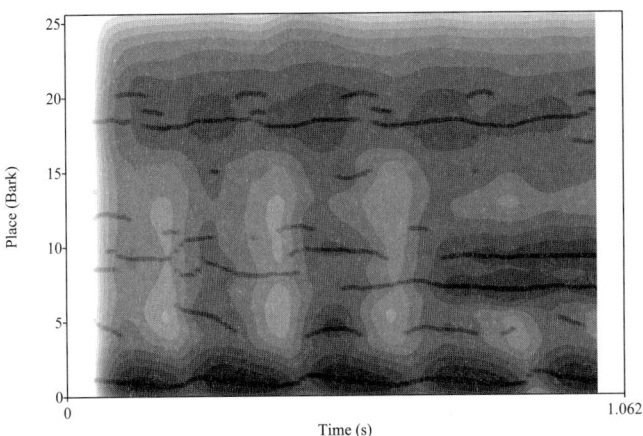

Figure 4: Cochleagram of the same short segment (fig. 3)

Taking a long-term average spectrum (LTAS) with frequency bins df = 10 Hz of a segment (2'26" – 2'31") of *Fight for your right* confirms that much of the spectral energy is concentrated below 200 Hz, with peaks at ca. 55 and 85 Hz, respectively (figure 5).

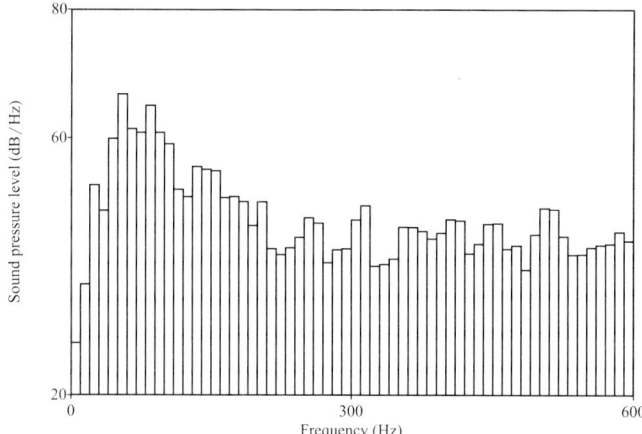

Figure 5: LTAS (0 – 600 Hz; df = 10 Hz) of sound segment

The *Gabber-track* that was created with the purpose to demonstrate features of this style (see Volkwein 2001) shows a similar temporal and spectral organization than does *Fight for your right*. Again, we see in the cochleagram (figure 5) a high frequency of sound bursts per time unit and a strong condensation of energy in the bass and low mid frequency bands as well as another condensation zone at Bark[z] 15-19.

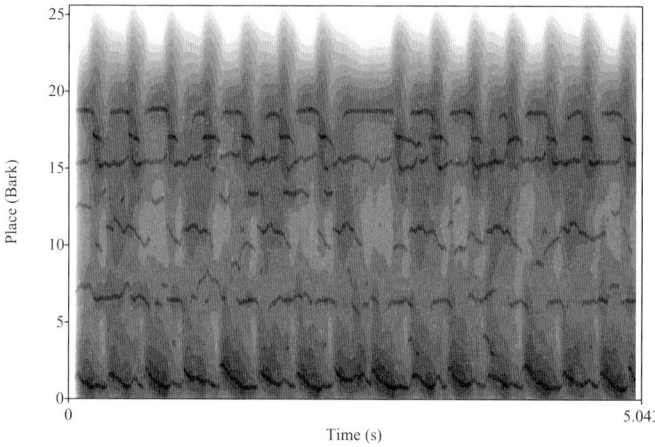

Figure 6: Cochleagram, *Gabber-Track*, segment of 4'75"

The LTAS (0-1kHz, df=10 Hz, figure 6) of the same segment shows a peak at 50-60 Hz as well as an almost continuous rise of level (dB) per bin with decreasing frequency from 1 kHz down to 50 Hz.

27

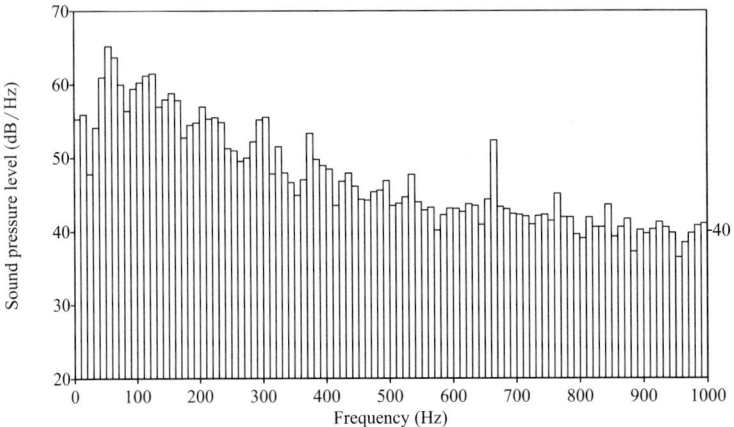

Figure 7: *Gabber-track*, LTAS 0 – 1 kHz, df = 10 Hz. Peak level at 50-60 Hz.

In certain respects, the spectral envelope resembles a so-called equal-loudness curve in that the reduced sensitivity of the ear at lower frequencies is compensated by higher SPL (dB). We will return to this phenomenon found in many modern music productions in chapter 5.

The next example is *The Hype* that is considered as Hard Trance, and was played in German discotheques and clubs regularly. Much of the piece (of which we analyzed a segment beginning at 6'35" of the recording) consists of the typical meter and rhythm pattern (4/4 with "four-to-the-floor" realized with a low frequency sound, and high frequency sounds marking the eights in between, resulting in the well-known "bum-tz-bum-tz-bum-tz-bum-tz"). The cochleagram (figure 8) exhibits this temporal and spectral structure very clearly.

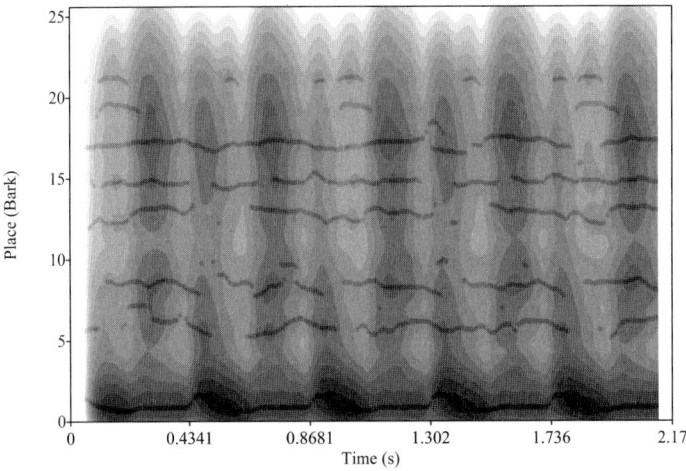

Figure 8: Cochleagram The Hype, 6'35" – 6'40"

To illustrate the emphasis of low frequencies, we take the excitation pattern of the basilar membrane (BM; see figure 9) at a given time (for this example, 1 second after onset). Excitation is strongest at Bark[z] 1 where the level (expressed in phon) is between ca. 72 and more than 80 phon.

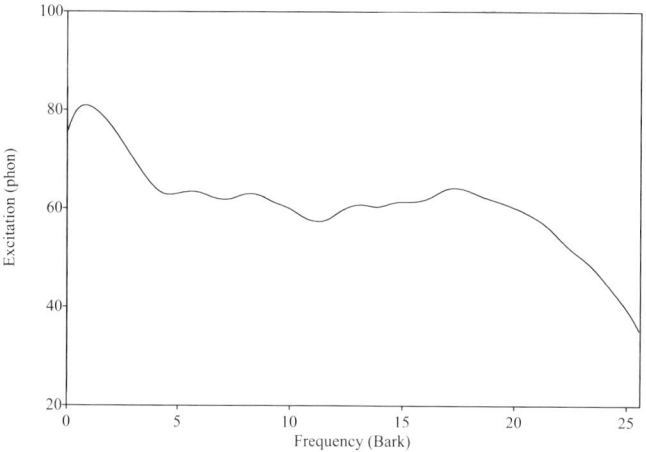

Figure 9: *The Hype*, excitation of BM calculated one second after onset of sound segment

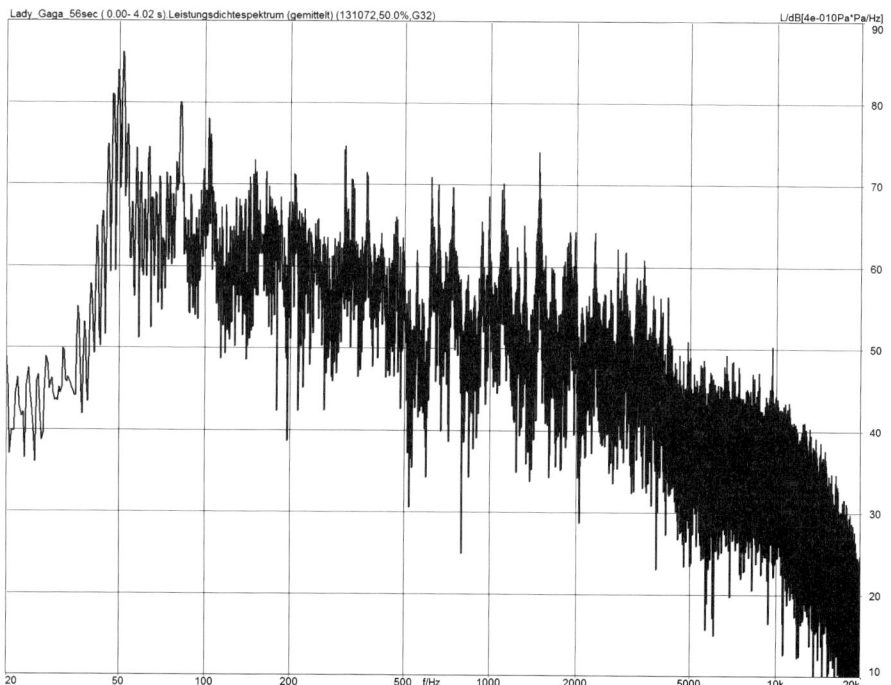

Figure 10: *Pokerface*, Power-density spectrum, ca. 4 seconds

Turning now to Lady Gaga and her 2008 hit, *Pokerface*, the production at first seems to fit more to pop music in general in that Gaga's voice plus a group of background singers is featured resulting in strong spectral components in the range of ca. 0.3 – 3 kHz. However, *Pokerface* contains also much energy at very low frequencies. The power-density spectrum for a segment of 4.04 seconds (window size:131072 samples, 50% overlap) has the strongest peaks at 45-55 Hz (figure 10).

Also, since the song employs the stereotypical bass drum pattern of "four-to-the floor" marking the meter in a disco-like manner, there is a sequence of pulses with peaks being ca. 500 ms apart (this corresponds to a tempo of the song of ca. 120 bpm). It should be noted that the dynamic range of the recording for the section analyzed varies only between ca. 82 and 87.5 dB (figure 11); the kick drum sound "sticks out" as a sequence of pulses from an already high dynamic level.

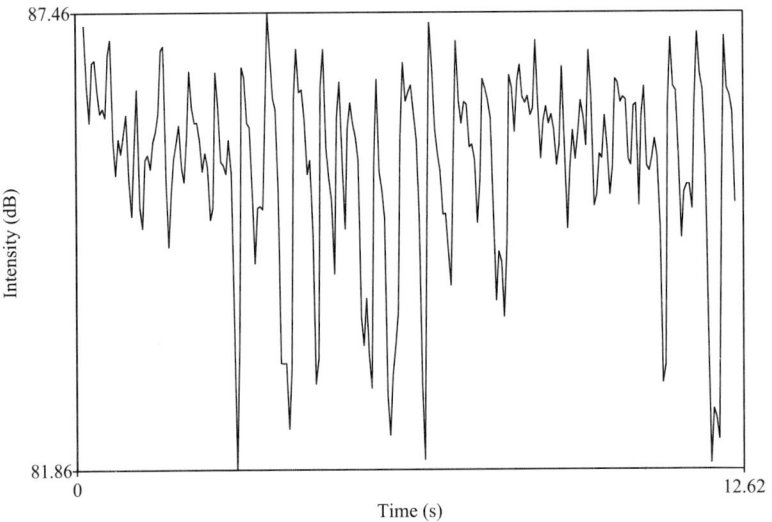

Figure 11: *Pokerface*: sound level [dB] over time, bass drum pulse sequence

Slipknot produces tracks that belong to the so-called trash metal genre for which high overall SPLs, high frequency of drum beats and other sounds per time unit, distortion of guitars and even voices as well as high spectral density seems typical. In regard to spectral energy, such tracks resemble broad-band noise, however, fast sequences of drum beats and bass notes result in a high number of pulses per time unit so that in effect such tracks as *People = Shit* are very dense in both spectral and temporal perspective (figure 12).

Within the segment of the recording shown in figure 12, energy varies only within a small range of less than 3 dB (min. = 83.1 dB; max = 86.04 dB; mean = 84.92 dB; SD =

0.499 dB[1]). This means the recording is very loud all the time yet appears static to the listener for the lack of variation in level or spectral composition.

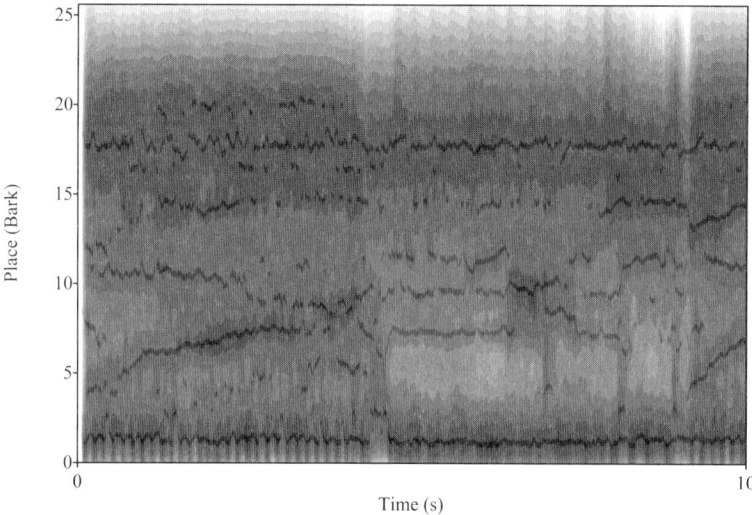

Figure 12: Slipknot: *People = Shit*, cochleagram for 10 seconds, spectral energy condensed in Bark[z] 1 – 22; fast pulse sequence in the bass at Bark[z] 1-2

4. Experimental investigation of sound pressure levels in a music club

To study possible effects of the music examples 1 – 5 described above on listeners visiting a music club discotheque, an experiment was run in a club in Hamburg (well-known for techno parties and similar events where various kinds of electronic dance music is presented by DJs). For the playback of the five samples (segments of 22 to 175 seconds duration taken from the recordings), a professional P.A. system installed in the club was used consisting of CD players, mixing desk, preamps, power amps, 31-band-equalizers, and four pairs of full-range loudspeaker cabinets mounted above the dance floor plus two large bass bins to the left and right of the dance floor containing sub-woofers (see figure 13).

The loudspeaker cabinets were custom designed and built by an audio firm in Hamburg specialised in the manufacture and installation of high power/high quality P.A. systems.

Frequency response of the 31-band-equalizers had been set to almost linear (with a few slight cuts of ca. -3 dB to suppress unwanted resonances in the room); for the experiment, equalizer and amp settings were left as had been chosen by audio engineers at the time the system was installed. The playback level of our music samples was

---

[1] The calculation of arithmetic mean (aM) and standard deviation (SD) in general presumes a linear scale of values (on a dimension or a variable). An interpretation of aM and SD for data expressed in a logarithmic unit (dB) therefore should consider the implications of the logarithmic nature of the data.

controlled by an employee of the club experienced with the system by operating the stereo sum faders of the mixing desk.

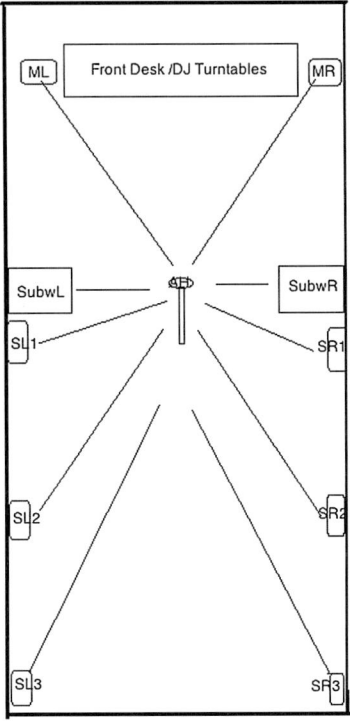

Figure 13: Schematic of measurement in music club/discotheque. ML = main fullrange speaker system front left; MR = main fullrange speaker system front right; SubwL = subwoofer cabinet left side of the dance floor; SbwR = subwoofer cabinet right side of the dance floor; SL1, SL2, SL 3 = supplementary fullrange speaker cabinets on the left side wall of the club; SR 1, SR2, SR 3 = supplementary fullrange speaker cabinets on the right side wall of the club; AH = artificial head (recording position central on the dance floor).

The sound radiated from the various speakers of the system was recorded with an artificial head and the ArtemiS 11 sound and vibration analysis software package (Head Acoustics). Recording on computer hard disc was done with 16 bit/44.1 kHz sampling. Equalization for the artificial head was set to linear in order to avoid any pre- or de-emphasis that can be necessary if playback of the recording via headphones or comparison of the sound recorded with the artificial head to normal microphone recordings is intended (not relevant for the present study).

The analysis of the recordings first was performed in regard to SPL over time. Since we want to compare different temporal and spectral weighting functions seemingly of relevance to models of loudness perception as well as the assessment of possible health risks arising from high SPLs in discotheques and music clubs, we employed three temporal (slow, fast, impulse) and two frequency weightings (A, C) that are widely in use in acoustic measurement and noise control. These temporal and frequency weightings that are implemented in acoustic hardware and software tools have been defined in technical terms (for details in regard to sound level meter construction and performance requirements, see European Norm EN61672-1 and EN61672-2, published 2002 [German edition 2003]).

For the temporal weighting, the following characteristics apply:

Weighting	Rise time	Decay time
Slow	1 s	1 s
Fast	125 ms	125 ms
Impulse	35 ms	1.5 s

Sound level meters give the SPL rms value as default.

Frequency weighting corresponds to filtering the signal (the transfer functions are readily available on the Internet) whereby the filter response is normalized to the frequency of 1 kHz that serves also as a reference point when comparing the different frequency weightings in regard to hearing and psychoacoustic parameters, e.g. loudness. Graphs of frequency weighting functions A, B, C are shown in figure 14.

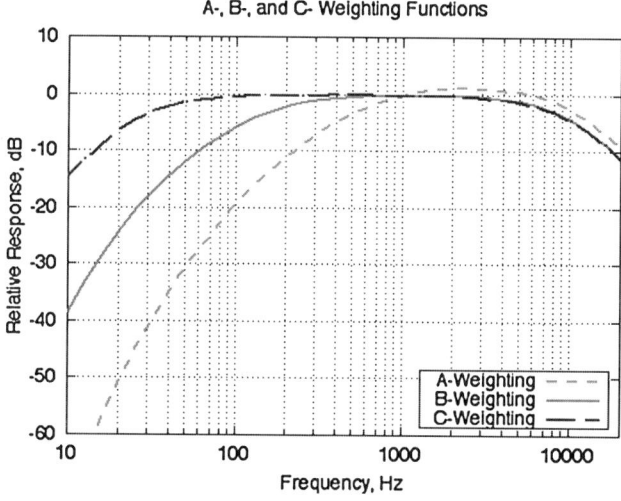

Figure 14: Frequency weighting functions A, B, C used in sound level metering

It is obvious that weighting A implies a strong cut of frequencies below 1 kHz, and particularly so for $f < 200$ Hz (where the roll off is about 10 dB/oct.). Weighting A includes a slight boost for frequencies from 2 – 6 kHz above 0 dB. Weighting B has a flat response from ca. 0.6 – 3 kHz, and rolls off to low frequencies more gently. Weighting C is flat from ca. 3 kHz down to about 100 Hz, from where on the roll off is very slight (taking 20 Hz as the lower frequency limit of hearing in humans, the cut at 20 Hz would amount to ca. -6 dB relative to 1 kHz).

Since only A and C weighting is used in most measurements nowadays (in addition, a linear frequency response defined as 'Z' may be chosen in some set-ups), we used these two weightings for all recordings.

Applied to 43 seconds of *Fight for your right*, temporal weighting 'fast' and frequency weighting A results in two sections with different peak and average level plotted as SPL over time in figure 15; there are two tracks representing the right and the left ear input, respectively. The first section (of ca. 15" duration) consists of four segments with an average level at ca. 107 dB[A], and each of the segments has a short peak slightly above 110 dB[A]. The second section shows a regular sequence of peaks at ca. 104 dB[A], and an average level of ca. 102 dB[A].

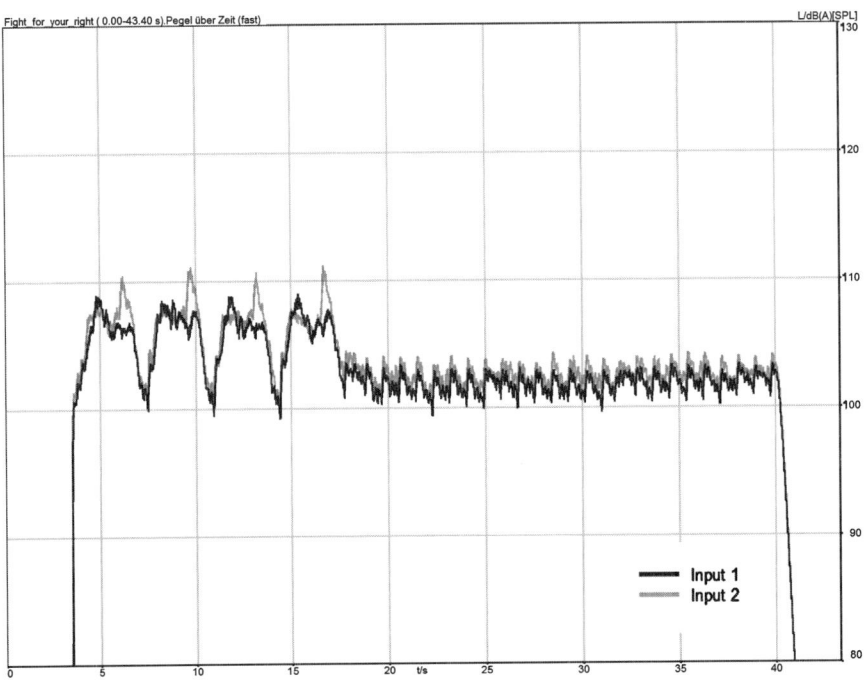

Figure 15: Fight for your right, SPL (dB[A]) ./. time (temporal weighting 'fast')

In contrast, if the same part of *Fight for your right* is processed with the temporal weighting 'fast' and frequency weighting C, a regular sequence of peaks at about 117-118 dB[C] is found together with an average level of ca. 115 dB[C]. It is of interest to note that the frequency of peaks in the dB[C]-weighting is about double that of the dB[A]-weighting notwithstanding temporal weighting 'fast' is identical in both runs. While we see 6 peaks in a time span of about five seconds in the dB[A]-weighting (cf. figure 15, second section, time 18" – 40"), there are 12 peaks in about the same time in the dB[C]-weighting (figure 16).

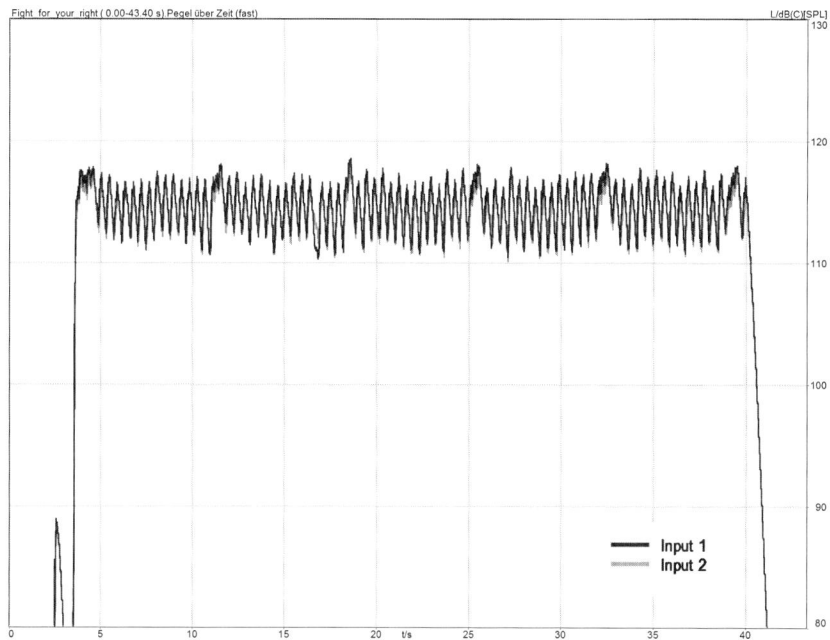

Figure 16: *Fight for your right*, SPL ./. time, dB[C], temporal weighting 'fast'

We now turn to *The Hype*, of which a long segment of 175" was analyzed first with 'slow' and then 'fast' temporal weighting, and dB[A] frequency weighting in both runs. The results are presented in figures 17 and 18, respectively.

Comparing the two plots, one sees that the SPL traces do not differ much, as can be expected. The magnitude of SPL at any given time is quite similar, however, the temporal resolution of course is much better with the 'fast' weighting, which indicates many short peaks and thus retains the actual intensity structure of the music recording while the 'slow' weighting acts like smoothening the SPL trace by low pass filtering (moving average) whereby the 'spiky' temporal structure of the music recording almost disappears.

A similar result is obtained in regard to temporal resolution when we apply 'slow' and 'fast' combined with dB[C]-weighting (see figures 19, 20). However, the dB[C]-weighting, preserving most of the energy contained in low frequency bands, not only leads to an increase of SPL of, on average 10 dB compared to the dB[A]-weighting, but also eliminates some of the dips left in the traces plotted in figures 17 and 18.

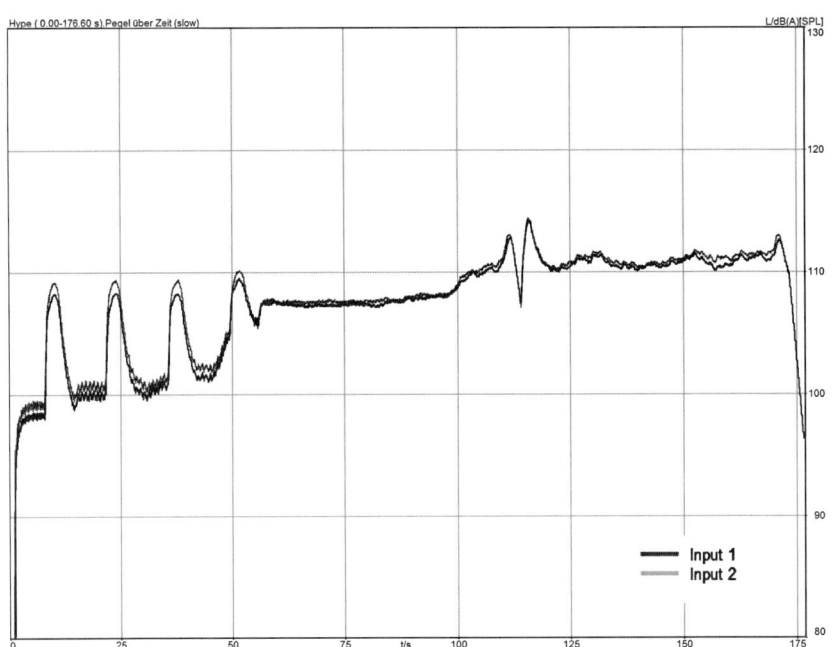

Figure 17: *The Hype*, SPL(dB[A]) ./. time (temporal weighting 'slow')

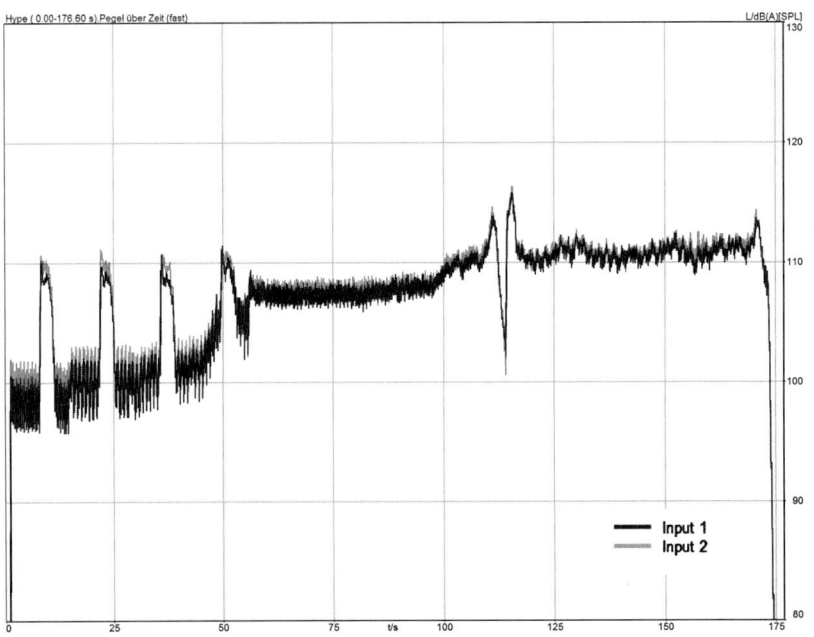

Figure 18: *The Hype*, SPL(dB[A]) ./. time (temporal weighting 'fast')

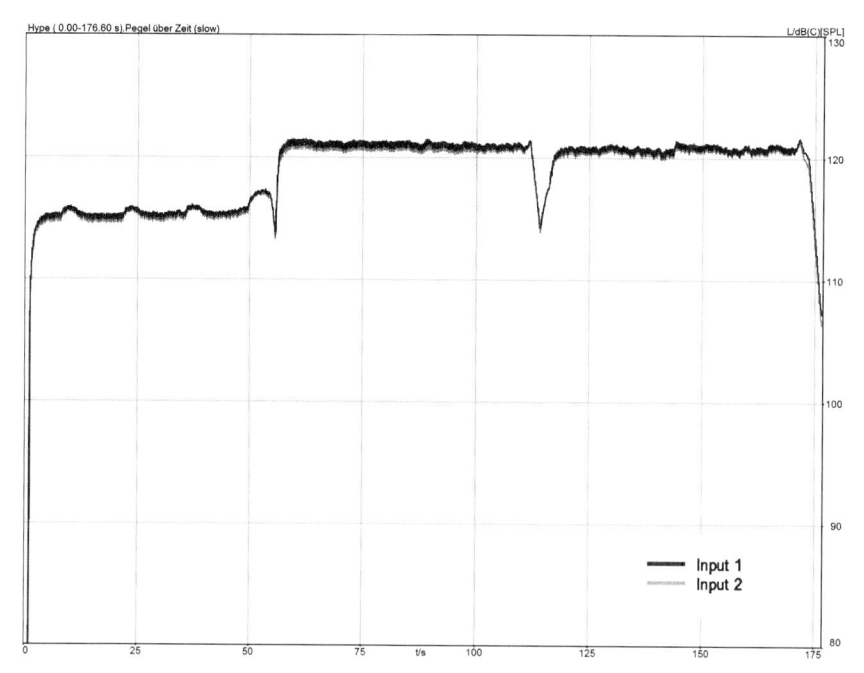

Figure 19: *The Hype*, SPL(dB[C]) ./. time (temporal weighting 'slow')

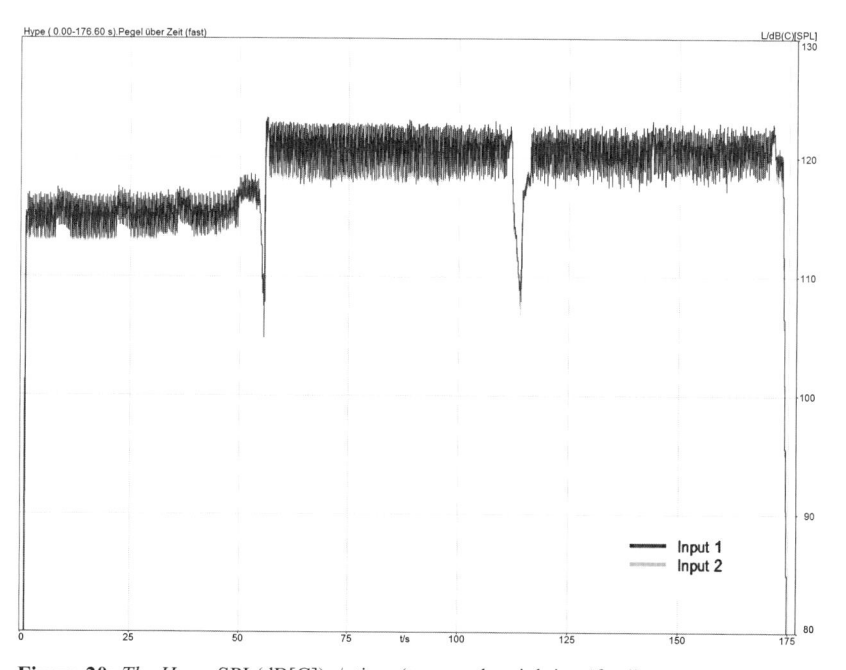

Figure 20: *The Hype*, SPL(dB[C]) ./. time (temporal weighting 'fast')

Turning finally to the temporal weighting 'impulse' combined with the two frequency weightings (A, C), we see not so much improvement in temporal resolution (cf. figures 19, 20) but again a significant increase in SPL when 'impulse' is chosen in conjunction with the dB[C]-weighting (figure 21). Here SPL reaches a plateau of ca. 124 dB[C] for the second and third sections of *The Hype* (spanning from 55" to 170" of the sound example, see figs. 19, 20).

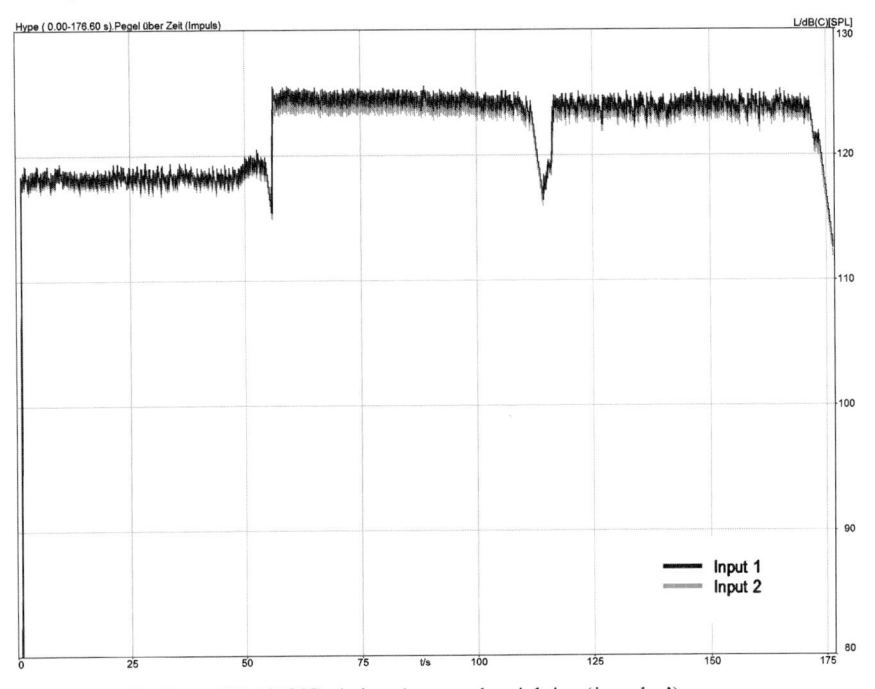

Figure 21: *The Hype*, SPL(dB[C]) ./. time (temporal weighting 'impulse')

In effect, SPL for 'impulse/dB[C]' in these sections is at least 12 dB above the two dB[A] readings shown in figs. 17 and 18, which converge in overall SPL magnitude notwithstanding different temporal weightings. The dB[A] readings for the two sections indicate SPLs from ca. 108 to ca. 112 dB while the dB[C] readings come close to 121 dB (slow) and 122 dB (fast), and even to 124-125 dB (impulse). Hence the difference in SPL between dB[A]-weighting and dB[C]-weighting can be estimated as 12 dB on average, and probably more when 'impulse' temporal weighting is applied to particularly 'spiky' music based on pulse-like sounds as is the case in *The Hype*. It should be noted that especially this sound example was played back in the music club at about the level that is usually chosen in actual events that take place in this club on weekends (according to the employee of the club operating the sound system). The other examples were played back probably slightly below the level commonly found at real "techno parties" or similar events. At least the system in the club even at the very loud playback of *The Hype* still had some 'headroom' so that significantly higher SPLs than those recorded could be realized (of course, at the cost of increasing distortion caused by nonlinear behaviour of the system, most of all, deformation of loudspeaker membranes notwithstanding stiffness at very high levels).

In the *Gabber-Track*, the difference in SPL with frequency weightings (A, C) and temporal weighting 'fast' (applied in both runs) to a segment of 55 seconds is not just as pronounced as in *The Hype*; on average, the difference in the *Gabber-Track* is ca. 9-10 dB (102 dB[A] versus 111-112 dB[C]. The difference is even less in *Pokerface* (ca. 105 dB[A] versus ca. 112 dB[C] for a segment of 65 seconds; temporal weighting 'fast' in both runs), where the SPL in this 'electro pop' in general varies a bit more with time than it does in the other four tracks.

For *People = Shit*, the A-weighting plus either 'slow' or 'fast' yields a SPL of 105-106 dB[A] on average. The C-weighting plus 'slow' results in a SPL slightly above 110 dB[C], and for 'fast' of about 111 dB[C]. The C-weighting combined with 'impulse' gives an SPL of ca. 112 dB[C]. Different temporal weighting in this specimen of 'trash metal' may not lead to significant changes in overall SPL curves because the sound of *People = Shit* constitutes an almost continuous broad-band noise signal in regard to both spectral and temporal energy distribution (see fig. 12).

Summing up these findings, one sees that the frequency weightings (A, C) account for most of the differences in SPL measured in five sound examples. In addition, temporal weighting can enlarge the difference, as was the case for *The Hype*. With dB[C] chosen as frequency weighting, the SPL rose another 2 dB when 'impulse' was applied instead of 'fast'.

As with other sound phenomena, temporal weighting for music must be chosen so as to match the actual structure of the material that is investigated. For music employing many short bursts of sound along the time axis, weighting 'fast' may be sufficient; in case music is based on sequences of pulse-like sounds, 'impulse' weighting can be more adequate in regard to picking up these pulses.

5. Ear models and loudness perception

Investigation of loudness sensation perhaps began with the seminal work of Harvey Fletcher (1940, see Hartmann 1998, ch. 4) and was continued by Stevens (1936, 1955) and later by Zwicker and colleagues (Zwicker et al. 1957, Zwicker & Scharf 1965). Several models of loudness sensation and perception are based on the concept of the critical band (CB; see Moore 1995, Hartmann 1998, Schneider & Tsatsishvili 2011 [this volume]), which can be viewed as a form of the auditory filter (AF) on the level of the cochlear partition (CP). Since the CP (including the basilar membrane, BM; see Pickles 2008) in humans is about 32 mm long (from base to apex if stretched along one dimension, x), one can assume that elongation is maximum for certain frequencies at certain places. Given that sine tones of f[Hz] and a SPL of A[dB] are used as stimuli, one may expect clear maxima due to hydromechanical models of the cochlea developed by Georg von Békésy (1961) and other researchers (cf. Keidel 1975, de Boer 1993). Such considerations in fact led to functions that relate frequency to place, and to defining sections along the BM corresponding in size to CBs. Accordingly, it was hypothesized that CBs cover (almost) equal distances along the BM and that one CB was estimated to have a size of "approximately 1 mm in the frequency region from about 400 to about 6600 cps, that is, from a point 9 mm from the apex to a point 27 mm from the apex" (Greenwood

1961, 1351). It should be noted that the CBs were viewed as non-overlapping (that is, positioned on the BM "end-to-end").

Considerations to relate loudness sensation to the acoustic power contained within a certain frequency band argue that the loudness arising from several (sine) tones closely spaced on the frequency axis is proportional to the acoustic power within a certain band that was labelled 'Frequenzgruppe' (Bauch 1956). Of course, in a linear approach and assuming additivity the sum of the energies contained in each spectral component within a frequency band would equal the energy contained in the respective band or 'Frequenzgruppe' as a whole.

In their experiments, Zwicker and colleagues found that perceived loudness of a four-tone complex was dependent on whether these tones fell into one CB or not. Their hypothesis was "that within a critical band the loudness is independent of spacing of the tones, and that, when the over-all spacing ΔF exceeds a critical value, the loudness increases" (Zwicker et al. 1957, 549). Another method to estimate the bandwidth of CBs was to present noise bands to subjects where an increase in perceived loudness was observed if the bandwidth of the noise exceeded a critical value (cf. also Greenwood 1961).

With the CB model and a 'Bark' scale of 24 non-overlapping CBs once established[2], the next step was to consider summation of loudness across several such CBs and to find an estimate for the overall loudness attributed to broad-band signals. The concept put forward by Zwicker and colleagues (Zwicker & Scharf 1965, Zwicker 1982) in a first step relates the physical spectrum of the auditory stimulus to excitation patterns on the BM (and, subsequently, on the neural level), which are dependent on the spacing and the level of spectral components, on the one hand, and the bandwidth of the AF that typically increases with stimulus level (cf. Moore & Glasberg 1983, Moore 1993, 2008), on the other. In regard to excitation, Zwicker (1982, 113) conceded that the slopes of auditory filters in reality can not be expected to be so steep as to cut off precisely at certain frequencies marking the very ends of CBs. Also, masking within CBs was taken into account. In a second step, specific loudness N' is calculated for each of the 24 bands (expressed in Bark[z]), whereby a relation (similar to Weber's "law") between the degree of excitation and a specific loudness is assumed to exist like

(35) $\Delta N' / N' = k(\Delta E / E)$ with k = proportionality constant.

A small increase in specific loudness $\Delta N'$ thus is due to a proportional increase in excitation, ΔE. If $E = 0$, N' must also be zero. From equation (35) a differential equation can be derived that is integratable (again, similar to the approach Fechner [1860] took with the Weber fraction; cf. Plattig 1975). The equation set up by Zwicker (1982, 131) for N' includes thresholds for both excitation and specific loudness which must not be considered here in detail. However, we may point to the fact that Zwicker regarded the following equation to hold for high signal levels

---

[2] Named after Heinrich Barkhausen, a well-known acoustician and engineer who introduced the unit ‚phon' relevant to loudness perception. For the Bark scale, see Zwicker 1982, Hartmann 1998, Schneider & Tsatsichvili 2011).

(36) $N' \sim (\Delta E / E_0)^k$

where E is excitation at a specific frequency, and E_0 is a reference level of excitation defined by a reference intensity ($I_0 = 10^{-12}$ W/m²).

What is of interest here is the form of a power law that had been advocated by Stevens for all sensory modalities (Stevens 1957; see below) and that Zwicker accepted as valid in regard to loudness sensation and perception.

After calculation of specific loudness N' for each frequency band (Bark[z]), overall loudness N in a third step is calculated as an integral across specific loudness(es) like

(37) $N = \int_0^{24\,\text{Bark}} N' dz$ and is expressed in a unit called *sone* (Stevens 1936; see below).

To sum up Zwicker's approach, it proceeds from the spectrum of the physical stimulus as input to the BM filter bank. More precisely, the spectrum is taken as the long-term power spectrum of a sound (cf. Marozeau 2011) that is analyzed into frequency bins corresponding to the Bark scale and is averaged according to some time constant. While the filter bandwidth corresponds to the Bark[z] scale, excitation is more complex due to effects of level and masking. Specific loudness for each band is calculated taking into account thresholds in quiet as points of reference. Overall loudness finally is obtained from integrating specific loudness(es) across 24 Bark.

In regard to theory and methodology, Zwicker's approach implies that the 'psychophysical law' as formulated by Stevens (1957) holds. Stevens' claim was that a 'psychophysical law' applicable to various sensory modalities and dimensions would be (different from Fechner's formulation of a logarithmic correspondence of stimulus R and sensation S) a power function like

(38) $S = kR^n$

where k is a constant and the exponent n is specific for certain classes of stimuli, on the one hand, and dimensions of sensation (like loudness, brightness, tone height, etc.), on the other. However, Stevens himself observed that his approach, based on psychophysical methods like magnitude estimation, fractionation, and equisection of arbitrary frequency ratios, did not work very well for sensation of 'pitch' or, regarding his experimental paradigm, rather tone height as a correlate to the frequency of sine tones since subjects found it hard to neglect elementary experience of musical intervals (whereas Fechner's "law" accounts for such perceptual phenomena as 'octave equivalence'). Stevens had to admit that subjects protested against magnitude estimation of pitch, on the one hand, and that the data he and his co-workers obtained were "highly variable" (Stevens & Galanter 1957, 407). The scale construct known as 'mel scale' advocated by Stevens (& Volkmann 1940) has since met with severe criticism, and has been dismissed as irrelevant in the light of elementary musical experience[3].

For loudness sensation, things might be different since there seem to be no evident rules from common experience like there is 'octave equivalence' and musical consonance in regard to pitch and interval perception. Stevens' approach of equisection asking subjects to adjust the level of sounds to make them appear "half as loud" or "twice as loud" as a reference at least seems more plausible in regard to loudness than similar procedures ("half as high", "double as high") had turned out with respect to the sensation of pitch. However, Stevens (1971, 431, 437f.) noted that "equal intervals are not judged equal at different locations on a prothetic continuum" (such as loudness), and that, therefore, "a 5-sone interval does not sound the same size at different locations on the loudness continuum"[4]. In other words, subjective loudness estimates and judgment of degrees of loudness are dependent on level (as well as on other parameters such as frequency and duration of sine tones, bandwidth of noise signals, etc.).

For loudness sensation the exponent in equation (38) in general was set to 0.3 following experimental data according to which the loudness for certain stimuli doubles if the intensity level of the signal is increased by 10 dB. Taking equation (33), we find $\log_{10}[2] = 0.30103$ for the exponent. Sensation of loudness in this way is related to the intensity of the sound raised to the power $n \sim 0.3$. With $n < 1$, the relation of intensity to loudness can be regarded as a compressive function. As in Fechnerian psychophysics, a threshold of sensation S_0 is assumed (cf. Marozeau 2011) so that the magnitude of loudness sensation according to the Stevens power function would be

$$(39) \quad S = S_0 \cdot (I / I_0)^{0,3}$$

Taking sound pressure level instead of intensity (cf. equation 34), the loudness of a sound in general would be proportional to its RMS pressure raised to the power 0.6 (cf. Moore 2008, 131). The reservation "in general" is made here because the exponent 0.3 (equation 39) does not apply to all kinds of sounds and at all levels. In fact, a range of exponents has been reported to fit to certain types of stimuli as well as experimental conditions. Also, a modified version of the loudness function called INEX (Inflected Exponential) has been issued that is somewhat steeper than the conventional power 'law' near threshold and at sound pressure levels above ca. 70 dB, and less steep at moderate levels (ca. 40 – 70 dB SPL; see Florentine & Epstein 2006). Further, some studies on loudness sensation found that the relation of intensity to loudness for certain frequency bands and levels was closer to a logarithmic than to a power function[5]. In

---

[3] For a more detailed discussion, see Attneave & Olson 1971, Schneider 1997, 410-413, Greenwood 1997.

[4] It is not possible, at this point, to discuss theory and methodology of scaling, and in particular the problems concerning ratio scales as proposed by Stevens and colleagues. For a justification of his approach, see Stevens 1957, 1971, 1974, and for a more critical examination e.g. Sixtl 1982, 111f., Niederée & Narens 1996, Niederée & Mausfeld 1996, Greenwood 1997, Laming 1997.

[5] For reviews of research, see e.g. Hellbrück 1993, Moore 2008, Jesteadt & Leibold 2011. As has been argued already by Wagenaar (1975) and can be demonstrated fairly easily using programs like Mathematica or Matlab, a logarithmic function (Fechner) and a power function (Stevens) are very

addition, there have been some more "ecologically valid" experiments indicating that doubling of subjective loudness sensation is effected by a rise of level by 6 dB (as would be expected from equation 19, above) rather than 10 dB (Warren 1982, Helbrück 1993). Stevens proposed the *sone* scale as suited to express and compare magnitudes of subjective loudness. In loudness scaling, a sine tone of 1 kHz with a SPL of 40 dB represents a loudness (German: *Lautstärke*) of 40 phon. According to Stevens' approach, such a stimulus is assigned a subjective loudness (German: *Lautheit*) of 1 sone. A stimulus that is sensed twice as loud will be given 2 sone, a stimulus that appears half as loud 0.5 sone, etc. For levels above 40 phon, a relation was established from experimental data according to which an increase in level by 10 phon (or, in more general terms, 10 dB) means doubling subjective loudness sensation (in sone). Hence a simple relation to the phon scale exists:

Phon:	40	50	60	70	80	90	100	110	120	130	140
Sone:	1	2	4	8	16	32	64	128	256	512	1024

The sone scale no doubt is a very elegant construct from a formal point of view since each scale step corresponding to an increase of 10 phon *Lautstärke* can be expressed as 2^n sone *Lautheit*[6]. As to the construction of the sone scale, there has been substantial criticism in regard to data acquisition, data analysis and statistical procedures that led Stevens to claim an increase of 10 dB sound intensity would correspond to a doubling of subjective loudness. One of the arguments was that Stevens had used heterogeneous data from various samples representing different stimuli and conditions to form a distribution of means from which he calculated another mean to finally find the 10 dB-rule. Also, it was objected that Stevens missed to properly indicate the variances for each sub-sample (cf. Sader 1966, 46ff.), and that the range of loudness judgements reported by Stevens and other researchers apparently was so broad that a 10 dB-rule seems poorly supported by facts (cf. Warren 1982/2008, 110-111).

Continuing yet expanding Zwicker's efforts, Moore and Glasberg (1983) proposed a more refined model of the AF and a CB concept based on Equivalent Rectangular Bandwidth (ERB) suited to calculate excitation patterns by making use of the derived filter shapes. This model has been improved later on to cover a wider frequency range and to account for various parameters relevant for loudness perception (Moore, Peters & Glasberg 1990, Moore, Glasberg & Baer 1997, Glasberg & Moore 1990, 2006, Moore 2008). Again, the input is the physical sound spectrum that, after filtering (including outer and middle ear transfer), yields the excitation pattern. After specific loudness N', which can be viewed as 'loudness density' per CB (expressed in sones/Bark[z] or in sones/ERB$_N$, cf. Moore 2008, 133f.), is computed per ERB, overall loudness for a monaural hearing condition results from summing the specific loudness across the ERB-

---

similar or almost identical in shape depending on parameter settings. Given the variance found in sets of empirical data on loudness, a logarithmic function or a power function may fit equally well.

[6] In English terminology, loudness may indicate both *Lautstärke* and *Lautheit*. To avoid confusion, one may distinguish between loudness level (*Lautstärke*) and subjective loudness (*Lautheit*).

scale (a brief description of the main stages of the model is also provided by Marozeau 2011).

The models developed by Zwicker and colleagues as well as Moore and colleagues in their original versions were directed to monaural (monotic) hearing. Binaural (diotic) hearing, which involves presentation of the signal to both ears and loudness summation across two channels, had been a topic in research for a long time. In a number of studies, loudness summation indeed was regarded as a linear sum of the loudness sensations registered at each ear in particular if simple sounds such as pure tones were presented (e.g., Marks 1978). The theoretical ratio for the monaural/monotic listening condition compared to binaural/diotic loudness then should be close to 1 : 2. A number of studies following different experimental setups however produced ratios from ca. 1 : 1.2 to 1 : 1.8. Consequently, loudness summation seems to differ from simple additivity[7]. One of the reasons might be inhibition effective between the two ears already on the level of the peripheral auditory system (cf. Moore & Glasberg 2007), or on a higher level along the auditory pathway. As is fairly well-known from neuroanatomy and neurophysiology, there are several nuclei along the auditory pathway which connect to contralateral nuclei (n. cochlearis dorsalis; n. olivaris metencephali; n. lemnisci lateralis; colliculus inferior) in a complex crossover network where information coming from the right and the left ear is exchanged or combined and analyzed with respect to a number of features to facilitate, among other tasks, spatial hearing (cf. Keidel 1975, Ehret 1997, Yin 2002, Casseday, Fremouw & Covey 2002, Pickles 2008). Spatial hearing basically rests on two sources of information, namely temporal based on sensory pickup and neural evaluation of a phase difference between the signals arriving at the left and the right ear, and level differences between the respective signals. Given the functional organization of brain-stem and midbrain nuclei, loudness summation could possibly be performed at these stages of the auditory pathway after processing of signals in the cochlea and transduction into neural spike trains has been carried out. One reason to assume processing of especially temporal features (such as fast impulse sequences or amplitude modulation) on the level of the brainstem and midbrain is that neurons capable to detect and encode relatively high modulation rates apparently have been identified on this level (cf. Ehret 1997, Langner 2007). In addition, from an evolutionary point of view one may argue that processing of auditory signals in mammals has to be achieved in quasi-real time in order to provide information useful or even necessary for survival. Therefore, processing on the level of the brainstem and midbrain leading to appropriate motor action can be achieved faster than involving central processing. In fact, the speed of neural processing decreases from peripheral stages towards the cortex.

How the SPL of a given audio signal is exactly transformed into a (micro)mechanical response of the cochlea and after transduction is exactly encoded into neural spike trains is still a matter of debate (cf. Pickles 2008, ch. 9). As a first stage, one can see that for

---

[7] Gigerenzer (1982, 247ff.) refuted the hypothesis of simple additivity for loudness summation on theoretical grounds (demonstrating invalidity of conditions necessary to apply the commutative law to binaural hearing). Laming (1997, 97-104), who in his book provides a thorough critique of Stevens' construction of ratio scales, went even further in pointing to inconsistencies in studies on loudness summation (e.g., Marks 1978), strongly questioning not only the hypothesis of additivity but even the possibility to find a single exponent for the power law matching data from different experimental designs and conditions.

sine tones of low frequency (up to perhaps 400 Hz) peak velocity of the stapes footplate leads to peak pressure in the cochlea fluid; also, peak displacement of the CP/BM corresponds to peak pressure within the cochlear fluid with no phase lag, whereas BM motion lags behind vibration of the stapes by 2.5 to 4 cycles for high frequencies (cf. Patuzzi 1996, 221f.). The amount of phase lag itself seems to be dependent on sound intensity. There are a number of indications that loudness (level) of a given sound corresponds to CP/BM vibration, and that loudness (SPL [dB]) seems to increase approximately proportional to BM velocity [µm/sec] squared (Epstein 2011)[8]. However, compression comes into play already at rather low sound levels of $L > 30$ dB SPL, and grows with intensity. Compression that seems to work over a wide frequency band (see Lopez-Poveda et al. 2003) and is about 0.2-0.3 dB/dB even at low characteristic frequencies (Plack & Drga 2003) often is attributed to reduced gain of the 'cochlear amplifier' (involving outer hair cells, OHC). Also, one must take into account the spread of bandwidth (usually measured in ERB_N) with rising level that results in broader excitation patterns and, correspondingly, an increase in specific loudness N'. According to model data, bandwidth for excitation patterns grows quite strongly with level so that for a sinusoidal of 1 kHz the frequency band corresponding to a level of 80 or 90 dB SPL is quite large (bandwidth depending on whether the input to the AF or its output is taken as the variable determining the shape of the excitation pattern; cf. Moore 1993, 73f.). However, it is argued that, at least for low level stimuli, increase of bandwidth will not result in a corresponding increase in specific loudness N' since, with a larger number of ERBs involved, the shape of the excitation pattern is broadened, yet at the same time flattened (cf. Moore 1993, 2008). If one considers the area under the curve as equivalent in some form to the energy relevant to loudness sensation, then the area (or, rather, its integral) can be regarded as almost constant. This, however, holds only for very low levels.

In regard to extremely loud, broadband signals with pulse-like temporal structure such as the music examples employed in this study, some other factors have to be taken into account. First, for such signals sharp excitation peaks on the BM/CP as found at low levels are likely to disappear. Instead, broad excitation zones can be expected. Second, with SPL dB[C] > 110 dB longitudinal coupling along the length of the CP/BM seems feasible. From a micromechanical point of view, longitudinal coupling has been viewed as weak because of a lack of tension in the BM in the longitudinal direction as well as structural stiffness indicating properties of a thin plate rather than that of a thin membrane under tension (cf. Patuzzi 1996, 207f.). However, from a function of human loudness (expressed in sones) based on Chinchilla BM velocity data obtained at 10 kHz, one may hypothesize that, for a single sine tone of 7 – 9 kHz presented at a level of 110 dB, BM velocity amplitude would be close to 10000 µm/s (cf. Epstein 2011, Fig. 4.6)[9]. Since the cochlea is a nonlinear system not only at the base but also at the apex region (see Cheatham 2004), compression considerably greater than 1 : 2 or 0.5 dB/dB results from both mechanical and hair cell nonlinearities[10]. Compression had been reported

---

[8] For a model calculation of BM velocitiy, see de Boer 1996, 268ff.
[9] Remember that the velocity of sound in a plane wave propagating in air at the threshold of hearing is about 0.00000005 m/s = 0.05µm).
[10] For a general model of cochlear mechanics including nonlinear effects see de Boer 1996.

previously to grow for BM displacement above ca. 40 dB SPL according to a power function with the ubiquitous exponent 0.3 (see Delgutte 1996, 167f.).

The actual amount of energy per Bark[z] contained in musical signals that are very dense in temporal and spectral structure (see figures 6, 8, 9, 12 above) perhaps is enough to drive parts of the cochlear transducer into saturation and possibly into distortion especially when the SPL in playback reaches or even exceeds 120 dB[C]. For example, specific loudness as calculated for a short segment (130 ms) of *The Hype* (figure 22) recorded with an artificial head in a music club shows that, consequent to strong excitation effected by the music (figure 9), specific loudness also has a clear maximum in the very low bass range. If we sum the specific loudness N' over the range where energy is actually present (i.e., 23 Bark[z]), the resulting loudness is about 100 Phon (left ear: 99.8 phon, right ear: 100.1 phon).

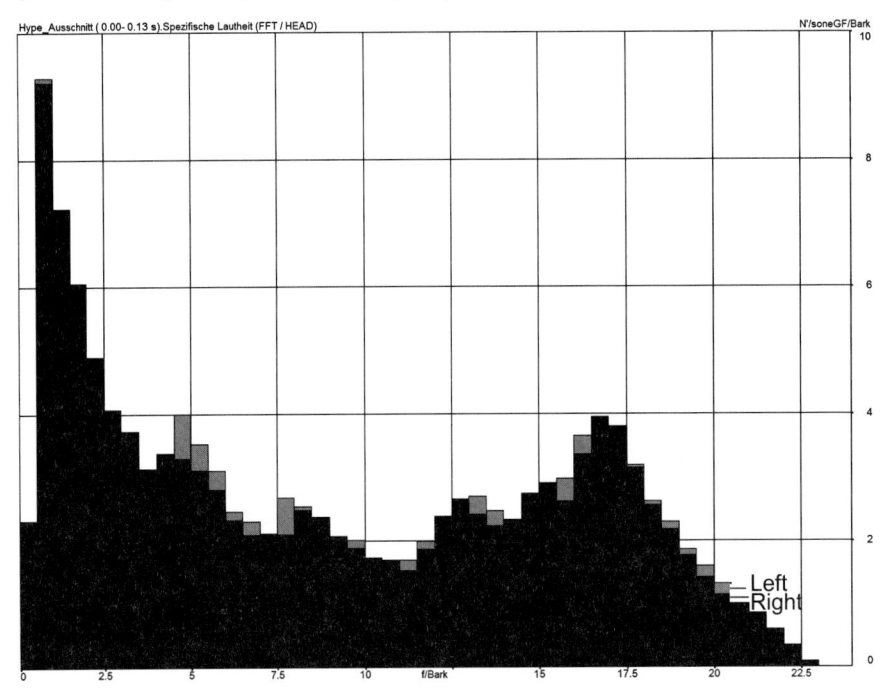

Figure 22: *The Hype*, specific loudness N' (sone) / Bark[z] 0-24

In fact, for this kind of music played back from a professional P.A. system loudness is very high almost all the time. As can be expected, the curve for SPL dB[C] over time (figures 20, 21) translates into equally high levels of loudness (figure 23).

Comparing the two plots, one sees that the SPL traces do not differ much, as can be expected. The magnitude of SPL at any given time is quite similar, however, the temporal resolution of course is much better with the 'fast' weighting, which indicates many short peaks and thus retains the actual intensity structure of the music recording while the 'slow' weighting acts like smoothening the SPL trace by low pass filtering (moving average) whereby the 'spiky' temporal structure of the music recording almost disappears.

A similar result is obtained in regard to temporal resolution when we apply 'slow' and 'fast' combined with dB[C]-weighting (see figures 19, 20). However, the dB[C]-weighting, preserving most of the energy contained in low frequency bands, not only leads to an increase of SPL of, on average 10 dB compared to the dB[A]-weighting, but also eliminates some of the dips left in the traces plotted in figures 17 and 18.

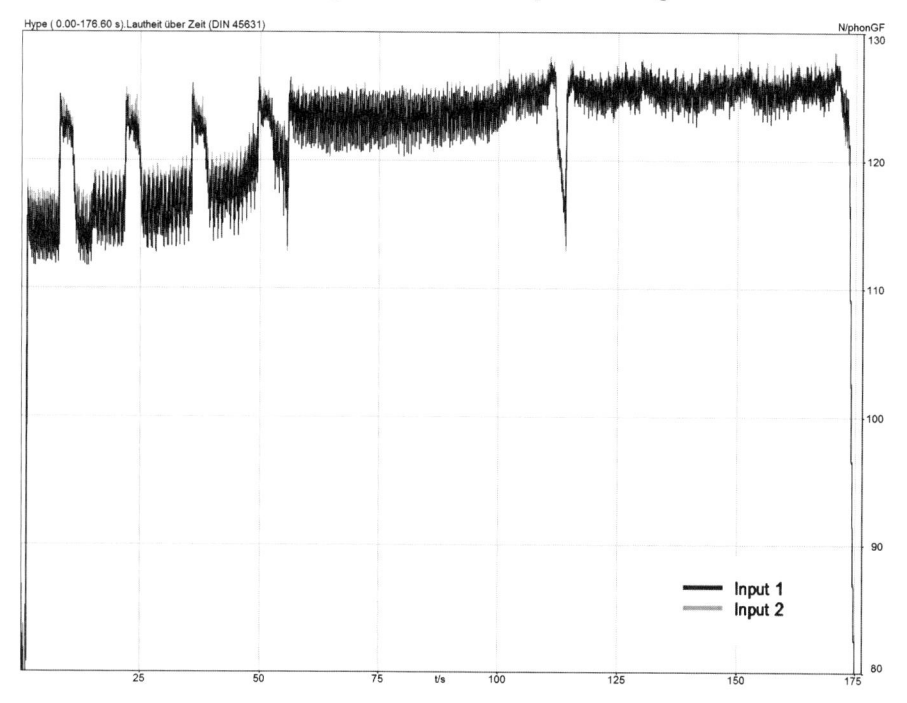

Figure 23: *The Hype*, Loudness (phon) / time (sec) for two ear channels

As one can see, in section 2 of the recording the overall loudness level reaches 123-125 phon, and in section 3 even more than 125 phon. As a third aspect relevant to neurophysiological processing of such sound signals, one can surmise that, at such high levels, saturation of many auditory nerve fibers (ANF) is likely to occur even if there are fibers with a high threshold (Delgutte 1996, 176ff.) and a 'sloping saturation' characteristic (Pickles 2008, chs. 4 and 9) in response to stimuli with higher intensity. Of course, one has to take the high number of fibers (about 30.000 in the human AN) into account which, as part of a system of combined sequential and parallel neural signal processing, suffice to cover a huge dynamic range of about 120 dB (while a single ANF can 'handle' a dynamic range of about 30 - 40 dB). Further, there is attenuation that can be effected by the musculus stapedius (which is activated by high SPL whereas the m. tensor tympani is not!) and by efferent circuits originating on the level of the n. olivaris metencephali. The medial olivocochlear bundle provides a reflex-like trigger that apparently attenuates the 'cochlear amplifier' as well as the activity in ANF. As is typical in feedback loops, increasing intensity of input leading to increasing activity of the afferent arm of the auditory pathway will also give rise to increasing activity of the efferent arm. Hence, it is no surprise that attenuation effected by the olivocochlear bundle is reported to increase with stimulus bandwidth. However, as a comparison of the SPL dB[C] recorded for *The Hype* to the sensation of loudness N (both plotted against time, see figures 20, 22) demonstrates, the effect of attenuation (at least in the model employed for our measurements) is very slight and does not yield a significant gain reduction necessary to prevent the auditory system exposed to such sounds in a music club or discotheque from damage. Also, as is obvious from figure 22, the "spiky" excitation pattern per time unit resulting from the pulse-like sound structure remains on the level of overall loudness sensation.

In the literature on loudness sensation and perception, a broad range of phenomena resulting from lateral inhibition, suppression, masking, adaptation, fatigue, etc. has been reported. Taken one by one or in combinations, all such effects condition loudness perception to some extent. Therefore, a comprehensive explanation how loudness of vastly different types of stimuli presented under various conditions is encoded in the cochlea and in the AN will be difficult to find. A hypothesis advanced by Fletcher and Munson as early as 1933 according to which loudness would correspond to the total discharge rate of all ANF within a certain interval has been questioned as perhaps being to simple. The *auditory nerve spike count*-hypothesis, as it was called (Relkin & Doucet 1997), assumes that the total spike rate produced by an array of neurons per time unit correlates with intensity of the sound stimulus so that with growing intensity (SPL dB) an proportional increase of spike rate should be observed. There have been some studies, however, which suggested that the increase in (observed or estimated) overall spike rate would be less than the increase in loudness. One of the possible reasons for this could be the fact that the number of neurons that can be stimulated with sine tones at moderate levels is not constant along the CP/BM. For such stimuli, spike rate decreases with increasing frequency. On the other hand, efferent innervation of the BM at the apex is reduced compared to the base (which is one factor to explain reduced sensitivity for low frequencies). Surprisingly, findings obtained with impaired subjects who have suffered damage of OHC indicate that loudness sensation grows steeper with intensity above a certain level than in normal hearing subjects (so-called loudness recruitment; cf. Smeds & Leijon 2011). This indicates that a control circuit of OHC and IHC assumed to prevent the hearing system from overload (cf. Hellbrück 1993, 103f.) partially breaks down consequent to damage of the OHC (and related CB/BM structures).

Given that broadband signals are presented at high SPL such as the music examples discussed in this study, there are very strong excitation patterns for each CP/BM resulting from the density and intensity of spectral components (see figure 9). We are safe to assume that the high amount of energy contained in the signal per time unit must be represented in the spatio-temporal patterns of spike trains in the AN. Since the rate of spikes per neuron is limited (by refractory period and dynamical saturation; see Pickles 2008), total neural activity representing the intensity of sound must be somehow distributed over the array of the ca. 30.000 AN fibres. Hence, a spatio-temporal representation seems a plausible model (though we do not know yet how this works in detail, and how afferent-efferent circuits modulate the processing of spike data along the auditory pathway). It has been suggested recently from fMRI data that spectral loudness summation is achieved in the primary auditory cortex (AI; see Röhl et al. 2010) since it was not traceable with the methodology employed on the level of the inferior colliculus. However, another fMRI study using broadband noise as stimulus found increased activiation with increasing level in the cochlear nucleus (CN), superior olive (SO), inferior colliculus (IC), corpus geniculatum mediale (CGM), and in auditory cortical areas (Sigalovsky & Melcher 2006). This indicates that processing of loudness involves all the major relays along the auditory pathway from the brainstem through the thalamus (CGM, which is regarded essential for feature extraction from complex input) up to cortical areas. In addition, cortical brain activation as revealed by fMRI recordings seems to grow with perceived loudness rather than with stimulus intensity (Langers et al. 2007) indicating that a final evaluation of the neural input is executed on the cortical level.

In regard to temporal aspects of sensation and perception, one has to distinguish resolution capabilities from integration. Temporal resolution (depending on the type of stimulus) can be as fine as 3-10 ms while integration typically spans over 200-300 ms (cf. Viemeister & Plack 1993, 143ff.). For simple signals such as sine tones, temporal integration is known to depend on the ratio of intensity and duration in such a way that, in order to maintain a certain threshold, SPL must increase by 3 dB if presentation time of the stimulus is halved (Pedersen & Elberling 1972). With respect to music, many subjects can identify two tones presented one after another as separate in time and different in pitch as well as in timbre if each of the two tones lasts for about 30-50 ms. The absolute time needed to identify musical tones depends on their pitch (fundamental frequency [Hz] and period length [ms]), on spectral characteristics (number and strength of harmonics) as well as on SPL and other factors (e.g., musical training, attention). Unless tones are comprised of inharmonic spectral components or subjected to signifycant amplitude and/or frequency modulation, pitch, timbre and loudness of most elementary musical signals can be judged by ear within ca. 60-150 ms. For complex sounds such as chords or sonorities, identification (which involves cognitive processes such as categorization and access to memory) probably needs more time so that an integration constant of 200-300 ms seems appropriate. As many studies have demonstrated, our sense of hearing is capable to trace very short temporal events of a few ms (e.g., a gap in a noise signal or inter-aural time differences) and thus provides excellent time resolution capability, on the one hand. On the other, identification and evaluation of complex signals needs longer time constants. Since music very often includes many fast events as well as dynamic changes and variations of spectral energy distribution, it is essentially a time-varying, non-stationary process. This holds true also for loudness perception where one can distinguish (a) instantaneous loudness, (b) short-term loudness, and (c) long-term loudness, each based on a different time constant. There are several loudness models that have been implemented to deal with time-varying sounds (cf. Rennies et al. 2010, Marozeau 2011). It was found that, with fixed integration constants performance of such models was uneven for different types of sounds since some (e.g. sounds undergoing slow modulation) would require rather long integration constants. In fact, it seems necessary to adapt integration constants to the nature of sounds, especially if these have non-stationary characteristics. If, for example, a single integration constant of 100 ms is chosen (as in some models or calculations), this must be regarded as kind of a compromise solution.

It should be noted, in this context, that the LTAS and excitation patterns calculated in this article from sound examples have been based on segments of the signal covering at least one period of a pulse-like temporal sound structure (see figures 2, 3, 23). It can be shown that spectral flux and dynamic change within such a 'pulse' is slight so that taking such a segment as one 'event' in regard to short-term loudness seems justified.

6. Techno, discos, decibels, and politics: some conclusions

As has been demonstrated in this article, genres of modern pop and rock music have a pulse-like temporal organization and a dense spectral composition with energy amassed especially in the low and very low frequency region. Such characteristics were already featured in much of the so-called 'disco' music and in hiphop and techno productions as well as in some metal-oriented rock genres of the 1980s. Techno perhaps was *the* genre where pulsed sounds and a 'spiky' sound structure were widely in use[11]. Meanwhile, 'spiky' music is by no means restricted to techno, hard trance or similar genres but is commonplace even among conventional pop. As but one additional example, we may point to a production that went up straight in the U.S. pop and in the U.S. R & B charts in 2002, Eryka Badu's *Love of my life (Ode to HipHop)*[12]. This number, which may appear quite unobstrusive as a medium tempo song featuring a female voice, in fact is full of pulse-like elements grouped into short segments of about 10" each that are repeated over and over. An analysis of such a segment (figure 24) reveals the pulse-like temporal organization whereby one phrase (≈10.5 seconds) is divided into four sub-groups. Within each such sub-group of about 2.4 seconds duration, there are four very strong short pulses coming from an electronic bass drum (or a similarly synthesized sound). Counting the strong pulses, we find 44 within 30 seconds of music.

The structure of such music, which indeed was and is extremely 'popular'[13], is of interest since it is the "stuff" that gets played a lot in discotheques, on the one hand, and is heard by young people by means of mobile mp3-players and similar devices, on the other. The risk of afflicting damage to the hearing system seems particularly high with pulse-type 'spiky' sounds since high energy levels are reached in very short time. Moreover, there are observations from experiments in hearing according to which subjects seem to systematically underrate the objective loudness level of sound presented to an occluded ear (Keidser et al. 2000). In a test situation involving a loudness matching task, normal hearing subjects on average chose a level of about +10 dB (measured at the eardrum) for a 500 Hz octave band signal compared to the open ear

---

[11] On top of that, 'techno pulse' has a specific meaning denoting "the part of a techno song when the music gets lower and then comes in full strength, it can be compared to the breakdown of hardcore music". Further, there is a drug called 'pulse' that seems to induce rapid bodily movements (*"Dude, we pulsed last night and i couldn't quit dancing!" "I love listening to techno music while I pulse, don't you?"* http://www.urbandictionary.com/define.php?term=techno%20pulse).

[12] Erykah Badu ft. Common, *Love of my life (Ode to Hip Hop)* reached no. 9 in the U.S. pop charts and no. 1 in the U.S. R & B charts.

[13] Besides conventional CD publication, the song plus a video are available from several internet platforms.

condition. Though the stimuli used in this experiment were quite different from pop and rock music, the finding that the level was raised by about 10 dB when the ear was occluded to produce equal loudness sensation indicates that the use of earphones when listening to music could have a similar effect (especially in low frequency regions). At least this is an issue that warrants further investigation.

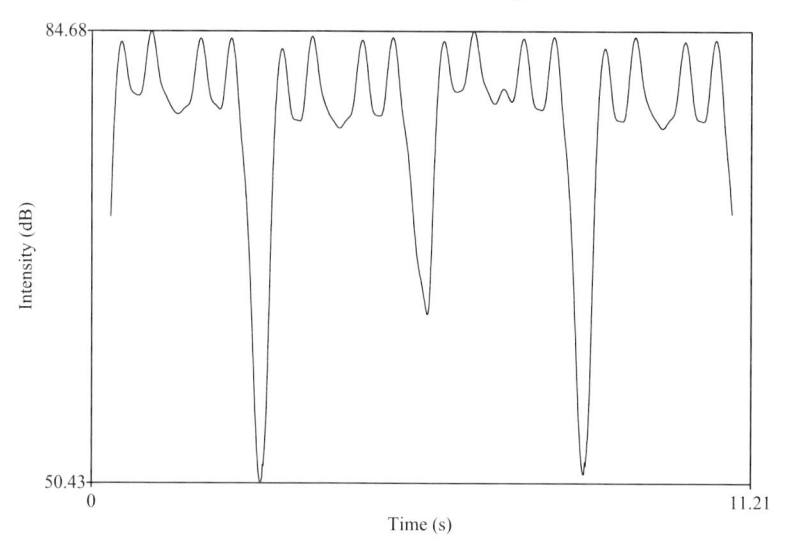

Figure 24: Erykah Badu ft. Common: *Love of my life* (*Ode to Hip Hop*): pulse-like structure per phrase and sub-group (4 x 4 strong pulses per 10.5")

The fact that music as recorded on CD is maximized in spectral energy over the bandwidth of hearing as well as in its temporal organization (as is obvious from the measurements shown in figs. 4, 6, 8, 12, 23) follows two goals: artists and, more so, producers want to achieve maximum loudness to attract in particular young customers, and to sell their ware that, as is evident in many cases, has more "punch" than the product of the competitor. To the same token, radio stations addressing young people strive to "outperform" their rival stations by being "louder" than the rest. For studio productions, already in the 1980 and 1990s hardware and software tools known as "aural exciter" and "loudness maximizer" became available which are used to increase spectral density and overall level per time unit, however, at the cost of also increasing distortion (cf. Chalupper 2000). In the course of this unfortunate developments based on the availability of CDs (allowing for a considerably higher dynamic range than LPs made from vinyl compound) as well as a broad range of analogue and digital tools for shaping dynamics (e.g., multi-band compressors, transient limiters), a veritable "loudness war" or "level war" broke out (for relevant measurements and background information, see v. Ruschkowski 2008). CDs since the early 1980 have become louder every year, meaning the average SPL [dB] per song or album has gone up to the very 'ceiling' of 0 dB-FS (FS = full scale, the upper limit of undistorted level in a digital audio system), and not infrequently even beyond this level into distortion. At present, many if not most CDs from pop and rock genres are produced so as to evoke maximum loudness sensation in

51

listeners. To this end, a special mastering process that includes spectral and dynamic shaping follows the production of the music that finally is evaluated as "fit for airplay" (broadcast) if it as loud as, or even louder than, rival products.

The effects such products might elicit in music listeners/consumers as well as in a more general perspective of music developments are manifold. First, making music productions such as songs or instrumental pieces appear louder means one has to reduce dynamics by applying a higher ratio of compression. In fact, the "loudest" present-day productions from the heavy metal genre such as "Death Magnetic" from Metallica (2008) use only a very small fraction (about 3 dB) of the dynamic range the CD standard offers (theoretically ca. 96 dB; for technical reasons, the actual peak level found in most recordings is < 90 dB). Second, increasing level by sacrificing dynamics results in static loudness that persists on a high level (cf. figure 12). In regard to music perception, such productions diminish variety and thereby reduce the amount of information available to listeners (one might get bored soon)[14]. In regard to hearing, music that is highly compressed in recordings up to so-called "brickwall limiting" (compression ratio ∞ : 1) means that, when listening to such music presented via loudspeakers or earphones, energy transport to the ear and energy consumption by the hearing system is near maximum all the time with practically no gap or break for whatever recovery. This in turn implies that cochlear motion and velocity amplitude are driven to saturation (and, correspondingly, deflection of hair cell stereocilia by shearing forces).

The effects of exposure to loud (SPL > 90 dB[C]) or even very loud music (SPL > 110 dB[C]) have been studied since the 1970s (see the review provided by Clark 1991). At first, the focus was on live music events such as rock concerts and listening to music from personal cassette players (PCP, e.g., the Sony Walkman) by earphones (Hellbrück & Schick 1989). It was found quite early that certain earphones could produce very high SPL of up to 124 dB[A] though most users interviewed in experiments kept the preferred listening level of the music of their choice around 90 dB[A] (cf. Clark 1991, 177). However, an estimate of risks based on a large sample of (n = 1364) subjects that were screened with high-definition audiometry (Meyer-Bisch 1996) showed that exposure time to loud music heard from PCP was a factor besides SPL that had to be taken into account. Signs of auditory suffering (tinnitus, hearing fatigue) increased in subjects using PCP extensively even though hearing loss was not yet detectable or relatively slight (up to 4 dB at 4 kHz) while such effects were much more pronounced in subjects visiting discotheques or attending rock concerts on a regular basis. With increasing exposure time and higher levels from music either heard in live music concerts or via earphones the possibility to develop "classical" signs of damage such as temporary threshold shift (TTS) or permanent threshold shift (PTS) for certain frequency bands grows. Persons who visit discotheques frequently may suffer TTS or PTS. For example, in a relatively large sample of pupils (13 – 19 years old) subjected to audiometry a PTS of 2-4 dB for 2 and 4 kHz was found, and a PTS of 3-7 dB for those pupils who were used to listen to music at home for hours besides visiting discos (cf. Babisch et al. 1988).

Of 141 patients treated in the HNO Klinik of the University of Würzburg between 1993 and 2003 for traumata resulting from exposure to loud sound at discos and rock

---

[14] There is a movement against the 'loudness war' that seeks to recapture and reinstall proper dynamics in pop and rock music productions; cf. www.turnmeup.org

concerts, more than half suffered ototraumatic effects at both ears (cf. Elberg 2010). All patients except one reported a tinnitus on one ear or on both sides. Hearing loss typically was found in the frequency band from 3 – 6 kHz; on average, hearing loss at 4 kHz was 21.2 dB. For 24 patients treated in the University HNO hospital at Hamburg 1994-97 after exposure to very loud sound (from rock concerts and discotheques to parties, and (ab)use of the 'Walkman'), some showed a hearing loss of up to 40-60 dB at 4 kHz, often combined with ipsilateral tinnitus at the same frequency (Metternich & Brusis 1999).

As can be expected, the risk for developing hearing loss is particularly high for persons working in discotheques and music clubs. In a study conducted at Birmingham, it was found that four subjects (out of 13) working up to 16 hours per week in music entertainment venues had developed permanent hearing loss to the extent of > 30 dB for high and low frequencies at both ears (Sadhra et al. 2002). For the staff of discotheques, Meyer-Bisch (1996, 138) observed "characteristic ototraumatic lesions, especially in disc jockeys". He also had measured SPL in several French discotheques; his recordings "were closer to 105 dBA or even 110 dBA in 1994" than keeping to an upper limit of < 100 dB[A]. Similar results were obtained in discotheques at Berlin (cf. Plontke & Zenner 2004, 130-132) where most of the levels recorded in 1984 and in 1994/97 were at or above 100 dB[A]. Measurements obtained in 15 discotheques all over Germany gave averaged SPL from 96.8 dB[A] to 106.1 dB[A] (Leitmann 2003). More recent data from measurements carried out 2005/06 in 20 discotheques in Bavaria again demonstrate that SPL of 100 dB[A] are common practice, and that SPL averaged over intervals of 30 minutes can reach or even exceed 110 dB[A] (Twardella et al. 2007). Also, this study showed once more that SPL increases in most discotheques from 11 p.m. to 2 a.m. by about 6 dB[A], that is, 2 dB[A] per hour. It should be noted that even very high SPL (at or above 100 dB[A]) are judged to be "adequate" or even "too low" by a majority of disco visitors, and that about 60% of the visitors interviewed apparently don't care about possible damage to the hearing system (cf. Leitmann 2003).

There have been speculations why a considerable number of disco visitors seem to prefer high or very high SPL notwithstanding the risk of hearing loss. Some of the factors that might be of relevance concern the human body and bodily motion. As can be checked out empirically, a person standing relatively close to subwoofer speaker systems (distance < 5 m) literally can be "shaken" by techno or similar music that comprises many pulse-like sounds with fundamental frequencies at 40-80 Hz if the SPL exceeds 110 dB[A] or, in a more adequate weighting (see below), 120 dB[C]. In this regard, it has been argued that humans as well as other vertebrates have preserved, in the course of evolution, a certain capacity to process sound with parts of the vestibular system (macula sacculi) in addition to the cochlea (Todd & Cody 2000). The hypothesis tested in experiments was that, in particular for pulse-like stimuli of considerable intensity (> 90-95 dB[A, Impulse-weighted] and for low frequencies a specific response can be expected that can be recorded as so-called myogenic vestibularly evoked potentials (MVEP). In fact, such responses were found after stimulation with either a single percussive sound (ca. 100 ms duration, main spectral components at ca. 100 and 240 Hz), or with a pulse train (Todd & Cody 2000, Todd 2001). The saccular response seems to have peaks for best frequencies (probably around 200 Hz) and for a level of 105 dB[AI]. In fact, this is about the level often registered in discotheques (see above) as well as in live rock concerts. A level of about 105 dB[AI] has, therefore, been tentatively labelled the "rock'n'roll threshold" (cf. Todd & Cody 2000) as a majority of persons attending rock concerts may expect just this sound pressure level to give them a bodily "feel" of the music

Though many visitors to discotheques, music clubs and open air or stadium concerts may esteem high or even very high SPL, such levels as we have recorded in a music club using the house P.A. (figures 16, 19-21, 23) are suited to cause hearing loss especially if visitors are exposed to the music for several hours or visit discotheques frequently. In regard to risks of hearing loss, a so-called equal-energy principle has been a matter of debate. In short, this principle that plays a certain role in noise control and protection of industrial workers against noise assumes that energy input from sound is accumulated over time. Hence, a daily exposure level ($L_{Ex,8h} = L_{aeq,8h} = L_{EP,d}$) or a weekly noise exposure level $L_{EX,w}$ for a typical working week of 5 days x 8 hours = 40 h is calculated (see, e.g. Maute 2006). According to ISO-1999 standard (1990, section 3.6), noise exposure can also be calculated in Pa^2 h. The noise dosis B for a period T can be found from equ. 40:

(40) $$B = \int_0^T |p_A(t)|^n \, dt$$ with sound pressure level p_A (A-weighted)

Applying the equal-energy-hypothesis (EEH), a 100% of the weekly (noise or other sound) dose will be absorbed after a person has been exposed to sound at a level of 85 dB[A] for 40 h. The same dose will be consumed at 95 dB[A] after 4 h, at 98 dB[A] after 2 h, and at 101 dB[A] after only one hour. This concept implies that a single visit per week to a discotheque for 4 hours where the average SPL on the dance floor typically is at or above 100 dB[A] already leads to a critical "overdose". Looking closer, things are even worse. Applying the rule whereby an increase by 3 dB doubles the power, and setting a lower risk limit at 80 dB[A] for a weekly noise exposure of 5 x 8 = 40 h (as is the case in legal regulations[15]), the critical dose would be obtained at 96 dB[A] after only one hour. Since levels around 95 dB[A] have been measured in the bar area of discotheques, this means that employees serving drinks at the bar can do so for one hour without protecting their ears, and after one hour must wear appropriate earplugs or use other devices for protection.

In regard to music, sound power and loudness levels, two factors have to be given special consideration: one relates to the spectral composition of rock and pop music (including techno and similar genres), the other to their temporal structure. As is obvious from figs. 5, 7 and 9 (above), in music such as played in discos and clubs, much if not most of the spectral energy is concentrated at low or even very low frequencies. For example, taking the spectrum of a small segment of Erykah Badu's *Love of my life*

---

[15] Of importance is the European noise regulation 2003/10/EG which is part of German national law effective March 2007 (Verordnung zum Schutz der Beschäftigten vor Gefährdungen durch Lärm und Vibrationen vom 6. März 2007, BGBl. I, S. 261). The relevant measures are found in §§ 6, 8 of this law.

including a beat of the electronic bass drum, we find the strongest components at the very bottom:

Frequency (Hz)	Power (dB/Hz)
46.8	65.61
62.44	60.19
97.1	58.39

If we would apply frequency-weighting A (cf. fig. 14) to these components, their power would be cut by ca. -20dB (at 97.1 Hz) to about -30 dB (at 46.8 Hz). This would certainly change the character of the music, which is designed and produced to have a low frequency fundament comprising a pulse-like temporal organization (fig. 24). In this connection, it is interesting to see that the extent to which low frequency components have achieved a boost in *Fight for your right* and in the *Gabber* track (cf. figs. 7, 9) is more than enough to compensate reduced sensitivity of our hearing system at low or even very low frequencies. Hence, such audio productions contain enough energy at the very base of hearing (in about the range from A_0 to C_2) to convey tonal and spectral information (for which auditory analysis is difficult, see Schneider & Tsatsishvili 2011) even if such music would be presented at low levels. This, however, would be quite untypical. Taking the spectral and temporal structure of such music as analyzed in this article (and hundreds if not thousands of similar pieces) as in fact it is, and also taking into account the reality of huge and powerful sound systems including subwoofers installed in discotheques and assembled on stage at clubs or stadiums, we find again the same overemphasis of bass in the music played back from such a system (see fig. 22) that is an essential feature of the original CD recording. Therefore, employing frequency-weighting A for sound level measurements in clubs, discotheques or at live concerts is totally inadequate as it simply cuts away much of the power actually present at low frequencies. Measurements of SPL involving dB[A]-weighting are thus flawed because the levels in discotheques and live music clubs are so high (about 110-135 dB, flat response) that a weighting function representing the inverse of the loudness contour closest to this level certainly cannot be the A-filter (which corresponds to the loudness contour representing the threshold of hearing and would be suited only to levels of 30-40 dB). Consequently, employing frequency-weighting A in sound levelling at discotheques or live rock concerts means measurements systematically underrate the real SPL prevalent at a certain place and time by, typically, 10-15 dB[16]. The difference is already obvious when comparing dB[A] to dB[C] readings (figs. 15-21). At high or very high levels, either frequency weighting C, which corresponds close enough to the behaviour of the auditory system to yield realistic results, or, alternatively, measurement not weighted in regard to spectral energy should be chosen.

---

[16] It was found also that subjective loudness estimates typically are 15 dB *above* dB[A] readings (cf. Gummlich 1992, 109). It has been demonstrated (cf. Zwicker & Fastl 1986) that, for certain stimuli, dB[A] readings may drastically deviate from subjective loudness judgements, to the point where dB[A] data are useless.

Further, one has to take temporal features of sound into account. In many environmental noise measurements, a more or less continuous noise level (resulting from traffic on a motorway or a machine running at constant speed) can be recorded with long integration constants (such as 'slow'). Also, it is long-standing practice in noise control to obtain "equivalent" levels L_{eq} from impulse or other short and strong sound bursts by applying various techniques of averaging SPL over time (see Kötter 1989, Schick 1990, Maute 2006). Averaging over time of course means eliminating impulses or similar pulse-like sounds. It has been objected to L_{eq} approaches that these are unsuited to predict noise-induced hearing loss (NIHL). In animal experiments involving 58 chinchillas[17] it was demonstrated that the actual loss of sensory cells relevant for hearing is not just dependent on the amount of energy absorbed but also on the temporal and the spectral structure of noise signals (Hamernik & Qiu 2001). The experiment thus showed equal amounts of energy can have different hazardous effects. A measure relevant to assess the hazardous potential of sounds in addition to energy is the degree of peakedness (expressed as the kurtosis β of the amplitude distribution). Meanwhile, kurtosis as a criterion has been incorporated into noise metrics for risk assessment (cf. Goley et al. 2011).

Given that much if not most of techno music as well as other contemporary rock and pop music is essentially pulse-based and 'spiky' in temporal structure, the temporal weighting function 'slow' is unsuited whereas 'fast' is more appropriate to pick up the short peaks (figs. 16, 18, 20). Alternatively, 'impulse' can be tried (fig. 21) depending on the signal.

In conclusion, we may point to political debates concerning health risks from loud music such as presented in discotheques and at live rock/pop concerts. In Switzerland, already in 1996 a legal regulation was established which sets the SPL limit to 93 dB[A] averaged per hour[18]. Meanwhile, a revised version was developed which would allow 100 dB[A] at the loudest spot of the dance floor for a maximum time of just 0.5 h. In Germany, after much discussions in specialist's panels devoted to 'Soziakusis' and 'Diskothekenlärm', the health ministers' conference convened in the summer of 2007 to make a decision according to which relevant organizations of the music and entertainment business should be asked to agree that all parties involved (e.g., discotheques, DJs, clubs, P.A. services, etc.) should strive for an average SPL in concerts and discotheques below 100 dB[A][19]. As the soft formulation of this goal indicates, the health ministers sought an agreement on a voluntary basis. However, measurements carried out in 20 discotheques in Bavaria 2005-06 (Twardella et al.) and in 27 discotheques at Hamburg in the autumn of 2007 revealed that the voluntary 100 dB[A] limit was not always respected. To the contrary, at Hamburg the SPL averaged over all 27 venues that had been inspected for level control was at 103 dB[A] (median and aM),

---

[17] In all of these poor creatures and in many more (ab)used in later experiments by the same team, the left cochlea was destroyed surgically. Animal experiments such as these are highly questionable from an ethical point of view notwithstanding small benefits that might result for assessment of hearing loss risks.

[18] Der Schweizerische Bundesrat: Verordnung über den Schutz des Publikums von Veranstaltungen vor gesundheitsgefährdenden Schalleinwirkungen und Laserstrahlen (Schall- und Laser-Verordnung) 1996.

[19] Beschluss der 78. Gesundheitsministerkonferenz der Länder vom 1.7.2005, TOP 7.1

with four venues reaching even 107 dB[A][20]. The seemingly small difference of 3 dB above the limit of course must be viewed in terms of the increase in pressure and intensity (see table 1).

The facts that are of relevance for assessment of hearing loss risks affected by very loud music are: (1) the average SPL measured in many discotheques and at live concerts (as L_{Aeq}) in many instances has been found to exceed 100 dB[A]. (2) Frequency weighting A for reasons explained above is totally inadequate as it systematically underrates levels in particular in loud music comprising a lot of "deep end" (low and very low frequencies). It must be remembered that frequency weighting "A" was accepted as a compromise, way back in 1967, consequent to discussions that involved various political, economic, and technical aspects on national as well as international levels (cf. Gummlich 1992; see also Schick 1990). Frequency weighting "A" certainly wasn't the best solution in regard to facts and conditions known from acoustics and psycho-acoustics. Arguments put forward in favour of "A" included that devices for level measurements should be manufactured and bought at low cost, and that operating had to be kept simple (Gummlich 1992, 111).

In order to obtain a more realistic picture, the least we can do is applying frequency weighting "C" as well as using appropriate temporal weighting. (3) Expressed in dB[C], average SPL in discotheques, clubs, and at live concerts are actually in the range from ca. 110 – 125 dB[C] (see figs. 16, 19-21). This is the reality we must deal with. There are some approaches to reduce SPL in music clubs by technical means (e.g., Sandell et al. 2007), and there are also discussions at present to limit the power available for earphones connected to personal media players in order to prevent users from hazardous levels. (4) Since much if not most of the music presented in discotheques, clubs, and at concerts contains pulse-like elements, L_{eq} seems unsuited as a valid noise metric since it eliminates the impact of impulses (see above). To account for pulsed sounds in particularly 'spiky' music from such genres as techno, a measure of peakedness as has been introduced in noise assessment studies recently (cf. Goley et al. 2011) seems inevitable. In sum, we must look at the real structure of technically produced and reproduced music in their technical and social context instead of playing down health risks by means of "A" weighting and L_{Aeq} averaging.

References

Ahnert, Wolfgang, Frank Steffen 1993. *Beschallungstechnik. Grundlagen und Praxis*. Stuttgart: Hirzel.

Attneave, Fred, Richard Olson 1971. Pitch as a medium: A new approach to psychophysical scaling. *Am. Journal Psych.* 84, 147-166,

Babisch, W., H. Ising, D. Dziombowski 1988. Einfluß von Diskothekbesuchen und Musikgewohnheiten auf die Hörfähigkeit von Jugendlichen. *Zeitschrift für Lärmbekämpfung* 35, 1-9.

Bauch, H. 1956. Die Bedeutung der Frequenzgruppe für die Lautheit von Tönen. *Acustica* 6, 40-45.

Békésy, Georg von 1961. *Experiments in Hearing*. New York: McGraw – Hill.

---

[20] Freie und Hansestadt Hamburg. Amt für Gesundheit und Verbraucherschutz. Bericht über Messung in Hamburger Diskotheken. (28.02.2008).

Casseday, John, Thane Fremouw, Ellen Covey 2002. The Inferior Colliculus: A Hub for the Central Auditory System. In Donata Oertel, Richard Fay, Arthur Popper (eds.). *Integrative Functions in the Mammalian Auditory Pathway*. New York: Springer, ch. 7, 238ff.

Chalupper, Josef 2000. Aural Exciter and Loudness Maximizer: What's Psychoacoustic about "Psychoacoustic Processors"? *109th AES Convention in Los Angeles, USA, 22.-25.9.2000, Audio Engineering Society Preprint*, Nr. 5208.

Cheatham, Mary Ann 2004. Nonlinearities at the apex of the cochlea: implications for auditory perception. In Daniel Pressnitzer et al. (eds.). *Auditory Signal Processing: Physiology, Psychoacoustics, and Models*. New York: Springer, 1-6.

Clark, William 1991. Noise exposure from leisure activities: A review. *Journal Acoust. Soc. Am.* 90, 175-181.

De Boer, Egbert 1996. Mechanics of the Cochlea: Modeling Efforts. In Peter Dallos, Athur Popper, Richard Fay (eds.). *The Cochlea*. New York: Springer, 258-317.

Delgutte, Bertrand 1996. Physiological Models for basic auditory Percepts. In Harold Hawkins et al. (eds.). *Auditory Computation*. New York, Berlin: Springer 157-220.

Ehret, Günter 1997. The Auditory Midbrain, a "Shunting Yard" of Acoustical Information Processing. In G. Ehret, R. Romand (eds.). *The Central Auditory System*. Oxford: Oxford Univ. Pr., 259-316.

Elberg, Peter 2010. *Lärmtrauma nach Diskotheken- und Rockkonzertbesuchen*. Med. Diss. Univ. Würzburg 2010.

Epstein, Michael 2011. Correlates of Loudness. In Mary Florentine, Athur Popper, Richard Fay (eds.). *Loudness*. New York: Springer, 89-106.

Florentine, Mary, Michael Epstein 2006. To honor Stevens and repeal his law (For the auditory system). In Diana Kornbrot et al. (eds.). *Fechner Day 2006*. Hatfield: Univ. of Hertfordshire Pr., 37-41.

Gehrtsen, Christian, Helmut Vogel 1993. *Physik*. 17th ed. Berlin: Springer.

Gigerenzer, Gerd 1981. *Messung und Modellbildung in der Psychologie*. München: Reinhardt.

Glasberg, Brian, Brian Moore 1990. Derivation of auditory filter shapes from notched-noise data. *Hearing Res.* 47, 103-138.

Glasberg, Brian, Brian Moore 2006. Prediction of absolute thresholds and equal-loudness contours using a modified loudness model. *Journal Acoust. Soc. Am.* 120, 585-588.

Goley, G. Steven, Won Joon Song, Jay Kim 2011. Kurtosis corrected sound pressure level as a noise metric for risk assessment of occupational noises. *Journal Acoust. Soc. Am.* 129, 1475-1481.

Greenwood, Donald 1961. Critical Bandwidth and the Frequency Coordiantes of the Basilar Membrane. *Journal Acoust. Soc. Am.* 33, 1344-1356.

Greenwood, Donald 1990. A cochlear frequency-position function for several species – 29 years later. *Journal Acoust. Soc. Am.* 87, 2592-2605.

Greenwood, Donald 1997. The Mel Scales disqualifying bias and consistency of pitch-difference equisections in 1956 with equal cochlear distances and equal frequency ratios. *Hearing Res.* 103, 199-224.

Gummlich, H. 1989. Zur Entwicklung der Geräuschbewertung in Wissenschaft und Administration. *Zeitschrift für Lärmbekämpfung* 36, 105-113.

Hamernik, Roger, Wei Qiu 2001. Energy-independent factors influencing noise-induced hearing loss in the chinchilla model. *Journal Acoust. Soc. Am.* 110, 3163-3168.

Hartmann, William 1998. *Signals, Sound, and Sensation.* New York: AIP/Springer.

Hellbrück, Jürgen 1993. *Hören. Physiologie, Psychologie und Pathologie.* Göttingen, Toronto: Hogrefe.

Hellbrück, Jürgen, August Schick 1989. Zehn Jahre Walkman – Grund zum Feiern oder Anlaß zur Sorge? *Zeitschr. für Lärmbekämpfung* 36, 121-129.

Jesteadt, Walt, Lori Leibold 2011. Loudness in the Laboratory, Part I: Steady-State Sounds. In Mary Florentine, Athur Popper, Richard Fay (eds.). *Loudness.* New York: Springer, 109-144.

Junger, Miguel, David Feit 1993. *Sound, Structures, and their Interaction.* Repr. New York: American Inst. of Physics.

Jurado, Carlos, Brian Moore 2010. Frequency selectivity for frequencies below 100 Hz: Comparisons with mid-frequencies. *Journal Acoust. Soc. Am.* 128, 3585-3596.

Keidel, Wolf D. (ed.). *Physiologie des Gehörs. Akustische Informationsverarbeitung.* Stuttgart: Thieme.

Keidser, Gitte, Rickard Katsch, Harvey Dillon, Frances Grant 2000. Relative loudness perception of low and high frequency sounds in the open and occluded ear. *Journal Acoust. Soc. Am.* 107, 3351-3357.

Kötter, J. 1989. Meßtechnische Erfassung impulshaltiger Geräusche in der Nachbarschaft. *Zeitschr. für Lärmbekämpfung* 36, 130-135.

Laming, Donald (1997). *The Measurement of Sensation.* Oxford, New York: Oxford Univ. Pr.

Langers, Dave, Walter Backes, Pim van Dijk 2007. Brain Activation in Relation to Sound Intensity and Loudness. In Birger Kollmeier et al. (eds.). *Hearing. From Sensory Processing to Perception.* Berlin: Springer, 227-234.

Langner, Jörg 2007. Die zeitliche Verarbeitung periodischer Signale im Hörsystem. Neuronale Repräsentation von Tonhöhe, Klang und Harmonizität. *Zeitschrift für Audiologie* 46, 8-21,

Leitmann, T. 2003. Lautstärke in Diskotheken. Eine Abschätzung des Gehörschadenrisikos bei jungen Erwachsenen. *Zeitschrift für Lärmbekämpfung* 50, H. 5, 140-146.

Lopez-Poveda, Enrique, Christopher Plack, Ray Meddis 2003. Cochlear nonlinearity between 500 and 8000 Hz in listeners with normal hearing. *Journal Acoust. Soc. Am.* 113, 951-960.

Marks, Lawrence 1978. Binaural summation of the loudness of pure tones. *Journal Acoust. Soc. Am.* 64, 107-113.

Marozeau, Jeremy 2011. Models of loudness. In Mary Florentine, Arthur Popper, Richard Fay (eds.). *Loudness.* New York: Springer, 261-284.

Maute, Dieter 2006. *Technische Akustik und Lärmschutz.* München: Hanser.

Metternich, Frank, T. Brusis 1999. Akute Gehörschäden und Tinnitus durch überlaute Unterhaltungsmusik. *Laryngo-Rhino-Otol.* 78, 614-619.

Meyer-Bisch, Christian 1996. Epidemiological Evaluation of Hearing Damage related to strongly amplified Music (Personal Cassette Players, Discotheques, Rock concerts). High-definition audiometric survey on 1364 subjects. *Audiology* 35, 121-142.

Moore, Brian 1993. Frequency Analysis and Pitch Perception. In W. A. Yost, A.N. Popper, R. Fay (eds.). *Human Psychophysics*. New York: Springer, 56-115.

Moore, Brian 1995. Frequency Analysis and Masking. In B. Moore (ed.). *Hearing* 2nd ed. San Diego, Orlando: Academic Pr., 161-205.

Moore, Brian 2008. *Introduction to the Psychology of Hearing*. 5th ed. Bingley: Emerald.

Moore, Brian, Brian Glasberg 1983. Suggested formulae for calculating auditory-filter bandwidths and excitation patterns. *Journal Acoust. Soc. Am.* 74, 750-753.

Moore, Brian, Brian Glasberg 2007. Modeling binaural loudness. *Journal Acoust. Soc. Am.* 121, 1604-1612.

Moore, Brian, Brian Glasberg, Thomas Baer 1997. A Model for the prediction of thresholds, loudness and partial loudness. *Journal Audio Eng. Soc.* 45, 224-240.

Moore, Brian, Robert Peters, Brian Glasberg 1990. Auditory filter shapes at low center frequencies. *Journal Acoust. Soc. Am.* 88, 132-140.

Morse, Philip 1981. *Vibration and Sound*. Reprint (New York): Am. Inst. of Physics.

Morse, Philip, K. Uno Ingard (1986). *Theoretical Acoustics*. Paperback ed. Princeton: Princeton U. Pr.

Niederée, Reinhard, Louis Narens 1996. Axiomatische Meßtheorie. In *Handbuch Quantitative Methoden,* hrsg. von Edgar Erdfelder et al., Weinheim: Beltz/Psychologie Verlags-Union, 369-384.

Niederée, Reinhard, Rainer Mausfeld 1996. Skalenniveau, Invarianz und "Bedeutsamkeit". In *Handbuch Quantitative Methoden,* hrsg. von Edgar Erdfelder et al., Weinheim: Beltz/Psychologie Verlags-Union, 385-398.

Patuzzi, Robert 1996. Cochlear Micromechanics and Macromechanics. In Peter Dallos, Arthur Popper, Richard Fay (eds.). *The Cochlea*. New York: Springer 1996, 186-257.

Pedersen, C. Brake, C. Elberling 1972. Temporal Integration of acoustic energy in normal hearing persons. *Acta Oto-laryng*. 74, 398-405.

Pickles, James 2008. *An Introduction to the physiology of hearing*. 3rd ed. Bingley: Emerald.

Plack, Christopher, Vit Drga 2003. Psychophysical evidence for auditory compression at low characteristic frequencies. *Journal Acoust. Soc. Am.* 113, 1574-1586.

Plattig, Karl-Heinz 1975. Äußeres Ohr und Mittelohr (Reizleitung). In Wolf D. Keidel (Hrsg*.)*. *Physiologie des Gehörs. Akustische Informationsverarbeitung*. Stuttgart: Thieme, 44-63.

Plattig, K.-H. 1975. Psychophysiologie und Psychoakustik des Gehörs. In W.D. Keidel (ed.). *Physiologie des Gehörs. Akustische Informationsverarbeitung*. Stuttgart: Thieme, 359-380.

Plontke, Stefan, Hans-Peter Zenner 2004. Aktuelle Gesichtspunkte zu Hörschäden durch Berufs- und Freizeitlärm. *Laryngo-Rhino-Otol*. 83, Suppl. 1, 122-164.

Recknagel, Alfred 1986. *Physik. Schwingungen und Wellen. Wärmelehre*. 14th ed. Berlin: VEB Verlag Technik.

Relkin, Evan, John Doucet 1997. Is loudness simply proportional to the auditory nerve spike count? *Journal Acoust. Soc. Am.* 101, 2735-2740.

Rennies, Jan, Jesko Verhey, Hugo Fastl 2010. Comparison of loudness models for time-varying sounds. *Acta Acustica united with Acustica* 96, 383-396.

Röhl, Markus, Birger Kollmeier, Stefan Uppenkamp 2010. Spectral Loudness Summation takes place in the Primary Auditory Cortex. *Human Brain Mapping* (Online Sept. 2010).

Roederer, Juan 1975. *Introduction to the Physics and Psychophysics of Music.* 2nd ed. New York: Springer.

Ruschkowski, Arne von 2008. Loudness war. In Albrecht Schneider (ed.). *Systematic and Comparative Musicology: Concepts, Methods, Findings.* Frankfurt/M.: P. Lang, 213-230 (=Hamburger Jahrbuch für Musikwissenschaft 24).

Sader, Manfred 1966. *Lautheit und Lärm: gehörpsychologische Fragen der Schall-Intensität.* Göttingen: Hogrefe.

Sadhra, S., C. Jackson, T. Ryder, M. Brown 2002. Noise Exposure and Hearing Loss among Student Employees working in University entertainment Venues. *Annals Occup. Hyg.* 46, 455-463.

Sandell, J., A. Berntson, G. Blomgren, K. Kähäri 2007. Acoustic Intervention in a Live Music Club. *Acta Acustica united with Acustica* 93, 843-849.

Schick, August 1990. *Schallbewertung.* Berlin: Springer.

Schneider, Albecht 1997. *Tonhöhe – Skala – Klang. Akustische, tonometrische und psycho-akustische Studien auf vergleichender Grundlage.* Bonn: Orpheus-Verlag.

Schneider, Albrecht, Arne von Ruschkowski, Rolf Bader 2009. Klangliche Rauhigkeit, ihre Wahrnehmung und Messung. In R. Bader (Ed*.). Musical Acoustics, Neurocognition and Psychology of Music.* (=Hamburger Jahrbuch für Musikwissenschaft 25). Frankfurt/M. etc.: P. Lang, 103-148.

Schneider, Albrecht, Valeri Tsatsishvili 2011. Perception of musical intervals at very low frequencies: some experimental findings. *Hamburger Jahrbuch für Musikwissenschaft* 28, 99-125.

Sigalovsky, Irina, Jennifer Melcher 2006. Effects of sound level on fMRI activation in human brainstem, thalamic and cortical centers. *Hearing Res.* 215, 67-76.

Sixtl, Friedrich 1982. *Meßmethoden der Psychologie. Theoretische Grundlagen und Methoden.* 2nd ed. Weinheim, Basel: Beltz.

Smeds, Karolina, Arne Leijon 2011. Loudness and hearing loss. In Mary Florentine, Athur Popper, Richard Fay (eds.). *Loudness.* New York: Springer, 223-260.

Stevens, Stanley S. 1936. A Scale for the Measurement of psychological magnitude: loudness. *Psych. Rev.* 43, 405-416.

Stevens, Stanley S. 1955. The measurement of loudness. *Journal Acoust. Soc. Am.* 27, 815-829.

Stevens, Stanley S. 1957. On the Psychophysical Law. *Psych. Rev.* 64, 153-181.

Stevens, Stanley S. 1971. Issues in psychophysical Measurement. *Psych. Rev.* 78, 426-450.

Stevens, Stanley S. 1974. Perceptual Magnitude and its Measurement. In *Handbook of Perception, Vol. II: Psychophysical Judgment and Measurement*, ed. by Edward Carterette and Morton Friedman, New York etc.: Academic Pr., 361-389.

Stevens, Stanley S., J. Volkmann 1940. The Relation of pitch to frequency: a revised scale. *Am. Journal Psych.* 53, 329-353.

Stevens, Stanley S., Eugene Galanter 1957. Ratio Scales and Category Scales for a dozen perceptual Continua. *Journal Exp. Psych.* 54, 377-411.

Streppel, Michael, Martin Walger, Hasso von Wedel, Elisabeth Gaber 2006. *Hörstörungen und Tinnitus*. (=Gesundheitsberichterstattung des Bundes, H. 29). Berlin: Robert-Koch-Institut.

Todd, Neil 2001. Evidence for a behavioral significance of saccular arousal sensitivity in humans. *Journal Acoust. Soc. Am.* 110, 380-390.

Todd, Neil, Frederick Cody 2000. Vestibular Responses to loud dance music: a physiological Basis of the „Rock'n'Roll threshold"? *Journal Acoust. Soc. Am.* 107, 496-500.

Twardella, Dorothee, Andrea Wellhöfer, Christian Wiedemann, Hubert Gail, Gerhard Prestele, Roland Scholz 2007. *Messprogramm Schallpegel in Diskotheken. Zusammenfassung wesentlicher Ergebnisse* (München: Bayerisches Landesamt für Gesundheit usw. und Bayerisches Landesamt für Umwelt).

Viemeister, Neal, Christopher Plack 1993. Time Analysis. In William Yost, Arthur Popper, Richard Fay (eds.). *Human Psychophysics*. New York: Springer, 116-154.

Volkwein, Barbara 2001. *What's Techno? Geschichte, Diskurse und musikalische Gestalt elektronischer Unterhaltungsmusik*. Phil. Diss. Univ. Hamburg.

Wagenaar, W. 1975. Stevens vs. Fechner: A plea for dismissal of the case. *Acta Psychol.* 39, 225-235.

Warren, Richard 1982. *Auditory Perception. A new Synthesis*. New York, Oxford: Pergamon Pr. (revised edition: *Auditory Perception. A new Analysis and Synthesis*. Cambridge: Cambridge Univ. Pr. 1999, 3rd ed. 2008.

Webers, Johannes. *Tonstudiotechnik*. 4th ed. München: Franzis.

Weinzierl, Stefan 2008. Grundlagen. In S. Weinzierl (ed.). *Handbuch der Audiotechnik*. Berlin: Springer, 1-40.

Yin, Tom 2002. Neural Mechanisms of Encoding Binaural Localization cues in the Auditory Brainstem. In D. Oertel, R. Fay, A. Popper (eds.). *Integrative Functions in the Mammalian Auditory Pathway*. New York: Springer, ch. 4, 99-159.

Zwicker, Eberhard 1982. *Psychoakustik*. Berlin: Springer.

Zwicker, E., G. Flottorp, S. Stevens 1957. Critical Band Width in Loudness Summation. *Journal Acoust. Soc. Am.* 29, 548-557.

Zwicker, E., B. Scharf 1965. A model of loudness summation. *Psych. Rev.* 72, 3-26.

Zwicker, Eberhard, Hugo Fastl 1986. Sinnvolle Lärmmessung und Lärmgrenzwerte. *Zeitschrift für Lärmforschung* 33, 61-67.

Zwicker, Eberhard, Hugo Fastl 1999. *Psychoacoustics. Facts and Models*. 2nd ed. Berlin, New York: Springer.

Daniel Müllensiefen
Geraint Wiggins

Polynomial Functions as a Representation of Melodic Phrase Contour

Abstract

The present paper explores a novel way of characterising the contour of melodic phrases. Melodic contour is represented by a curve that can be derived from fitting a polynomial equation to the pitch values given the note onsets. To represent contour numerically, we consider the coefficients of the polynomial equation as well as the time limits of the melodic phrase. After a brief review of different theoretical, didactic, analytic, and computational approaches to melodic contour, a detailed step-by-step description is provided of how polynomials can be fitted to melodic phrases. In two application examples, it is demonstrated how polynomial contour can be used as a basis for the computational processing of melodic information. The first application estimates the frequency of occurrence or prevalence of a phrase contour: a probabilistic model is constructed based on a large sample of phrases from popular melodies using a standard density estimation procedure to obtain an indicator of contour occurrence frequency. The second application is a similarity measure that exploits polynomial curves graphically and is based on Tversky's (1977) ratio model of similarity. Further applications of the approach as well as quantitative tests of the existing ones are discussed as options for future work.

1 Introduction

1.1 Background

Melodic contour is often regarded as one of the most important features in the analysis and composition of melodic music, i.e. music that is mainly conceived as consisting of one or several horizontal lines or voices. Throughout history theorists have stressed the importance of the melodic line for the construction of a *good melody*. Examples include Ernst Toch, who, in his *Melodienlehre* (1923), defines a melody as consisting of a line of pitches ("Tonhöhenlinie") and a rhythm, and Knud Jeppesen (1935), who mentions in his counterpoint text book the importance of a good balance between melodic skips and related step-wise motion, as well as the special role that contour extrema have in the construction of melodic lines. Rules to relate contour extrema to each other in a musically meaningful fashion are also given by Paul Hindemith in his *Unterweisung im Tonsatz* Bd. I (1940). The notion of melodic contour features even more prominently in Walter Piston's book on counter point (1950) where he introduces "the melodic curve" as a concept for describing and structuring melodies in the very first chapter. A recent survey of 24 historical melody composition treatises from the 1700s to the present (Winkelhaus, 2004) identifies melodic contour as one of the basic global characteristics according to which melodies can be defined, classified, and constructed. Popular song and melody writing books concur, and employ the concept of "melodic contour" (Perricone, 2000; Bradford, 2005) or "melodic shape" (Kachulis, 2003) for their respecttive instruction methods.

Music analysts, too, make frequent use of the concept of contour when they describe and interrelate sections of melodies or melodic phrases. Meyer (1956) demonstrates the basic perceptual Gestalt laws of *good continuation, completion* and *closure* by the "motion" of a melodic line within a number of examples. Kunst uses the "melodic curve" as a structural descriptor within his logical approach to analysis (1978, e.g. 113). Grabner (1959) classifies the possibilities for the melodic motion ("melodischer Verlauf") of instrumental melodies and also proposes principles of alteration and variation of melodic motives and phrases. Kühn, in his *Formenlehre der Musik* (1987), points out that alterations of rhythmic and melodic motion ("Tonhöhenverlauf (Diasthematik)") are often balanced, especially in compositions from the classical era, to maintain the understandability or recognisability of the melodic unit. The same point is made by Rosen (1971) in several of his in-depth analyses of compositions in the classical style. De la Motte in his workbook on melody (1993) uses the term melodic arch ("melodischer Bogen") to denote the gross motion of pitch over time. Like many of the aforementioned authors he stresses the balance between steps and skips, the role of the melodic range, and the direction of contours of subsequent segments of a melody.

From the very beginning of the discipline of music cognition, in the 1970s, and probably inspired by extensive analytic and compositional literature, researchers have investigated the question of how of melodies are perceived by a listener and what role melodic contour plays in perception. One of the most active and influential researchers has been W. Jay Dowling, who has demonstrated in several studies the importance of contour for melodic memory, particularly if melodic phrases are transposed, not presented in context, or with other musical parameters that carry little information (e.g. Dowling & Fujitani, 1971; Dowling & Bartlett, 1981; Dowling & Harwood, 1986; Dowling et al., 1995). Dowling (1978) published a very influential theory of melodic memory, according to which, melodic contour and scale information are the main informational dimensions processed in memory and are probably sufficient to reconstruct the full melody. In addition, several psychological studies by other authors have confirmed the important role that contour plays in the reconstruction of other melodic parameters in memory (e.g., Idson & Massaro, 1978; Eiting, 1984; Cutietta& Booth, 1996). The requirements for contour to act as an effective cognitive representation are that the contour of a phrase has to be simple (few changes of direction, symmetrical structure) and that the task does not allow for direct encoding of absolute pitch structure (i.e., the task involves transposition; see e.g. Idson & Massaro, 1976; Cuddy & Lyons, 1981; Taylor & Pembrook, 1984; Edworthy, 1985; Boltz & Jones, 1986). One outcome from a study by Dowling and colleagues from 1995 is the conclusion that the encoding of contour as a conscious process is of great importance when listeners are aware of the memory task and try consciously to reconstruct other parameters in memory as well. In contrast, the encoding of interval and scale information appears to be a rather automatic process that does not require voluntary attention. Taken together with evidence from infant studies (e.g., Trehub et al., 1984), these experimental findings demonstrate that melodic contour is a very important concept for the conscious perception of melodies.

Therefore, given the great and obvious usefulness of contour as an abstracted feature, it is no surprise that there have been several attempts to define melodic contour formally in order to enable the algorithmic computation of a contour representation for any given melodic phrase.

One of the most simple and reductive definitions and implementations of melodic contour was proposed by David Huron (1996). His definition of contour is based on the pitch height of the first and last notes of a melodic phrase and the mean average pitch[1] of all notes in between. Huron describes phrase contour in terms of the relationships between the first note and the average note and the average note and the last note, expressed simply as higher, lower or equal, with no information about the size of the interval. From the combination of these two free parameters with three different possible values, Huron defines nine distinct contour classes to which any melodic phrase can be assigned. The classes are named according to the two-dimensional visual shapes the three notes describe: *convex, concave, ascending, descending, horizontal, horizontal-descending, horizontal-ascending, ascending-horizontal,* and *descending-horizontal.* A classification into effectively the same nine contour classes is used by Galvin et al. (2007) to test the auditory discrimination abilities of cochlear implant users. In that study, which makes no reference to Huron's work, the nine contour classes are employed for not analytical purposes but to generate test stimuli, with absolute frequency level, interval size, and contour being the three independent dimensions of the artificial test melodies.

The advantages of Huron's contour definition are that a) any melodic phrase can simply be assigned to one out of nine contour categories, b) the categories are easily distinguishable and correspond in part to contour description used by theorists (see, e.g., the close correspondence to the five categories defined by Perricone, 2000), and c) the contour classes are very easy and quick to compute. Comparing melodic contours is very straightforward since the only existing relation between contour classes is identity or difference.

The drawbacks of Huron's contour definition are that it reflects neither the rhythmic dimension nor the length of the melodic phrase. Furthermore, it does not represent any difference between melodies with very wide or very narrow pitch range—an attribute that is considered important by many theorists. For example, both the simple three-note motif c' d' c' and a long melody with many interval skips and extensive scalar movements, but which happens to start and end on low notes, would be simplistically allocated to the same *convex* contour.

While Huron's definition of melodic contour is probably the most reductive one, the so-called *step contour* as defined by Steinbeck (1982), Juhasz (2000), Eerola and Toiviainen (2004) and others is the most literal contour definition. Here, each note is represented by its onset and duration and its pitch height. The contour of a melody can therefore be represented graphically as a step curve where the x-axis represents time and the y-axis is pitch. For the duration of every note starting at its onset on the x-axis, the curve denotes a constant pitch height value (y) until the onset of the next notes. In order to make the step curve representation invariant with respect to absolute pitch height and absolute time, only pitch intervals and inter-onset time intervals are used. The time and

---

[1] The average note is, of course, only a notional note, and may not occur in the melody.

pitch height dimension can be normalised to start at 0 of the coordinate system (i.e., the first onset starts at time 0 and either the first or the lowest pitch value is assigned the value 0 as well).

The advantage of the step contour representation lies in its precision: every contour movement, even by the shortest and most insignificant note, is represented. The disadvantage is that it does not summarise or abstract the melodic contour at all and the space of melodic contours is as large as the space of melodies. So this representation does not usefully assist comparison between, or classification of, melodic contours.

Between these two extremes of strong reduction (Huron contour) and information-preserving transformation (step contour) many alternative ways of representing melodic contour have been proposed in the literature. There is not space here to review all of them here in depth. Nonetheless, it is worth at least mentioning some of the elegant ideas that have been suggested in order to define and implement melodic contour. The definitions of contour differ according to the purpose for which the contour information is required.

Interpolation contour as proposed by Steinbeck (1982) or Zhou & Kankanhalli (2003) can be regarded as a sophistication of the step curve representation. Like in these two publications, this representation is often employed as a first transformation and reduction stage in melodic similarity measures. The basic idea is to join the turning points or extrema of a melody by straight lines. Minor contour changes such as those generated by change notes, appoggiature, and other ornaments should be excluded as they are not considered important for the overall contour motion; rules for doing so differ between authors (Müllensiefen & Frieler, 2004). To implement this representation of contour, the sequence of length and gradient values have been used, and this usually results in an effective reduction of the melodic data. Alternatively, if melodic contour is used just as a transformation, without the intention of reducing or summarising melodic data, then taking pitch height values at onset points or at regular intervals from the interpolation line is another option (e.g., Steinbeck, 1982).

Schmuckler (1999) compares tonal and dodecaphonic melodies with an algorithmic similarity measure which uses melodic contour as its core representation. He models melodic contour as a smooth up and downward motion, which is approximated by overlaid sine waves. Fourier analysis is then applied, to obtain a set of Fourier components from the ranked pitch and raw onset values. Schmuckler uses only the first six amplitude and phase coefficients to represent the contour of every melody. In contrast to Schmuckler's own experiments with dodecaphonic and artificial tonal melodies, Müllensiefen & Frieler (2004) found Schmuckler's contour-based similarity to have predictive power when compared to the similarity judgements of human experts on popular melodies.

Another family of contour representations is characterised by inclusion of all notes in the melody, but reducing the pitch representation to ordinal relations (e.g., onset note 2 higher than onset note 1) defined exclusively between adjacent notes. The simplest and widest-spread of this family is the *Parsons' code* which records whether the second note in a contiguous pair is lower or higher than, or equal to the first (symbols conventionally denoting these relations are - , + , 0, respectively). Parsons' *Directory of tunes and musical themes* (1975) lists many thousands of mainly classical melodies using this representation. However, empirical evidence from cochlear implant users (Galvin et al.,

2007) suggests that most listeners are able to retain a more precise, yet still approximate, representation of interval size than merely the direction of the interval movement as encoded by the Parsons code. To this end, intervals have been classified into five and seven (Kim et al., 2000), and into nine different classes (Pauws, 2002; Müllensiefen & Frieler, 2004). In this last case, scale intervals are grouped together into discrete classes which become less discriminatory as interval size increases. For example, Müllensiefen and Frieler (2004, p.152) assign a unison to class 0, upward and downward seconds are classes +1/-1, thirds are classes +2/-2, fourths and fifths are +3/-3, and all intervals smaller or greater than that are coded as +4/-4. A strong argument in favour of this family of contour representations is that it seems to approximate human perception in as much as humans tend to be able to make very reliable judgements about the direction and approximate size of an interval. The negative aspect of the Parsons' code and related contour schemes is certainly the fact that they do not admit exact inference about pitch height relations for non-adjacent notes.

A few approaches related to the Parsons' code overcome this problem by filling a matrix between all possible pairs of notes with and indicator of interval direction (1 if note i is lower than note j or 0 otherwise) between row element i and column element j. Since these models cover ordinal relations between all note pairs of a melody, they are sometimes referred to as *combinatorial models of contour* (Shmulevich, 2004). Most of them are rooted in the theoretical models of Friedmann (1985) and Marvin and Laprade (1987), subsequently elaborated by other researchers (e.g., Quinn, 1999). The information contained in the contour relation matrix can be exploited for various purposes, one of which is to determine the similarity between two melodies of equal length by the *contour similarity index* (CSIM; see Marvin & Laprade, 1987, and Polansky, 1996). The CISM has been shown to be equivalent to Kendall's τ, a long-established ordinal measure of concordance, and is suspected not to be very robust to structural permutations of melodies (Shmulevich, 2004). While combinatorial contour models are far more comprehensive than the representation from the Parsons' code family, in that they contain information about non-adjacent notes, they may retain more information than human listeners can actually process in real time. A listener may only compare the pitch height of a given note to other notes in its temporal vicinity (e.g., within a time window which corresponds to working memory span of 2-3 seconds; see Baddeley, 1997). But, because the contour relation matrix is uniform, the interval between notes 1 and 2 is of equal importance to the one between, say, note 5 and note 55 of a very long melody. In sum, the combinatorial contour models do not reflect the linear nature of a melodic line but rather a holistic conception of contour. Also, unless some summarising method is performed on the contour relation matrix, the combinatorial models do not reduce, but inappropriately include ornaments and change notes.

1.2 Motivation

From the previous section, it emerges that there is neither a single notion of what melodic contour really is, nor a single application of it. Instead, different ways of looking at the directional movement of pitch height over time in a melody have emerged for different theoretic, didactic, analytic, and practical purposes. In the present paper, we do not aim to decide how melodic contour should be defined correctly; nor are we trying to compare different approaches or to reconcile diverging concepts of contour. Instead, we develop a new method of defining and actually computing melodic contour from a series of onset and pitch height values. This new method is ultimately designed to represent melodic phrases of a large collection of popular melodies as part of the M^4S project at Goldsmiths[2]. It aims to overcome some of the disadvantages of existing contour definitions and implementations. For the present purpose, some important requirements for the new contour representation are:

- The musical unit that it is primarily designed to work on is the melodic phrase – which is defined as a shorter segment of a melody that induces a certain perception of closure towards its end. Several algorithmic melody segmenters produce segmentations of melodies that correspond roughly to these assumptions (e.g. Cambouropoulos, 2001; Temperley, 2001; for an overview, see Pearce et al., 2010). The contour computation is designed to work on the output of such segmenters.
- A good balance between summarising the melodic events of a melodic phrase and discriminating between a large number of phrases should be maintained, to make melodic contour a feature which is helpful in grouping melodic phrases together and in searching and retrieving melodies from a large collection.
- The representation should be robust to minor variations in pitch and time, and do some degree of smoothing over melodic ornamentation.
- The linear evolution of a melodic phrase as generally perceived by human listeners should be emphasised, and intuitively it should be possible to relate the new contour representation to the conventional representation of a melody in staff notation.

A second aim of this paper is to demonstrate the potential of our polynomial contour representation as a means of describing and modelling a large collection of melodies, and as a basis for the construction of similarity measures between pairs of melodies.

2 A new method for computing melodic contour

The basic idea of this new method for representing the contour of melodic phrases is very simple: Imagine one connects all the notes of a melody in staff notation, like the one in Fig. 1, with a smooth line.

Fig. 1: First two phrases of the well-known French tune *Ah vous-dirai-je, Maman*; in English-speaking countries often sung to the lyrics of the nursery rhyme *Twinkle, twinkle little star*; in German-speaking countries it is known as the Christmas carol *Morgen kommt der Weihnachtsmann*.

Just as in this example, for many melodic phrases the result would be a curved line, maybe going up and down a few times. To represent these smooth and short curves

---

[2] see http://www.doc.gold.ac.uk/isms/mmm/

numerically we use polynomial equations, like the one in eqn. 1, a polynomial of order 6 (meaning that the highest exponent for any term in this monovariate equation is 6).

(1) $\quad y = 65.987 - 1.589 \cdot x + 0.589 \cdot x^2 - 0.13 \cdot x^4 + 0.024 \cdot x^5 + 0.004 \cdot x^6 - 0.001 \cdot x^7$

When computed over the range of $x \in$ [-4.2, 4.2] this equation corresponds to the graph in Fig. 2, which seems intuitively to fit the contour of the melody in Fig. 1 quite well. There is a sharp rise in the first half of the graph which approaches MIDI pitch 69 corresponding to the A4 at the beginning of bar 2. After that the curve falls down smoothly towards the end.

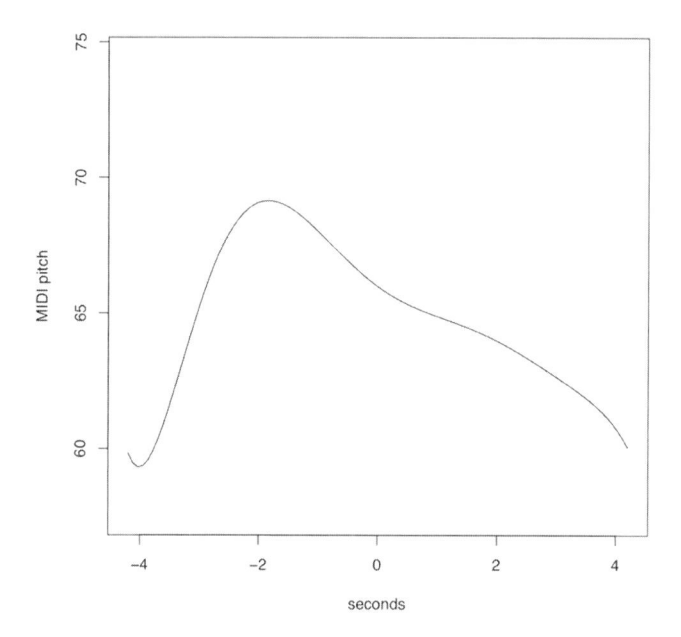

Fig. 2: Polynomial contour curve corresponding to Eq. 1 and derived from the first two phrases of *Ah vous dirai-je, Maman*.

If the second phrase (bars 3-4) of the same melody is modelled on its own we obtain the smooth descending line depicted in Fig. 3.

The contour curve for the second phrase is characterised by only three components: An additive constant (63.571) that corresponds to the central pitch level, between D#4 and E4, a negative linear component ($-1.369 \cdot x$) which is responsible for the overall downward motion, and a smaller negative quadratic component ($-0.298 \cdot x^2$) which adds a bit of smoothness to the curve.

The polynomial curve for the first phrase (bars 1–2) only is given in Fig. 4.

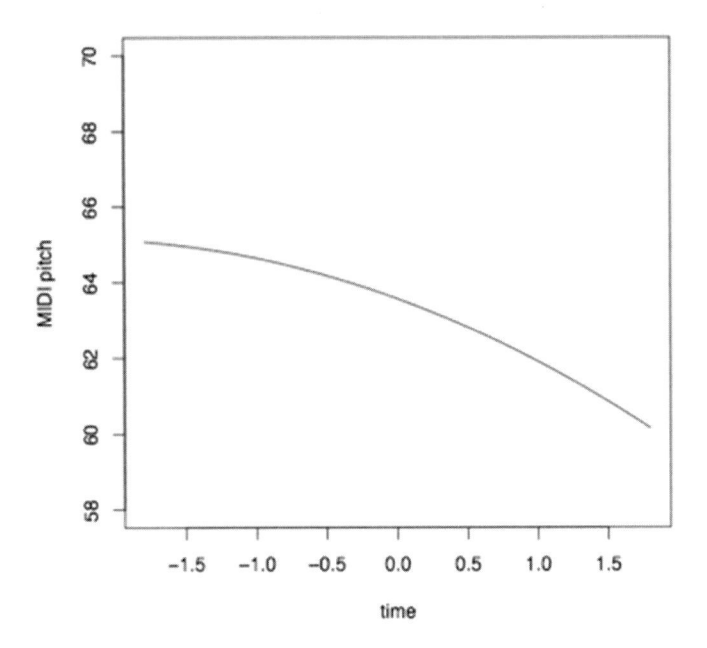

Fig. 3: Polynomial contour curve derived from the second phrase of *Ah vous dirai-je, Maman*. The corresponding polynomial equation is: $y = 63.571 - 1.369 \cdot x - 0.298 \cdot x^2$

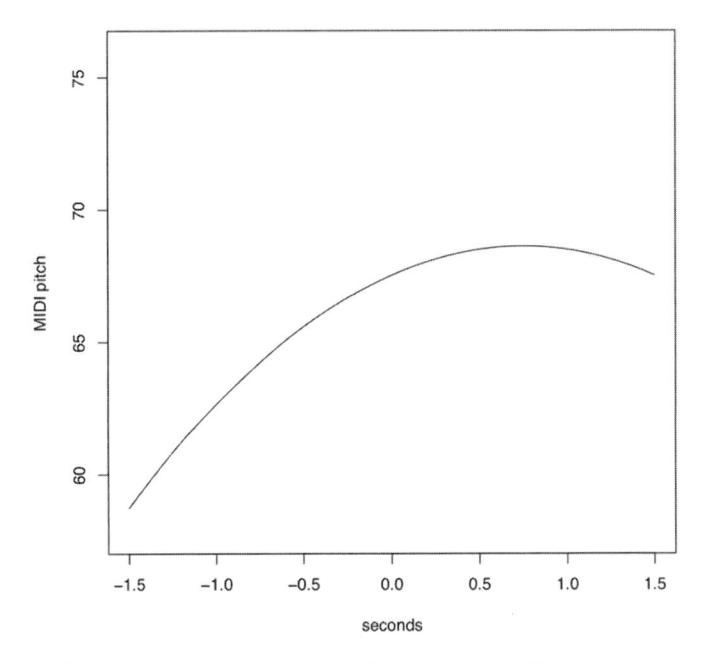

Fig. 4: Polynomial contour curve derived from the first phrase of *Ah vous dirai-je, Maman*. The corresponding polynomial equation is: $y = 67.524 + 2.929 \cdot x - 1.925 \cdot x^2$

The curve of the first phrase is dominated by a strong positive 1st-order component (2.929 · x) which is responsible for the overall ascending trend of the curve. The comparatively weaker quadratic component generates the directional turn at the end of the phrase (A4 to G4).

In comparison, if we drop the last note (G4) from the first phrase, and fit a contour curve to the first six notes (C C G G A A) we obtain, as a result, an almost straight line characterised by the additive constant, an even stronger linear component (3.429 · x) and a very small quadratic component that models the lower steepness of the contour going only a major second up from G4 to A4 (Fig. 5).

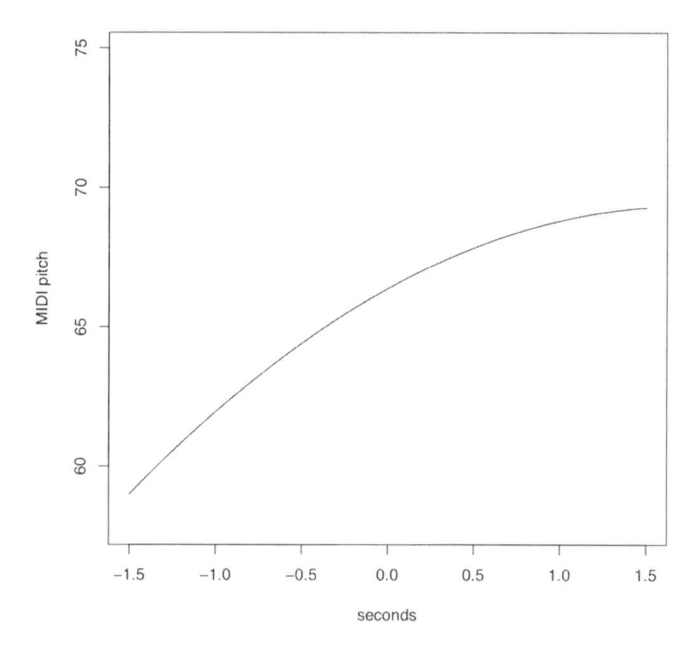

Fig. 5: Polynomial contour curve derived from the incomplete first phrase (first 6 notes) of *Ah vous dirai-je, Maman*. The corresponding polynomial equation is: $y = 64.375 + 3.429 \cdot x - 0.992 \cdot x^2$

This simple example makes the central points about the polynomial contour representation very clear: It is possible to represent a melodic phrase by a polynomial. The polynomial curve aims at connecting the pitches of the phrase in a smooth way and thus captures the up- and downward motion of the phrase over time. The coefficients of the polynomial equation can be interpreted as a numerical representation of the melodic phrase.

Polynomials have some advantages that make them suitable for describing melodic contours. They are elegant in the sense that they only make use of the three most basic arithmetic operations (add, subtract, multiply). Simple shapes (lines, parabolas) correspond to simple polynomial equations (i.e., few and lower-order coefficients). Simple shapes can be added to form more complex ones. Polynomials are good for describing symmetrical behaviour (i.e. up and downward motion). They are simplest when describing motions with only a few directional changes, which makes them suitable for most short melodic phrases.

3 How to compute polynomial contour

The idea of representing the contour of a melody by a polynomial equation whose curve is fitted to the notes of a melody was first proposed by Steinbeck (1982). The main purpose for Steinbeck was to find a compact representation that could be used for measuring the similarity between folk melodies. Although his description of how to derive a polynomial contour representation from melodic data is quite detailed (ibid., pp. 116-121) he did not make use of the polynomial contour representation for the clustering of folk melodies that he presents later in his book but resorted to aggregate features. This is probably due to the computational limitations regarding speed and arithmetic accuracy at his disposal in the early 1980s.

Frieler et al. (in press) took up Steinbeck's original idea and represented a large collection of melodic phrases from highly commercial western pop songs by coefficients of fitted polynomials. Like Steinbeck's, the purpose of their investigation was to cluster melodic phrases into a small number of discrete classes. In their results, Frieler et al. compare clusterings performed on the basis of polynomial contour to the contour classification as generated by Huron's contour representation and find general agreement between the two methods. They stress that one of the additional benefits of the clustering based on polynomial contour is the fact that, unlike Huron's method, information about the relation between an individual melodic phrase and the centre of the cluster it belongs to is retained. Thus, a distinction can be made between phrases that are very typical for a class of phrases and those that can be considered as rather atypical or outliers. The approach we present here for obtaining and working with a polynomial contour representation differs in a number of ways from Steinbeck's original idea and from the empirical adaptation as engineered by Frieler and collaborators. We will highlight these differences of the present implementation from its predecessors below, where appropriate. The computation of polynomial contour is carried out in four consecutive steps:

1. Representation and selection of melodic data: segmentation and phrase length limits

A melody m is represented as a series of pairs of pitch and onset time value (p_i, t_i) for each note n_i of the melody m. In principle, the units for these values could be represented with reference to any suitable measurement system. In practice, we use MIDI pitch since the main collection of popular music we are currently investigating has MIDI as its source format. The decision to use absolute timing information in milliseconds instead of metrical time as measured in fractions of a beat is rooted in the assumption that from a certain point on the tempo of a melodic phrase acts on the perception of melodic contour and the variation in tempo in our collection of popular songs is too large (range 6bpm to 303bpm) to be ignored. Our definition of contour is supposed to work on melodic phrases as units. However, just as with melodic contour itself, there exists a considerable debate among music theorists and psychologists about what constitutes a melodic phrase and how a continuous melodic line should be segmented or grouped into shorter meaningful units (e.g., Temperley, 2001; Pearce, Müllensiefen, & Wiggins, 2010). Several algorithms have been proposed for segmenting melodies into consecutive phrases and a few comparative studies have tested these segmentation algorithms with respect to their cognitive validity (e.g., Thom et al., 2002; Müllensiefen et al, 2008; de Nooijer et al., 2008). We chose Grouper, David Temperley's rule-based algorithm (Temperley, 2001), as a segmenter since it has performed well in comparative studies using different melody collections and because it can handle unquantised data by using a built-in quantisation mechanism. For each melody m, Grouper produces melodic phrase boundaries according to which the notes of a melody can be grouped together into a number of phrases φ_i. The number of notes naturally varies between phrases. In order to obtain a homogeneous collection of melodic phrases for the present study, we only consider phrases with a length within the 95-percentile around the mean phrase length (9.28 notes) from the Essen folk song collection (Schaffrath, 1995)[3]. To put it differently, we discard all phrases that have a number of notes significantly different from the mean phrase length of a large collection of popular melodies with manually annotated phrase segmentations. The 95-percentile corresponds with limits of *4 < N < 16* for the number of notes of a melodic phrase. Also, as we are using absolute timing information, it is necessary to set a limit to the phrase duration as measured in milliseconds. 95% of the 399,672 melodic phrases in the M^4S database, resulting from the segmentation by Grouper and between 5 and 15 notes long, have a duration between 0.98 and 6.85 seconds. We limit ourselves to the analysis of melodic phrases within these absolute time limits.

Unlike Steinbeck and Frieler et al., we do not standardise the duration of the phrases to unit time. This would eliminate effects of phrase lengths in terms of absolute time or number of notes and tempo. However, we do assume that the natural length of a melodic phrase makes a difference to contour perception, which we would like to be reflected in the polynomial model. Frieler et al. are also aware of the perceptual importance of phrase length (as measured in the number of notes in a phrase) and retain this information in a variable separate from the polynomial model.

2. Transformation of melodic data: Centring around the origin

To exploit the symmetrical nature of the polynomial function (reflectively symmetrical with respect to the y-axis for even exponents, and rotationally symmetrical around the origin for odd exponents), we centre each melodic phrase around the origin on the time scale. This is achieved by shifting all onset values to the left on the time scale according to equation 2:

(2) $\quad t'_i = t_i - (t_1 + \frac{t_n - t_1}{2})$

Under the assumption that many melodic phrases have a more or less symmetrical structure, centring around the origin reduces the number of parameters to be estimated and is therefore a clear improvement which has not been considered by Steinbeck nor Frieler et al.

---

[3] The grouping into phrases in the Essen folk song collection was carried out manually by expert musicologists and folk song collectors.

3. Fitting the full model

As we are striving towards a summary representation of contour, we set $\lfloor n/2 \rfloor +1$ for a phrase φ with n notes as an upper limit for the number of free parameters to estimate. For a given phrase φ with n notes the full polynomial model is therefore defined as

$$(3) \quad p = c_0 + c_1 t + c_2 t^2 + \ldots + c_m t^m$$

where $m = \lfloor n/2 \rfloor$. To obtain the parameters, c_i, we use least squares regression and treat the exponential transformations, $t, t^2 \ldots t^{n/2}$, of the onset variable t as predictors and pitch height p as the response variable. Only the actual time and pitch values (t_i, p_i) of the melodic phrase are used in the regression procedure. The result is a numerical value for each of the parameters $c_0, \ldots, c_{\lfloor n/2 \rfloor}$.

4. Variable selection

Least squares regression generally overfits the data of the response variable – that is to say, the regression model is likely not to be robust to minor variations in the data. In our case this could mean that melodic phrases with similar contours would be represented by hugely different sets of polynomial parameters. Therefore, we apply Bayes' Information Criterion (BIC) as a standard variable selection procedure that balances the fit to the response variable against the complexity (number of terms) of the model. The stepwise search through the model space is done backwards (starting from the full model) and forwards (starting from the c_0 parameter alone), and, at each step, predictor variables that lead to a better BIC value are included or excluded from the model. Most of the time, this variable selection process results in a final contour model where the number of predictor variables necessary to predict p is considerably smaller than $n/2 +1$. Since all predictor variables are considered for inclusion or exclusion at each step the resulting model does not necessarily consist exclusively of exponential transformations of t with neighbouring exponents (e.g., $p = c_0 + c_1 t + c_2 t^2 + c_3 t^3 + c_4 t^4$). Instead, in many instances just a single transformation of t (e.g., $p = c_0 + c_3 t^3$) is selected, or predictor variables with non-adjacent exponents form the model (e.g., $p = c_0 + c_1 t + c_3 t^3 + c_6 t^6$).

The variable selection process ensures that the polynomial model is not over-fitted and this is a major advantage over the procedures suggested by Steinbeck and Frieler et al. who respectively determined the upper limit for the order of the polynomial with regard to the fix point precision of the computer used and the use of a fixed order (e.g., 2 or 4) for the polynomials fitted to all phrases of a collection regardless of their melodic structure.

The result of the variable selection process is a set of polynomial coefficients that are taken to represent the melodic phrase that has been modelled. This includes the coefficients that have a numerical value $\neq 0$ as well as the information about which variables (exponential transforms of t) were not selected for the contour model and therefore have a value of 0. Since the length limit of a phrase is 15 notes and the complexity limit is $\lfloor 15/2 \rfloor = 7$, we represent each melodic phrase as an 8-dimensional vector

$$<c_0, c_1, c_2, c_3, c_4, c_5, c_6, c_7>$$

where the c_i are the coefficients of the polynomial terms[4]. In addition to the polynomial coefficients, the shifted limits on the time axis which correspond to the onset of the first and last note of the phrase are also part of contour representation.

4 Applications

This new representation allows several interesting analytical and computational applications.

4.1 Density estimation from a probabilistic model

Like Huron (1996), we are interested in the distribution of melodic phrase contours in large collections of melodies. Knowing what very common and very uncommon contours look like can inform, for example, the automatic detection of unusual phrases in a melody or the construction of cognitive models of melodic processing which are based on the assumptions that frequency information, acquired by statistical learning, is an important aspect of many cognitive mechanisms. Also, knowledge about the distribution of melodic contours for different musical repertoires can help identify the structural characteristics of different styles, and supports theorising about musical universals and the compositional and performative constraints for vocal melodies in general (see, e.g., Huron, 2006).

To model a collection of polynomial phrase contour representations, we first standardise the coefficients for each phrase to make them comparable. We use the *z-transformation*, which normalises the raw coefficients c_i of each of the 376,423 phrases[5] from our pop song database, according to the mean and standard deviation of the coefficients of each phrase, as shown in Eqn. 4; s_c is the standard deviation. Note that the standardisation is done separately for each phrase.

$$(4) \quad c'_i = \frac{c_i - \overline{c}}{s_c}$$

The z-transformation reduces differences between contours with respect to the interval range and temporal span. For example, arch-like contours ranging for two octaves or for only a fifth will have very similar sets of coefficients. Similarly, arch-like contours span-

---

[4] However in practice, when applied to a collection of 376,423 melodic phrases from popular melodies the variable corresponding to the polynomial component of order 7 was never selected. Thus, for modelling our collection of popular melodies we represent polynomial contour only as a 7-dimensional vector.

[5] The melodies were all taken from the vocal line of the song. In general, the MIDI transcriptions of the pop songs are very accurate but due to their commercial nature they sometimes contain transposed melodic segments in unsingable registers, or instrumental melodies which were saved to the vocal track of the MIDI file. Since our aim is here the characterisation of phrases from vocal melodies, we excluded all phrases with a central pitch (1st coefficient) smaller than MIDI pitch 36 or larger than 96 (most of which are probably computer generated and not actually sung phrases), as well as all phrases with coefficients outside the 99.9% percentile for any coefficient. As a result, from the original 379,703 phrases 3,280 were excluded.

ning five crotchets (e.g., 1 second) or 17 crotchets (e.g., 4s) having similar coefficient values after z-transformation. The transformed coefficients do not reflect the absolute dimensions of the original curve, but information about the relative sizes within the set of coefficients is retained. Therefore, we regard the z-transformation to be a sensible step because we are interested, at this stage, in the coarse outline of the melodic contour, and not in individual details of length, tempo, duration, or interval range. Also, for this comparative contour modelling, we are not interested in the absolute pitch of the phrase, and so we disregard the additive constant, c_0, which is the zeroth-order component of the contour vector.

To model the distribution of melodic phrase contours, we make use of a statistical procedure known as Gaussian mixture modelling (e.g., McLachlan & Peel, 2000). This probabilistic model approximates an empirical multi-dimensional distribution by a mixture of multidimensional normal or Gaussian distributions. Each Gaussian distribution is characterised by only three parameters, its weight in the mixture, its mean, and its variance. The three parameters are estimated in such a way that the probabilities of each object (i.e., phrase contour) belonging to any of the Gaussians is maximised.

For technical reasons[6], we used a subsample of coefficients from 30,000 melodic phrases drawn at random from the overall 376,423 phrases. The model that fits this sample best is a 17-component *EEV* model with equal volume and equal shape but variable orientation of the components. The density distribution of only the first (linear) and second (quadratic) standardised coefficients is visualised in Figs. 6 and 7.

However, interpreting the density distributions of z-transformed coefficients is difficult and musicologically not very interesting. In that respect, an interpretation of the components of the mixture model as clusters of phrases is more rewarding. We return to this below.

With the help of the mixture model, any new melodic phrase, represented by a set of polynomial coefficients, can be assigned a density in the model space. This density can be interpreted as indicating the frequency of occurrence or prevalence of the melodic contour in the model space. As raw density numbers are difficult to interpret and depend on the dimensionality of the data and on peculiarities of the density estimation procedure, we express the prevalence in terms of the percentile into which a given phrase falls with respect to the distribution of density values. We therefore compute the distribution of densities for a new and randomly selected set of 30,000 phrases with respect to the existing model. We compute the 1-percentile boundaries of the distribution for this new set of phrases and we then can determine the percentile that corresponds to the density of the new melodic phrase contour.

---

[6] The algorithm we used for maximum-likelihood estimation as implemented in the library MCLUST of the statistical programming language R is very memory intensive and therefore sets an effective limit for the number of phrases to be modelled in the same model.

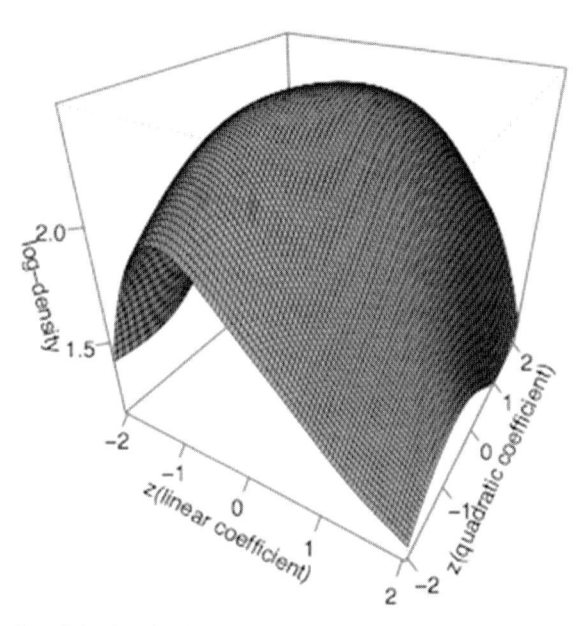

Fig. 6: Perspective plot of the log-density of the distribution of the z-transformed first and second polynomial coefficients according to a 17-component Gaussian Mixture Model. The density is marginalised over the other four coefficients.

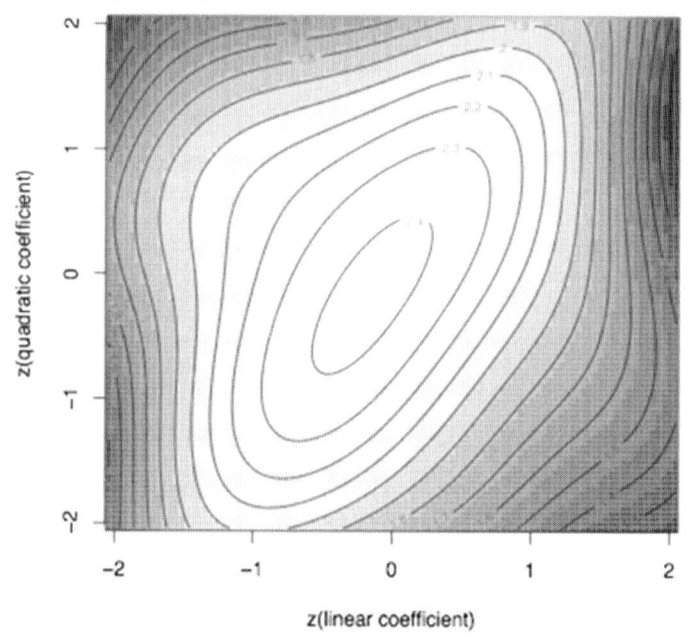

Fig. 7: Heat plot of the density of the distribution of the first and second polynomial coefficients according to a 17-component Gaussian Mixture Model. Lighter colours correspond to a higher density. The contour circles denote regions with equal density.

For the contour of *Ah vous dirai-je Maman*, as displayed in Fig. 2, we obtain a logarithmic density value of 7.33. This corresponds to the 100th percentile of the distribution of density values of 30,000 randomly sampled melodic phrases; i.e., the contour of the melody is more common than 99% of all phrase contours. Therefore, relatively speaking, the melody displayed in Fig.1 can be considered to have a very common melodic shape.

The first and the second phrase of the same melody as displayed in Figs. 3 and 4 both have a density of approximately 5.42 and 7.49 respectively which means that they are in the 78th and 100th percentile, i.e. phrase is less common and phrase 2 is slightly more common than the contour of the first two phrases modelled together.

In comparison, we obtain a considerably lower density value for the 1st phrase of the melody of the national anthem of the USA (see Figs. 8 and 9). The density value is 3.868 which corresponds to the 41st percentile, that is, 40% of the 30,000 randomly sampled phrases have a less common contour.

Fig. 8: First phrase of the melody from the US national anthem.

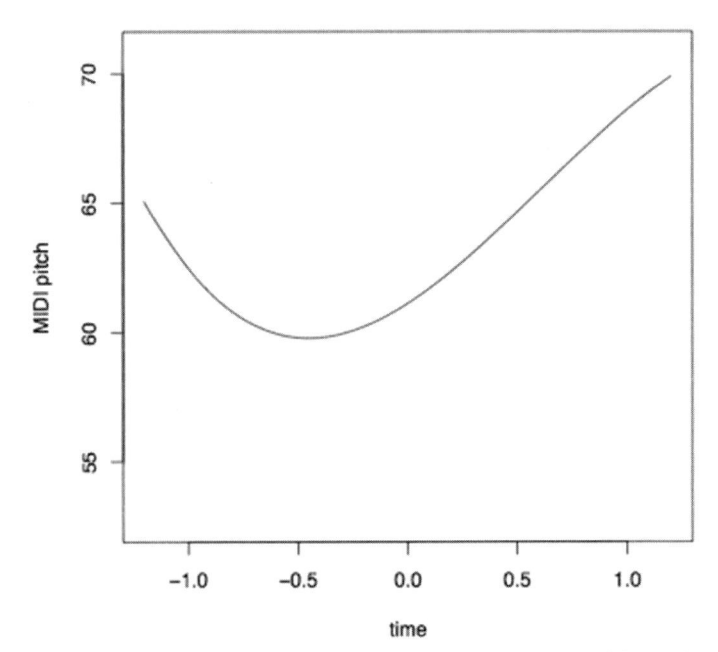

Fig. 9: Contour curve corresponding to the phrase in Fig. 8. The polynomial equation is: $y = 61.1 + 5.44 \cdot x + 4.44 \cdot x^2 - 2.38 \cdot x^3$

Apart from density estimation, Gaussian mixture models can also be exploited for clustering melodic phrases. Each multi-dimensional component can be interpreted as a separate cluster and all phrases with the highest probability of being generated from that component are considered to belong to that cluster. Due to the space limitations of this contribution, we cannot go into detail here, but a comparison to the contour-based clustering or grouping of melodic phrases as carried out by Steinbeck (1982), Huron (1996), Juhasz (2000, 2009), or Frieler et al. (in press) would certainly be a very interesting next step.

4.2 Similarity measurement via integration

Similarity measurement has been the primary aim of most analytical and computational studies on melodic contour. We now show very briefly how the polynomial contour representation of melodic phrases can serve very straightforwardly as base representation for determining the similarity relationship between two phrases.

As an example we consider the polynomial contours of several phrases taken from Beethoven's famous theme from the 4th movement of the 9th symphony, also known as *Ode to Joy* (Fig. 10).

Fig. 10: Ode to Joy

We choose phrase 1 (bars 1, 2, and the first note in bar 3), phrase 2 (bars 3, 4), phrase 5 (bar 9), phrase 6 (bar 10), and phrase 7 (bar 11 and first 3 notes in bar 12) as example phrases for our small test set. Their polynomial contours are depicted in Figs. 11–15.

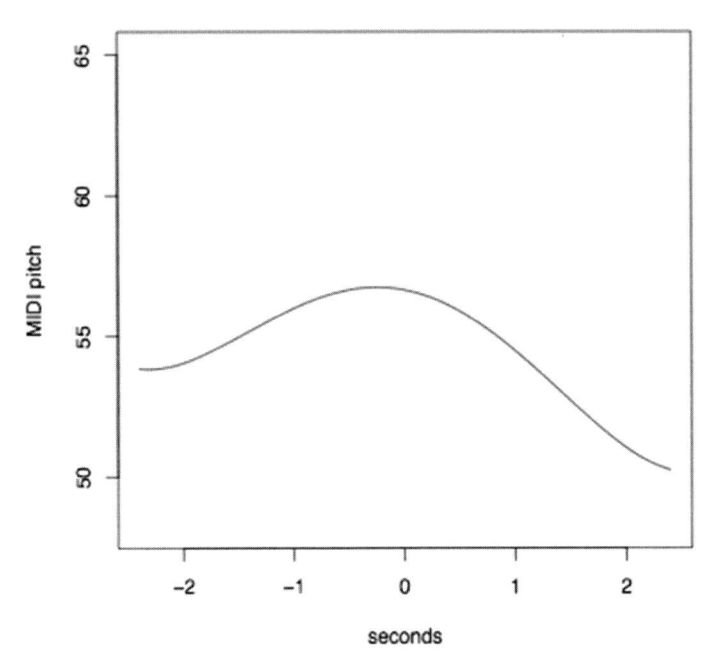

Fig. 11: Polynomial contour of *Ode to Joy*, 1st phrase

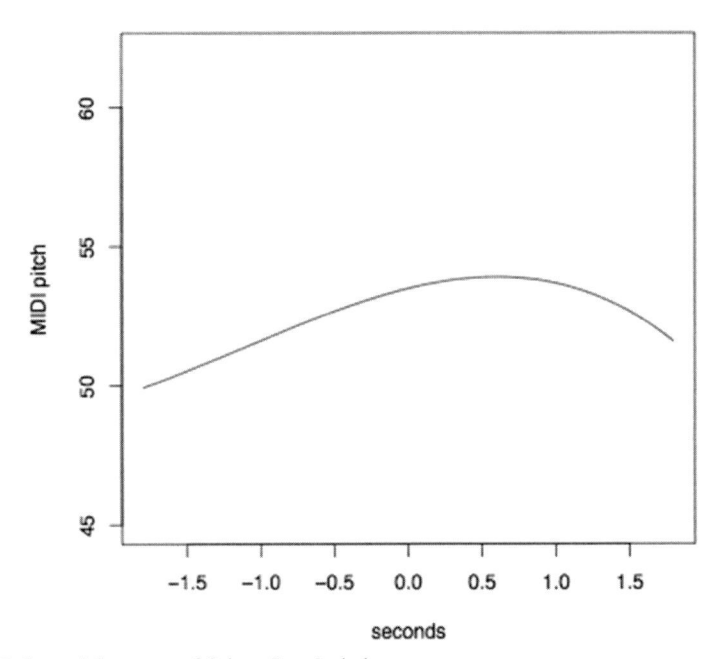

Fig. 12: Polynomial contour of Ode to Joy, 2nd phrase

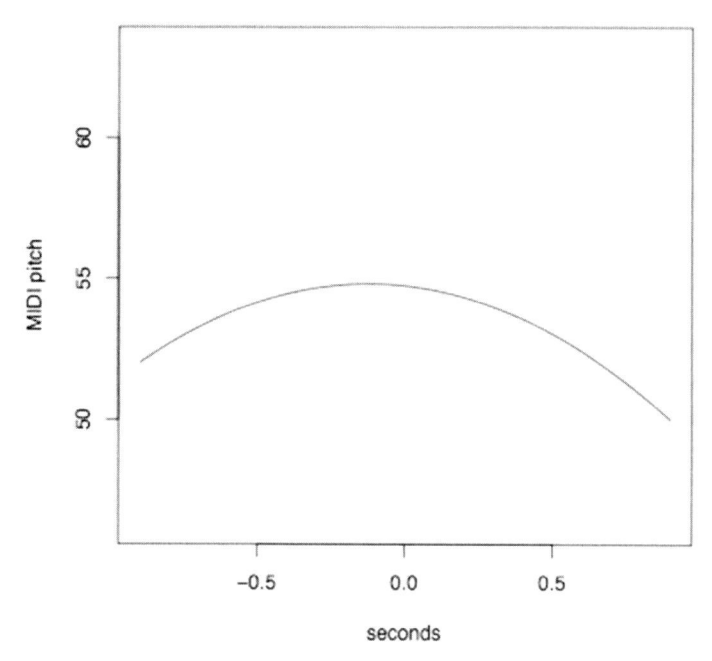

Fig. 13: Polynomial contour of Ode to Joy, 5th phrase

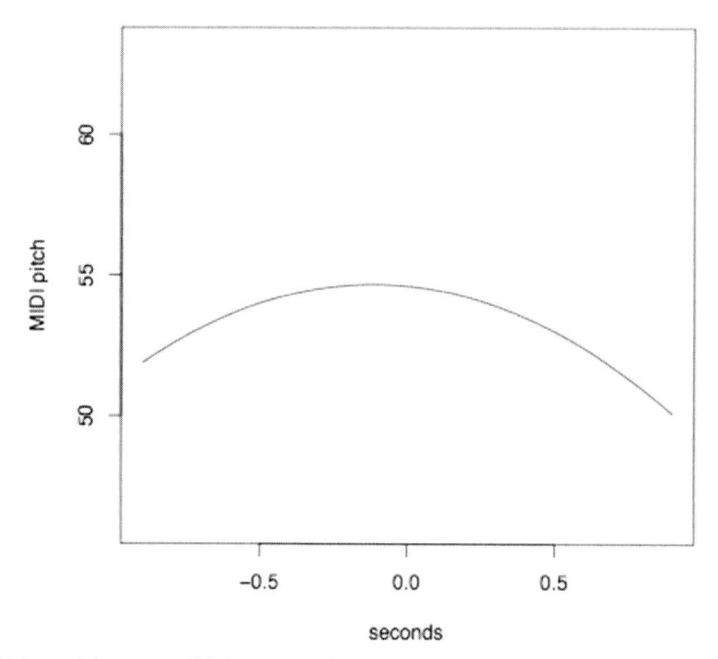

Fig. 14: Polynomial contour of Ode to Joy, 6th phrase

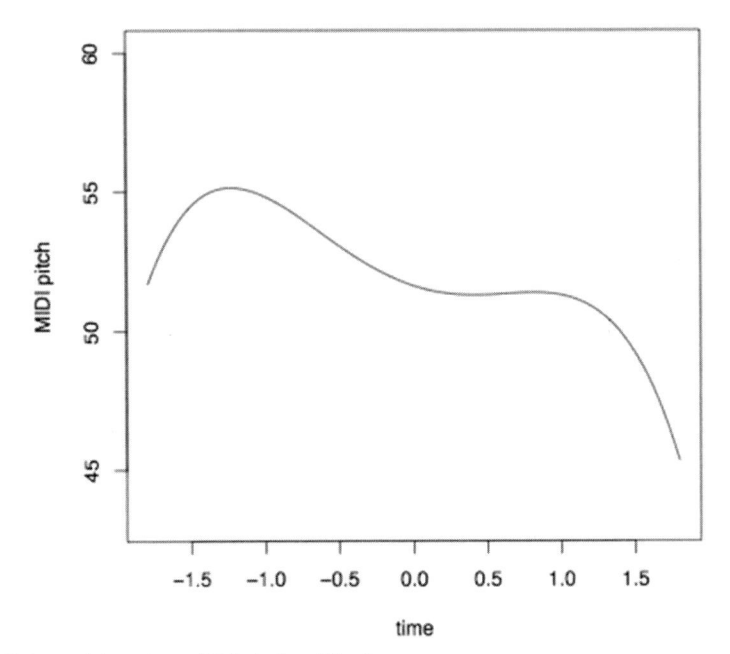

Fig. 15: Polynomial contour of Ode to Joy, 7th phrase

All the phrases are to a certain degree similar, in that their overall shape could be described as arch-like. However, they differ in length, the relation between the first and last note (overall rising vs. falling motion), and the range between the lowest and highest pitch in the phrase. We compare these phrases from Beethoven's *Ode to Joy* also to the first and second phrase of *Ah vous dirai-je, Maman* (Fig. 1), and the first phrase of the US national anthem (Fig. 8).

To measure the pairwise similarity between these phrases, we propose a new similarity measure based on Tversky's ratio model of similarity (1977) and a graphical interpretation of the polynomial curves. We assume that the area under the polynomial curve characterises the contour of a melodic phrase and that the overlap between the areas under the curves of two polynomials reflects their degree of similarity.

The polynomial functions $p(x)$ and $q(x)$ derived from melodies m and n as well as the time limits of the melodies to the left and the right of the origin $x_{p,-T}$, $x_{p,T}$, and $x_{q,-T}$, $x_{q,T}$ are the input to the procedure. First, the additive constant a in $p(x)$ and $q(x)$ is replaced by a value such that the lowest value of the polynomial curve within the limits is 0.[7] In the following we only give the equations concerning the transformations of $p(x)$. $q(x)$ is transformed correspondingly.

(5) $\quad a' = a - \min(p(x)); x \in [-T, T]$

---

[7] This is only one possible way to transform two phrases into the same pitch range. Other possibilities which need to be explored in the future include offsetting the two phrases by their respective average pitches or by their central or key pitches.

Then we compute the areas below each polynomial curve by integrating the polynomial function in its limits.

(6) $$P = \int_{-T}^{T} p'(x)$$

Then we compute the two difference functions between the two polynomials:

(7) $$d(x) = p'(x) - q'(x)$$

This is done simply by subtracting each coefficient value of one function from its correspondent value in the other function. We denote the ranges of values for which $d(x)>0$ with R_i, each of which comprises a start and end point j and k.
We then integrate over all positive ranges and sum the resulting areas.

(8) $$D = \sum_{i=1}^{R} \int_{j}^{k} d(x)$$

This leaves us with four area values, P, Q, D, and E. The intersection between the areas under the two curves is then given by

(9) $$P \cap Q = P - D = Q - E$$

For computing a similarity between the two melodic phrases we make use of the ratio model of similarity originally proposed by Tversky (1977, p. 333) for measuring the similarity between two objects a and b via their feature sets A and B.

(10) $$s(a,b) = \frac{f(A \cap B)}{f(A \cap B) + \alpha f(A - B) + \beta f(B - A)}, \alpha, \beta \geq 0$$

Here $f(A \cap B)$ is a function that measures the salience or prominence of the features present in both melodies to the notion of similarity. By analogy, $f(A - B)$ and $f(B - A)$ measures the salience of the features only present in one of a and b respectively. The choice of the weights α and β sets the focus of the similarity comparison. A straightforward implementation of the ratio model in terms of our melodic contour representation is achieved by using the areas as values of the salience functions and setting $\alpha=\beta=1$:

(11) $$s(m,n) = \frac{P \cap Q}{P \cap Q + D + E}$$

The similarity measure has a range of possible values between 0 (no similarity) and 1 (maximal similarity/identity).

Table 1: The similarity values obtained by the similarity measure in eqn. 11 for all pairs of melodic phrases of our test set.

	Ode_p1	Ode_p2	Ode_p5	Ode_p6	Ode_p7	US_nat_p1	Ah_p1
Ode_p1	1						
Ode_p2	0.51	1					
Ode_p5	0.56	0.67	1				
Ode_p6	0.53	0.68	0.95	1			
Ode_p7	0.73	0.37	0.48	0.46	1		
US_nat_p1	0.38	0.42	0.3	0.3	0.38	1	
Ah_p1	0.57	0.38	0.41	0.39	0.2	0.41	1
Ah_p2	0.6	0.47	0.74	0.74	0.49	0.31	0.33

The highest similarity value of 0.95 is obtained for phrase 5 and 6 from *Ode to Joy*, the full results being given in Table 1. Both phrases are one measure long, have a clear arch-like shape, the same pitches at start and end and a narrow interval range of 4 and 5 semitones respectively. The high contour similarity is reflected by the closeness of the polynomial curves and the very small area between them as depicted in Fig. 16.

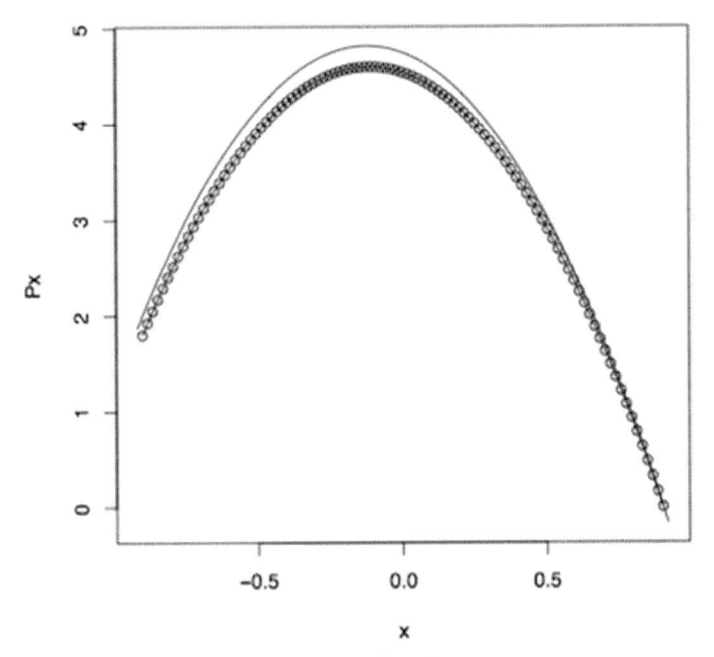

Fig. 16: Contour curves for phrases 5 and 6 from Ode to Joy.

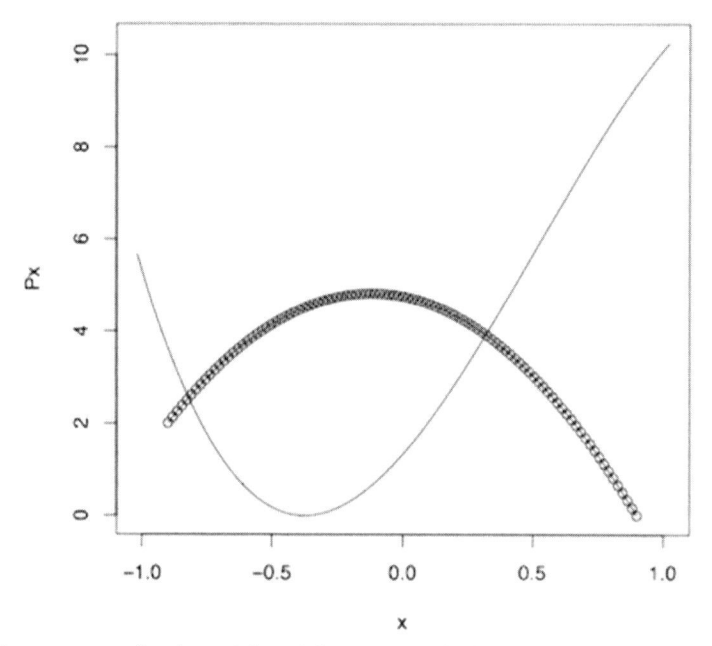

Fig. 17: Contour curves for phrase 5 from *Ode to Joy* and the first phrase of the US national anthem.

The other similarity values in table 1 between the 5 phrases from *Ode to Joy* cover a middle range between 0.37 and 0.73. Their common feature is the arch-like overall motion. Generally, higher values are obtained for phrases of approximately the same length (*s(p2,p5)*, *s(p2,p6)*) and phrases of approximately the same length and the same interval between start and end note (*s(p1,p7)*).

In contrast, clearly lower similarity values are obtained for the comparisons of the arch-like contours from *Ode to Joy* to the first phrase of the US national anthem, which describes something of a *J*-shape. Fig. 17 shows the small overlap between the areas under the curves of the latter phrase and phrase 5 from *Ode to Joy*.

5 Summary and options for future work

In this paper, we have introduced a new method for representing the contour of melodic phrases based on fitting a polynomial to the pitches of the phrase. In our approach, the melodic contour of a phrase is represented by a finite set of polynomial coefficients and the time limits that mark the start and end of the polynomial curve. We have given a detailed description of how the fitting is carried out in order to enable other researchers to implement their own version of this idea. We have explained several principled implementation decisions during the fitting process, where exploring alternatives might be a worthwhile enterprise. Among the decisions to be challenged are the length and duration limits of the phrases to be modelled by a polynomial, the decision not to normalise to unity with regard to pitch and time, and the z-transformation of the resulting coefficients.

We have presented two applications that make use of the polynomial contour representation and sketched the options for clustering large collections of melodic phrases. The first application allows one to estimate the probability density of a melodic contour with respect to a Gaussian mixture model created from a sample of 30,000 phrases randomly drawn from a pop song collection. The density model of phrase contours can be a very useful tool for a number of music information retrieval applications that deal with melodic data. In addition, cognitive models of music processing can be informed by density estimates of phrase contour assuming that the model density is closely related to the prevalence of a melodic contour (in popular music).

As a second application, we have defined a similarity measure that takes two polynomial curves as drawn within their corresponding limits and compares the areas enclosed between the curves. The degree of overlap between areas is then interpreted as the degree of (contour) similarity between the two melodic phrases.

Both applications have been tested by example in this paper and the results are plausible, easy to interpret, and intuitively convincing. However, a rigorous empirical verification of both applications, with large suitable datasets and more specifically selected qualitative examples, is necessary to evaluate the utility of the polynomial contour representation for theoretical, analytical, and empirical research on melodies. This is our next step.

Acknowledgements

We would like to thank Jamie Forth for comments and feedback on the manuscript of this article. Daniel Müllensiefen's contribution to this work was supported by EPSRC research grant EP/D038855/1.

References

Baddeley, A. (1997). *Human Memory.Theory and Practice.* Hove: Psychology Press.

Boltz, M. & Jones, M.R. (1986). Does rule Recursion Make Melodies Easier to reproduce? If Not, What Does? *Cognitive Psychology*, 389–431.

Bradford, C. (2005). Heart & Soul: Revealing the Craft of Songwriting. London: Sanctuary.

Cambouropoulos, E. (2001). The local boundary detection model (LBDM) and its applications in the study of expressive timing. *Proceedings of the International Computer Music Conference* (pp. 17–22).

Cuddy, L.L. & Lyons, H.I. (1981). Musical Pattern Recognition: A Comparison of Listening to and Studying Structures and Tonal Ambiguities. *Psychomusicology, 1*(1), 15–33.

de la Motte, Diether. (1993). *Melodie: Ein Lese- und Arbeitsbuch.* München, Kassel: dtv / Bärenreiter.

de Nooijer, J., Wiering, F., Volk, A. &Tabachneck-Schijf, Hermi J.M. (2008). Cognition-based segmentation for music information retrieval systems. In C. Tsougras & R. Parncutt (Ed.), *Proceedings of the fourth Conference on Interdisciplinary Musicology (CIM2008).*

Dowling, W.J. & Bartlett, J.C. (1981).The importance of interval information in long-term memory for melodies. *Psychomusicology, 1*, 30–49.

Dowling, W.J. & Fujitani, D.S. (1971).Contour, Interval, and Pitch Recognition in Memory for Melodies. *The Journal of the Acoustical Society of America, 49*(2, Part 2), 524–531.

Dowling, W.J. & Harwood, D.L. (1986). Melody: Attention and Memory. In Dowling, W.J. & Harwood, D.L. (Ed.), *Music Cognition* (pp. 124–152). Orlando: Academic Press.

Dowling, W.J., Kwak, S. & Andrews, M.W. (1995). The timne course of recognition of novel melodies. *Perception and Psychophysics, 57*(2), 136–149.

Edworthy, J. (1985). Interval and Contour in Melody Processing. *Music Perception, 2*(3), 375–388.

Eerola, T. & Toiviainen, P. (2004). MIR in Matlab: The MIDI Toolbox. Proceedings of the 5th International Conference on Music Information Retrieval.

Eiting, M. H. (1984). Perceptual Similarities between Musical Motifs. *Music Perception, 2*(1), 78–94.

Friedmann, M. L. (1985). A methodology for the discussion of contour: its application to Schoenberg's music. *Journal of Music Theory, 31*, 268–274.

Frieler, K., Müllensiefen, D. & Riedemann, F. (in press). Statistical search for melodic prototypes. Staaatliches Institut für Musikforschung.

Galvin, J.J., Fu, Q.J. & Nogaki, G. (2007). Melodic Contour Identification by Cochlear Implant Listeners. *Ear & Hearing, 28*(3), 302–319

Grabner, H. (1959). *Allgemeine Musiklehre.* Kassel: Bärenreiter.

Hindemith, P. (1940). *Unterweisung im Tonsatz: Bd. 1: Theoretischer Teil.* Mainz: Schott.

Huron, D. (1996). The Melodic Arch in Western Folksongs. *Computing in Musicology*, 10, 3-23.

Idson, W.L. & Massaro, D. W. (1976). Cross-octave masking of single tones and musical sequences: The effects of structure on auditory recognition. *Perception & Psychophysics, 19*(2), 155–175

Idson, W.L. &Massaro, D.W. (1978). A bidimensional model of pitch in the recognition of melodies. *Perception & Psychophysics, 24*(6), 551–565.

Jeppesen, K. (1935). *Kontrapunkt.* Leipzig.

Juhász, Z. (2009). Automatic Segmentation and Comparative Study of Motives in Eleven Folk Song Collections using Self-Organizing Maps and Multidimensional Mapping. *Journal of New Music Research, 38*(1), 71-85.

Juhász, Z. (2000). A Model of Variation in the Music of a Hungarian Ethnic Group. *Journal of New Music Research, 29*(2), 159–172.

Kachulis, J. (2003). *The Songwriter's Workshop: Melody.* Boston, MA: Berklee Press.

Kim, Y.E., Chai, W., Garcia, R. &Vercoe, B. (2000). Analysis of a Contour-based Representation for Melody.*Proceedings of the 1st Conference on Music Information Retrieval.*

Kühn, C. (1987). *Formenlehre der Musik.* München, Kassel: dtv / Bärenreiter.

Marvin, E.W. & Laprade, P. (1987).relating musical contours: extensions of a theory for contour. *Journal of Music Theory, 31*, 225–267.

McLachlan, G. & Peel, D. (2000).*Finite Mixture Models:* Wiley-Interscience.

Meyer, L. B. (1956). *Emotion and Meaning in Music:* University of Chicago Press.

Müllensiefen, D. & Frieler, K. (2004). Cognitive Adequacy in the Measurement of Melodic Similarity: Algorithmic vs. Human Judgments. *Computing in Musicology, 13*, 147–176.

Parsons, D. (1979). *Directory of tunes and musical themes.* New York: Spencer Brown.

Pauws, S. (2002). Cuby hum: A fully Operational Query by Humming System. *Proceedings of the 3rd International Conference on Music Information Retrieval* (pp. 187–196).

Pearce, M. T., Müllensiefen, D. T, & Wiggins, G. A. (2010). The role of expectation and probabilistic learning in auditory boundary perception: A model comparison. *Perception, 9*, 1367–1391.

Perricone, J. (2000). *Melody in Songwriting: Tools and Techniques for Writing Hit Songs.* Boston, MA: Berklee Press.

Piston, W. (1950). *Counterpoint* .London: Victor Gollancz.

Polansky, L. (1996). Morphological metrics. *Journal of New Music Research, 25*, 289–368.

Quinn, I. (1999). The combinatorial model of pitch contour. *Music Perception, 16*, 439–456.

Rosen, C. (1976). *The classical style: Haydn, Mozart, Beethoven.* London: Faber.

Schaffrath, H. (1995). *The Essen Folksong Collection in the Kern Format.* Huron, D. (Ed.): Center for Computer Assisted research in the Humanities.

Schmuckler, M. A. (1999). Testing Models of Melodic Contour Similarity. *Music Perception, 16*(3), 109–150.

Shmulevich, I. (2004). A Note on the Pitch Contour Similarity Index. *Journal of New Music Research, 33*(1), 17–18.

Steinbeck, W. (1982). *Struktur und Ähnlichkeit: Methoden automatisierter Melodieanalyse.* Kassel: Bärenreiter.

Taylor, J. A. & Pembrook, R. G. (1984). Strategies in Memory for Short Melodies: An Extension of Otto Ortmann's 1933 Study. *Psychomusicology, 3*(1), 16–35.

Temperley, D. (2001). *The Cognition of Basic Musical Structures.* Cambridge, MA: MIT Press.

Thom, B., Spevak, C. & Höthker, K. (2002). Melodic segmentation: Evaluating the performance of algorithms and musical experts. *Proceedings of the 2002 International Computer Music Conference.*

Toch, E. (1923). *Melodielehre: EinBeitrag zur Musiktheorie.* Berlin.

Trehub, S. E., Bull, D. & Thorpe, L. A. (1984). Infants' perception of melodies: the role of melodic contour. *Child Development, 55*, 821–830.

Tversky, A. (1977). Features of Similarity. *Psychological Review, 84*(4), 327–352.

Zhou, Y. & Kankanhalli, M. S. (2003). Melody alignment and Similarity Metric for Content-Based Music Retrieval. *Proceedingsof SPIE-IS&T Electronic Imaging.* SPIE Vol. 5021, 2003, 112-121.

Klaus Frieler[1]
Frank Höger
Jörg Korries

Meloworks - An Integrated Retrieval, Analysis and E-learning Platform for Melody Research

Abstract

In this paper we present the first release of a new integrated melody search and analysis online platform called *Meloworks*. It is built upon a database which incorporates currently about 7,000 tunes from the Essen folk song collection. Songs can be searched and retrieved and statistically analyzed using a modular analysis framework based on symbolical computations.

1. Introduction

Most likely, techniques of music information retrieval were first enterprised in the fields of ethno- and comparative musicology as early as 1949 (Bronson, 1949), since these disciplines had to deal which large amounts of musical data (field recordings, printed folk song collections etc.). Main research objectives have been and still are categorisation and classification of vocal and instrumental folk music with regard to ethnical and geographical origin or functional and melodic types. To this end, different feature sets (e.g. phrase and accents structures, tonality, cadences, melodic contour, etc.) are utilised. Specific indexing techniques were developed for content-based retrieval of melodies[2], which is inseparably intertwined with analytical and classificatory reasoning, e.g., by employing the concept of "tune families" based on melodic features (Bayard, 1950).[3] Early examples of computational projects in ethnomusicology are Alan Lomax' famous Cantrometics project (Lomax, 1968), which was based on manually extracted feature vectors of folk songs recordings from all over the world, or the automated classification of Slavonic folk tunes with the help of the Wrocław Taxonomy by Anna Czekanowska and co-workers in Poland (Czekanowska, 1972). The recently emerging efforts (e.g. Kranenburg, 2009; Tzanetakis et al. 2009) of connecting music information retrieval to folk song research via computational musicology is—in some way—like bringing music information retrieval "back home".

However, to our view there is one more ingredient needed for a real up-to-date research in this area, namely music psychology. Algorithms of computational musicology could be built upon and greatly enhanced by results from music psychological research, thereby boosting its ecological validity. In return, we believe that music psychology

---

[1] Corresponding author: klaus.frieler@uni-hamburg.de
[2] One of the first example being Ilmari Krohn's classification system for Finnish Folk song from 1903; his system being adopted by Bartok and Kodaly later on (Kranenburg et al., 2009).
[3] For an overview on this topic see again Kranenburg et al. (2009).

should be informed and supplemented by statistical investigations of large music corpora, since statistical approaches to music cognition are becoming more and more relevant besides rule-based thinking (cf. Gigerenzer, 1987; Huron, 2004). This coincides nicely with the many approaches taken in current Music Information Retrieval (MIR) employing statistical, particularly Bayesian methods. The success of these methods where the evaluation is mostly based on human judgments, hints to an integrated view. Human perception is mostly determined by enculturation built upon innate biological systems, i.e., statistical learning from a music environment under certain constraints. Furthermore, there are a lot of socially determined factors, which to a great extend do not depend directly on the musical objects themselves but on the semiotics of the social and cultural context, e.g., the image of a pop star or the ritualistic use of shamanistic songs or church hymns, which is basically the object of ethnological or sociological studies. The real-world behaviour of music users is thus determined by psychological (mostly low-level) and socio-ethnological (mostly high-level or extra-musical) factors. To build successful applications MIR needs to be informed by the fields of ethnomusicology (in the broadest sense), music psychology (including neuromusicology), and music sociology. On the other hand, these fields could greatly benefit from technologies developed in a MIR context.

One more point might serve to illustrate this. The on-going trend of cultural heritage institution to digitise their collections, particularly of field recordings, produces demands and new application areas for MIR techniques, including state-of-the-art audio-based techniques[4]. Ethnomusicology in this regard calls for MIR techniques in a highly integrated manner.

Our contribution, *Meloworks,* is just a small step on the way to a fully integrated system as envisioned above. Nevertheless, we already laid the groundwork for a general framework which finally might evolve into a work bench for "computational ethnomusicpsychology", and which we are going to describe in more detail in the following sections.

2. Goals

The *Meloworks* projects aims at an integrated, easily accessible system for retrieval and analysis of monophonic folks songs. It is designed as a flexible, extendable, yet easy-to-use system which can serve for serious scientific research as well as an educational tool for learners and beginners in the field of computational (ethno-)musicology.

3. System

An overview of the system is depicted in Fig.1. The core component is a MySQL database, which currently comprises about 7,000 songs from the Essen Collection (Schaffrath, 1992). The songs are stored as chains of annotated note events along with

---

[4] Notably, already in 1975 attempts to classify folks songs on the basis of field recordings had been adventured in Scandinavia (Sevåg, 1975).

the original EsAC code and metadata. This double coding of songs allows for flexible and complete ways of retrieval and analysis. The data was imported with specialized scripts from the original EsAC text files. For the future, it is planned that songs can be added to the database via the web interface, which is the main access point to the system[5]. The web interface enables basic retrieval and analysis operations. Song data and analysis results are displayed together in the browser window for easy comparison. Songs can be listened to by a single click on a flash player integrated in the interface. Additionally, there are export options for further external use: Songs can be exported as text files in EsAC format and analysis results can be retrieved as CSV files.

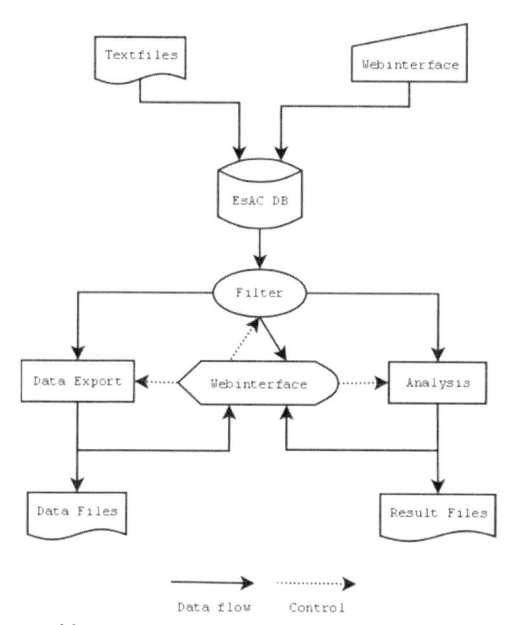

Fig. 1: *Meloworks* system architecture.

The system was implemented with state-of-the-art web development techniques. The backend is built with Ruby on Rails and the frontend features modern web design and AJAX technology.

3.1 Retrieval

Selection of melodies is currently only possible on grounds of the historical EsAC song collections (e.g. Kinderlieder, Old-german songs, Ballads, etc.), more elaborate options are under construction. The user can choose a whole collection or just a single song from the collection for analysis. On these selections various algorithms can be applied.

---

[5] A beta version of Meloworks is currently available online for the public under: http://www.meloworks.uni-hamburg.de/meloworks/login.

3.2 Analysis

The analysis module is based on the conceptual mathematical frameworks of melodic transformations and transformation chains (Frieler, 2009), resp. multiple viewpoints (Conklin & Anagnostopoulou, 2001). The basic objects in this framework are sequences of tone events, which are represented by onset, pitch and duration. Pitch is thought here as an index in a predefined tone system, which is a necessary generalisation to allow for non-western melodies. Since EsAC does not explicitly specify a tone system, we currently employ the standard MIDI system for indexing tones from the western equal-tempered system. In this framework, a melody of length N is a map

$$\mu : [0:N[\to \mathbb{R} \times [0:127[\times \mathbb{R}_0^+$$
$$n \mapsto (t_n, p_n, d_n),$$

where t_n are onsets, p_n MIDI pitches, and d_n durations. The map must be strictly monotonic in the first argument, i. e., $i<j \Leftrightarrow t_i<t_j$. Furthermore, monophonic melodies must fulfill the condition $t_i+d_i \leq t_{i+1}$ for all $i \in [0:N-1[$.

For many analytical tasks, it is desirable to measure durations not in seconds (or ticks) but in units of tatums. Since the EsAC durations are already denoted using a system of basic rhythmic units (quaver, semi-quaver etc.), we additionally store duration information in the database as integer multiples of basic units. Let $\tau(\mu)$ denote the tatum of a melody, then the integer durations are calculated as $d'_i = d_i/\tau(\mu) \in \mathbb{N}$.

EsAC provides meter information, crucial for many analysis applications. Consequently, each tone is annotated by a metrical position. Let B be the coding space of metrical positions consisting of triples (m, b, s) with m denoting the bar index, b the beat index in a bar, and d the subdivision position in a beat (measured in tatums or ticks). Furthermore, let S be the space of time signatures of pairs (b, t), where b is the number of beats per bar and t the number of tatums (or ticks) per beat. We then define a metrical annotation M for a melody μ of length N as a map $M(\mu):[0:N[\to B \times S$. For melodies with changing or free meter (which are quite frequent in folk songs), it is necessary to store the metrical context coded as time signatures together with the metrical positions[6].

Phrase information is of central importance for folk song research, and its availability is a unique feature of EsAC compared to other symbolical data formats. Hence, phrase indices are stored for every note event.

Meloworks currently features 9 melodic transformations which can be combined with n-gram transformations up to n=4. An n-gram transformation for a sequence $\sigma : [0:N[\to X$ with domain X is a sequence of length N-n of sequences of length n over X. Clearly, a unigram transformation is the identity map. For a non-trivial example, let n = 3. Then a trigram transformation of σ has elements

---

[6] Of course, certain consistency conditions need to be fulfilled by such metrical annotations, but we cannot go into detail here.

$$3_\sigma(i) = (\sigma(i), \sigma(i+1), \sigma(i+2)), 0 \leq i \leq N-3.$$

Let μ be a melody of length N. The 9 melodic transformations in *Meloworks* are the following.

1. **Durations**. This transformation maps μ on a sequence of length N of tatum durations $d'_i = d_i/\tau(\mu)$.
2. **Duration ratios**. This transformation maps μ on a sequence of length N-1 of duration ratios, i.e. $r_i = d_{i+1}/d_i$. Durations ratios are displayed in the form "1:1", "1:2", "2:1" etc.
3. **Interonset intervals**. Interonset intervals are defined as the time between two subsequent note onsets. Formally, we map μ on a sequence of length N-1 with elements $\Delta t_i = t_{i+1}-t_i$. Interonset intervals are often used instead of durations for analytical purposes.
4. **Semitone intervals**. In the MIDI indexing scheme, pitches are normally assumed to be from the 12-TET system. Thus, the difference of pitch indices is simply the interval between the pitches in semitones. In this case, this transformation is a sequence of length N-1 with elements $\Delta p_i = p_{i+1}-p_i$. If in the future the database will contain also music from non-equal-tempered tone systems, a differentiation between "index differences in a tone system" and "musical intervals" has to be introduced.
5. **Parsons Code**. The Parsons transformation of μ is a sequence of length N-1 with elements $sgn(p_{i+1}-p_i)$, where $sgn(x)$ is the usual signum-operator. Thus, ascending intervals will be mapped onto +1 (displayed as **U**, for "Up"), unisones onto 0 (displayed as **S**, for "Same") and descending intervals onto -1 (displayed as **D**, for "Down"). Parsons code is sometimes referred to as melodic contour in the literature.
6. **Pitch classes**. This transformation is based on the notion of octave equivalence, which allows separating pitch into the psychophysical dimension of chroma quality and octave position. In *Meloworks* the pitch class transformation uses the key information as provided by EsAC as a reference point. Furthermore, it assumes 12-TET. Let T be the reference key pitch, we then define the pitch class of a MIDI pitch p with regard to T in 12-TET as $p_T = [p-T]_{12} = (p-T) \mod 12$. Clearly, the tonic and its super- and sub-octaves will be mapped onto 0.
7. **Diatonic pitch classes**. The EsAC code is based on diatonic thinking, i.e., on heptatonic scales. The diatonic pitch class transformation for a given reference pitch T, the tonic of μ, is established by mapping the pitch classes p_T according to $\{0\} \rightarrow 1$, $\{1,2\} \rightarrow 2$, $\{3,4\} \rightarrow 3$, $\{5,6\} \rightarrow 4$, $\{7\} \rightarrow 5$, $\{8,9\} \rightarrow 6$, $\{10,11\} \rightarrow 7$. Strictly speaking, the mapping of the tritone $p_T=6$ onto the raised fourth is ambiguous, it could be as well conceived as a flatted fifth. However, for folk songs this is not a big issue, since tritones are generally quite rare, and if they occur, then mostly as raised fourths in the role of the leading tone to the dominant.
8. **Tonal pitches**. The tonal pitch transformation with reference tonic T(μ) is the sequence of translated pitches $p'_i = p_i-T$. According to the EsAC specification, the tonic needs to be chosen from the middle octave, i.e., $T \in [60:71]$.

9. **Metrical circle map**. The metrical circle map is based on the idea of cyclic time. To this end, every bar of a melody is divided into M equal segments and the metrical positions of note events are mapped onto the according segment index $k \in [0 : M-1[$. For a more detailed description see (Frieler, 2007). The parameter M can be chosen in the web interface.

This set of transformations is clearly not exhaustive and still under development.

Frequency distributions and statistical values are calculated from the resulting transformations and three different display options can be chosen:

1. The transformation can be viewed directly for each melody.
2. Histograms of frequency distributions are shown for each song. They can be conveniently compared to the corresponding frequency distributions as calculated over the whole song selection.
3. Summaries of numerical statistics can be viewed, again for each song separately and for the whole selection. The statistics comprise number of elements, number of classes, mode, entropy, redundancy[7], as well as arithmetic mean, standard deviation, median, minimum, maximum, and range if applicable for a given transformation.

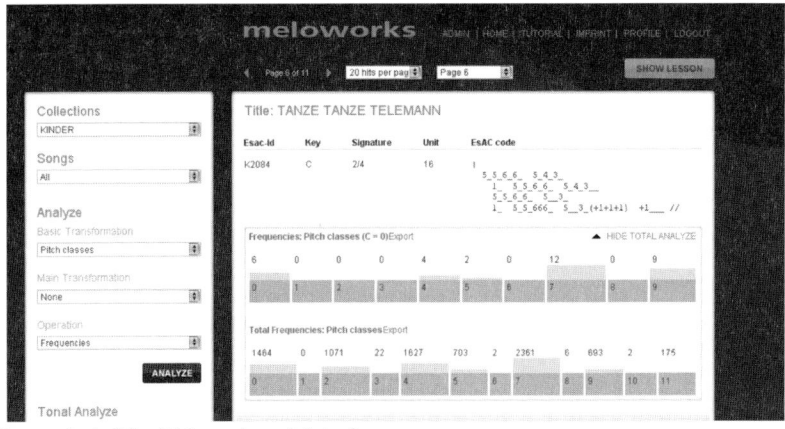

Fig. 2: Screenshot of the *Meloworks* web interface.

There is yet another analysis option in *Meloworks* of a slightly different kind, which is dedicated to tonal analysis as given by the Krumhansl-Schmuckler algorithm (see Temperley, 2001 for a discussion of this class of algorithms). For a given selection of songs, the user can choose between six different key profiles that represent weight-vectors for tonalities which are cross-correlated with tone profiles calculated from the songs for each possible transposition. The highest cross-correlation indicates the tonality. All correlations for mode and key are displayed for each song of the current selection.

---

[7] Redundancy is defined here as normalized (sample) entropy subtracted from 1.

Furthermore, the winning tonality is compared to the tonality as contained in the EsAC data and percentages of correctly classified melodies are calculated. This allows the comparison of different key profiles for different song sets. In a future version, more degrees of freedom of the Krumhansl-Schmuckler algorithm will be adjustable, in particular, users will be able to enter their own key profiles.

3.3 Learning

Besides the use for research, a platform like *Meloworks* offers excellent learning and teaching opportunities. *Meloworks* lends itself quite naturally for employing the educational paradigm of "explorative learning" (Bundesassistentenkonferenz, 1970) in workshops and classes. Students can delve into the principles of ethnomusicology using the different collections by formulating their own research questions and conducting desktop experiments with the online workbench. Furthermore, students are introduced to the basics of computational musicology and - thus - ultimately to MIR. Last but not least, (statistical) music psychological questions can be easily explored with the help of *Meloworks*, which could even be helpful as training cases for statistics classes.

We already collected some experience with employing *Meloworks* (and its prototype *Melex*[8]) in universitary workshops on melody research and cognition and received very promising results and very positive feedback from the participants.

4. Future Work

Meloworks can be regarded as a prototype for an integrated system as described in the introduction. Many extensions and improvements can be thought of.

- **Data**. More data need to be integrated. In the literature, up to 10,000, sometimes even 14,000 songs are reported for the EsAC collection. We incorporated up to now the songs which are available through the offical EsAC web site[9], plus the collections of Luxembourgian, Lorrainian and Irish Songs by Damien Sagrillo (Sagrillo, 1999), and a set of about 200 songs from Warmia handed down to us by Ewa Dahlig-Turek, the maintainer of the EsAC collection. A collection of ca. 2,000 Hungarian songs is at our disposal, however with insufficient metadata, hence they are not yet included. Furthermore, we already started collecting transcriptions of monophonic jazz solos coded to EsAC.
- **Retrieval**. One of the most urgent points is the development of retrieval options. These should comprise extensive search by metadata as well as by musical content. The latter will be based on search methods as they are used for example in *Themefinder*[10]. Usability studies could be of great help since designing a satisfactory search interface for melodic content is, in our view, quite challenging. The transformations of the analysis module could be of great help here as well.

---

[8] *Melex* is based on the same concepts, but written entirely in Javascript with only a few songs incorporated without an underlying database. It is still accessible under http://melex.muo-on.org.
[9] http://www.esac-data.org
[10] http://www.themefinder.org

- **Analysis**. The analysis module can be greatly extended while sticking to the modular system of transformation chains as far as possible. Music psychologically inspired transformations (e.g., contour, accents) and well-known algorithms from folk song research have highest priority here. Last but not least, a module for similarity calculations is highly desirable and of particular interest for retrieval methods as well. More far out ideas are a) the implementation of an API that would allow accessing the database and the analysis modules remotely, and b) a flexible scripting engine for analysis and retrieval.
- **Display & Export**. EsAC code is well readable after short training but more traditional forms of display as common western notation should be provided as well. This can be viewed as part of a more general conversion engine, for exporting melodies in various other symbolical formats (e.g. MIDI, MusicXML, Lilypond).
- **Usability**. A detailed user rights system could allow incorporating copyrighted material (e.g., pop songs) as well. Users could be given the possibility to save and load retrieval and analysis results for later reuse.

5. Conclusion

We presented here the first beta release of an integrated analysis and retrieval workbench for melodies which already has been proven very useful for explorative (E-) learning scenarios. The big picture as painted in the introduction is a distant prospect, but a reasonable step in this direction has been done, though the need for further improvements is still huge. We sincerely hope that we will be able to continue working on *Meloworks* in the future.

Acknowledgments

This work was partly supported by a "Seminare ans Netz" E-learning grant from the University of Hamburg. The web design was carried out by Tino König (http://www.macdoct.de).

6. References

B. Bayard (1950). Prolegomena to a Study of the Principal Melodic Families of British-American Folk Song, *Journal of American Folklore*, Vol.63, No.247, pp.1–44.

B. Bronson (1949). Mechanical Help in Study of Folk Songs. *Journal of American Folklore*, Vol.62, No.244, pp. 81–86.

Bundesassistentenkonferenz (1970). Forschendes Lernen – Wissenschaftliches Prüfen. Universitätsverlag Webler, Bielefeld, (reprint 2009).

A. Czekanowska (1972). *Ludowe melodie wąskiego zakresu w krajach słowiańskich*. [Narrow-Range Melodies in Slavic Countries], Kraków.

D. Conklin and C. Anagnostopoulou (2001) Representation and discovery of multiple viewpoint patterns. *Proceedings of the 2001 International Computer Music Conference*, ICMA, San Francisco.

K. Frieler (2007). *Visualizing Music on the Metrical Circle. Proceedings of the 8th International Symposium on Music Information Retrieval*, ISMIR2007. Wien: OCG.

G. Gigerenzer, D. J. Murray (1987). *Cognition as Intuitive Statistics*. Hillsdale, NJ: Erlbaum.

D. Huron (2004). *Sweet Anticipation.* Cambridge, MA: MIT Press.

P. Kranenburg, J. Garbers, A. Volk, F. Wiering, L.P. Grijp, and R.C. Veltkamp (2009). Collaboration Perspectives for Folk Song Research and Music Information Retrieval: The Indispensable Role of Computational Musicology. *Journal of Interdersiciplinary Music Studies*, doi:10.4407/jima, 2009.11.006.

A. Lomax (1968). *Folk Song Style and Culture.* Washington: American Association for the Advancement of Science.

D. Sagrillo (1999). *Melodiegestalten im luxemburgischen Volkslied: Zur Anwendung computergestützter Verfahren bei der Klassifikation von Volksliedabschnitten.* Bonn: Holos.

H. Schaffrath (1992) The ESAC databases and MAPPET software. *Computing in Musicology,* Vol. 8, No. 66.

R. Sevåg (1975). Ethnomusicology and Automatic Transcription of Melodies. *NIF Newsletter.* Vol.2–3, pp.17–18.

D. Temperley (2001). *Cognition of Basic Musical Structures.* Cambridge, MA: MIT Press.

G. Tzanetakis, A. Kapur, W. A. Schloss and M. Wright (2009). Computational Ethnomusicology. *Journal of Interdisciplinary Music Studies,* Vol. 1, No. 2.

Albrecht Schneider
Valeri Tsatsishvili

Perception of Musical Intervals at Very Low Frequencies: Some Experimental Findings

Summary

Interval recognition of musical intervals (major second, minor third, major third, fourth, tritone, fifth) at very low frequencies of pairs of complex tones was studied in an experiment carried out with two samples of subjects at Hamburg (Germany) and Jyväskylä (Finland).

Pairs of complex harmonic tones were generated representing the six musical intervals. Each complex tone comprised five harmonic components with frequency ratios 1:2:3:4:5 and amplitudes $A = 1/n$, $n = 1, 2, 3, 4, 5$. Fundamental frequencies of the lower complex tone were set at 31.5 Hz, 40 Hz, 50 Hz, 63 Hz, and 80 Hz (corresponding to ISO frequencies for 1/3-octave band filters). Thus the design of the experiment consisted of six intervals times five fundamental frequencies (= 30 sound stimuli). The stimuli were presented to subjects in two runs, and in different order.

Interval recognition scores in general were low, however, data from the experiments indicate a gradual difference between a very low number of correct judgements at 31.5 Hz and 40 Hz, on the one hand, and improved scores at 50 Hz, 63 Hz, and 80 Hz, respectively, on the other. Results of the experiments as well as pitch perception and interval recognition in general are discussed in regard to concepts of Critical Bands (CBs) with special emphasis given to low frequencies ($f < 100$ Hz).

Zusammenfassung

Die Wahrnehmung musikalischer Intervalle (große Sekunde, kleine Terz, große Terz, Quarte, Tritonus, Quinte) in sehr tiefen Frequenzlagen wurde experimentell an zwei Stichproben von ProbandInnen in Hamburg (n = 22) und Jyväskylä (n = 13) untersucht. Dazu wurden Paare komplexer harmonischer Töne gebildet und mit diesen die sechs Intervalle dargestellt, wobei jeder Ton aus fünf Harmonischen mit den Frequenzverhältnissen 1:2:3:4:5 und den Amplituden $A = 1/n$, $n = 1, 2, 3, 4, 5$ besteht. Die Grundfrequenz des jeweils tieferen komplexen Tons wurde auf 31.5 Hz, 40 Hz, 50 Hz, 63 Hz und 80 Hz eingestellt (dies sind ISO-Frequenzwerte für 1/3-Oktav-Bandfilter). Der Versuchsplan bestand also aus sechs Intervallen kombiniert mit fünf Grundfrequenzen, mithin aus 30 Klangbeispielen, die den ProbandInnen jeweils zweimal (in verschiedener Reihenfolge) dargeboten wurden.

Die Anzahl richtig erkannter Intervalle war insgesamt niedrig, jedoch zeigen sich deutliche Unterschiede zwischen den Ergebnissen bei Grundfrequenzen von 31.5 Hz und 40 Hz auf der einen Seite, 50 Hz, 63 Hz und 80 Hz auf der anderen. Die experimentellen Befunde werden mit Bezug auf Konzepte 'kritischer Bandbreiten' (bzw. 'Frequenzgruppen') unter besonderer Berücksichtigung der Wahrnehmung von Tonhöhen bei tiefen Frequenzen ($f < 100$ Hz) erörtert.

1. Introduction

The range of hearing for so-called pure tones (sinusoidals with a frequency f [Hz] and an amplitude A [dB]) for humans usually is given as, roughly, 18 Hz to 18 kHz (Plattig 1975), or 20 Hz to 16 kHz (e.g., Zwicker & Fastl 1999). Tones not far below 20 Hz are sensed as a series of pulses, and tones above 15-16 kHz are not audible for most humans (although, for a number of other mammals). However, the threshold of hearing for sine tones or complex tones is dependent on sound pressure level (SPL) as well as on conditions such as monaural or binaural presentation of the signal. Also, the upper limit of 16 kHz may apply to young persons while many elderly people tend to experience a decrease of sensitivity at higher frequencies, or even partial loss of hearing for certain frequency bands. The lower frequency range down to 20 Hz seems to be less affected by age, though in general a certain variability concerning the frequency range and sensitivity of hearing is observed in samples of subjects. Factors such as frequent exposure to noise or very loud music (see Schneider & von Ruschkowski 2011; this volume) can have considerable influence on the frequency range of hearing, and on partial loss of sensitivity for certain frequency bands known as 'spectral dips'.

While perceptual phenomena such as pitch, masking, and roughness have been studied in great detail for the frequency range from about 100 Hz up to 4-5 kHz (see, e.g. Zwicker 1982, Zwicker & Fastl 1999, Moore 1995, 2008), the frequency range below 100 Hz down to the limit at ca. 20 Hz has been given much less attention though it is of importance in regard to music and perception. The lower limit for melodic pitch in some psychoacoustic experiments was found at about 30 Hz (cf. Pressnitzer et al. 2001). The fundamental frequency of the lowest note A_0 ($A_{,,}$ in Helmholtz designation) on a grand piano tuned to A4 (a') = 440 Hz is 27.5 Hz. On a large organ such as that built by Arp Schnitger for the St. Jakobi church of Hamburg, the fundamental frequency f_1 of the note A of the pedal when played with the Prinzipal 32' is at 30.48 Hz[1]. The pitch of the complex sound radiated from this pipe can be determined by ear quite easily since the sound contains a number of harmonics (of which no. 1 and 2 are strongest, and no. 4 strong enough to be identifiable as the double octave of the fundamental); in addition, the time signal after onset (in the quasi-stationary segment of the sound) is stable with a period of ~33 ms corresponding to a frequency f_0 with which the temporal envelope repeats at 30.3 Hz. Evidently, in the sound in question $f_1 = f_0$ so that there are two cues for pitch perception, one spectral and one temporal. Both could be used either in conjunction or independently to derive a salient pitch assigned to the sound stimulus. Since the periodicity inherent in the time series is stable after the transient part of the sound, pitch can be securely determined by means of an autocorrelation (AC) algorithm (figure 1):

---

[1] Recording made on DAT (16 bit/48 kHz) by the first author in 1995; analysis was done with Spectro 3.0 on a NeXT (FFT: 131072 samples, zero pad factor 4.0, Hanning). The fundamental of a harmonic spectrum in this paper is designated as f_1 and not as f_0 since, obviously, it is the first part of a harmonic series and not the „nullest". The original tuning of the Schnitger organ at St. Jakobi is a' = 495.45 Hz. Compass of the pedal is C D – d'.

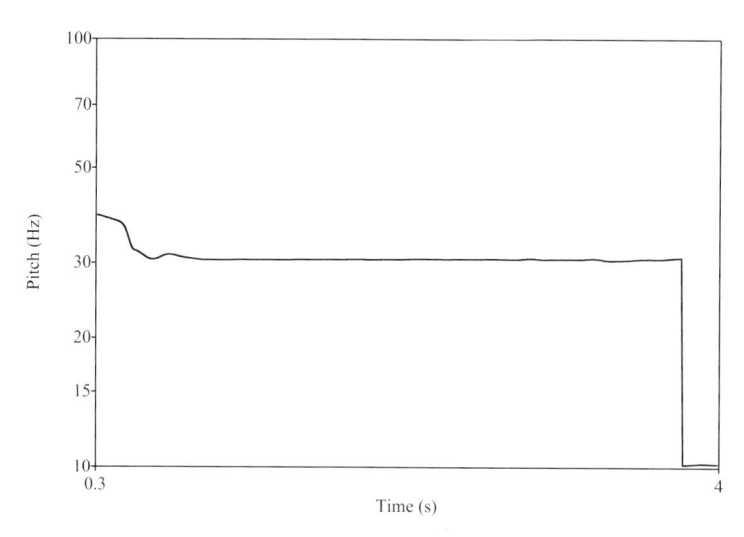

Figure 1: Schnitger-organ St. Jakobi, Hamburg. Prinzipal 32', pedal, note A

Things are more complicated if two complex sounds with fundamental frequencies below 100 Hz are presented simultaneously. For example, two notes that are played on a small grand piano with A_0 as the bottom note result in intervals that are not just as easy to analyze by ear. One can try by listening to the minor third $A_0 - C_1$, the major third $A_0 - C\#_1$, the fourth $A_0 - D_1$, or the fifth $A_0 - E_1$. Apparently, there are reasons why determination of such intervals by ear poses problems to subjects asked to make judgements. Some have to do with the acoustics of the instrument, others with the nature of our hearing system.

First, in a piano or grand piano, the strings in the bass are made from a core of steel wound with one or even two layers of wire so that the diameter of such strings is not infinitesimal small in relation to effective string length set to transversal vibration (see Fletcher & Rossing 1991, 316-318). Consequently, such strings cannot be considered as one-dimensional continua yet must rather be regarded as thin bars where stiffness and also mass has to be taken into account. The effect of the relative stiffness of a thick string is a certain amount of frequency dispersion causing inharmonicity in the respective spectrum[2]. The thick bass strings corresponding to notes from A_0 on produce harmonics that deviate to some extent from ideal frequencies n x f_1 Hz, n = 2, 3, 4, ... relative to a fundamental frequency f_1. Hence the pitch even of a single thick bass string in a piano is not just as clear and salient as is that of a strictly periodic complex tone with harmonics falling right into place at n x f_1. With two notes played simultaneously in the very low register, pitch and interval analysis becomes even more difficult. To demonstrate the issue, a cochleagram of the fifth $A_0 - E_1$ recorded with an artificial head to simulate human ear characteristics is shown in figure 2. The cochleagram is a repre-

---

[2] For the present article, we measured inharmonicity of the A_0 string spectrum of a historical Steinway O (effective length of A_0 string ≈ 137 cm) grand piano. Relative to the fundamental at 24.3675 Hz (determined with a frequency at peak algorithm; FFT = 65536 samples, zero-pad factor 2.0, Hanning), the 10th harmonic was 199 cent sharp, the 20th harmonic even 296 cents (about a minor third).

sentation of signal energy falling into a number of auditory filters (see below) located along the cochlear partition. The ordinate (y) in this case ranges from 0 – 25.6 Bark (where Bark indicates a certain bandwidth along the cochlear partition), the abscissa (x) is the time axis so that a quasi-continuous temporal and spatial representation of energy distribution over time results. The relative strength of energy at a certain place and time is marked by grey scales (the darker, the more energy).

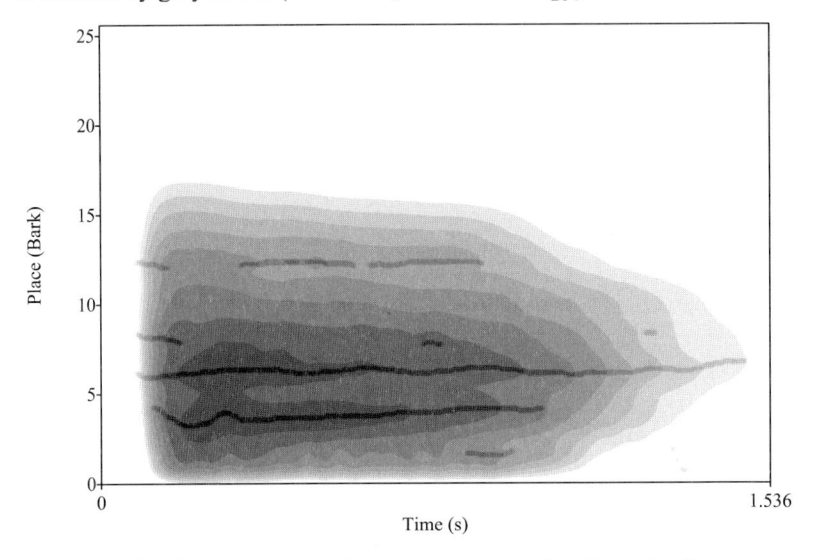

Figure 2: Fifths $A_0 - E_1$, played on Steinway (recorded with artificial head)

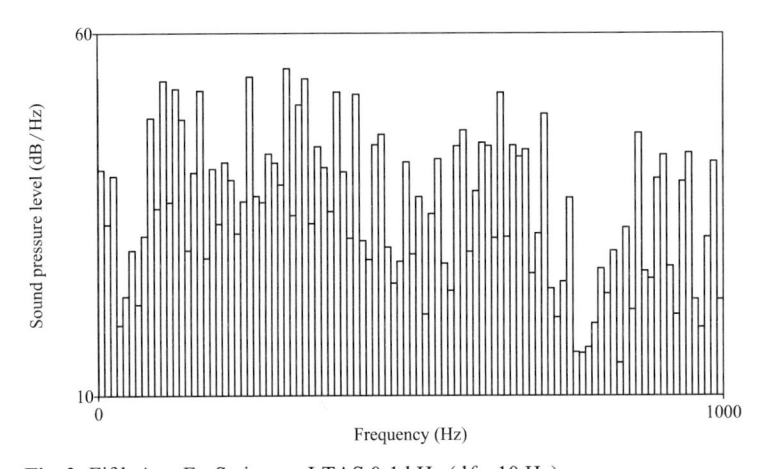

Fig. 3: Fifth $A_0 - E_1$, Steinway, LTAS 0-1 kHz (df = 10 Hz)

Second, as one can see, spectral energy is concentrated in the low frequency bands, which correspond to units 1 – 10 on a Bark scale (as to this construct, see below). The long-term average spectrum (LTAS) of the same sound (figure 3) reveals that the fundamental frequencies of the complex tones A_0 and E_1 forming the interval of a fifth are relatively weak in level when compared to spectral components above 80 Hz representing harmonics of the two fundamentals. In fact, the relative SPL of the harmonics indicates that the level difference between a fundamental (either A_0 or E_1) and its harmonics nos. 2 - 5 amounts to ca. 8 – 20 dB. Consequently, identification of the interval by the fundamental frequencies of the two complex tones seems very difficult if not impossible. Of course, identification of an interval can also be achieved by drawing to higher harmonics, which are available in this sound (that contains relevant spectral energy up to ca. 2.5 kHz) in significant number, though progressively detuned with increasing frequency.

In case harmonic frequencies f_n in the two complex tones forming the interval were exactly n x f_1, the level difference would not matter that much since it would still be possible to derive the fundamental frequencies by means of either an AC analysis or, alternatively, a subharmonic matching (SHM) process (see Terhardt 1998, Schneider & Frieler 2009). Both approaches, however, do not work perfectly anymore when frequencies of string partials deviate substantially from harmonic ratios as in this case. Figure 4 shows the result of both the AC and the SHM analysis plotted into the same graph[3]:

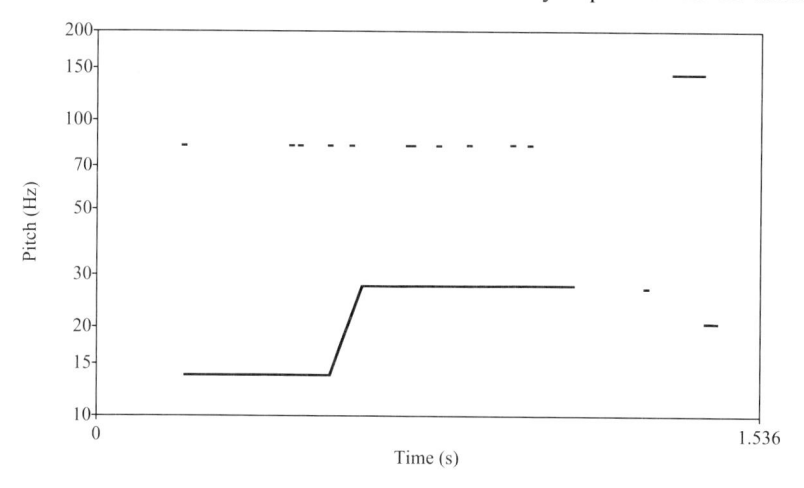

Figure 4: Pitch analyses (AC, SHM) of fifth $A_0 - E_1$ played on a small grand piano

In this plot the solid line results from the AC analysis, and the dotted line at ca. 80 Hz from the SHM analysis. The AC analysis first indicates a very low pitch at about 14 Hz and then makes a jump to about 27-28 Hz (the fundamental of A_0). Since 14 Hz is about half of the fundamental frequency, this is a subharmonic ratio ($f \approx 1/2 f_1$). The dotted line points to the second harmonic of E_1, which is much stronger than the fundamental near 41 Hz.

Looking at the result, one could say the analyses were moderately, though not completely, successful. The algorithms employed can detect 'pitch candidates' at low frequencies that correspond either to spectral components or come relatively close to the

---

[3] Analyses were made with the Praat software and also with Audacity.

f_0 of the complex sound. Of course, one can run behavioural experiments where subjects are asked to make judgements concerning the size of musical intervals under certain conditions, for example, in the low or even very low frequency region. We will return to this below in section 3.

2. Critical Band Concepts and musical intervals at low frequencies

The concept of Critical Bands (CBs) emerged from experiments in which detection of a sine tone in a noise-band masker was central. Such experiments were conducted by Harvey Fletcher around 1940 and later on by Eberhard Zwicker and colleagues as well as by other researchers (cf. Moore 1993, 1995, 2005; Zwicker 1982, Zwicker & Fastl 1999, Hartmann 1998, 249-258). CB concepts were applied to studies on masking thresholds, loudness perception, and on finding the bandwidth(s) auf 'auditory filters' as well as a correlation between the spatial dimension of the cochlear partition and the place where excitation is maximum for certain frequencies (see below). In many publications, reference is made to the basilar membrane (BM) even though motion of the entire cochlear partition (CP) needs to be studied in regard to cochlear models (cf. de Boer 1996).

The CB concept implies a model of the auditory filter, its shape, bandwidth and dynamical behaviour (cf. Moore 1993, 2005). The CP including the BM is usually conceived as being divided in k CBs ($24 \leq k \leq 40$) that can be understood as weighting functions describing the response behaviour of the CP following excitation. Technically, the CP (BM) response to various stimuli can be modelled with a chain of k band-pass filters, which are "wired" in parallel and are overlapping on the frequency dimension. The unit for the CB according to the concept proposed by Zwicker (1982, 51-53, 64-67) is the "Bark"[4], whereby the BM is divided into 24 Bark. With respect to the Bark scale, Zwicker assumed the following relations to exist:

24 Bark = 32 mm of BM = 640 jnd of pitch = 2400 mel = 3600 inner hair cells

Consequently, 1 Bark would cover ca. 1.3 mm of the BM, within which about 27 jnd (just noticeable difference or frequency limen df) should be distinguishable.

The CB into which any given frequency f [Hz] falls can be calculated using the formula (cf. Traunmüller 1990)

(1) $z = [26.81 / (1 + 1960 / f)] - 0.53$

Inversely, one can calculate f from z like

(2) $f = 1960 / [26.81 / (z + 0.53) - 1]$

The CB concept in regard to musical intervals postulates that subjects are unable to separate two sine tones of frequency f_1, f_2 presented simultaneously and to identify the

---

[4] Commemorating the many achievements of the German physicist and professor of electric engineering, Heinrich Barkhausen, who introduced the "phon" as a unit for loudness.

interval between them securely if these two frequencies fall into the same critical band. Instead, subjects experience roughness and beats if two pure tones with frequencies f_1, f_2 are located in the same CB and interact in typical ways (e.g., Plomp & Levelt 1965, Roederer 1975, 28-31).

Table 1: Critical Bands (Bark-rate[z], frequencies, cents)

Bark z	Frequency[Hz] lower	upper	center	Bandwidth[Hz]	Cents	Interval
0	0	100	50	100	unclear	?
1	100	200	150	100	1200	octave
2	200	300	250	100	702	fifth
3	300	400	350	100	498	fourth
4	400	510	450	110	421	major third (enlarged)
5	510	630	570	120	366	major third (narrowed)
6	630	770	700	140	347	neutral third
7	770	920	840	150	308	minor third
8	920	1080	1000	160	278	narrowed minor third
9	1080	1270	1170	190	281	narrowed minor third
10	1270	1480	1370	210	265	
11	1480	1720	1600	240	260	
12	1720	2000	1800	280	261	
13	2000	2320	2150	320	257	
14	2320	2700	2500	380	262	
15	2700	3150	2900	450	267	
16	3150	3700	3400	550	279	
17	3700	4400	4000	700	300	minor third
18	4400	5300	4800	900	322	minor third
19	5300	6400	5800	1100	326	minor third
20	6400	7700	7000	1300	320	minor third
21	7700	9500	8500	1800	364	neutral third
22	9500	12000	10500	2500	404	major third
23	12000	15500	13500	3500	443	
24	15500					

Since the "classical" CB concept originally relates to the technical standard of 1/3-octave band-pass filters, one would perhaps expect a bandwidth of CBs above a centre frequency of 500 Hz corresponding, roughly, to one third of an octave, that is, to an interval about the size of a major third. This size, however, cannot be generalized even though several CBs (Bark[z] 4, 5, 23; see table 2) are near this interval. To simplify matters, Zwicker made certain assumptions concerning the bandwidth of CBs, in particular in the frequency region ranging from 500 to 100 Hz, and again for frequencies below 100 Hz. One assumption was that "the lowest critical band ranges from 0 Hz to 100 Hz", another calls for "constant bandwidth of 100 Hz up to a centre frequency of 500 Hz" (Zwicker & Fastl 1999, 158). Both assumptions seem problematic in regard to musical interval perception. This is an issue that needs some elaboration:

To express the bandwidth of CBs (and similarly of ERBs, see below) in a unit relevant for precise definition of musical interval size independent of absolute frequency, the frequencies given by Zwicker (1982, 52; Zwicker & Fastl 1999, 159) have been transformed into cents for Bark[z] 1 – 24. Also, a function fitting the cent values for Bark[z] 1 - 14 has been given along with a graph of the function (cf. Schneider et al. 2009, 109-111). The frequency and cent values for 24 CBs are listed in table 1.

What is puzzling with these values is, first of all, the bandwidth of the lowest CB. If it is indeed taken to cover frequencies from 0 to 100 Hz, no interval in terms of cents can be assigned since the calculation of cents rests on a quotient $f_2/f_1 \geq 1$, precluding division by zero. The lower frequency threshold for sensation of a pitch from sinusoidals usually is around 20 Hz, the lower limit for melodic pitch in some psychoacoustic experiments was found at about 30 Hz (Pressnitzer et al. 2001). If we accept a lower limit of pitch around 25 Hz, this means the lowest CB in regard to pitch perception would range from ca. 100 Hz to ca. 25 Hz, comprising thus no less than two octaves (100 – 50 Hz, 50 – 25 Hz). According to CB theory, identification of intervals presented simultaneously within this single CB (25 – 100 Hz) should be limited and probably impossible for the width of this CB (equivalent in size to about two octaves). On the one hand, one should thus expect that identification of musical intervals considerably smaller than one octave might be impeded. On the other, a simple experience one can have playing musical intervals located within the two lowermost octaves $A_0 - A_1$ and $A_1 - A_2$ (= $A_{,,} - A_{,}$ and $A_{,} - A$) on a piano is that interval identification is still possible to a certain degree, and especially so in the second octave $A_1 - A_2$ (= $A_{,} - A$). Of course, the strings corresponding to all the notes from A_0 on produce harmonics in addition to a fundamental frequency f_1 that can be used as cues for pitch (notwithstanding the harmonics are all sharp in frequency). Hence one could hypothesize that pitch perception as well as interval recognition for such stimuli is facilitated by using the information contained both in harmonics above f_1 as well as in the periodicities inherent in the complex wave shape. However, for the very low notes of a grand piano, interval identification is not easy since, in addition to the low register, there can be significant inharmonicity in the spectrum of each tone caused by the stiffness of the thick bass strings[5]. Increase of spectral inharmonicity implies relative loss of strict periodicity of the time function (et vice versa). The pitch evoked by such sounds hence is not as salient and clear, as is the pitch of piano tones at higher fundamental frequencies. With two notes played simultaneously in the very low register, pitch and interval analysis becomes even more difficult.

As an alternative to the "classical" CB concept and the Bark-scale (critical-band-rate scale [z]) as formulated by Zwicker (1982, 51-53), the ERB (Equivalent rectangular bandwidth) scale was established based on the so-called roex model of the auditory filter (roex = rounded exponent; see Moore & Glasberg 1983, Moore 1993, 1995). Calculation of the ERB was done by fitting a function to experimental data; the equation is

(3) $ERB = Af^2 + Bf + C$

---

[5] Taking stiffness into account, calculation of the transverse motion of a thick piano string leads to a 4th order differential equation; cf. Fletcher & Rossing 1991, 61.

where f ist the center frequency in kHz and A, B, and C are parameters for which suitable numerical values must be found. For practical applications, one can use

(4) ERB = 6.23x 10^{-6} (f_c) + 93.39 $10^{-3} f_c$ + 28.52,

with f_c = center frequency in Hz. Another formula that leads to similar results is

(5) ERB = 24.7 (4.37f_c /1000 + 1)

An ERB scale can be calculated by using

(6) ERB[E] = 11.17 ln [(f + 312) / (f + 14675] + 43

Initially, the ERB scale was devised to cover the frequency range above 100 Hz (up to 6.5 kHz). Different from the Bark scale assuming constant bandwidth of 100 Hz below 500 Hz (see above), the ERB was found to decrease also below 500 Hz; for a center frequency f_c = 125 Hz a bandwidth of ca. 40 Hz was given. In additional experiments, the ERB at 100 Hz and 200 Hz was found, on average, as 36 Hz and 47 Hz, respectively. Using equation (5), calculation of ERB for center frequencies below 100 Hz is straightforward. In figure 5, the ERB for center frequencies proceeding in steps of 10 Hz from 30 Hz to 200 is plotted, resulting in a linear increase of ERB (df [Hz]) with increasing center frequency f_c[Hz]. Assuming that one ERB corresponds to about 0.86 mm of BM, the average number of non-overlapping ERB for a human BM of ca. 34 mm length would be about 39.5 (as compared to 24 Bark[z] representing a frequency range from 0 Hz to ca. 16 kHz).

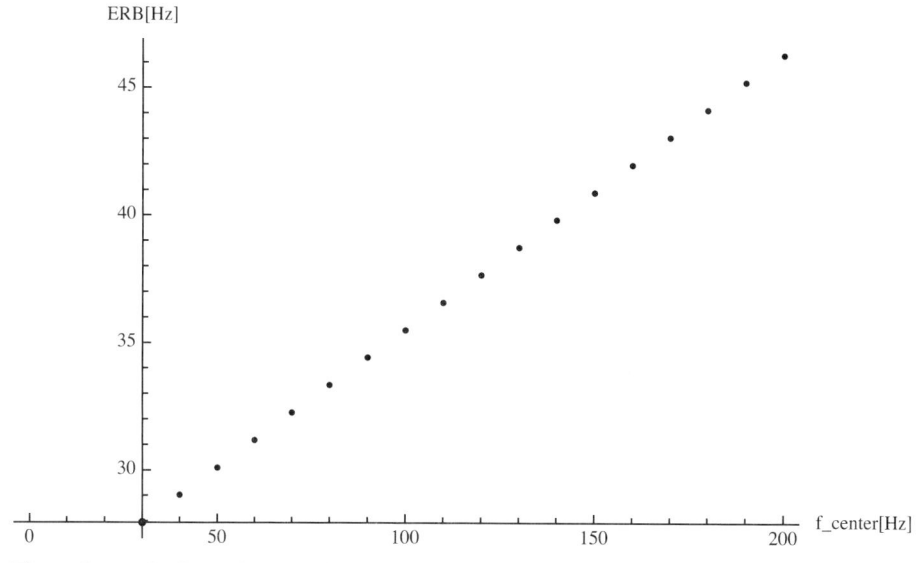

Figure 5: ERB[Hz] as a function of center frequency (f_c = 30 – 200 Hz)

If all ERB values are transformed from Hz into cents to give them perceptual (as well as musical) meaning, the data summarized in table 2 and plotted in figure 6 result.

Table 2: ERB values and corresponding cents for center frequencies f_c 30 – 200 Hz

f_c [Hz]	cents	f_c [Hz]	cents	f_c [Hz]	cents
30	1752	100	621	180	427
40	1315	110	581	190	414
50	1073	120	548	200	402
60	921	130	496		
70	811	140	475		
80	732	160	457		
90	670	170	441		

A graph can be fitted to the cent values; the function for the graph is

(7) 42.1215 + 2785.11 e^-0.02x + 1.78551 x

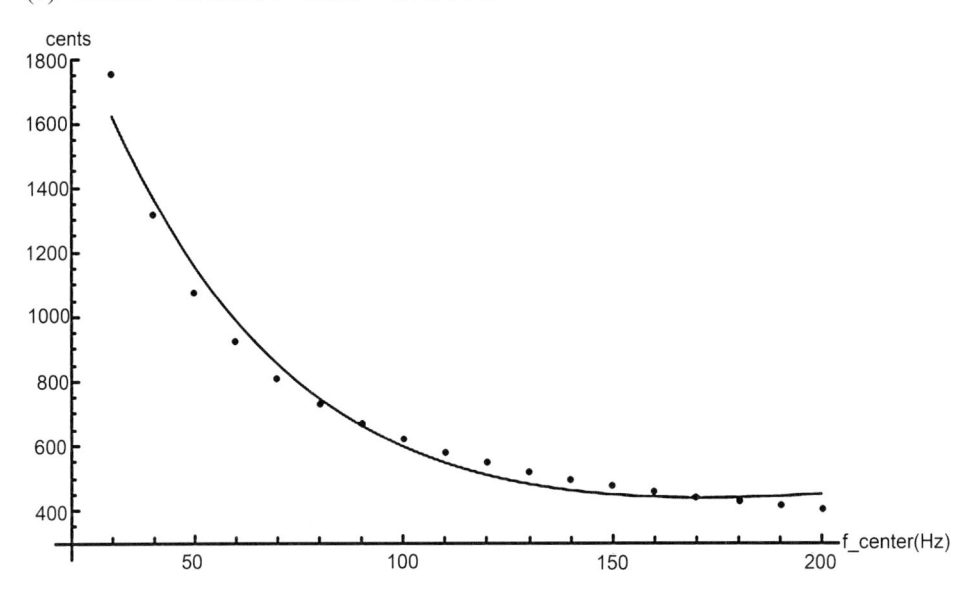

Figure 6: Cents corresponding to ERB center frequencies f_c 30 – 200 Hz

From the data in table 2, it is evident that the ERB calculated for a center frequency of 200 Hz is about the size of a major third (400 cents in equal temperament, 386 cents in just intonation), and that the ERB for a center frequency of 100 Hz is somewhat larger than a tritone, and smaller than a perfect fifth (3/2 = 702 cents). Still, for a very low center frequency of 50 Hz the ERB is less than a major seventh. However, these values are hypothetical since they stem from calculation and need to be checked against empirical evidence (see below). In particular, it is not clear if the linear relationship of ERB to center frequency (see figure 5) holds for frequencies below 100 Hz.

3. Some experimental data

To explore interval identification in the very low frequency region, an experiment was designed which offered a range of musical intervals to be judged in size by subjects. The experiment was carried out at Hamburg and at Jyväskylä, in 2010. At Hamburg, a sample of $n = 22$ subjects (students in musicology at Hamburg University, most of them beginners in their first semester) took part. At Jyväskylä, the experiment was run with a smaller sample of $n = 13$ subjects (see below).

At Hamburg, subjects were offered 30 sound examples in two runs (30 + 30 = 60) played back from an audio system suited to reproduce low frequencies down to 40 Hz with a relatively flat frequency response, and frequencies below 40 Hz with decreasing SPL[6]. Playback level was set to an average SPL of 72 dB[A] for a distance of 1 m from the source and was controlled by a sound level meter. Subjects were seated in a classroom of, roughly 12 x 12 x 3 m (constructed so as to absorb a certain amount of acoustic energy at its floor and walls and suited for recording of music) at a distance of ca. 5 – 8 m from the two loudspeaker cabinets. The sound examples were generated with Mathematica© at 44.1 kHz/16 bit sampling as two-track mono (both channels containing identical signals). All 30 stimuli were composed of pairs of complex tones whereby each tone had five harmonics with amplitudes A = 1/n as shown in figure 7: The reason why we chose sounds including a few harmonics simply was to provide at least 'semi-musical' stimuli (instead of pairs of sine tones) that come closer to a real-life listening situation. Of course one can argue that thereby an unwanted leakage of spectral energy into one or two neighbouring CBs might occur that could influence interval judgements.

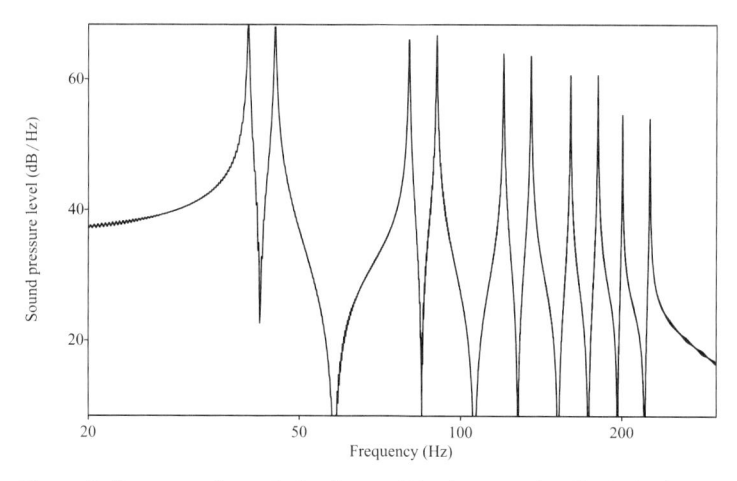

Figure 7: Spectrum of sound stimulus no. 7 (major second at 40 Hz fundamental frequency)

---

[6] Tandberg 3000 Integrated Amp; ElectroVoice Sentry 500 (frequency response 40 Hz – 18 kHz ± 3 dB; Output SPL 96 dB/W/m)

Tones lasted for 3 seconds with an exponential decay of the envelope (see figure 8) and were repeated twice with an interval of one second between sounds. The break between consecutive stimuli available to subjects to make their judgements was about 15 seconds.

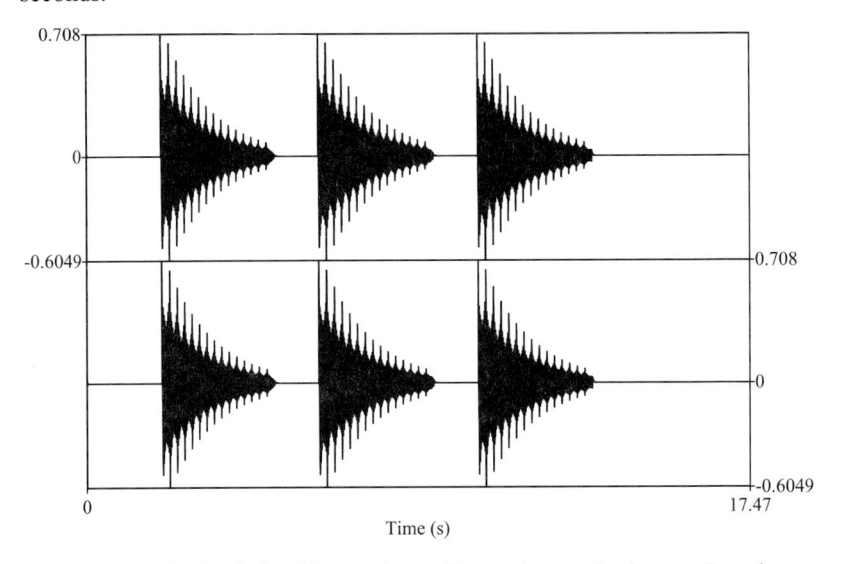

Figure 8: sound stimuli for CB experiment (figure shows stimulus no. 7: major second at 40 Hz fundamental frequency of the lower complex tone)

Pairs of complex tones formed six musical intervals (major second, minor third, major third, fourth, tritone, fifths) whose size was 2, 3, 4, 5, 6 and 7 semitones, respectively. Intervals are in just intonation so that the fundamental frequencies and harmonics are forming simple integer ratios (like 3/2, 4/3, 5/4, etc.). This was done to install a maximum of periodicity in the time function and of harmonicity in the spectra (two cues relevant for interval recognition; cf. Schneider & Frieler 2009). The intervals were located on the frequency scale so that the fundamental frequency of the lower complex tone was at 31.5 Hz, 40 Hz, 50 Hz, 63 Hz, and 80 Hz (these are center frequencies for standard [ISO] 1/3-octave filters). Thus the design was six musical intervals times five fundamental frequencies making up 30 stimuli which were played back in two runs: first (A) in a regular pattern (the sequence of intervals from major second to fifth at 31.5 Hz, then at 40 Hz, 50 Hz, etc.) and, after a break of about fifteen minutes, (B) in random order.

Subjects were instructed about the task of making judgements about the size of musical intervals. Information was provided that each interval could have any size from one (minor second) to eleven semi-tones (major seventh). Subjects then were asked to listen to the sound examples and to estimate the size of the interval realized with each of the sound stimuli, as well as to indicate the size on a sheet that offered 11 alternatives (from 1 semi-tone for the minor second to 11 semi-tones for the major seventh) for each stimulus.

The results of the experiment for two runs (A, B) are summarized in table 3:

Table 3: Fundamental frequencies, intervals, correct identifications (n = 22 subjects, 2 runs)

Hz	Interval	no. of correct identifications A, B	
31.5	major second	1	1
31.5	minor third	3	1
31.5	major third	2	2
31.5	fourth	2	6
31.5	tritone	2	1
31.5	fifth	3	1
	Sum	13	12 (A + B = 25 → 9.5% correct)
40	major second	2	0
40	minor third	3	4
40	major third	5	2
40	fourth	5	5
40	tritone	2	4
40	fifth	3	0
	Sum	20	15 (A + B = 35 → 13.25% correct)
50	major second	3	5
50	minor third	0	2
50	major third	5	4
50	fourth	3	10
50	tritone	6	5
50	fifth	4	2
	Sum	21	28 (A + B = 49 → 18.5% correct)
63	major second	6	2
63	minor third	4	3
63	major third	3	4
63	fourth	5	1
63	tritone	5	1
63	fifth	10	5
	Sum	33	16 (A + B = 49 → 18.5% correct)
80	major second	6	1
80	minor third	4	4
80	major third	5	7
80	fourth	7	4
80	tritone	7	0
80	fifth	6	8
	Sum	35	24 (A + B = 59 → ca. 22.5% correct)
	Total	122	95 (A + B = 217 → ca. 16.5% correct)

Table 4: t-tests for pairs of data sets (fundamental frequencies) per interval category

Category	Run (A, B)	Set 1[Hz]	Set 2[Hz]	p
Major second	A	31.5	50	0.107
Major second	A	31.5	80	0.021
Major second	B	40	50	0.003
Major second	B	40	63	0.108
Major second	B	50	80	0.011
Minor third	A	31.5	80	0.208
Minor third	B	31.5	50	0.100
Minor third	B	40	50	0.025
Minor third	B	40	63	0.007
Minor third	B	40	80	0.165
Major third	A	31.5	50	0.178
Major third	A	50	63	0.145
Major third	B	31.5	40	0.015
Major third	B	31.5	50	0.003
Major third	B	40	80	0.026
Major third	B	50	80	0.042
Fourth	B	40	80	0.038
Fourth	B	50	80	0.027
Tritone	A	40	63	0.263
Tritone	B	31.5	40	0.001
Tritone	B	31.5	50	0.048
Tritone	B	31.5	63	0.022
Tritone	B	40	50	0.000
Tritone	B	40	63	0.015
Tritone	B	40	80	0.001
Tritone	B	50	80	0.211
Fifth	A	31.5	50	0.058
Fifth	A	31.5	63	0.054
Fifth	A	40	50	0.097
Fifth	A	40	63	0.116
Fifth	B	31.5	50	0.033
Fifth	B	40	50	0.026
Fifth	B	50	63	0.025
Fifth	B	50	80	0.059

From the data it is obvious that interval identification was poor in particular for the two groups of stimuli with fundamental frequency of the lower tone at 31.5 Hz and 40 Hz, respectively. Performance improved towards higher fundamental frequencies, but still the rate of correct answers was only around 22.5% for the 80 Hz condition. If a criterion of 50% correct interval estimates is regarded as the chance level, the percentage of 'hits' of this sample of subjects remains far below chance. There are indications, though, that the performance of individuals varied markedly since in the ordered presentation (A) the range of 'hits' was from 0 to 14 (with a mean of 5.55, SD = 3.67, median = 5) and in the random presentation (B) from 1 to 10 (mean = 4.52, SD = 2.23, median = 4). The scores for subjects in both runs (A, B) correlate at $r_{xy} = 0.369$ and, alternatively, Spearman's rho [|r(s)|] = -0.323 (both r_{xy} and rho are only slightly below p = 0.05), indicating that the two modes of presentation did not have decisive effects on judgements.

To check differences in performance further, a series of t-tests covering pairs of data sets representing the five different fundamental frequencies (31.5 Hz, 40 Hz, etc.) within each interval category (major second, minor third, etc.) for both runs (A, B) were carried out. Results of several t-tests (table 4) indicated marked differences between conditions. In regard to criteria of reliability and validity, one of course has to bear in mind the relatively small number of correct interval estimates per condition (see table 3).

Though the outcome of the t-tests can not be said to be unequivocal in every respect, it seems to indicate at least a trend: apparently, there is a *gradual* difference in subject's performance between intervals presented at the two lowermost fundamental frequencies (31.5 Hz, 40 Hz) and the three higher fundamental frequencies (50 Hz, 63, Hz, 80 Hz). An interpretation of the data provided in tables 3 and 4 as well as in the following section will be given in chapter 4 below.

Similar to Hamburg, the experiment was conducted in Finland where 13 participants consisting of graduate students, undergraduate students and staff members of Music Department at the University of Jyväskylä were presented with the same stimuli used in the experiment described above. The experiment took place in the control room of the university recording studio, using a Genelec active speaker system (with subwoofer) capable to produce very low frequencies. Results are provided in the table 5.

In the figure (below) correct answers are summed for each fundamental frequency group. In the figure correct recognition rate shows consistent increasing pattern for second run (B) of the experiment while it is not observable for the first run (A). However, in both experiments correct interval recognition rates are higher for the last three (50Hz, 63Hz, 80Hz) groups, which is in agreement with the Hamburg experiment. Analysis of variance showed significant difference between fundamental frequency group means ($p \ll 0.05$). Detailed between group comparisons revealed only two combination of groups to be significantly different: 40Hz, 63Hz and 40Hz, 80Hz. However, further analysis did not reveal any significant correlations between the rest of the groups and interval recognition rates, which might be due to the rather small sample size.

Table 5: Fundamental frequencies, intervals, correct identifications (n = 13 subjects, 2 runs)

Hz	Interval	no. of correct identifications A, B	
31.5	major second	2	1
31.5	minor third	1	0
31.5	major third	3	0
31.5	fourth	3	2
31.5	tritone	2	1
31.5	fifth	0	1
	Sum	11	5 (A + B = 16 → 11% correct)
40	major second	1	4
40	minor third	0	0
40	major third	0	1
40	fourth	2	1
40	tritone	1	0
40	fifth	1	1
	Sum	5	7 (A + B = 12 → 8% correct)
50	major second	1	3
50	minor third	2	2
50	major third	6	2
50	fourth	5	3
50	tritone	0	0
50	fifth	3	3
	Sum	17	13 (A + B = 30 → 21% correct)
63	major second	4	3
63	minor third	1	2
63	major third	2	0
63	fourth	7	4
63	tritone	5	5
63	fifth	5	4
	Sum	24	18 (A + B = 42 → 29% correct)
80	major second	4	2
80	minor third	1	2
80	major third	3	2
80	fourth	3	3
80	tritone		2 7
80	fifth	7	4
	Sum	20	20 (A + B = 40 → 28% correct)
	Total	77	63 (A + B = 140 → 17,95% correct)

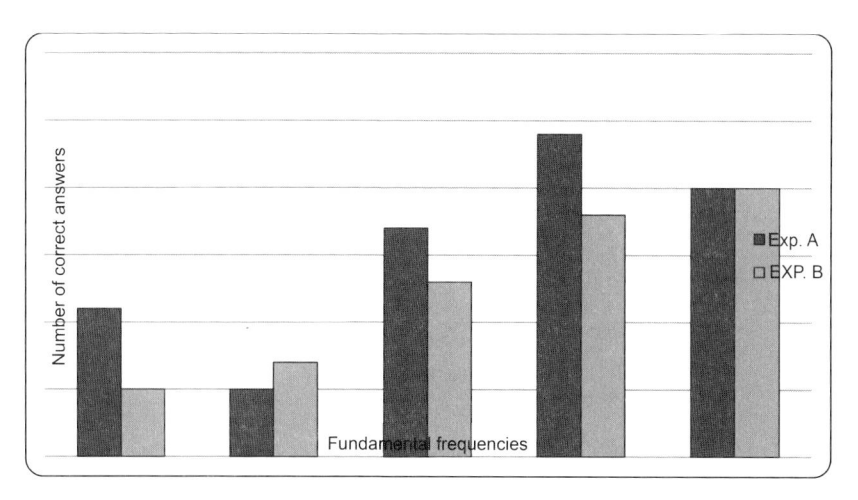

Figure 9: Relationship between correct recognition rate and fundamental frequencies.

4. Discussion

From the overall very poor results for the first two conditions (fundamental frequency of the lower tone of the interval at 31.5 Hz and 40 Hz, respectively) found in both experiments (Hamburg and Jyväskylä subjects, respectively), and considerably better results for the next three conditions (fundamental frequency of the lower complex tone of the interval at 50 Hz, 63 Hz and 80 Hz, respectively), one may hypothesize that there could be a region possibly near 50 Hz where the lowest auditory filter band and the next higher filter band join (with some overlap). Also, failure of most subjects to identify musical intervals at very low fundamental frequencies could have to do with the bandwidth and shape of the lowest CB conceived as a filter. In fact, there is evidence available from experimental data as well as from auditory modelling to support such an interpretation.

One has to remember that one aspect of CB concepts is to find a correlation between stimulus frequency f[Hz] and position x[mm] of excitation on the CP (including BM). One early approach to CB estimates led to the formulation of an exponential function $CB = 10^{(ax+b)}$, in which x is the distance along the cochlear partition (Greenwood 1961). The function was refined later on, taking fresh physiological data from humans and several other species into account. The function that relates frequency to position was given by Greenwood (1990) as

(8) $F = A(10^{ax} - k)$,

where A is a constant (for humans, $A = 165.4$ to yield frequency in Hz) and $a = 0.06$ if the distance x is to be expressed in mm. The integration constant k, if set to 0.88, yields a lower frequency limit of 20 Hz.

Summing up the findings from a number of studies covering man as well as other mammals, Greenwood (1990, 2602) asserts that, "over most of the basilar membrane, and most of the frequency range, log frequency versus basilar position is nearly a straight line". Looking at the data and the graphs provided by Greenwood (1990), a straight line seems an appropriate fit for a frequency range of, roughly, 500 Hz to 8 kHz or even 10 kHz. Below 500 Hz, however, the fit is not linear anymore and flattens with decreasing frequency, most of all, below 200 Hz. Redrawing a section of Greenwood's fig. 1 (1990, 2594: bottom panel) in enlarged format, the relation of frequency to BM position for frequencies for 20 Hz to 200 Hz and distances from apex of ca. 0.35 mm (origin of the y-axis) to about 4 mm on BM (CP) would come close to figure 10.

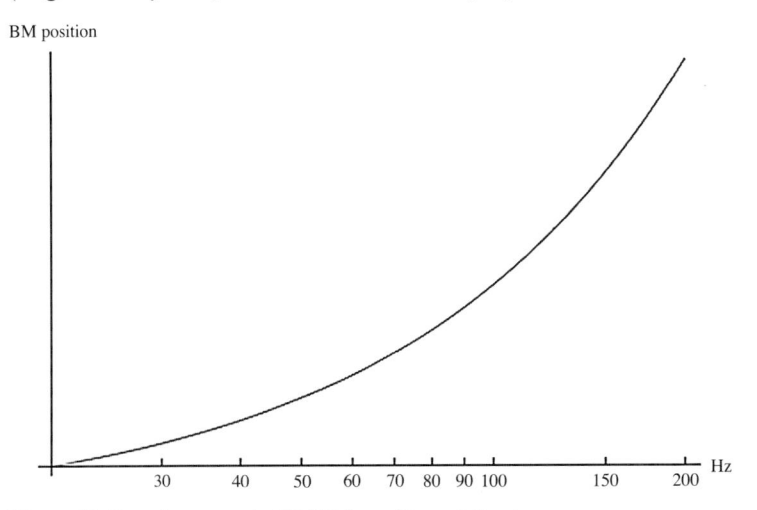

Figure 10: Low frequency to CP (BM) position relative to apex

According to figure 10, the maximum of excitation on the BM for a steady-state sine tone of 20 Hz would be very close to the helicotrema in the apical turn of the cochlea (see Pickles 2008), where the scala media and the cochlear partition "taper prematurely to a blind end, leaving a small, perilymph-filled fluid junction between the scala tympani and the scala vestibuli" (Patuzzi 1996, 206). The function of the helicotrema has been described both as a shunt between the scala vestibuli and the scala tympani, and as an "acoustic plug" that would block pressure fluctuations between the two due to fluid mass and viscosity. The cut-off frequency below which the helicotrema functions like a shunt has been given as 400 Hz (Patuzzi 1996, 221).

Discussions of apex and helicotrema function give rather uneven results (for a summary of questionable animal experiments up to 2000, see Robles & Ruggero 2001, 1315ff.). In regard to the middle-ear sound transfer function (METF) and the input impedance of the cochlea, measurements on human temporal bones recovered from dead persons yielded that the ear canal sound pressure to the scala vestibuli sound pressure transfer function (GME; i.e., the ratio of the two pressures) is nearly flat at a level of ca. 2 dB (average from 11 human cochleae) in the frequency range from 50 Hz to 100 Hz, and that also the phase angle is almost flat (it decreases slightly towards 50 Hz; cf. Aibara et al. 2001, 104, Fig. 2). The ear canal sound pressure to stapes footplate velocity transfer function (SVTF; in [mm s^{-1}/PA]) shows only a slight increase from 50 Hz to 100 Hz (while the phase angle remains flat at about 80 degrees; see Aibara et al. 2001,

Fig. 3). The cochlear input impedance at 50 Hz is ca. 21 GΩ (MKS), and is just slightly higher than at 100 Hz (Aibara et al. 2001, Fig. 4). From these data one may infer that for stimulus frequencies from 100 Hz down to 50 Hz no significant change in performance parameters of the cochlea must be expected. In addition, a simple electrical model of the cochlea demonstrated the system was functional for stimulus frequencies down to 50 Hz as long as the helicotrema was not too small (and the impedance accordingly relatively low; cf. Schick 1994). However, in another study the effect the helicotrema has on decreasing sensitivity below 100 Hz was estimated at 6dB/octave, and a combination of filter effects resulting from the helicotrema, the highpass characteristic of the middle ear function (leading to a slope of approx. -6dB/oct. below 1 kHz) as well as a similar characteristic of the inner hair cell velocity would lead to a reduction of sensitivity of about 18 dB/octave below 100 Hz (Cheatham & Dallos 2001, 2041, Fig. 7). The estimate of the combined filter effects below 1000 Hz would yield a curve of sensitivity that corresponds roughly to the lower threshold of the hearing curve as well as equal-loudness contours for very soft signals. A similar curve was obtained from measurements performed on living subjects with a method based on the $2f_1 - f_2$ distortion product otoacoustic emission, DPOAE (see Marquart et al. 2007). However, the graph(s) derived from DPOAE recordings showed a notch and a peak at 45 Hz and at 60 Hz, respectively, which have been interpreted as caused by apical reflection of travelling waves at very low frequencies and a distinct shift in impedance due to inertia of the perilymph passing through the helicotrema. In a more general way, it has been suggested in previous studies that the high sensitivity of the BM (CP) for characteristic frequencies (CF) and the compressive nonlinearity attributable to the "cochlear amplifier" (cf. Zenner 1994, Pickles 2008) might be less prominent at the apex compared to the base of the BM (cf. Robles & Ruggero 2001). Besides various filter effects (see above), this is another factor that could account for reduced frequency resolution at very low frequencies.

Recently, estimates for the auditory filter (AF) at very low frequencies were published (Jurado & Moore 2010) using the notched-noise method and the ERB approach (Moore & Glasberg 1983, Moore et al. 1990) as well as taking the middle ear transfer function (METF) into account. Auditory filter shapes were derived for signal frequencies from 50 to 1000 Hz, and were presented for two different models, one comprising the METF cascaded with the AF, the other reflecting the system-as-a-whole. Two filters covering the very "bottom" of the frequency range (ca. 10 – 100 Hz) with center frequencies of 50 and 63 Hz, respectively (cf. Jurado & Moore 2010, 3594, Fig. 6) have shallow lower skirts and broadly overlap, indicating poor frequency selectivity as well as restricted dynamic range. In fact, the dynamic range of the derived filters decreased sharply below 125 Hz. Moreover, frequency selectivity for low frequencies (50 Hz, 63 Hz) was found to depend strongly on the (assumed) METF below 50 Hz. From the derived filter shapes, which are asymmetric with rather shallow lower skirts also at 80 Hz and still at 100 Hz, as well as from other evidence available from experiments and observations one may conclude that the performance of peripheral auditory filtering as realized in the cochlea (CP, BM) works reasonably well down to 63 or even 50 Hz, but then declines markedly towards the lower limit of pitch. In particular, if the shape of the AF at very low frequencies is as broad as has been estimated (Jurado & Moore 2010), interval recognition will be very poor since fundamental frequencies of pairs of complex tones are likely to fall into one CB (possibly somewhat different in bandwidth from calculated "linear" ERB as listed in table 2).

Interval judgements then would be hampered unless sufficient information concerning pitch and interval relations can be drawn from higher harmonics.

Data from our experiments, limited as they were, indicate that recognition of intervals ranging from a major second (204 cent) to the fifth (702 cent) was particularly poor for fundamental frequencies of the lower complex tone at 31.5 Hz and 40 Hz, respectively. Put in absolute frequency values, fundamentals for the two complex tones forming a fifth at 31.5 Hz are 15.75 Hz apart (31.5 ←→ 47.25 Hz). For the fifth at 40 Hz, the respective frequency distance is 20 Hz. If we assume an AF centred at 40 Hz, the (calculated) ERB would be about 29 Hz that must be distributed evenly (assuming, for reasons of simplicity, symmetry of the filter) to the lower as well as to the higher end of the respective frequency band, leading to a lower cut-off at about 25 Hz and a higher cut-off near 55 Hz. For intervals of complex tones at 40 Hz, the fundamentals of the major second, the minor third, the major third and even the fourth (at 53.32 Hz) would remain within the same CB as defined by the ERB while the fundamental of the tritone would fall just outside the limit of the CB. For an AF centred at 80 Hz, the ERB would be 33.33 Hz, again to be distributed evenly about the center frequency. Hence, a similar situation in regard to fundamentals falling into the same CB would occur, so that interval recognition at 80 Hz should not improve (while it does according to our experimental data). Consequent to the observation of marked differences between responses to intervals presented at 40 Hz and 80 Hz fundamental frequency, respectively, one has to consider the possibility that the ERB of an AF with f_c = 80 Hz may differ somehow from the theoretical value as calculated. Further, there might be additional cues relevant for interval recognition that should be taken into account (see below).

Besides fundamental frequencies, all complex tones combined into pairs for interval recognition comprised four harmonics so that subjects possibly could make use of some spectral information as well as from the periodicity inherent in particular in the sounds corresponding to consonant intervals like the major third (frequency ratios 5/4), the fourth (4/3) and the fifth (3/2). Contrary to the smoothness of periodic waveshapes representing consonant intervals, subjects could use audible beats as occurring with major seconds (frequency ratios 9/8) as a cue for interval recognition.

In order to check periodicity detection for the type of stimuli employed, both AC and SHM algorithms were applied to five sounds representing the major third at 31.5 Hz, 40 Hz, 50 Hz, 63 Hz, and 80 Hz, respectively (figure 11).

The AC analysis (lower half of figure 11) did not turn out a pitch candidate for the major third placed at 31.5 Hz, but gave stable results for the major third at 40 Hz, 50 Hz, 63 Hz, and 80 Hz, where the pitch frequencies indicated are at 10 Hz, 12.5 Hz, 15.75 Hz, and 20 Hz, respectively. Of course, these are common denominators inherent in the pairs of fundamental frequencies of the pairs of complex tones (40 Hz : 50 Hz, 50 Hz : 62.5 Hz, 63 Hz : 78,75 Hz, 80 Hz : 100 Hz). The SHM analysis (upper half of figure 11) for the major third at 31.5 Hz produces an unstable pitch estimate that covers a range from 30.34 Hz (min) to 39.1 Hz (max). The pitch candidates calculated for the other four sounds are very close to the fundamental frequency of each of the lower complex tones of a pair of tones forming the interval of the major third.

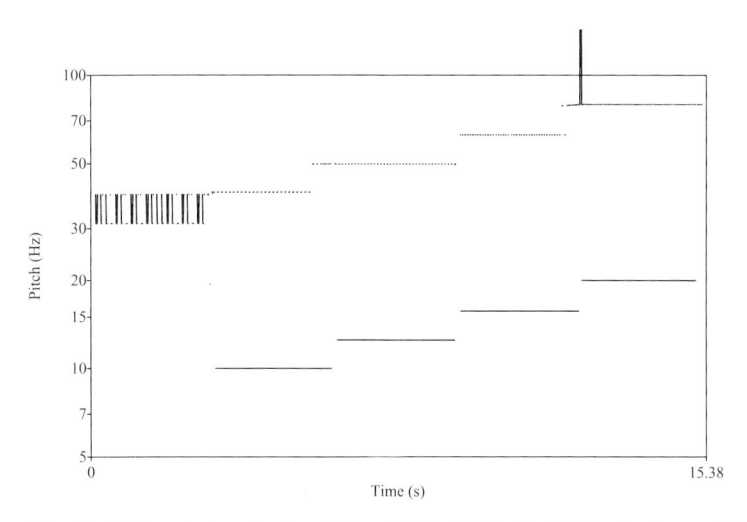

Fig. 11: Pitch analysis of major third at {31.5, 40, 50, 63, 80} Hz fundamental frequency

Table 6: AC analysis of five major thirds at {31.5, 40, 50, 63, 80} fundamental frequency

Major third	candidate (no.)	lag (ms) →	Component (Hz)
31.5 Hz : 39.37 Hz	1	31.4	~32
	2	25.2	~40
	3	76.1	~13
	4	95.5	~10
40 Hz : 50 Hz	1	19.9	~50
	2	24.8	~40
	3	60.0	~17
	4	75.1	~13
50 Hz : 62.5 Hz	1	46.4	~22
	2	80.4	~12
63 Hz : 78.75 Hz	1	12.6	~79
	2	15.8	~63
	3	38.1	~26
	4	47.6	~21
	5	63.5	~16
	6	79.3	~13
	7	88.9	~11
80 Hz : 100 Hz	1	46.6	~21
	2	50.0	20
	3	22.2	~45
	4	37.7	~27
	5	60.0	~17
	6	12.4	~81
	7	28.2	~35
	8	10	100

Another AC analysis algorithm[7] yields the lags (ms) and corresponding frequencies (Hz) listed in table 6, which includes both spectral components as well as possible virtual pitches resulting from periodicities. The order in which components appear for each of the five major thirds reflects the relative strength of autocorrelation per (pitch/frequency) candidate.

The results of the periodicity analysis are also of interest to musical interval recognition since each interval, if played in just intonation (as was the case with the stimuli used in this experiment), will give a perfectly periodic waveshape. For example, the third 40 Hz : 50 Hz as shown in figure 12 has a period length of $T = 100$ ms $= 0.1$ seconds that is fixed except that the overall amplitude decreases over time according to the damping factor $e^{\wedge}(-\delta t)$ included in the calculation of the waveshape. Since $f = 1/T$, the frequency with which the envelope repeats is 10 Hz. Assuming that our sense of hearing is capable to perform 'periodicity detection' making use of some form of AC analysis to assign a pitch to a periodic wavetrain[8], 10 Hz would be the low pitch fitting as a "root" to the two complex tones forming the major third. Indeed, such a pitch candidate was found in the first AC analysis (figure 11). One can infer from such a model that the two complex tones forming the major third with a ratio of fundamental frequencies as well as of harmonics of 4 : 5 may be imagined as parts of a harmonic chord comprising components at frequency ratios 1 : 2 : 3 : 4 : 5. While 4 : 5 are presented in the stimulus (and, hence, are real in regard to perception), 1 is inherent in the periodicity of the wavetrain resulting from 4 : 5 played simultaneously (phase-locked, see figure 12), and can, at least in principal, be perceived as a virtual pitch in "root position".

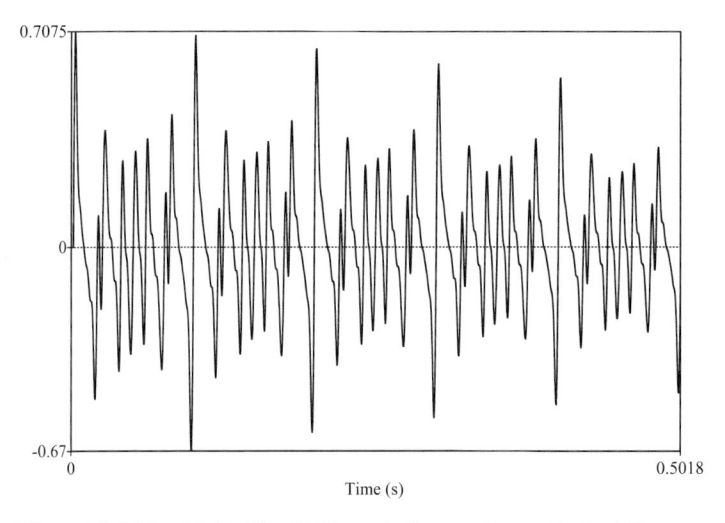

Figure 12: Major third 40 Hz: 50 Hz, periodic waveform with $T = 100$ ms

---

[7] Available in the Audacity package (analysis parameter settings: extended AC, FFT size 16384, Gauss 3.5-window).

[8] Notwithstanding the simplicity of the concept that has been implemented in various auditory models, this is still an issue mostly because convincing physiological evidence for a 'delay line' capable to realize a lag of up to 100 ms is not at hand; for a summary of modelling approaches, see de Cheveigné 2005.

In this respect, it should be noted that a harmonic chord 3 : 4 : 5 made of three complex tones with fundamental frequencies at 300 Hz, 400 Hz, and 500 Hz, and seven harmonics each, when processed with a model of the auditory periphery (AMS, Meddis & O'Mard 1997), yields a pattern of periodicities in the output that include 10 ms = 100 Hz as well as a complete series of subharmonics (frequency ratios 1/1, 1/2, 1/3, 1/4, etc.) below 100 Hz plus a number of additional periodicities representing frequencies above 100 Hz (cf. Schneider & Frieler 2009). The chance that an AC or a SHM analysis (both of which draw on periodicities inherent in complex tones or other sounds) can find common periodicities in a combination of complex tones increases with the number of successive harmonics per complex tone. Also, absolute frequencies play a role insofar a series of subharmonics (as in SHM) for several complex tones down to a common "root" can be formed much easier if the spectral components from which the calculation starts are in a frequency region well above 200 Hz. If the spectral components have already very low frequencies (as is the case in our stimuli), both AC and SHM analysis can lead to unrealistic virtual pitch estimates or may even fail for certain conditions. This is what happened with the major third placed at 31.5 Hz (see figure 11) where the AC analysis turns out "undefined" as pitch frequency, and where the virtual pitch estimates for the major thirds placed at 40 Hz, 50 Hz, and 63 Hz yield frequencies so low as to be of little or no relevance in regard to pitch perception. Even for the 80 Hz condition the virtual pitch would be only 20 Hz.

In addition to periodicity analysis drawing on the temporal envelope, brightness could also be a factor relevant to interval recognition. With increasing fundamental frequency of the lower complex tone from 31.5 Hz up to 80 Hz, and, correspondingly, a shift of all intervals up the frequency axis, the phenomenal quality of 'brightness' increases due to a rise of the spectral centroid of the sounds. For example, for the five major thirds brightness (calculated as the normalized spectral centroid with a phase vocoder[9]) increases from about 10-11 for the interval placed at 31.5 Hz fundamental frequency of the lower component to about 20-21 for the same interval at 80 Hz (see figure 13). Hence the brightness almost doubles within the five conditions.

Since brightness is an integral component of pitch in regard to pitch perception (cf. Schneider 1997, 404-430), increasing brightness of sounds can add to precision of perceptual analysis. It should be noted, though, that in the 'semi-musical' sound stimuli designed for the experiment, the number of harmonics per complex tone and the spectral energy contained in these is much smaller as in complex tones recorded from a grand piano at the same fundamental frequencies. Hence, the spectral information available from the harmonics contained in the sounds we used in our experiment seems quite limited.

---

[9] For the calculation the sndan software (Beauchamp 1995) running on a NeXT was used with an FFT length of 16384 sample points and a Hamming window.

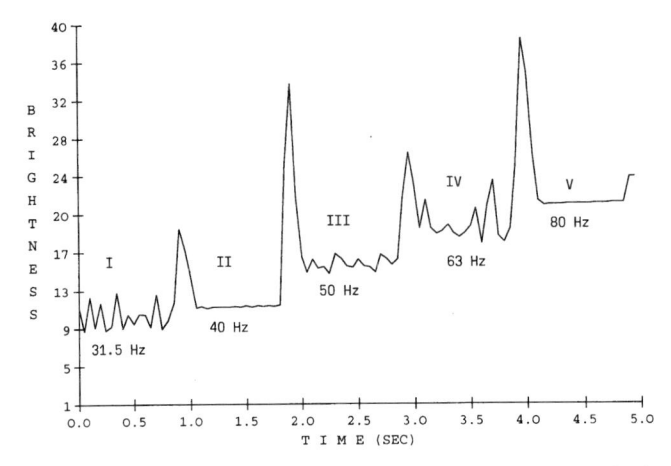

Figure 13: Brightness calculated for the five major thirds with fundamental frequencies of the lower complex tone at 31.5, 40, 50, 63, and 80 Hz

5. Conclusion

Perception of musical intervals and interval recognition at low frequencies was studied with an experiment designed to offer 'semi-musical' sound stimuli, which contain four harmonics in addition to the fundamental frequency of each complex tone, and which have amplitudes decreasing with ordinary number n like $A = 1/n$. Notwithstanding some spectral information was available to subjects besides (and complementing) that contained in the pairs of fundamental frequencies forming musical intervals (major second, minor third, major third, fourth, tritone, fifth), interval ratings were poor in particular if the fundamental frequency of the lower complex tone was at 31.5 Hz and 40 Hz. Scores improved for the 50 Hz and 63 Hz condition, respectively, and again at 80 Hz fundamental frequency of the lower complex tone. There are several factors (discussed in chapter 4 of the present article) that can explain poor interval recognition at very low frequencies, among them being mechanical and physiological properties of the cochlear partition near the apex and the helicotrema. Also, periodicity analysis in hearing that leads to a low virtual pitch imagined as the "root" of the two complex tones forming a musical interval may provide no relevant information or fail altogether if the complex tones are too low in fundamental frequency, on the one hand, and have only few harmonics, on the other (as is the case with our stimuli). However, spectral centroid frequency and, correspondingly, phenomenal brightness of pairs of complex tones increase considerably with the stepwise shift of fundamental frequencies from 31.5 Hz up to 40 Hz, 50 Hz, 63 Hz, and 80 Hz. Since brightness is an important factor in pitch and timbre perception, it may be hypothesized that interval recognition at 80 Hz fundamental frequency can be achieved with more ease and reliability than at 40 Hz because the musical interval formed by two complex tones becomes more pronounced as a qualitative configuration (or 'Gestalt') with increasing brightness of the complex sound stimulus. Increasing brightness thus may in part account for higher scores at 50 Hz, 63 Hz, and 80 Hz fundamental frequency. Finally, the "true" size of CB below $f < 150$ Hz seems difficult to estimate since the AF apparently is rather broad with shallow lower skirts at center frequencies below ca. 150 Hz or even 100 Hz. Though the assumption according to which the lowest CB of the Bark scale would stretch from 0 to 100 Hz, with the next CB assigned to the frequency range from 100 to 200 Hz seems questionable, also the concept of the ERB scale that would expect an almost constant decrease of bandwidth proportional to center frequency may not fully apply at very low frequencies (f_c < 80 Hz). Due to decreasing sharpness of the skirts of the AF with decreasing center frequency (cf. Jurado & Moore 2010), the bandwidth of the AF would increase rather than decrease, a circumstance that in part accounts for poor interval recognition in very low frequency bands as was found in our experiments.

Postscript (July 2011)

After this article had been completed, another article by Jurado and Moore on the shape and function of the auditory filter (AF) at frequencies below 100 Hz appeared (Carlos Jurado, Christian Pedersen, Brian Moore: Psychophysical tuning curves for frequencies below 100 Hz. *Journal Acoust. Soc. Am.* 129, 2011, 3166-3180). The psychophysical tuning curves (PTC) were measured for sinusoidals at 31.5, 50, 50, 63, and 80 Hz (that is, for the same center frequencies as in our study presented here), with sinusoidal and narrowband-noise maskers. The middle-ear transfer function (METF) was taken into account and showed an effect on the AF shape especially for frequencies below 40 Hz. The PTC as measured by Jurado et al. (2010, 2011) demonstrates relatively poor frequency selectivity for frequencies < 100 Hz due to shallow skirts of the AF. The CF of the "bottom" auditory filter (closest to the apex) according to Jurado et al. 2001, 3179 "appears to be located between 40 and 50 Hz". This again indicates that the conventional Bark scale (with frequencies < 100 Hz summarily assigned to one AF or CB) may not be precise enough to account for actual perception.

References

Aibara, Ryuichi, Joseph Welsh, Sunil Puria, Richard Goode 2001. Human middle-ear transfer function and cochlear input impedance. *Hearing Res.* 152, 100-109.

Beauchamp, James 1995. New methods for computer analysis and synthesis of musical sounds. *32nd Czech Conference on Acoustics. Speech – music – hearing.* Prague, 7-15.

Cheatham, M., P. Dallos 2001. Inner hair cell response patterns: Implications for low-frequency hearing. *Journal Acoust. Soc. Am.* 110, 2034-2044.

de Boer, Egbert 1996. Mechanics of the Cochlea: Modeling Efforts. In P. Dallos, A.N. Popper, R. Fay (eds.). *The Cochlea.* New York: Springer, 258-317.

de Cheveigné, Alain 2005. Pitch Perception Models. In Christopher Plack, Andrew Oxenham, Richard Fay, Arthur Popper (eds.). *Pitch. Neural Coding and Perception.* New York: Springer, 169-233.

Fletcher, Neville, Thomas Rossing 1991. *The Physics of Musical Instruments.* New York, Berlin: Springer.

Greenwood, Donald 1961. Critical bandwidth and the frequency coordinates of the basilar membrane. *Journal Acoust. Soc. Am.* 33, 1344-1356.

Greenwood, Donald 1990. A cochlear frequency-position function for several species – 29 years later. *Journal Acoust. Soc. Am.* 87, 2592-2605.

Hartmann, William 1991. *Signals, Sound, and Sensation.* New York: AIP/Springer.

Jurado, Carlos, Brian Moore 2010. Frequency selectivity for frequencies below 100 Hz: Comparisons with mid-frequencies. *Journal Acoust. Soc. Am.* 128, 3585-3596.

Marquardt, Torsten, Johannes Hensel, Dieter Mrowinski, Günther Scholz 2007. Low-frequency characteristics of human and guinea pig cochleae. *Journal Acoust. Soc. Am.* 121, 3628-3638.

Meddis, Ray, Lowel O'Mard 1997. A unitary model of pitch perception. *Journal Acoust. Soc. Am.* 102, 1811-1820.

Moore, Brian 1993. Frequency Analysis and Pitch Perception. In W. A. Yost, A.N. Popper, R. Fay (eds.). *Human Psychophysics.* New York: Springer, 56-115.

Moore, Brian 1995. Frequency Analysis and Masking. In B. Moore (ed.). *Hearing.* San Diego, Orlando: Academic Pr., 161-205.

Moore, Brian 2005. Basic Psychophysics of human spectral processing. *Intern. Rev. of Neurobiology* Vol. 70, 49-86.

Moore, Brian 2008. *Introduction to the psychology of hearing.* 5th ed. Bingley: Emerald.

Moore, Brian, Brian Glasberg 1983. Suggested formulae for calculating auditory-filter bandwidths and excitation patterns. *Journal Acoust. Soc. Am.* 74, 750-753.

Moore, Brian, Robert Peters, Brian Glasberg 1990. Auditory filter shapes at low center frequencies. *Journal Acoust. Soc. Am.* 88, 132-140.

Patuzzi, Robert 1996. Cochlear Micromechanis and Macromechanics. In P. Dallos, A.N. Popper, R. Fay (eds.). *The Cochlea.* New York: Springer, 186-257.

Pickles, James 2008. *An Introduction to the physiology of hearing.* 3rd ed. Bingley: Emerald.

Plattig, K.-H. 1975. Psychophysiologie und Psychoakustik des Gehörs. In W.D. Keidel (ed.). *Physiologie des Gehörs. Akustische Informationsverarbeitung.* Stuttgart: Thieme, 359-380.

Plomp, R., W. Levelt 1965. Tonal Consonance and Critical Bandwidth. *Journal Acoust. Soc. Am.* 38, 548-560.

Pressnitzer, Daniel, Roy Patterson. Katrin Krumbholz 2001. The lower limit of melodic pitch. *Journal Acoust. Soc. Am.* 109. 2074-2084.

Robles, Luis, Mario Ruggero 2001. Mechanics of mammalian cochlea. *Physiol. Rev.* 81, 1305-1352.

Schick, Fritz 1994. The Helicotrema and the Frequency Resolution in the Inner ear. *Acustica* 80, 463-470.

Schneider, Albrecht 1997. *Tonhöhe – Skala – Klang. Akustische, tonometrische und psychoakustische Studien auf vergleichender Grundlage.* Bonn: Orpheus-Verlag.

Schneider, Albrecht, Klaus Frieler 2009. Perception of harmonic and inharmonic sounds: results from ear models. In S. Ystad, R. Kronland-Martinet, K. Jensen (eds.). *Computer Music Modeling and Retrieval. Genesis of Meaning in Sound and Music.* (=Lecture Notes in Computer Science, Vol. 5493). Berlin, New York: Springer, 18-44.

Schneider, Albrecht, Arne von Ruschkowski, Rolf Bader 2009. Klangliche Rauhigkeit, ihre Wahrnehmung und Messung. In R. Bader (Ed.). *Musical Acoustics, Neurocognition and Psychology of Music*. (=Hamburger Jahrbuch für Musikwissenschaft 25). Frankfurt/M. etc.: P. Lang, 103-148.

Schneider, Albrecht, Arne von Ruschkowski 2011. Techno, Decibels, and Politics: an empirical study of modern dance music productions, sound pressure levels, and 'loudness perception'. *Hamburger Jahrbuch für Musikwissenschaft* 28, 13-62.

Terhardt, Ernst 1998. *Akustische Kommunikation*. Berlin, New York: Springer.

Traunmüller, H. 1990. Analytical expressions for the tonotopic sensory scale. *Journal Acoust. Soc. Am.* 88, 97-100.

Zenner, Hans-Peter 1994. *Hören. Physiologie, Biochemie, Zell- und Neurobiologie*. Stuttgart, New York: Thieme.

Zwicker, Eberhard 1982. *Psychoakustik*. Berlin: Springer.

Zwicker, Eberhard, Hugo Fastl 1999. *Psychoacoustics. Facts and Models*. 2nd ed. Berlin, New York: Springer.

Robert Mores

Nasality in Musical Sounds – a few Intermediate Results

Introduction

A recent meeting of reputated violin researchers and luthiers, held in Cambridge, led to this review. "Nasality" is one of the most frequently used and commonly understood terms if it comes to describe musical sounds. A recent study ranked this term among the top ten [Nyk09]. However, studies on perceived nasality in sounds often conclude without significant results, including those presented in Cambridge. A general understanding of which acoustical properties in a sound would lead to perceived nasality is still missing, and automated measurements of nasal content in recorded musical sounds seem to remain unachievable.

The violin research community still trusts the early definition of Dünnwald, who did a tremendous work in measuring more than 1000 violins and in defining four characteristic energy bands for violins. One of these bands he assigned the nasal band, and in the latest publication on this the band ranges from 700 Hz to 1600 Hz [Hei03]. In the strings community, these bands serve as reference today as well as the assigned terminology. However, the speech processing community has established other acoustical properties (APs) to capture nasality, and clinical research has also established its own perspective on nasality. This paper reviews these knowledge fields and relates the findings to musical sounds. The paper also covers some own studies on capturing nasality.

Nasality in Speech Processing

A brief look into history shows that after a period of fragmented research the community settled with some well accepted acoustical properties (AP). House and Stevens, searching for the ingredients of nasality in speech in 1956, found some prominence at 1kHz, an additional dip in the range between 700 Hz and 1800Hz and a reduced A1, the amplitude of the F1, the 1st formant [Hou56]. In 1958, Hattori identified a resonance at 250 Hz and a zero at 500 Hz [Hat58]. Two years later, Fant confirmed the reduction of A1 and additionally noticed an increase of bandwidth of F1, F1BW, and an extra formant at 2 kHz, seen in form of a split 3rd formant [Fan60]. Especially such early results may have caused the violin research in the 70s to assume that nasality is just a matter of extra energy somewhere in the range of 1 to 2 kHz. Such assumption can easily be forwarded with the argument that sinus resonances are simply an add-on to the oral resonances. In 1962 Dickson confirmed the contribution of an increased bandwidth for F1 but also for F2 [Dic62]. He also noticed an increase or decrease of amplitude and frequency of F1, F2 and F3. Fujimura and Lindqvist report the frequency-shift of F1 and an extra zero-pole around F1 [Fuj71]. One decade later Maeda observed a flattening of the spectra in the range of 300 Hz to 2500 Hz, which clearly seems to contradict some of the earlier observations [Mae82]. Hawkins and Stevens concluded in 1985, that it was the degree of prominence of an extra pole around F1 that would most likely feature nasality [Haw85]. Bognar and Fujisaki, in their study on the four French nasal vowels in 1986, found an upward frequency shift of F3 and a downward shift of F2, resulting in widening of the F2-F3 region with two extra pole-zero pairs between 220 Hz and 2150 Hz [Bog86]. Dang et al. linked observations in the spectrum with source features in 1994, when they assigned the lowest pole-zero pair to the maxillary sinuses [Dan94]. In summary, early research results are fragmented and do not encourage to build a general model.

Acoustical Properties	std0-1k	% extra poles	delta 1st - xpole	F1-FP0 & F1-FP1	A1-P0 & A1-P1	MFCC	F1BW & F1 profile	nPeaks 40dB	A1-H1
Glass 1985	x	x	x						
Maeda 1993				x					
Chen M. 1995					x				
Hasegawa 2004						x			
Pruthi 2007	x			x	x		x	x	x
Chen N. 2007					x				
our study				x	x		x		

Legend:
- std0-1k: std around center of mass 0-1kHz
- % xpoles: min/max values of % of time there are extra poles at low frequencies
- delta 1st – xpole: min/max values of differences between first pole and extra pole
- F1-FP0, F1-FP1: frequency differences between F1 and extra poles P0 and P1
- A1-P0, A1-P1: amplitude differences between F1 and extra poles P0 and P1
- MFCC: mel frequency correlation coeff.
- F1BW: bandwidth of F1
- F1 profile: signal energy after passing a 100Hz band filter in relation to passing a 1kHz band filter, both centered around F1
- nPeaks40dB: number of peaks within 40dB of the maximum amplitude in a spectral frame
- A1-H1: amplitude difference of F1 and 1st harmonic H1, two methods

Table 1: Acoustical properties for capturing nasality in speech sounds, as preferred in the speech processing community

Table 1 gives an overview of today's most well accepted APs for nasality in speech. Different sets of these APs are usually taken as knowledge-based parameters to solve binary nasality classification tasks. Most of these studies deliver an accuracy between 60% and 90%. Some of the APs introduced by Glass in 1985 are now expressed by the nasal poles P0 and P1 around F1 [Gla85]. Maeda and Chen proposed to use the relation of P0 and P1 to F1 in terms of frequency and amplitude, see table 1 [Mae93][Che95]. P0 and P1 are usually dominated or superimposed by F1 and F2. Therefore, P0 and P1 are usually difficult to separate, as shown in Figure 1. Even more difficult is the extraction of bandwidth or amplitude for these extra poles. The respective APs introduced by Maeda and Chen M. have been reused until now. Pruthi has resolved many issues in his dissertation and has demonstrated classification results with an accuracy of up to 96 %, 78 % and 70 % on the StoryDB, TIMIT and WS96/97 data sets, respectively, with an RBF kernel support vector machine (SVM) [Pru04]. He also changed the paradigm of static sinus resonance frequencies and identified the interdependence of nasal APs and vowel quality [Pru07]. The work of Chen N. is listed because it exemplarily demonstrates that the established APs are reused and that further accuracy progress is now expected by other, context-sensitive, measures, i.e. the statistical difference in A1-P1 measurements for vowels with adjacent nasal consonants (NVN, NVC, and CVN utterances) vs. vowels with no adjacent nasal consonants (CVC utterances).

The speech community seems to have settled with the search for appropriate APs, most of which are located around F1 and well below 1 kHz. However, reviewing the publications, it becomes clear, that the community is fully aware of the fact that there are many other APs around at higher frequencies and that earlier observations are true for individual test setups, however, with little chance for general modelling. Pruthi has shown in his simulations that velum movement raises extra poles and zeros across the full range between 1 kHz and 3 kHz, depending on the size of the coupling area between the vocal and the nasal tract, and depending on the vowel context [Pru05]. This confirms the complexity issue and explains the problem of agreeing upon APs in the range of higher frequencies. In recent research, the speech community rather moves away from finding appropriate APs towards using additional cues. Examples are phonetic context and murmur thresholds or energy over time fluctuations which seem helpful to resolve the categorical question of nasality for further speech recognition improvements [Ber07] [Haj04] [Che07]. Such speaker-specific approach is reasonable for speech recognition tasks when considering the finding that inter-speaker variance within categories may be larger than intra-speaker categorical distances [Eng06].

Perceptual Issues

Apart from the analysis and modelling piece of work, the perceptual studies deliver a likewise heterogeneous scenario. House and Stevens in their study in 1956 reduced A1 by 8 dB for a nasality response to reach the 50% level [Hou56]. Hattori et al. worked on poles and zeros in 1958 [Hat58]. Adding a pole around 250 Hz gave some perception of nasality, but adding the zero at 500 Hz did not, the combination of the two resulted in a much stronger perception of nasality. In 1982 Maeda confirmed the importance of spectral flattening at low frequencies in producing the perception of nasality by listening tests [Mae82]. In 1985, Hawkins and Stevens inserted a pole-zero pair in the vicinity of the first formant, wider spacing of the pole-zero pair was found to be necessary for the perception of nasality [Haw85]. Bognar and Fujisaki studied the perception of French vowels in 1986, identifying the role of the formant shifts and of existing pole-zero pairs for phonemic and phonetic judgements [Bog86]. They also found biasing problems in using French native speakers to resolve perceptual questions on nasality. This brief review demonstrates that the method of varying only singular parameters within the complex multi-variant scenario fails to deliver the prominent APs.

Cross-language studies confirm the necessity of careful test design for perceptual studies. In their study in 1968, Delattre and Monnot presented stimuli to French and American English speaking listeners, differing only in vowel duration [Del68]. Shorter vowels were more likely identified as oral whereas longer vowels were more likely identified as nasal. Lintz and Sherman found in 1961, that the perceived nasality was less severe for syllables with a plosive environment than for syllables with a fricative environment [Lin61]. Beddor and Strange did not find consistent differences in responses from Hindi and American English speaking test groups when they investigated oral-nasal distinction in vowels in 1982 [Bed82]. However, these researchers identified that perception of oral-nasal vowel distinction is categorical for Hindi speakers, and more continuous for speakers of American English. Hawkins and Stevens also did not find significant differences between American English, Gujarati, Hindi and Bengali speaking test groups when they compared the 50% crossover points of the identification functions in 1985 [Haw85]. Stevens again identified similar responses to nasality content when working with Portuguese, English and French speaking test groups in 1987 [Ste87]. However, British English speaking listeners preferred some murmur along with brief nasalization in the vowel, whereas French speaking listeners preferred a longer duration of nasalization in the vowel and gave little importance to the presence of murmur. Finally, Krakow and Beddor concluded in 1991 that nasal vowels presented in isolation or in oral context were more often correctly judged as nasal than when presented in the original nasal context, i.e. together with adjacent nasal consonants [Kra91]. In summary, even though there seem to be commonalities across languages, results from perceptual studies will still strongly depend on test group selection. For test persons with a language background containing phonemic nasalization, the trained categorical listening will likely be an obstacle to perceiving the degree of nasalization. And the results will also strongly depend on sound presentation, with or without phonemic context, oral or nasal context, duration of short-steady sounds, presentation with or without an onset, or, we could say with or without a plosive. All these aspects have not been considered so far in the studies on nasality in musical sounds.

Clinical studies

A quite different perspective on nasality opens up when reviewing clinical studies. Whereas the speech processing research aims at speech or speaker-specific feature extraction, clinical research aims at diagnosis and therapy of speech problems or inabilities. This different focus and context has led to other approaches in terms of analysis, modelling and creating data bases. Clearly, entries in the IPA chart, which represents vowel quality, or tongue position and pitch, will be shifted away from normal population for children with Down's syndrome, and nasality measurements are likely to fail for patients where the phonetic context is shifted due to conjoined cleft palates. In their clinical study in 2002, Baken and Orlikoff identified the following APs for nasality: larger F1BW, frequency shifts of formants, an extra pole between 250 Hz and 500 Hz, an extra zero around 500 Hz, irregular extra poles between formants, and a lower total signal energy [Bak02]. Some of these APs are similar to those found by the speech community, but in general these findings seem to stay behind the state of the art. The classification study of Zečević in 2002 aims at developing assisting tools for speech therapy [Zec02]. For classification with SVMs, he decided to extract the first four formants in terms of frequency, amplitude and bandwidth on the basis of LPC (two levels of order), ignoring the extra poles P0 and P1. The investigated data corpus NASAL contains more than 3000 sounds from 116 male, female and infant speakers, following some guidelines of the Rinophoniebogen [Hep91]. Sound samples are classified into four nasal categories by speech therapists. This data corpus is particularly interesting for musical acoustics not only because of its differentiated classification in terms of nasal quality but also because of its emphasis on stand-alone vowels. Although some of the observations on individual changes to formants contradict those made by the speech community, the overall classification accuracy achieved in individual studies is well comparable with results by the speech processing community.

Own studies between the disciplines

Improved property extraction from sounds and classification on a reduced set of properties

In a brief study we used APs according to Table 1, however only a small subset of these together with an improved extraction method. F1, P0 and P1 were extracted using the warped LPC ([Lai94]) and a root solver on the LPC coefficients. Figure 1 clearly demonstrates the superiority of warped LPC against LPC when searching for properties at low frequencies.

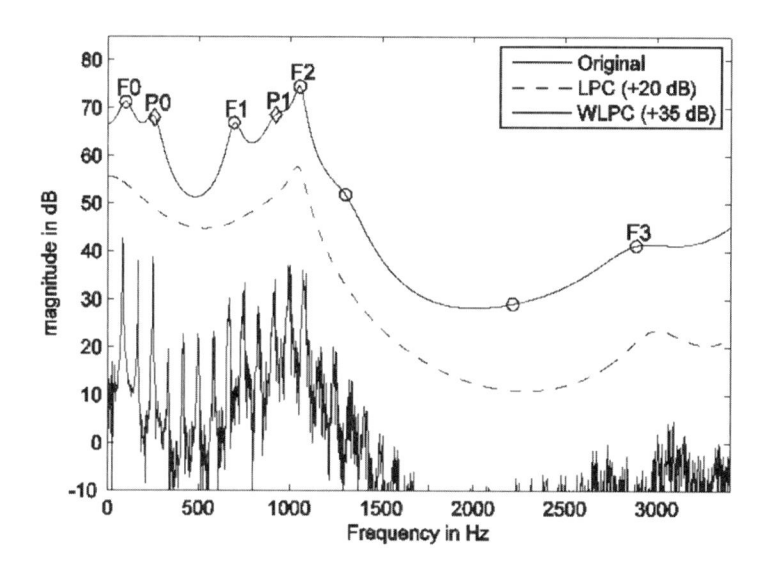

Figure 1: Nasal speech signal /a/ in the frequency domain and its related LPC (order n = 48 at 44.1 kHz sampling rate) and warped LPC (order n = 24 at 44.1 kHz sampling rate) spectrum.

Even though the warped LPC uses half the number of coefficients (n = 24 versus n = 48 at 44.1 kHz sampling rate), it does resolve the hidden P0 and P1 poles, whereas the LPC does not. This advantage remains at lower sampling rates. Solving the roots of the LPC coefficients allows for identifying bandwidth and frequency of the P0 and P1 poles even when these are masked by F1, see Figure 2. The model works without machine learning and achieves considerable classification accuracy. It has been shown that even a sparse AP set consisting only of F1-FP0, F1BW, A1-P0 and A1-P1 achieves 84 % accuracy, when used on adult female /a/ sounds from the data corpus NASAL, compared to the 94 % accuracy achieved in a 17 component AP set as suggested by Zečević, see Table 1 for abbreviations [Mal09].

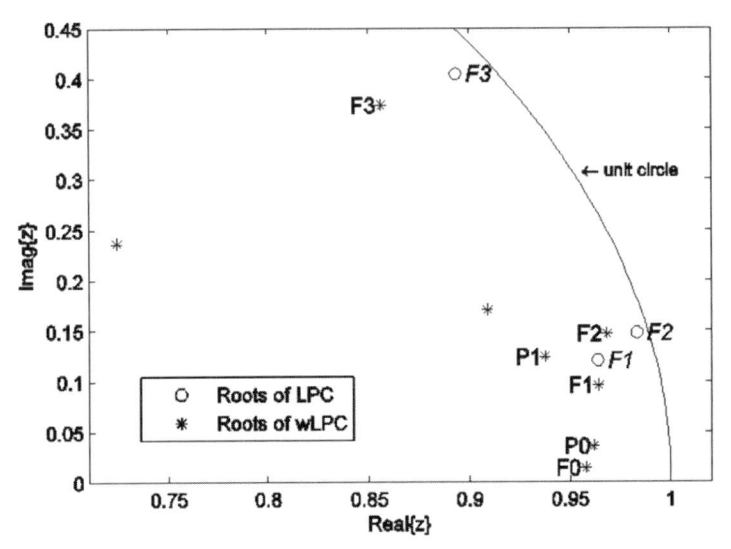

Figure 2: LPC and warped LPC coefficients of a nasal speech signal /a/ in the z-plane, for the related spectra see Fig. 1.

Study on the perceptual impact of extra poles P0 and P1

In another study we investigated the necessity of P0 and P1 for perception. We used an ordinary LPC of order 13 (11025 kHz sampling rate) on nasal and non-nasal speech. This low-order approach is just about able to capture the general formant structure, but not P0 or P1. In listening tests the perceptual distance between nasal and non-nasal vowels was significant, even when presented with synthesized pitch. Therefore, P0 and P1 are not necessarily the prominent cue to nasality perception, even though the speech community agreed, that these APs are well extractable and reliably accompany nasalized sounds.

Perception of nasalized voice attributes in musical sounds

We apply known APs to musical sounds to investigate perceptual impact. In an unpublished study in 2008, we post-processed near-field recordings from the "Schreiber" Stradivari 1712 violin, implementing individual APs from Baken and Orlikoff [Ker08]. Being asked on any perceptible change of sound, test persons gave all kinds of explanations but did not mention nasality at all. This very honest test confirms again that combinations of APs rather than individual APs will trigger perception of nasality.

Dünnwald's nasality band revisited

Another study corresponds to the Dünnwald definition of a nasal band [Hei03]. Dünnwald investigated more than 1000 violins, their body impulse response and related spectral characteristics. In this context he identified a correlation between nasal sounding violins and energy content in a frequency band from 700 Hz to 1600 Hz relative to the energy content in other frequency bands. Due to this observation, he assigned this band the nasal band, not necessarily claiming such relative energy content would cause the nasal perception. According to his findings we used recordings of valued violins and boosted the signal by 3 dB, 6 dB or 10 dB in bands from 600 Hz to 1000 Hz, 600 Hz to 1500 Hz, and 900 Hz to 1500 Hz. Subjects had to describe the change they perceived when listening to the modified sounds in comparison to the original sounds [Ker08]. Again, after listening to six different musical pieces, none of the test persons mentioned nasality when asked to describe perceived differences. The assumption lying behind Dünnwald's definition cannot be confirmed by the outcome of this test.

This result is not surprising and is in agreement with the findings of the speech community and the clinical research. Both do not support the idea of nasality being characterised by energy in a certain frequency band. The other research fields rather suggest that nasality relates to formant structures and complex pole-zero scenarios across all bands up to 4 kHz and beyond. In conclusion, Dünnwald's assignment is not in agreement with findings in other research fields and it cannot be confirmed by a simple and honest test.

Conclusions

Perception of nasal ingredients in musical sounds will be triggered by many possible AP combinations, but not necessarily by those agreed upon in the different fields of research, and not necessarily by those believed by the violin research community. A violin resonance profile offers enough pole-zero combinations over a wide range to trigger nasality, and most of the energy is outside the low frequency focus of speech research. Another problem occurs by applying results from voice research to musical sounds when the pitch is higher than that of voice, effectively requiring extensions of existing models and verification. We have to admit that understanding nasality in musical sounds will finally request a similar effort as does understanding nasality in speech. However, there has not even been developed a general model for nasality in speech.

The knowledge base on acoustical properties (APs) for nasality perception seems to be stronger in the fields of speech processing or clinical research than in musical acoustics. Models in the different fields are diverging, and the properties used in modelling do not necessarily correspond with the acoustical properties causing nasality perception. In addition, knowledge in the field of voice is not necessarily applicable to musical sounds. The most reliable APs found for nasality in speech do not translate to musical instruments, especially with high-pitch and multi-resonance sounds. In an honest listening test, the often cited Dünnwald definition for nasality cannot be confirmed. Knowledge-based modelling with a sparse AP set from the speech community, however, resulted in 80 % classification accuracy. Perceptual tests on nasality need very careful design, since results will largely be biased by language background, phonetic context and duration of sound presentations.

Acknowledgements

We thank Prof. R. Männer and his research group, University Mannheim, for providing the data corpus NASAL, and we thank the BMBF for funding the violin project, reference no. AiF 1767X07.

References

[Bak02] Baken, R.J., Orlikoff, R.F.: *Clinical Measurement of Voice and Speech*, Singular Publications, 2002.

[Bed82] Beddor, P. S., Strange, W., Cross language study of perception of the oralnasal distinction. *J. Acoust. Soc. Am. 71 (6)*, 1551–1561, 1982.

[Ber07] Berger, M. A., *Measurement of vowel nasalization by multi-dimensional acoustic analysis*, MSc thesis, University of Rochester, Rochester, New York, 2007.

[Bog86] Bognar, E., Fujisaki, H., Analysis, synthesis and perception of French nasal vowels. In: *Proceedings of ICASSP*. pp. 1601–1604, 1986.

[Che95] Chen, M. Y., Acoustic parameters of nasalized vowels in hearing-impaired and normal-hearing speakers. *J. Acoust. Soc. Am. 98 (5)*, 2443–2453, 1995.

[Che07] Chen, N.F., Vowel nasalization in American english: acoustic variability due to phonetic context, *ICPhS XVI Saarbrücken* Germany 2007, ID1171, 905-908.

[Dan94] Dang, J., Honda, K., Suzuki, H., Morphological and acoustical analysis of the nasal and the paranasal cavities. J. Acoust. Soc. Am. 96 (4), 2088–2100, 1994.

[Del86] Delattre, P., Monnot, M., The role of duration in the identification of French nasal vowels. *International Review of Applied Linguistics 6*, 267–288, 1968.

[Dic62] Dickson, D. R., Acoustic study of nasality. J. of Speech and Hearing Research 5 (2), 103–111, 1962.

[Eng06] Engwall, O., Delvaux, V., & Metens, T. Interspeaker Variation in the Articulation of French Nasal Vowels. In: *Proceedings of the Seventh International Seminar on Speech Production* (pp. 3-10). Ubatuba, Sao Paolo, Brazil, 2006.

[Fan60] Fant, G., *Acoustic Theory of Speech Production*. Mouton, The Hague, Netherlands, 1960.

[Fuj71] Fujimura, O., Lindqvist, J., Sweep tone measurements of vocal-tract characteristics. *J. Acoust. Soc. Am. 49*, 541–558, 1971.

[Gla85] Glass, J. R., Zue, V. W., Detection of nasalized vowels in American English. In: *Proceedings of ICASSP*. pp. 1569–1572, 1985.

[Has04] Hasegawa-Johnson, et. al., Landmark-based speech recognition: *Report of the 2004 Johns Hopkins summer workshop*. Tech. rep., 2004.

[Hat58] Hattori, S., Yamamoto, K., Fujimura, O., Nasalization of vowels in relation to nasals. *J. Acoust. Soc. Am. 30 (4)*, 267–274, 1958.

[Haw85] Hawkins, S., Stevens, K. N., Acoustic and perceptual correlates of the nonnasal-nasal distinction for vowels. *J. Acoust. Soc. Am. 77 (4)*, 1560–1575, 1985.

[Haj04] Hajro, N., *Automated nasal feature extraction*, MSc thesis, MIT, 2004.

[Hei03] Heike, G., Dünnwald, H.: Neuere Klanguntersuchungen an Geigen und ihre Beziehung zum Gesang, in: *Festschrift Jobst Peter Fricke zum 65. Geburtstag*, Systemische Musikwissenschaft published by Wolfgang Auhagen et. al., 2003.

[Hep91] Heppt, W.,et. al., Nasalanz – Ein neuer Begriff der objektiven Nasalitätsanalyse; *Laryngo-Rhino-Otologie 70*, pp. 169-228, 1991.

[Hou56] House, A. S., Stevens, K. N., Analog studies of the nasalization of vowels. *J. of Speech and Hearing Disorders 21 (2)*, 218–232, 1956.

[Jon62] Jones, D.: *An Outline of English Phonetics*, W. Heffer & Sons Ltd. Cambridge, 9th edition, 1962.

[Ker08] Kersten, J., *Sprechen versus Singen - eine Klanganalyse an Musikinstrumenten*, diplome thesis, faculty DMI, HAW, Hamburg, 2008.

[Kra91] Krakow, R. A., Beddor, P. S., Coarticulation and the perception of nasality. In: *Proceedings of the 12th International Congress of Phonetic Sciences*. pp. 38–41, 1991.

[Lin61] Lintz, L. B., Sherman, D., Phonetic elements and perception of nasality. *Journal of Speech and Hearing Research 4*, 381–396, 1961.

[Lai94] Laine, U. K., Karjalainen, M., Altosaar, T. "Warped linear prediction (wlp) in speech and audio processing," in: *Proc. IEEE Int. Conf. on Acoustics, Speech, and Signal Processing (ICASSP-94)*, Adelaide, Australia, 1994.

[Mae82] Maeda, S., Acoustic cues for vowel nasalization: A simulation study. *J. Acoust. Soc. Am. 72 (S1)*, S102, 1982.

[Mae93] Maeda, S., *Phonetics and Phonology: Nasals, Nasalization and the Velum*. Academic Press, Ch. Acoustics of vowel nasalization and articulatory shifts in French Nasal Vowels, pp. 147–167, 1993.

[Mal09] Malhotra, I., *Extraktion der Nasalität in Klängen – eine Werkzeugentwicklung unter MATLAB*, diplome thesis, faculty DMI, HAW, Hamburg, 2009.

[Nyk09] Nykänen, A., Johansson, Ö., Lundberg, J., Berg, J. (2009). "Modeling Perceptual Dimensions of Saxophone Sounds," *Acta Acustica united with Acustica, 95*, 539-549.

[Pru04] Pruthi, T., Espy-Wilson, C., Acoustic parameters for automatic detection of nasal manner. *Speech Communication 43 (3)*, 225–239, 2004.

[Pru05] Pruthi, T., Espy-Wilson, C., Simulating and understanding the effects of velar coupling area on nasalized vowel spectra. *J. Acoust. Soc. Am. 118 (3)*, 2024, 2005.

[Pru07] Pruthi, T., Analysis, *Vocal-Tract Modeling and Automatic Detection of Vowel Nasalization*, PhD dissertation, University of Maryland, 2007.

[Ste87] Stevens, K. N., Andrade, A., Viana, M. C., Perception of vowel nasalization in VC contexts: A cross-language study. *J. Acoust. Soc. Am. 82 (S1)*, p 119, 1987.

[Zec02] Zečević, A., *Ein sprachgestütztes Trainingssystem zur Evaluierung der Nasalität*, Dissertation, Universität Mannheim, 2002.

Florian Pfeifle

Air Modes in Stringed Lute-like Instruments from Africa and China

Summary

The article reports acoustical research carried out on non-western lute-like stringed instruments such as the West African *Gurumi* and the *Gimbri* as well as the Chinese *Ruan*. Measurements were obtained with a focus on air modes and the Helmholtz resonance.

1. Introduction: Cavity Modes and the Helmholtz frequency

A structural feature that can be found in many musical instruments is a body used as a resonator with an air volume enclosed (e.g. percussion instruments or stringed instruments like a guitar or violin). In certain cases these air volumes add important spectral components to the overall sound and timbre of the instrument. In a timpani, the air load from the kettle lowers the modal frequencies of the membrane and can be used to adjust the spectrum (cf. Fletcher & Rossing 1990, 2000). In some instruments the influence of the air load enclosed in a cavity on the radiation behaviour is rather small but nonetheless noticeable. For example, the air load in the cavity of a banjo plays only a minor role in regard to the spectrum of the sound that is radiated from the instrument though the air load influences the intensity of the sound (Gura & Bollmann 1999). In many string instruments the effect of the air filled cavity on the radiated sound is enhanced intentionally by one or several openings (sound holes) placed on the instrument's body as in the guitar, the banjo or in a number of bowed instruments. It is common knowledge that the lower air resonances enhance the radiation of the sound in the lower spectral range (Hutchings 1981/1988) thus giving an instrument more of a ‚fundament' or adding to the bass. The Helmholtz frequency often has a resonance peak around the fundamental frequency of the second lowest string (commonly found in guitars, or in bowed string instruments).

Even though there is a lot of research on air modes in instrument cavities, and on the Helmholtz frequency in particular, very little information so far can be found as to the actual influence of cavity modes on the sound of an instrument as is perceived as well as in regard of a possible influence cavity modes might have on the radiation behaviour of non-cavity modes.

The present article, which is based on the author's research project on the banjo (Bader & Pfeifle 2010) addresses vibration patterns and sound radiation behaviour of air modes and the Helmholtz frequency as found in three non-European lute instruments. All three instruments have a body with air enclosed and one or several sound hole(s). The main focus of this paper lies on the intensities of the air modes radiated from these instruments and the interaction air modes have with the other modes found in the radiated sound spectrum.

The present work is based on research on the acoustical behaviour of a banjo, which included the radiation patterns of a banjo's membrane. It was found that a membrane has the expected distinct radiation patterns of mode shapes as occurring in circular membranes but these mode shapes are stable over a certain frequency range and can be excited by various frequencies falling into that particular range. This means, if for instance a string has a partial whose frequency lies in that specific mode shape area it will be radiated in that mode shape. The intensity of the radiation strongly depends on the peak of the resonance frequency of that particular mode shape and how close the excitation frequency is to the maximum peak. This behaviour is depicted in figure 1[1], which shows the radiated spectrum of a *Banjo* membrane. The numbers in brackets correspond to the nodal diameters and circles of the modes.

Given this relation of string partials to membrane mode shapes as existing in the banjo, the question which arises here is whether a similar behaviour can be observed in cavity resonances of other string instruments.

2. Helmholtz frequency and air modes

Since my investigation reported in the following is primarily concerned with the radiation of sound from the sound hole(s) it is important to interpret the sound radiation correctly. In particular, one has to discern between the air modes of the cavity and the Helmholtz frequency. To this aim, a brief overview explaining the two phenomena is given here.

2.1 Helmholtz resonance

The formula for the Helmholtz frequency was originally developed to describe the resonance frequency of a Helmholtz resonator (cf. Helmholtz 1870, 60-83 and the Beilage II of that work), which was used as a mechanical ‚filter' for spectral analysis of complex sounds. It basically can be described as a piston of air in a neck or orifice interacting with a volume of air. This physical system can be expressed as a simple spring-mass system giving a resonance peak with a high Q-factor (Selamet & Radavich 1997).

The effect described above can be extended to objects of arbitrary geometries with accurate results (cf. Fletcher & Rossing 1990/2000).

An end correction δ_C was introduced by Lord Rayleigh (1894/1926/1945) to account for inertial fluid motion around the openings (cf. Chanaud 1998), and was further refined by Ingard (cf. Ingard 1947). This formulation can be applied to musical instruments of many kinds, the only properties that have to be known are the volume of the cavity V and the area of the opening r_O resulting in the well-known formula:

(1) $$f_H = \frac{c}{2\pi} \cdot \sqrt{\frac{2r_O \cdot \delta_C}{V}}$$

Even though this formula is only an approximation in many cases (Selamet & Radavich 1997 showed that the value of the end correction is linked to the geometry and therefore is not universal) it gives a good estimation of the Helmholtz frequency for many kinds of musical instruments. At this point it is important to note that the Helmholtz frequency

---

[1] See appendix for figures 1, 3, 5, 7, 9.

was originally defined for cavities with solid walls. In the case of the *gurumi* and the *gimbri* (types of lutes found in parts of Africa), this constraint is not met because one side of the interior space is confined by a membrane which has a much lower impedance compared to the rest of the body. The effect of this influence is not part of this work but is again mentioned in the measurement section and the conclusion.

2.2 Cavity modes in musical instruments

As mentioned above, the Helmholtz formula only describes an interacting air piston with the air volume of the cavity. The wave propagation behaviour through the neck (or orifice) and inside the cavity is neglected and must be described with the wave equation for air which is also known as the Helmholtz equation:

(2) $\nabla^2 P + k^2 P = 0$

where P is the acoustical pressure and $k = \omega/c$ is the wave number with ω being the angular frequency and c the sound propagation speed in the medium.

An analytical solution to this differential equation can only be given for simple geometries (cf. Selamet & Radavich 1997) so in musical instruments with arbitrarily shaped geometries a numerical method like FEM, BEM or FDM must be employed.

3. Measurements

3.1 Equipment and method

All measurements were done in an anechoic chamber of the Institute of Musicology, University of Hamburg. Sound radiated from the surface of each instrument under investigation was recorded with an 11 x 11 microphone array as described in (Bader 2010). With this method, reconstruction of the sound radiation behaviour is achieved by recording the sound pressure changes in the acoustical nearfield. From the data, the spatio-temporal radiation pattern is calculated and displayed in a graphical format.

For all measurements reported in the following, the instruments where excited by (a) a knock on the body with a small hammer or (b) by a finger plucking a string. No additional statistical or signal processing tools were used. All figures (as shown below) are the result of a single measurement.

3.2 Gurumi

The first instrument in this series of measurements is the West African *Gurumi*, a snakeskin covered lute with 2 strings. The body is made from a callabash and has a sound hole on the upper/front side facing the player (if played right-handed) as depicted in figure 2. This instrument is played with a typical West African finger technique[2], a technique which is mostly associated with griots or other West African lute players (cf. Carlin 2006 ; Lomax 2006). The instrument produces a nasal sound that is remarkably loud

---

[2] Relevant video material is found at Centre pour la formation et promotion musicales (CFPM) www.youtube.com/watch?v=41KLRaTqgXA

considering the rather small size of the instrument. This is a recurrent feature in membrane covered lutes where the membrane acts as an acoustical amplifier for the string sound (Hendler 1995).

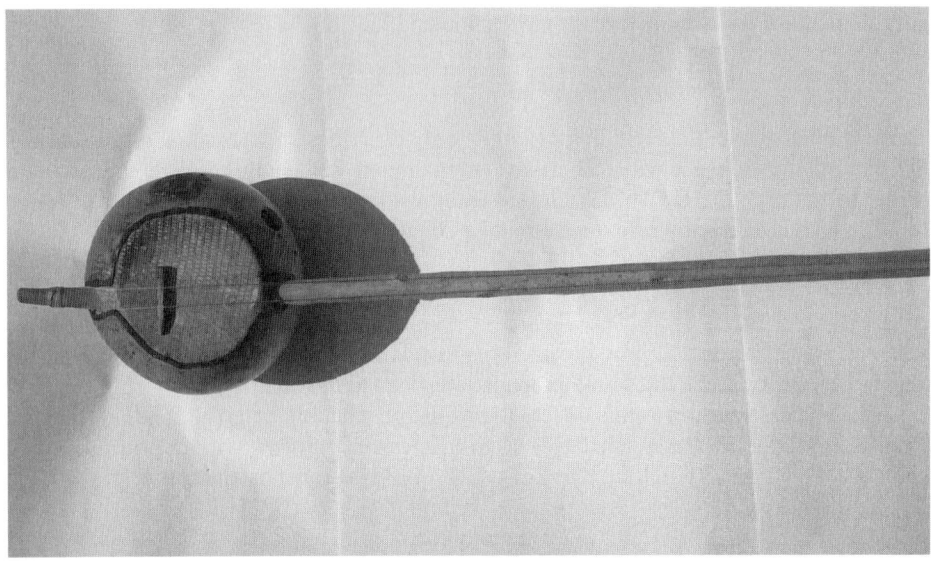

Fig. 2: West African Gurumi.

3.2.1 Helmholtz resonance and air modes of the Gurumi

To calculate the volume of this instrument the body can be approximated mathematically as a sphere volume minus a spherical cap volume. The volume of the complete sphere is:

(3) $\quad Volume_{Sph} = \frac{4}{3}\pi \cdot r^3 = \frac{4}{3}\pi \cdot (0.07m)^3 = 0.0014m^3$

The volume of the spherical cap is given through:

(4) $\quad Volume_{Cap} = \frac{\pi h^2}{3} \cdot (3r - h) = \frac{\pi (0.025m)^2}{3} \cdot (3 \cdot 0.07m - 0.025m) = 0.000121m^3$

The total volume now is

(5) $\quad Volume_{Sph} - Volume_{Cap} = 0.0014m^3 - 0.000121m^3 = 0.00132m^3$

Taking the volume and the measured size of the opening, the Helmholtz frequency of the *Gurumi* is approximately:

140

(6) $$f_H = \frac{c}{2\pi} \cdot \sqrt{\frac{r_0 \delta}{Volume}} = \frac{343 \frac{m}{s}}{2\pi} \cdot \sqrt{\frac{0.0125m \cdot 0.85}{0.00132m^3}} \approx 155 Hz$$

This frequency can be counterchecked by blowing over the opening and measuring the resulting sound with a spectrum analyzer. The Helmholtz-frequency was measured at about 153 Hz, so the calculated value is close to the actual measurement. As mentioned before, because the Helmholtz resonance is only defined for cavities with rigid walls, a membrane can directly influence the Helmholtz frequency. Dampening of the membrane with a finger at varying points changes the Helmholtz frequency in a range of about 30 Hz.

3.2.2 Measurements of the Gurumi

Figure 3a.1 and 3a.2 show the radiation patterns of the *Gurumi* when knocking on the membrane. The strings are damped, so only the body and the membrane can resonate.

As one can see in the figures 3a.1/3a.2, the calculated Helmholtz frequency of the *Gurumi* is not excited, but a coupling between a membrane mode and air mode can be seen at 182 Hz. To illustrate this, a measurement with the sound hole closed was taken and can be seen in figures 3b.1/3b.2.

As depicted in figure 3b.1/3b.2, the membrane mode at 182 Hz is still present but has a smaller amplitude than before. The other membrane mode can also be seen.

Figure 3c.1/3c.2 show the radiated sound spectrum of a plucked string with the fundamental frequency of 167 Hz. Figure 3c.1/3c.2 shows the expected behaviour. The fundamental tone of the plucked string is radiated in the frequency range of the coupled air membrane mode, whereas the first partial is radiated in the membrane only mode.

3.2.3 Intermediate results

As can be seen from figure 3a/b/c, the calculated Helmholtz frequency is not excited, neither from a knock on the membrane nor by a plucked string. An effect that supports the findings reported in (Bader & Pfeifle 2010) is that the mode of the membrane coupled to the air mode can be excited over a frequency range.

3.3 Gimbri

The *Gimbri* is a three-stringed lute from Mauretania. The body is covered by a membrane made from sheep skin. A two-legged wooden bridge supports the strings. This instrument is predominantly used by singers for their accompaniment. It is similar to other typical Griot lutes like the *Xalam* or *Ngoni* (lutes from the Maghreb, cf. Wegner, U. 1984). A part of the membrane is damped by the neck that runs underneath the sheep skin and acts as the string fixation at the opening of the membrane. Because of the dampening thereby effected, the duration of the tones played is shorter and they are a little bit darker and more percussive in sound compared to those of the *Gurumi*.

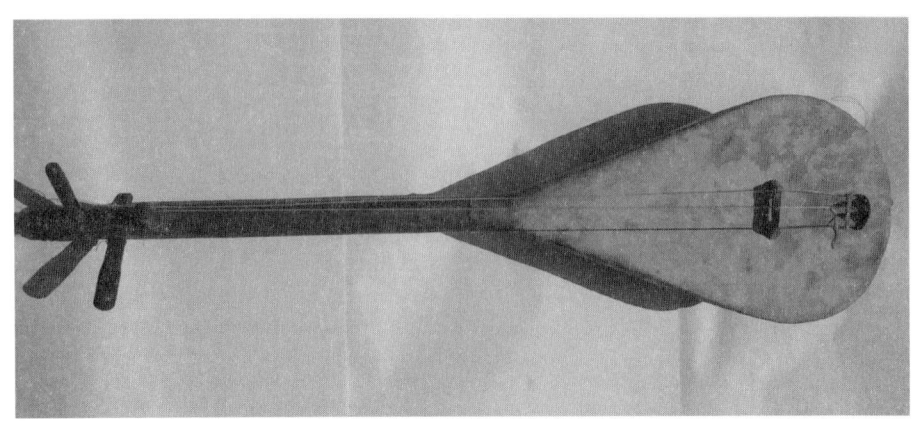

Fig. 4: *Gimbri* from Mauretania.

3.3.1 Helmholtz resonance and air modes of the Gimbri

Because the body of the *Gimbri* is irregularly shaped, its volume can only be approximated. So the Helmholtz frequency is measured by blowing over the opening. The resulting frequency is ≈ 85 *Hz*.

3.3.2 Measurements of the Gimbri

As in the measurements of the *Gurumi*, the strings are damped and the instrument is excited by a knock on the membrane. The resulting spectrum can be seen in figure 5a.1-4.

The radiation of the Helmholtz frequency can be seen in figure 5a.1. A coupled membrane air mode is depicted in figure 5a.2.

Figure 5a.3 shows modes of the neck under the membrane and modes of the membrane figure 5a.4.

Figure 5b.1-3 show the radiated spectrum when the instrument is excited by plucking a string, having a fundamental frequency of 135 *Hz*. The fundamental of the string at 135 *Hz* is radiated from the air hole and the membrane with a small amplitude compared to the second partial seen in figure 5b.2 and 5b.3 which is radiated only from the membrane.

3.3.3 Intermediate results for the Gimbri

As one can see from figure 5a/b, the Helmholtz frequency is excited when knocking on the membrane of the instrument. Similar to the *Gurumi*, a coupled air-membrane mode is excited (figure 5a.2).

The sound radiation pattern of the plucked string shows the expected behaviour. The fundamental and the partials are radiated in the specific mode shape range; since the second partial (401 *Hz*, figure 5b.3) is close to a resonance frequency peak of the membrane (378 *Hz*, figure 5a.3), it has a much larger amplitude than the other partials which are further afar from a resonance peak of a mode shape area.

3.4 Ruan

The *Ruan* is a four-stringed lute from China and one of the oldest Chinese string instruments (it is sometimes mentioned as the predecessor of the Pi'pa). Its round shaped body is made from wood and it has two sound holes on its front plate. The playing technique resembles the tremolo style of the Italian mandolin. It is mostly played with a plectrum made of animal horn or, more common nowadays, plastic. The *Ruan* is played in Chinese orchestral music as well as a solo instrument.

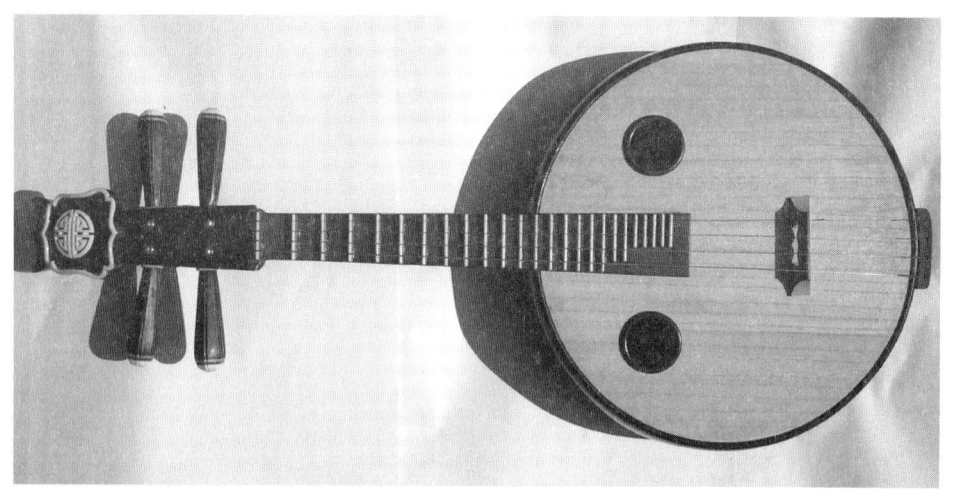

Fig. 6: *Ruan* from China.

3.4.1 Helmholtz resonance and air modes of the Ruan

The volume of the enclosed air can be approximated by calculating the volume of a equivalent cylinder:

(7) $\quad \pi \cdot r^2 \cdot height = \pi \cdot \left((0.17m)^2 \cdot 0.065m\right) = 0.0059 m^3$

The openings of the *Ruan* have a thickness of 1cm, therefore it is important to account for this parameter in the Helmholtz frequency formula. Following (Chanaud 1998) the Helmholtz formula in the extended notation by Rayleigh (Rayleigh 1926/1945) is

(8) $\quad f_H = \dfrac{c}{2\pi} \cdot \sqrt{\dfrac{A_O}{V \cdot (l_O + 2\delta_R)}}$,

where $\delta R = \delta * r_O$, l_O is the length, and A_O is the area of the openings. For the openings of the *Ruan* one can add the two areas of the sound holes ($A_{Og} = A_{O1} + A_{O2}$) to obtain an area-equivalent circle. The radius of that circle can now be calculated with

143

(9) $\quad r_{Og} = \sqrt{\dfrac{A_{Og}}{\pi}} = 0.0283m$.

With this and the known end correction the computed Helmholtz frequency is

(10) $\quad f_{H0} = \dfrac{343}{2\pi} \cdot \sqrt{\dfrac{2 \cdot (\pi \cdot 0.02^2)}{0.0059m^3 \cdot (0.01m + 2 \cdot 0.85 \cdot 0.0283m)}} = 147.8 Hz$

The Helmholtz resonance frequency of the *Ruan* when blowing over one of the holes is ≈147 *Hz*, so the computed and measured frequency are very similar.

3.4.2 Measurements of the Ruan

Figure 7a.1-6 show the vibrational behaviour of the *Ruan* resulting from a knock on the front plate. Then spectra resulting from a knock on the back plate will be adduced to reveal more details of the vibrational behaviour of the instruments (figure 8).

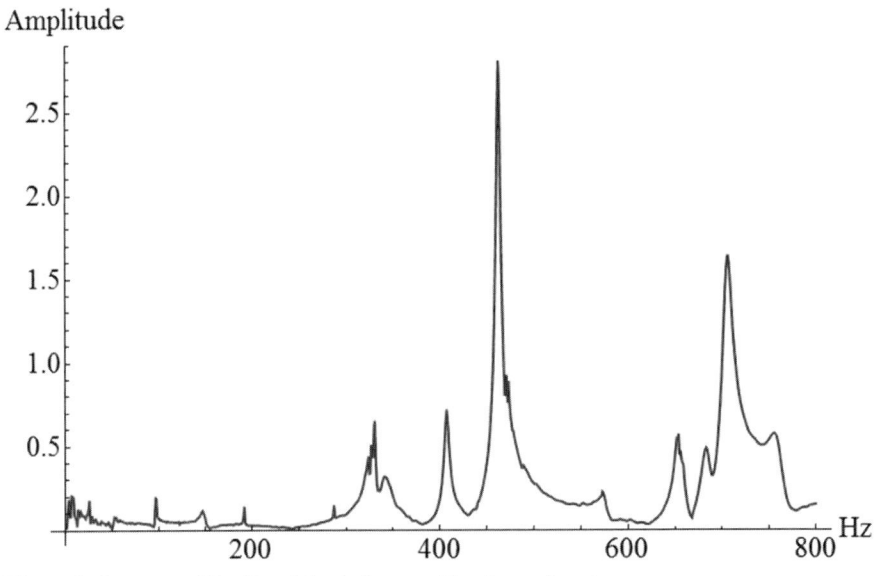

Figure 8: Spectrum of the *Ruan's* backplate resulting from a knock.

The radiation of the Helmholtz frequency through the sound holes can be seen in figure 7a.1. Three front-plate modes are visible in figures 7a.2-4. In figures 7a.5 and 7a.6 two modes are shown that are radiated almost exclusively through the sound holes.

If knocked on the backside, the *Ruan* produces spectra with several components that are identifiable by their peaks. As one can see in figure 8, two frequencies that are radiated through the holes on the front have strong peaks here. The data at hand might suggest that the spectral components at 465 *Hz* and 654 *Hz* are backplate modes. Some other resonances that might be attributed to vibrations of the backside can be also found in the frontal spectrum; however, to clarify whether those are backplate modes a third measurement was taken with one of the two frontal sound holes closed. A small towel was pushed into the right sound hole so that it was sealed and the volume of the cavity at the same time was reduced a bit. Taking the change in the sound hole area and the change in volume into account, the Helmholtz frequency had to be recalculated. With $r = 0.002$ the resulting Helmholtz frequency now is ≈107 *Hz*.

A knock on the front plate yielded the radiation patterns and the corresponding spectrum depicted in figure 9. As expected, the Helmholtz frequency can now be found at approximately 107 *Hz*.

The strong dual peak in the spectrum visible in figure 5a.2-3 and 7a.2-3 are two modes of similar radiation characteristics (0 nodal diameters, 1 nodal circle). These modes occur because of the non-isotropic characteristics of the wood. For the transversal wave propagation in the wooden front plate there are two different Youngs moduli in the x and the y direction.

Another effect becomes visible in figures 9a.4 and 9a.5: the modes visible in the pictures of the radiation patterns and indicated in the spectrum have a radiation characteristic that is similar to the modes depicted in figs. 7a.5 and 7a.6 above. Evidently, the mode frequencies relevant here are considerably lowered in case one of the openings is closed. To be sure, except for the two pairs of mode frequencies considered (575 *Hz* : 559 *Hz*; 652 *Hz* : 636 *Hz*), all other mode frequencies remain almost identical. Hence we may suppose that the two mode frequencies affected by closing one of the holes as well as changing the air volume contained in the cavity are those belonging to air modes.

4. Additional results and discussion

From the data and findings presented in this paper it is evident that the Helmholtz (resonance) frequency has been excited in two instruments, the *Ruan* and the *Gimbri*. The other two instruments, the *Gimbri* and the *Gurumi*, had a low air frequency that was coupled with a membrane mode. The most important finding, and the reason that has led to this research project, is that air modes in these lute-like instruments from Africa and China can be excited over a certain frequency range, a behaviour similar to the membrane of the banjo.

To illustrate the phenomenon in question further, the figures 7b.1/2 and 7c.1/2 show radiation patterns and the corresponding spectrum for the *Ruan* that emerge when the second and the third strings are plucked.

As is obvious from the spectrum (fig. 7b.1), the fundamental f_0 (first harmonic[3]) is by far the strongest component whereas the partial above the fundamental is much weaker. The radiation pattern (fig. 7b.1) indicates that the energy of the fundamental (which in this case does have the same frequency as the Helmholtz resonance) is radiated only through the sound holes while the next partial (2nd harmonic) is radiated in a mixed mode combining the air volume and a plate mode (fig. 7b.2).

---

[3] Due to some rather odd convention, the fundamental frequency of a harmonic complex sound or of a harmonic complex vibration is labeled f_0. Of course, the first harmonic is not the „nullest" partial.

Figures 7c.1/2 show the radiation behaviour of the third string. Here the fundamental f_0 is radiated through the holes but has a much smaller amplitude compared to the second string because the fundamental frequency is further away from the resonance peak of the Helmholtz. More energy is radiated in the second harmonic (fig. 7c.2).

5. Conclusion

This work has shown that previous findings that had been made on the membrane of the banjo (Bader & Pfeifle 2010) can be extended to air resonances of the cavities of the three lute-like instruments under investigation. There are several questions that arise from this work. The first and most important is the influence of an elastic cavity wall (a membrane) on the behaviour of the Helmholtz resonance and air modes. It is feasible to suppose that the moving membrane not only changes the volume of the enclosed air, an effect that can presumably be neglected because of the small amount of deflection of the membrane and the resulting small change in volume, but because of a forced excitation of the air volume through the movement of the membrane. As already mentioned in the measurements of the *Gurumi* and the *Gimbri*, the Helmholtz frequency changed drastically when the membrane was stiffened, so a further investigation of this effect would be worthwhile.

References

Bader, Rolf 2010. Reconstruction of Radiating Sound Fields using minimum Energy Method. *Jounal Acoust. Soc. Am*. 127, 300-308.

Bader, Rolf, Florian Pfeifle 2010. Membrane modes and air resonances of the banjo using physical modeling and microphone array measurements. *Journal Am. Acoust. Soc.* 127, 1870.

Carlin, Bob 2007. *The Birth of the Banjo. Joel Walker Sweeney and Early Minstrelsy*. Jefferson, NC: McFarland & Company, Inc.

Chanaud, R.C. 1994. Effects of Geomtery on the Resonance Frequency of Helmholtz Resonators. *Journal of Sound & Vibration*, 178, No. 3, 337-348,

Conway, Cecelia 2003. Black banjo songsters in Appalachia. *Black music research journal,* 23 (2003), Nr. 1-2.

Fletcher, Neville, Thomas Rossing 1990, 2000. *The Physics of musical instruments*. New York: Springer (2nd ed. 2000).

Gura, Philip F., James F. Bollman 1999, *America's instrument. The banjo in the Nineteenth Century.* Chapel Hill and London: The University of North Carolina Press.

Helmholtz, Hermann von 1870. *Die Lehre von den Tonempfindungen als physiologische Grundlage für die Theorie der Musik.* 3. Aufl. Braunschweig: Vieweg.

Hendler, Maximilian 1995. *Banjo. Altweltliche Wurzeln eines neuweltlichen Musikinstrumentes. Verschüttete Spuren zur Vor- und Frühgeschichte der Saiteninstrumente.* (=Afro-Amerikanische Schriften Bd. 1, hrsg. Von A. Dauer). Goettingen: Edition RE.

Hutchings, C.M. 1981. Klang und Akustik der Geige. *Spektrum der Wissenschaft* 12/1981, Dezember, 112 -122. original: *Scientific American*, October 1981

Ingard, K. U. 1953. On the theory and design of acoustic resonators. *Jounal Acoust. Soc. Am.* 25, 1037-1061.

Lomax, A. 2006. *American Patchwork: Appalachian Journey*. DVD Documentary.

Rayleigh, John William Strutt 1894/1926/1945. *Theory of Sound* (in 2 vols). London: Macmillan 1894 (2nd rev. and enlarged ed. 1926; repr. New York: Dover Publ. 1945).

Selamet, A., P.M. Radavich 1997. Circular concentric Helmholtz resonators. *Journal. Acoust. Soc. Am.* 101, 41-51.

Wegner, Ulrich 1984. *Afrikanische Saiteninstrumente*. Berlin: Staatliche Museen Preußischer Kulturbesitz.

Figures

In the following figures, the colours in the background of the spectra indicate frequency bands within which certain membrane modes can be elicited. The modes (m, n for m nodal diameters and n nodal circles) for each frequency band are given in brackets.

For comparison, Figure 1 shows the respective modes and five frequency bands (roughly, from 150 *Hz* to 1200 *Hz*) for a banjo membrane. Mode (0, 1) covers a frequency band from ca. 150 Hz to 370 *Hz*, mode (1, 1) from 410 *Hz* to 580 *Hz*, etc.

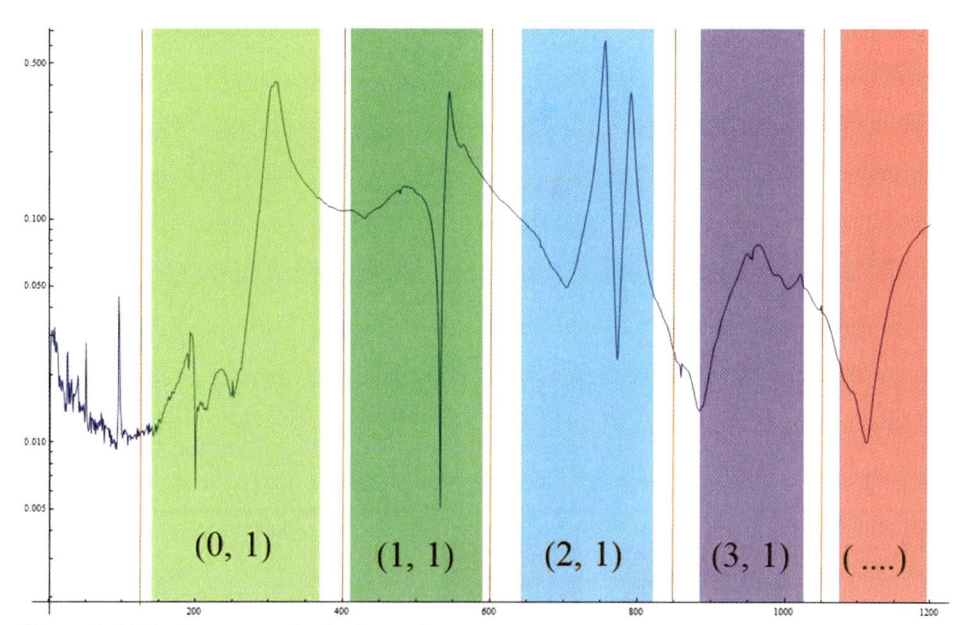

Figure 1: Mode shape areas of a *Banjo* membrane

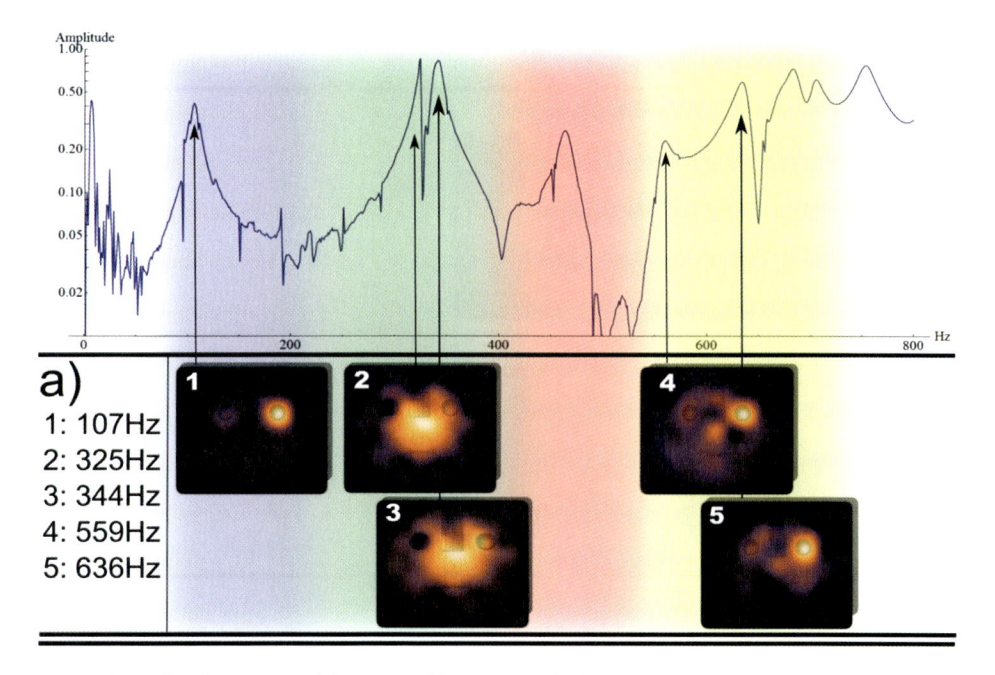

a)
1: 107Hz
2: 325Hz
3: 344Hz
4: 559Hz
5: 636Hz

Figure 9: Radiated spectrum of the *Ruan* with one sound hole closed.

149

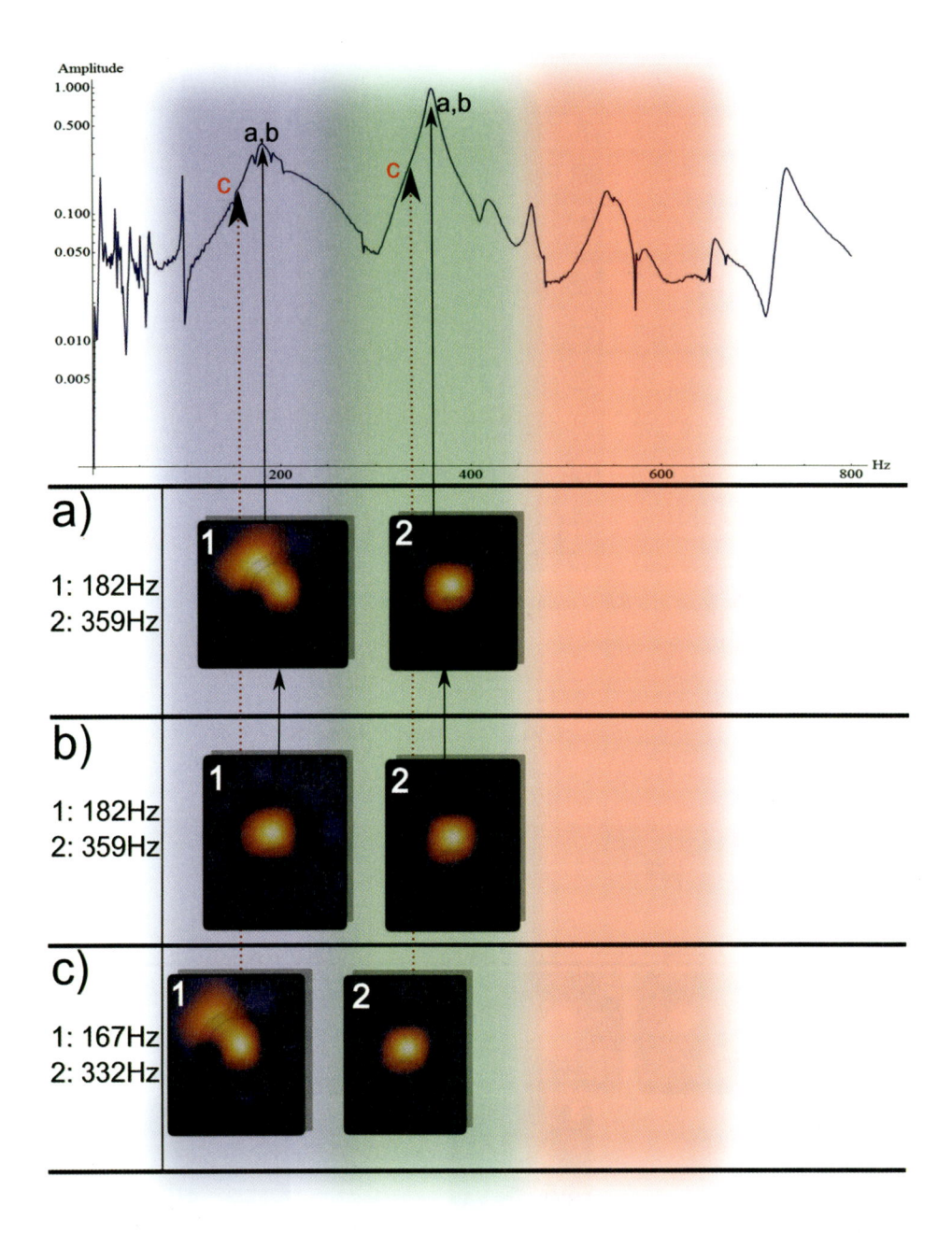

Figure 3: *Gurumi* measurements: a) knock on the membrane open sound hole. b) knock on the membrane closed sound hole c) plucked string, fundamental 167*Hz*

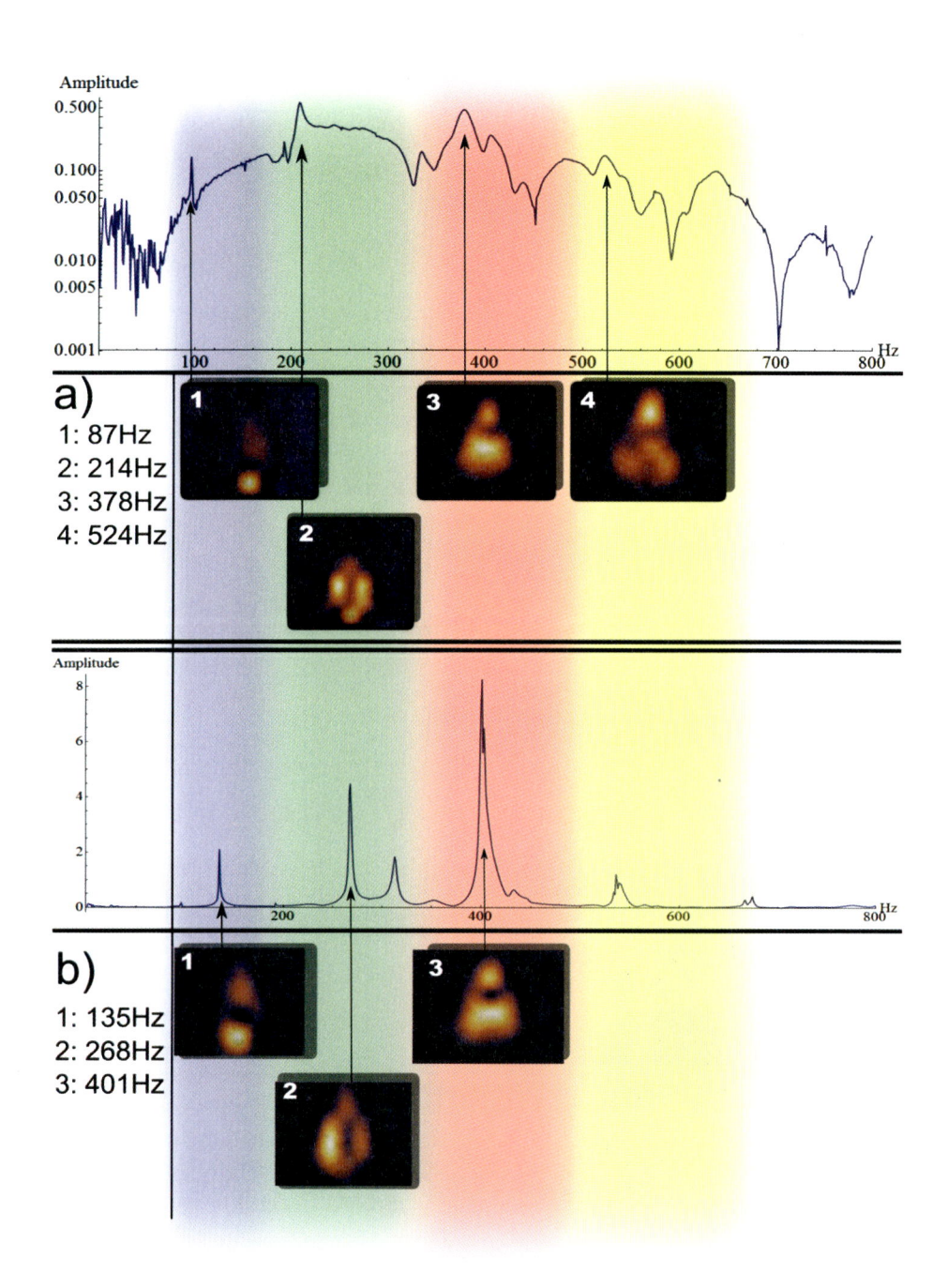

Figure 5: Spectrum and radiation patterns of the *Gimbri*.

151

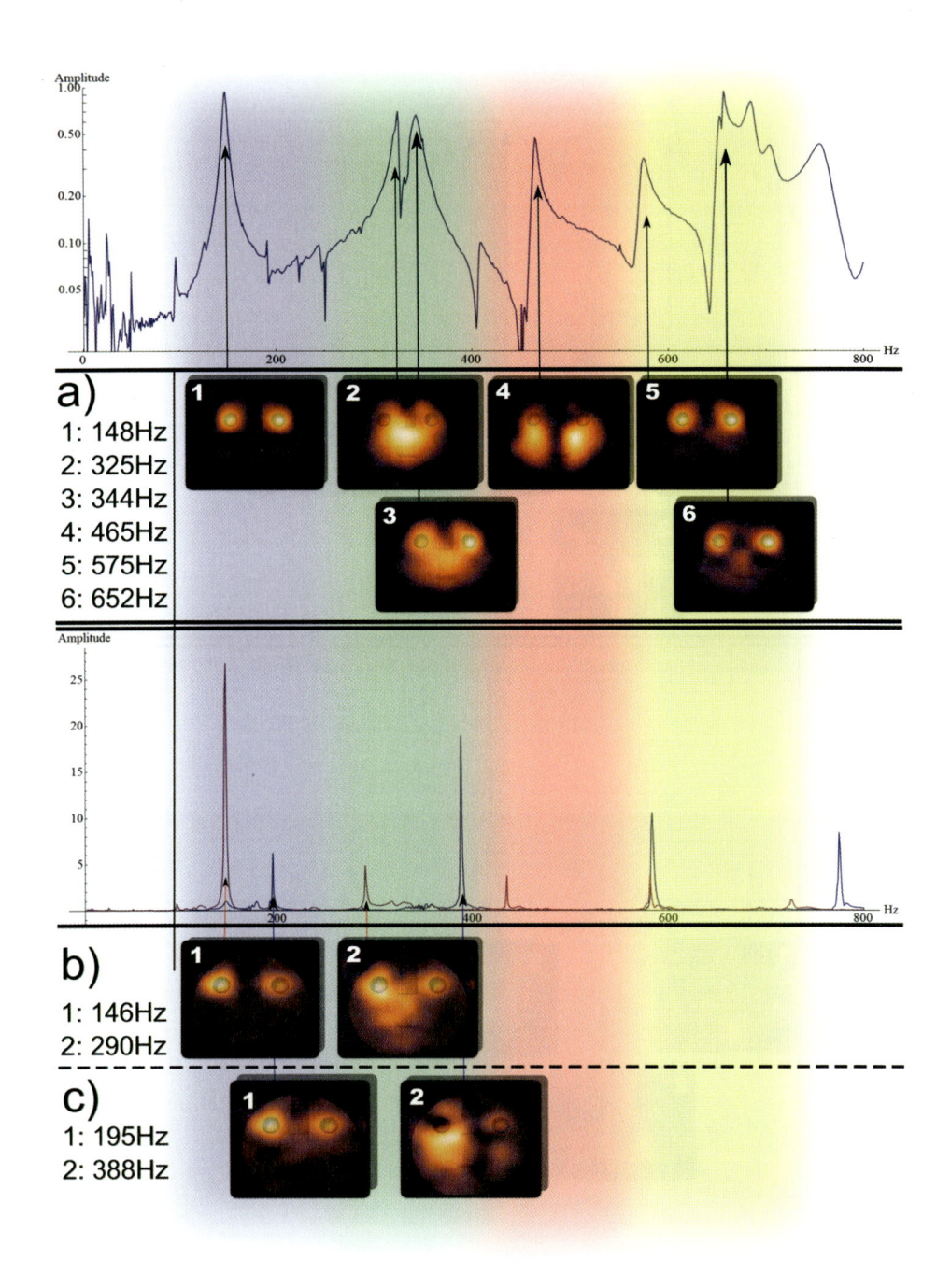

Figure 7: Spectrum and radiation patterns of the *Ruan*.

Tim Ziemer

Psychoacoustic Effects in Wave Field Synthesis Applications

Abstract

The present article compares ideas and methods of conventional audio techniques with wave field synthesis. Considering application areas and resulting needs of the listeners, psychoacoustic deliberations are derived to improve wave field synthesis, especially for musical performances with a small number of loudspeakers. A listening test shows the potential of combining wave field synthesis with systematically involved psychoacoustic deliberations.

Introduction

Wave field synthesis (WFS) is an audio reproducing technique which aims to physically recreate a natural wave field in a wide listening area. So far WFS is still in a state of research and development, not many WFS systems are available on the open market[1]. Wave field synthesis systems have numerous potential application areas[2]:
- Laboratories for matters of research and development
- Cinema/Theatre
- Clubs/Concert halls
- Conference Rooms/Lecture halls
- Car
- Virtual reality environments/Planetaria
- Home cinema/music installation

To date most of these areas are served by conventional audio systems such as stereo or 5.1 surround.

Functional principle of conventional audio systems

Conventional audio systems like stereo and 5.1 surround are usually based on either amplitude panning or time based panning between a pair of loudspeakers. Sometimes a combination of both panning techniques is used. As a result a virtual source ("phantom source") can be placed on the connection line between the two loudspeakers (the "loudspeaker base"). The wave field created by this technique is different from a natural wave field which would emerge from a real source at that position. But the human auditory system interprets the two loudspeaker signals in a way that is predictable due to years of research with listening tests[3]. This led to panning laws with quite good localization results of the phantom sources.

---

[1] To my knowledge only Fraunhofer sells WFS systems, see IOSONO.
[2] Concrete examples are itemized e.g. in IOSONO, Slavik/Weinzierl 2008, Audi AG 2010.
[3] Systematized in Blauert 1974.

A good localization, natural timbre, dynamics and temporal progress and real-time capability are the great advantages of conventional audio systems. But the main disadvantage is the restriction to one ideal listening position (the so-called "sweet spot"). Outside the sweet spot a listener localizes the phantom sources incorrectly. Furthermore conventional panning techniques show bad results for lateral phantom sources – so no real surround sound is possible due to missing lateral source positions and reflections.
Wave field synthesis can fill this gap and additionally overcome the sweet-spot restriction.

Functional principle of wave field synthesis

WFS is based on Green's second theorem (which describes the coherence between a function over a volume and the function over its surface) applied to the wave equation. This theoretically allows to create any wave field inside a volume if its complete surface has a controllable sound radiation, so a whole three-dimensional sound envelopment can be synthesized in a sense of holophony (similar to the idea of a visual holography). In this case no psychoacoustic considerations would be needed since the synthesized wave field equals a natural wave field.

But this approach demands an infinite number of sources completely surrounding a listening area. Actual applications use a finite number of loudspeakers with discrete positions, often arranged one- or two-dimensional only. This leads to synthesis errors like truncation and aliasing artifacts and a missing representation of height[4]. These synthesis errors result in wave fronts which arrive belatedly at the listening area, have unwanted propagation directions and contain the frequencies above the aliasing frequency. The errors are audible as high-pass echoes, which lead to an unwanted sound coloration, a disturbed localization or even the impression of several source positions[5].

Raising the number of loudspeakers to reduce the distance between them and to surround a listening area from all dimensions minimizes those errors. This led to WFS systems with hundreds of loudspeakers. But a great quantity of loudspeakers can also be a disadvantage for several reasons:
- Financial reasons (High acquisition costs for loudspeakers, installation and a computer with sufficient computational power)
- Aesthetic/visual/spatial reasons (A great quantity of loudspeakers may take up space, block the view or disturb the interior design)
- Performance practice (Real-time processing is difficult to achieve, since the signal for each loudspeaker is calculated individually from the same source signals: The more loudspeakers, the more simultaneous calculations are needed)
- Erroneous room reflections (The reflections of the loudspeakers do not correspond to the reflections of a source on the virtual source position. These erroneous reflections disturb locatability, sound color and spatial properties of the sound. This effect becomes worse the more loudspeakers are in use)

---

[4] See e.g. Ahrens/Rabenstein/Spors 2008.
[5] See Wierstorf/Spors/Raake 2010.

- Thermotechnical reasons (A high number of loudspeakers, amplifiers and computers generate heat which can make rooms unpleasantly warm and destroys the wave field synthesis if the temperature change – and thereby sound velocity change – is not considered within the calculation. Or disturbing noise is generated when cooling the room with air-conditioning.)

Especially for private use like home cinema or car, as well as for small applications like little clubs, chamber music halls or small laboratories, these disadvantages overweight the benefits. This means for many application areas there is a need to reduce the number of loudspeakers while keeping the sound quality in the listening area satisfying. One promising approach is to combine wave field synthesis with psychoacoustic techniques. Such a "psychoacoustic wave field synthesis" is only possible if the needs of the listeners are known.

Needs of the listeners

By physically reconstructing a natural wave field, one is always on the save side; if all physical parameters are recreated correctly, the perception will be as well. But due to unavoidable synthesis errors and a high effort it is meaningful to develop a wave field synthesis with systematic synthesis errors: Errors that are not audible by human listeners. Inventions like amplitude panning and mp3 established themselves because they systematized the coherence between physical nature and psychoacoustic nature of sound. The reproduced sound is not equal to the original sound but people unconsciously interpret it in a predictable way.

Many of the application areas enumerated above have musical aims exclusively or among other aims. Therefore the features of musical instruments are to be recreated by an audio system for all possible source positions, considering the acoustics of the performance room. Ideally these features are recreated for an extended listening area, so several listeners can have a natural listening experience, even when moving through the room.

The features of instrumental sounds are[6]:
- musical scale
- dynamics
- timbre of sound
- time envelope of the sound
- sound radiation characteristics

The first four features are easily reproducible by simply recording and playing back an instrumental sound by microphone and loudspeaker with flat frequency- and phase-response. But the sound radiation characteristic is represented by neither the panning laws nor conventional recording techniques.

The radiation characteristic leads to different amplitudes and phases per frequency and angle around the instrument. By this binaural signal the listener gets an impression about the "viewing direction" and width of the instrument. It makes the sound vivid and spatial. Once the radiation characteristic of an instrument is determined it can be calculated for any direction, reproduced from any mono signal and implemented into a wave

---

[6] According to Kostek 2005, 24.

field synthesis. It is determinable by simultaneously recording an instrument's sound from all directions[7] or by physically modeling the instrument. Then the wave field synthesis models the instrument as virtual point source with the measured directional radiation characteristic.

The room acoustics of the performance room can be recreated from impulse responses, from physical modeling of the room or from a combination of both approaches. Mirror sources are an easy way to recreate the early reflections of a room; for the late reverberation a simple reverb algorithm with the sound coloration of the impulse response is adequate.

Psychoacoustic criteria for wave field synthesis

The features of instrumental sounds do not necessarily have to be synthesized exactly in the whole listening area. Since the sound shall be satisfying for human listeners, only the perceived part of the physical sound needs to equal a natural situation. The auditory system entails certain peculiarities in regard to processing of sound which give us a clue which parameters need to be reconstructed and which are not. These peculiarities (critical bands, masking, auditory stream segregation) will be explained in detail later in this section.

Eliminating time: Wave field synthesis in the time domain needs a windowing mechanism which mutes all loudspeakers whose designated contribution to the wave field synthesis takes effect outside of the listening area only (i.e. whose position is on the opposite side of the virtual source position related to the listening area). If not muted, these speakers would only create a delayed sound with the wrong propagation direction since their contribution to the wave front curvature begins behind the listening area. This windowing always reduces the number of used loudspeakers.

In a loudspeaker system where the number of loudspeakers is already reduced, any speaker is indispensable, so a solution is needed which includes all speakers. An elegant way is to calculate the signals in frequency domain where the temporal aspect is eliminated. Then the wave field at the listening positions is the superposition of the loudspeaker spectra. Transforming these back to time domain offers a correct synthesis for stationary sounds. But since in music and speech quasi-stationary sounds do not last long the listening positions are to be close to another with similar distance to every speaker under consideration of sonic speed. For this case the solution stays approximately correct.

Critical bands (CB): The auditory sense processes sound not as a whole but in frequency bands[8]. Therefore it is reasonable to treat sounds in critical bands according to the Bark scale or to one third octave bands. Also the radiation characteristic of musical instruments is similar for frequencies within this interval.

Masking: Within those critical bands and between adjacent bands simultaneous masking appears. This means there is no need to treat all frequency components in one

---

[7] As done in the listening test, described in the following sections. Further information on the recording setup, see Bader 2010.
[8] See e.g. Moore 2008, Blauert 1974, 173 and Kostek 2005, 9.

band since the loudest component tends to mask all other found within the same CB[9]. This reduces the number of frequencies to be calculated to 25 (the loudest frequency per critical band).

Auditory Stream segregation: In the auditory system, complex signals are split vertically into frequency bands (corresponding, in principle, to critical bands) and horizontally into (speech or melody) phrases or into types of 'chunks'. Hence complex signals are analyzed according to psychoacoustic and cognitive processes, which designnate whether sounds are integrated into one auditory stream or segregated into different auditory streams[10]. Parameters for this grouping are especially:
- Closure
- Comparisons with other senses (esp. visual sense)
- Connectedness
- Gestaltpsychological aspects
  - Common fate
  - Similarity
  - Temporal and spatial proximity
- Harmonicity
- Intensity
- Spatial origin
- Timbre
- Pitch

Proximity of successive sounds leads to the impression of one common source. This explains the summing localization[11]. Sounds with synchronized on- and offset integrate into one stream and are heard as one complex sound, especially when they share pitch glides or micromodulations. So it can make the source position more clear if several frequency bands integrate into one stream, each band hinting at the same source position.

Precedence Effect: The precedence effect indicates that the sound events are localized solely in the direction of the first wave front arriving at the ears, so a frontal sound is localized correctly, even if lateral reflections reach the ear, since the first wavefront was already crucial for the localization. Premise is that the first and second arriving signal are integrated into one common auditory stream. If the arrival time interval is too big or the sounds distinctly distinguish in other parameters of the abovementioned list, separate sources are audible. The precedence effect can last for seconds and more[12].

Implementation of a psychoacoustic wave field synthesis

The above-mentioned deliberations are put into practice in an initial psychoacoustic wave field synthesis application with 15 loudspeakers with a distance of 0.65m between adjacent speakers, surrounding a 4m² sized listening area from three sides (see fig. 1). Q denotes the virtual source position, the contour with the arrow denote the viewing

---

[9] See Moore 2009.
[10] A comprehensive account of such processes is given by Bregman 1990.
[11] See Strube 1985, 69.
[12] See Blauert 1974, 224.

direction and the instrument's radiation characteristic. Y_{1-15} are the inwards facing loudspeakers, X_{1-15} are the listening positions which span the listening area. The following steps are the basis for a wave field synthesis[13]:

First the radiation characteristic of an instrument has to be detected for all frequency bands. Then the instrumental sound signal to be synthesized is transformed into the frequency domain, split into critical bands and the loudest frequency per band is chosen. The wave field for one frequency, excited by the instrumental sound for a given listening position, can be calculated by multiplying this sound with the directional factor and propagating it by means of a spherical wave. This value is to be created by the superposition of all loudspeaker signals to realize a wave field synthesis in frequency domain. This has to be done for all frequency bands. An inverse Fourier transform delivers the loudspeaker signals in time domain.

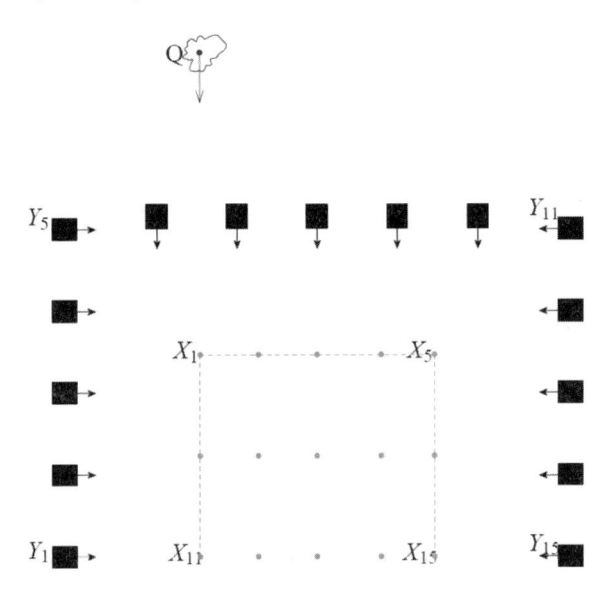

Figure1: Setup of the psychoacoustic wave field synthesis system.

Under neglect of room reflections the wave field is synthesized correctly in the frequency domain. But since the signals reach the listener position from several directions at different points in time, the precedence effect tends to steer the localization towards the nearest loudspeaker.

This effect is unwanted but its initiator can be used: The loudspeaker whose direction is most similar to the direction of the virtual source position (from the central listening position) plays his sound while the other loudspeaker signals fade in ("precedence-fade"). Due to summing localization the signals should still be perceived as coming from one common source. The duration of the fade is chosen to be long enough so that at any listening position the unfaded signal arrives before the first faded signal is faded in

---

[13] A detailed description is given in T. Ziemer, Octupole Speaker System.

completely. Furthermore the function has to be short enough for summing localization to occur and for the precedence effect to appear, which means a maximum of about 50 to 65ms[14].

In an initial test an exponential fading function was used to compare the psychoacoustic wave field synthesis with mono and stereo. Two groups of listeners, each consisting of five subjects, were asked to arbitrarily choose a position in the listening area. There they were allowed to turn torso and head during the test, as long as they do not move their feet. The subjects were advised to mark their own position and viewing direction and – during or after the musical presentation – the perceived source position or area on a map[15]. A violin piece was presented successively first in mono, then in stereo and in psychoacoustic WFS. The subjects are additionally asked if more than one source has been localized, how "natural" the sound appears (on a scale ranging from 1 "entirely unnatural" to 5 "entirely natural") and how spatial it sounds (on a range from 1 "not a bit" to 4 "very spatial"). These qualities were not described further so the subjects had to answer according to their own interpretation and did not pay attention to specific parameters of the sound.

The dots, connected by the bold lines, denote the loudspeaker positions. The gray lines every 10° are drawn for a better orientation. The gray bold rectangle is the listening area, the anthracite plot shows the number of subjects who localized the source at that angle. The dashed circles lie at 3, 5 and 7 subjects. The frame around the map shows the room walls. Adjacent to the figures the answers of the questionnaire are summarized for each performance.

As can be seen from fig. 2, the mono source is located quite correctly within a small area. All subjects perceived one distinct source position with a medium degree of naturalness and small to medium degree of spaciousness.

The range of perceived source positions in case of the stereo example is bigger than for mono (see fig. 3). This coincides with the inferior perceived distinctness. Furthermore half of the probands perceived several sources. Most salient of the stereo example is that the commonest perceived angle is not in the region of the phantom source but of the active speaker which is closer to the listening area. Stereo obviously suffers under the precedence effect since most probands are beyond the sweet spot. The sound is rated more naturally and spaciously sounding than the mono sound.

Figure 4 shows that the psychoacoustic WFS leads to a rather correct localization of the virtual source for most subjects but eight of ten perceived more than one source. A second region protrudes 90° shifted. The absolute distribution is wider than in the stereo or mono example. It has distinct heaps and valleys. The degree of spaciousness is higher than for mono and stereo but at the cost of distinctness. The naturalness is smaller than for the conventional audio performances.

---

[14] According to Blauert 1974, 180, an arrival time difference of 50ms or more leads to the impression of different sources, according to Dickreiter 1987, 129, an arrival time difference of more than 65ms leads to separately audible sound. Since the sounds are faded and not delayed, the fading maximal duration may be even longer.

[15] The plots with the results are projected on this map, see fig. 2 to 4.

Mono

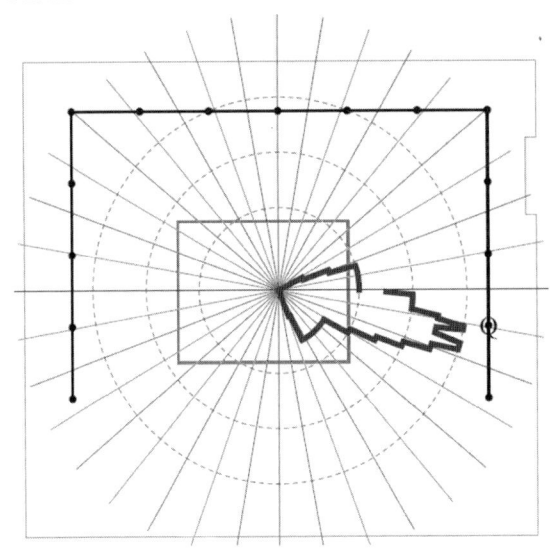

Figure 2: Perceived source direction of the musical performance in mono.

Several sources?
[0] "Yes" [10] "No"

Distinctness:
[0] 1 [0] 2 [0] 3 [5] 4 [5] 5
Modus: 4 and 5, Median: 4 to 5,
ar. Mean: 4.5

Naturalness:
[0] 1 [3] 2 [7] 3 [0] 4 [0] 5
Modus: 3, Median: 3,
ar. Mean: 2.7

Spaciousness:
[2] 1 [2] 2 [5] 3 [1] 4
Modus: 3, Median: 3,
ar. Mean: 2.5

Stereo

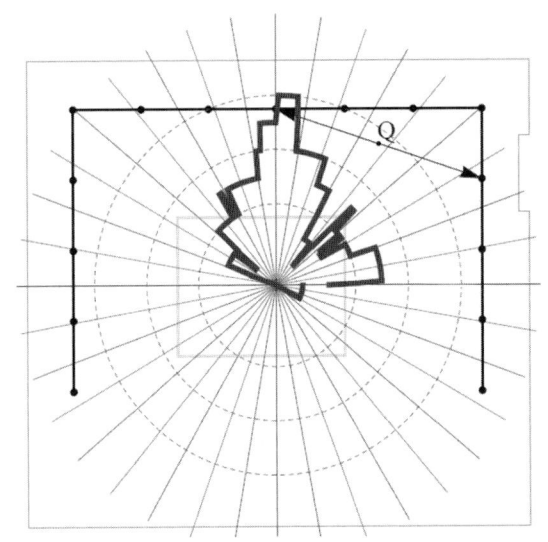

Figure 3: Perceived source direction of the musical performance in stereo.

Several sources?
[5] "Yes" [5] "No"

Distinctness:
[0] 1 [0] 2 [6] 3 [2] 4 [2] 5
Modus: 3, Median: 3,
ar. Mean: 3.6

Naturalness:
[0] 1 [1] 2 [7] 3 [2] 4 [0] 5
Modus: 3, Median: 3,
ar. Mean: 3.1

Spaciousness:
[0] 1 [4] 2 [5] 3 [1] 4
Modus: 3, Median: 3,
ar. Mean: 2.7

Psych. WFS

Several sources?
[8] "Yes" [2] "No"

Distinctness:
[0] 1 [7] 2 [1] 3 [2] 4 [0] 5
Modus: 2, Median: 2,
ar. Mean: 2.5

Naturalness: [2] 1 [3] 2 [3] 3
[2] 4 [0] 5
Modus: 2 and 3, Median: 2 to 3,
ar. Mean: 2.5

Spaciousness:
[1] 1 [1] 2 [4] 3 [4] 4
Modus: 3 and 4, Median: 3,
ar. Mean: 3.1

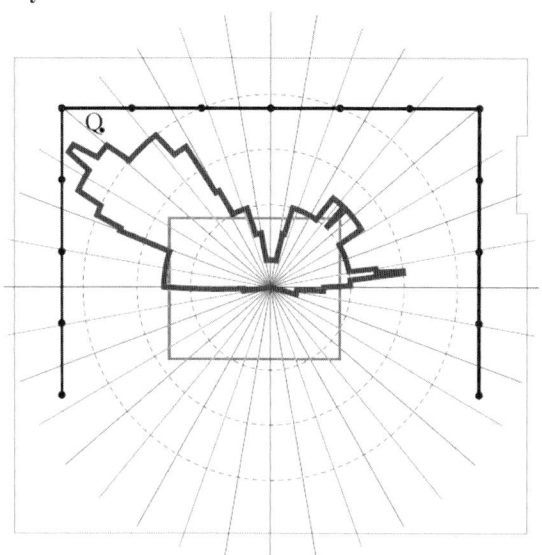

Figure 4: Perceived source direction of the musical performance with psychoacoustic wave field synthesis.

Conclusion

Knowledge about the human auditory system is already used in conventional audio systems like stereo. Wave field synthesis can widen the listening area and add the radiation characteristic of sources for a more natural performance. But artifacts become audible unless the number of loudspeakers is massively raised and consequently also the computational power and installation and operation costs. Combining wave field synthesis with psychoacoustic considerations is a way to keep the number of speakers small without losing fidelity. The basic psychoacoustic processes are already well-investigated and can be used for a satisfying psychoacoustic wave field synthesis. The preliminary listening test shows the potential of psychoacoustic considerations for wave field synthesis applications, especially with a small number of loudspeakers.

Further investigations, especially on the precedence effect for faded sounds, can make small psychoacoustic wave field synthesis application a competitive alternative to stereo and surround sound systems.

Further studies may answer current questions on the precedence fade:
– What fading function offers the best results?
– What fading duration offers the best results?
– Can different fading durations per loudspeaker improve the localization? (e.g. a fading duration for each loudspeaker which is shorter, the closer a loudspeaker lies towards the virtual source position → this conforms a "fading based panning", similar to time based panning or amplitude based panning in conventional stereo applications).

- Are different fading durations per frequency band meaningful? (the precedence effect may have a frequency dependency, as time based panning has).
- Is it useful to leave more than one loudspeaker signal unfaded for special cases? (e.g. if the virtual source position lies centered between two loudspeakers).

Literature

Ahrens, Jens & Sascha Spors 2008. Reproduction of a Plane-Wave Sound Field using Planar and Linear Arrays of Loudspeakers", on: *www.deutsche-telekom-laboratories.de/~sporssas/ publications/2008/Ahrens_Spors_ISCCSP08.pdf, 2008* – visited on 01.09.2010.

Ahrens, Jens, Rudolph Rabenstein & Sascha Spors 2008. The Theory of Wave Field Synthesis Revisited, in: *Audio Engineering Society Convention 124, 2008.*

Audi AG 2010. Neue Wege für den perfekten Klang. Die HiFi-Kompetenz bei Audi", on: *http://www.audi.de/de/brand/de/unternehmen/aktuelles.detail.2010~06~neue_wege_fuer_den.html 2010* (visited 05.05.2011).

Bader, Rolf 2010. Reconstruction of radiating sound fields using minimum energy method. *Journal of the Acoustical Society of America* 127, 300–308.

Berkhout, A. J. 1988. A Holographic Approach to Acoustic Control. *J. Audio Eng. Soc,* 36 (No. 12), 977–995.

Blauert, Jens 1974. *Räumliches Hören*, Stuttgart; Hirzel 1974.

Blauert, Jens 1985. *Räumliches Hören. Nachschrift - Neue Ergebnisse und Trends seit 1972*, Stuttgart: Hirzel 1985.

Bregman, Albert S. 1990. *Auditory Scene Analysis,* Cambridge, London: MIT Pr.

Dickreiter, Michael 1987. *Handbuch der Tonstudiotechnik,* Volume 1, 5th edition, München et al.: Saur.

IOSONO GmbH: "IOSONO for", on: *http://www.iosono-sound.com/* – visited on 23.01.2011.

Kostek, Bozena 2005. *Perception-Based Data Processing in Acoustics,* Berlin, New York: Springer.

Moore, Brian 2008. *Introduction to the psychology of hearing*. 5th ed. Bingley: Emerald.

Slavik, Karl & Stefan Weinzierl 2008. Wiedergabeverfahren, In Stefan Weinzierl (Hrsg.). *Handbuch der Audiotechnik*, Berlin, New York: Springer, 609–686.

Strube, Gerhard 1985. Lokalisation von Schallereignissen. In Herbert Bruhn, Rolf Oerter & Helmut Rösing: *Musikpsychologie. Ein Handbuch in Schlüsselbegriffen,* München, Wien: Urban & Schwarzenberg, 65-69.

Wierstorf, Hagen, Sascha Spors & Alexander Raake 2010. Die Rolle des Präzedenzeffektes bei der Wahrnehmung von räumlichen Aliasingartefakten bei der Wellenfeldsynthese", on: *http://www.deutsche-telekom-laboratories.de/~sporssas/publications/2010/Wierstorf_etal_ DAGA2010_praezedenzeffekt_aliasing_WFS.pdf* (visited 01.09.2010).

Ziemer, Tim 2009. Wave Field Synthesis by an Octupole Speaker System. Proceedings *SysMus09,* Ghent 2009, 89–93.

Orie Takada

Sound Radiation Patterns in Classical Singing Styles

Summary

Most musical instruments exhibit complex patterns of sound radiation, which change with direction, pitches played and other factors. The same holds true for the body of a singer (regarded as an instrument) singing with her or his voice but activating also parts of the chest, face, etc. A topic addressed in this paper is whether there are differences between ‚classical' and other styles of singing in regard to sound production and sound radiation. Changing patterns of sound radiation relating to 'chest voice' and 'head voice' as well as to 'Belcanto' and the so-called 'German singing-technique' were investigated with a microphone array comprising 128 microphones. The intonation of three tones (B3, B4, F5) shows that radiation patterns of the female singing voice depend on the vocal technique and the type of the vocalization employed, and on the pitch of the tone that is sung.

1. Introduction

In the available literature singing is analyzed from both a theoretical and practical point of view. For example, such books may discuss acoustical, physiological and phonatory aspects of singing (e.g., Sundberg 1987/1997). Very few studies as yet are directed to cognitive issues involved in singing though this is also an important field that needs to be studied. Further, motor control as related to cognition is of interest since any singer must learn in lessons and through exercises to control and coordinate those parts of the body relevant to sound production in singing. This implies that the singer knows which muscles, tendons, etc. must be activated, and to which degree, in order to shape the sound of the singing voice according to a certain style of music as well as to certain expressive features. In regard to measurable differences, it can be expected that the pattern of sound radiation changes if a singer adopts a different vocal technique or sings notes in a different register. Also, singers at times remark that certain parts of her or his body tend to vibrate while singing, and that the degree of such vibrations varies in line with the vocal technique employed. Hence there are indications that sound radiation from singers must not be restricted to the mouth though one may expect a maximum of energy radiated from there. To explore such issues, a research project reported in some preliminary form in this article was started (the author herself being a professional singer trained in "classical" music genres). One of the aspects investigated is if the radiation pattern of a singer's voice can be varied (in similar ways as the radiation pattern of instruments can be influenced by musicians), and to find the degree to which such variation is possible. Another, more general aspect is to further our understanding of physiological and other functions relevant to control the singer's body as well as the actual sound produced in singing.

2. Material and Methods

In the next paragraph, I will briefly introduce the objects of research in a descriptive way to allow for better understanding. Then I will present methods used in the analysis of the material.

2.1 Objects of research

Currently, I have been examining the differences between the radiation pattern of two types of voice registers known from their respective resonance areas as 'head voice' and 'chest voice'. Though these terms are widely used in a descriptive way, there seems to be no general definition for their utilization. In practice, the head voice is often used by female singers in classical singing, and in particular when producing notes in higher octaves. The chest voice is usually employed for notes in a lower frequency range. In addition to 'head voice' and 'chest voice', I also explore two different classical vocal techniques, namely 'Belcanto' (of Italian origin) and the so-called 'German singing technique'. The term 'Belcanto' unfortunately is also not clearly defined and thus is used for a range of phenomena. However, it is the most popular classical (mainly operatic) singing technique in the world and most classical singers are trained in this singing method at conservatories or similar music educational institutions. For performing in Belcanto style, it is important to have "sensations of openness in the nasopharynx" in order to open the throat area widely (Miller 1997, 78).The technique of "singing in the mask" is known as the most essential term for the Belcanto. What this "singing in the mask" means in practice is singing toward the paranasal sinuses (cf. Schiller-Institut 1996, 154) to the effect that the brilliant voice of the Belcanto should occur through this Italian singing method. The so-called 'German singing technique' also calls for opening the throat area. What differentiates it from Belcanto is the principle of singing toward the rear (of the head). One of the known pedagogical methods for this is "up the throat wall into the dome of the skull" (Miller 1997, 70).

For my investigation of the two voice registers ('head voice' and 'chest voice') I chose the note/tone B3, and for the two singing techniques, 'Belcanto' and 'German', I used the tones B4 and F5. For each trial I recorded my own singing voice and always sang the vowel "a".

2.2. Analysis Technique

In order to explore possible differences in singing style and register, the radiation pattern of the sound produced from singing was chosen as an acoustic parameter that is accessible through objective methods. For the study reported in this article, an 'acoustic camera' comprising an array of 128 microphones (developed at the Institute of Musicology, University of Hamburg) was employed. The array spacing is a regular grid with a grid constant of 3.9 cm. All microphones record the sound emitted from a source placed in front of the array in an anechoic room. Microphone signals are digitized at 24 bit/ 48 kHz and are fed into a computer where a self-developed software permits to calculate and display in a graphic format the radiation patterns of sources that have been recorded (see Bader et al. 2009, Bader 2010).

Among the instruments investigated so far have been ("classical") guitars where the dynamical, spatio-temporal process of radiation of sound has been studied in detail (cf. Bader 2010). It was shown that the radiation patterns depend on the timbral character as well as on the quality of a certain guitar.

By using the 'acoustic camera', I will try to determine whether the sound radiated from a singer comes only from her mouth, or may originate also from other parts of the body. Furthermore, it is intended to measure if radiation patterns of a singing voice change in correspondence to the voice register employed or the singing style adopted.

For the visualization of the radiation patterns, a code written in Mathematica was applied to the data. Thereby it was possible to show energy values of the voice radiation as well as to mark areas of radiation on a picture of the singer's upper body.

3. Results

In the following, the radiation patterns recorded from the two different kinds of voices and vocal techniques will be shown. When the radiation is emitted from several parts of the body, the respective areas will be included in the presentation. Beforehand, I would like to indicate that there are some areas shown on the pictures where radiation does not come directly from the body but from nearby the body instead. At present, it is not clear yet if such radiation results from room reflections, or from refractions caused by some part of the body; in fact, I hope to dissolve this issue in the near future.

For the recording the singer was placed at a distance of 3 cm in front of the acoustic camera. For all voices and vocal techniques five recordings with a length of 2 seconds were made in order to obtain reliable and valid results. They were analyzed in frequency up to approx. 7 kHz. Only such findings will be presented here which yielded the same or similar results in five trials.

3.1. Radiation Patterns of the Chest Voice and Head Voice in Tone B3

Although a difference in sound character was perceived by an assistant and myself during the recording, the plots of the fundamental sung with either chest voice or head voice show hardly any difference, as shown in Fig.1. Nevertheless, measurements revealed that the energy radiated when using the head voice was nine times as much as that of the chest voice.

At the 2nd partial however the energy value of the head voice decreases to half of that from the fundamental while the chest voice radiates just as much energy at the 2nd partial or shows only a slight increase. The radiation strength for both voice registers changes at each partial, depending on the pitch. However, the measurements show that up to 5 kHz both voices generally radiate sound from the mouth only. For higher frequency ranges the picture changes since there is a difference between the two voice registers, and radiation includes parts of the body other than the mouth. As is shown in Fig. 2, the plot for the two voices at 5600 Hz reveals that the radiation not only comes from the mouth, but also from the nose, the throat (near by the clavicle) and from parts of the head. For the chest voice it was found that, at 5617 Hz, the energy value recorded from the mouth equals that of the throat. Furthermore, when the plots from the chest voice and the head voice will be compared for the 7 kHz frequency range (Fig. 3), one can see that the radiation of both voices comes from many parts of the body. Note however that the head voice has completely lost radiation from the mouth and radiates sound only from the chin while the chest voice still shows direct radiation from the mouth. In addition, a very remarkable finding is that the energy radiated from other body parts can not only be as strong as the sound energy radiated from the mouth, but at times even stronger: at 7099 Hz, the chest voice yields energy values which are about equal for the mouth, the nose, the head, the throat and the left part of the chest area. Energy radiated from the middle of the chest in this case is slightly stronger than is energy radiated from the mouth.

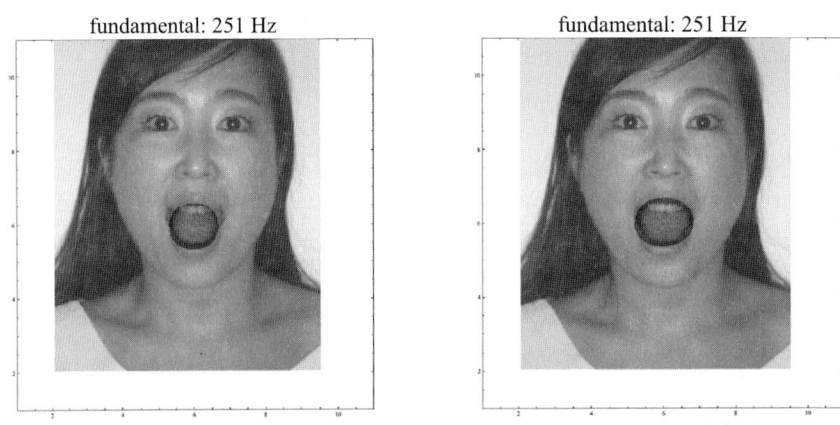

Fig. 1: Radiation of the fundamental of the chest voice (left) and head voice (right) in tone B3

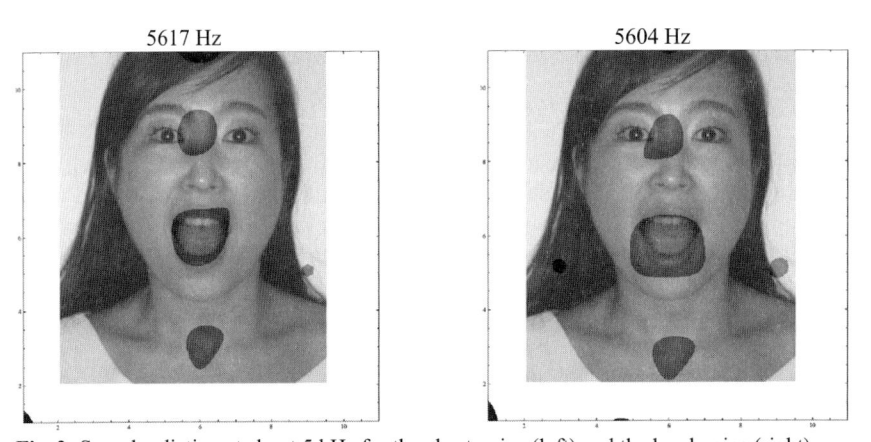

Fig. 2: Sound radiation at about 5 kHz for the chest voice (left) and the head voice (right)

7099 Hz   7095 Hz

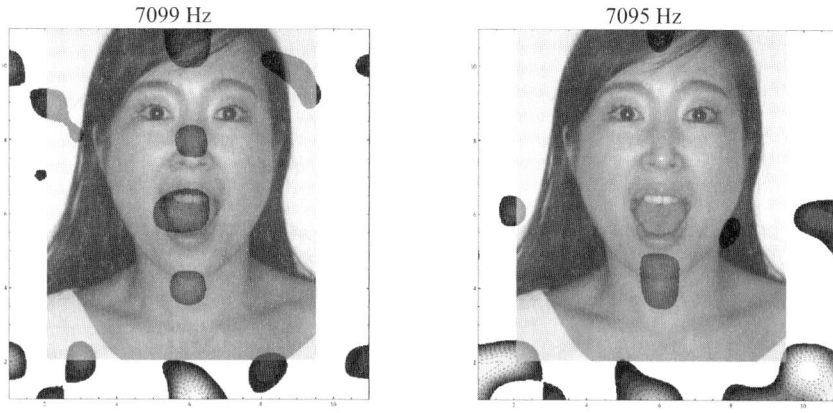

Fig. 3: Radiation fields and patterns of the chest voice (left) and head voice (right) in tone B3

3.2. Radiation Patterns for the Belcanto and German Singing Technique

For the Belcanto and German singing technique two different pitches (B4 and F5) were used. The respective results will be presented separately.

3.2.1. Case study 1: Note/tone B4

Similar to the fundamentals of the chest voice and the head voice in tone B3, there is no obvious difference between both singing techniques and their energy values are also equivalent. At the 2nd partial, the energy value for both voices increases up to twice the value of the fundamental, but in general the energy of the voice in Belcanto singing radiates somewhat stronger than when using the German singing technique (see Fig. 4).

fundamental: 520 Hz   fundamental: 522 Hz

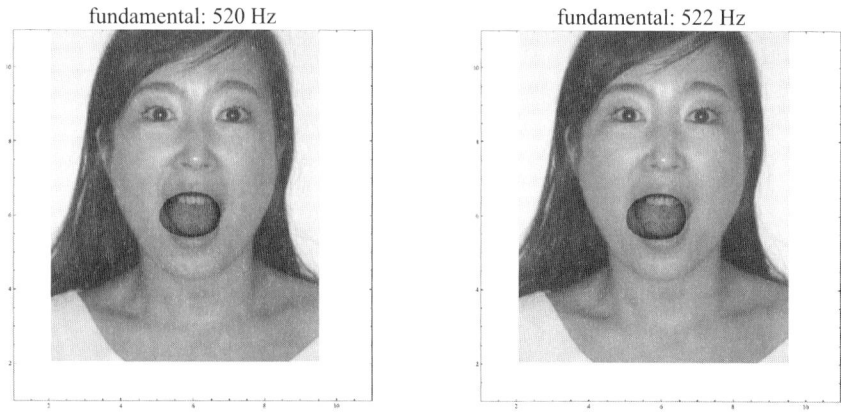

Fig. 4: Radiation of the fundamental in Belcanto (left) and in German singing technique (right) for the tone B4

As the plot of the head voice in Fig. 3 showed, there are some cases in which no radiation comes from the mouth. This effect appears even more clearly here for the tone B4: for 5700 Hz (see Fig. 5), the strongest radiation does not come directly from the mouth, but rather from the chin. In the case of Belcanto, at 6269 Hz direct radiation from the mouth can be seen to cover an area reduced in size, and at 7341 Hz only the chin-throat area appears in the plot. In general, in the high frequency range the radiation produced from Belcanto is located in parts of the head, neck and chest that are comparatively lower than those found for the same frequency range in the German singing technique. In this case, at 6218 Hz (Fig. 6), the strongest radiation also does not come directly from the mouth, significant additional radiation appears at the nose and cheek area as well as at the chest area . German singing shows sound radiation from the cheek and also from the forehead at 7283 Hz (Fig. 7); by comparison to Belcanto, a tendency for the sound radiation to be located on upper parts of the head and body can be observed in regard to high frequencies.

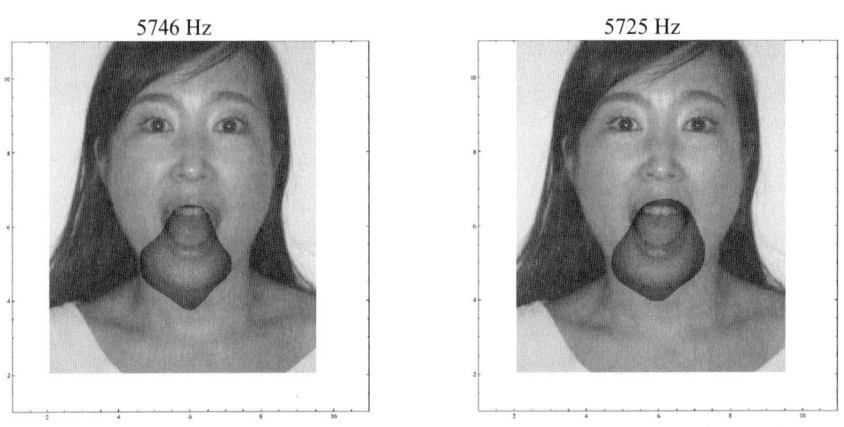

Fig. 5: Radiation pattern for Belcanto (left) and German singing technique (right), 5.7 kHz

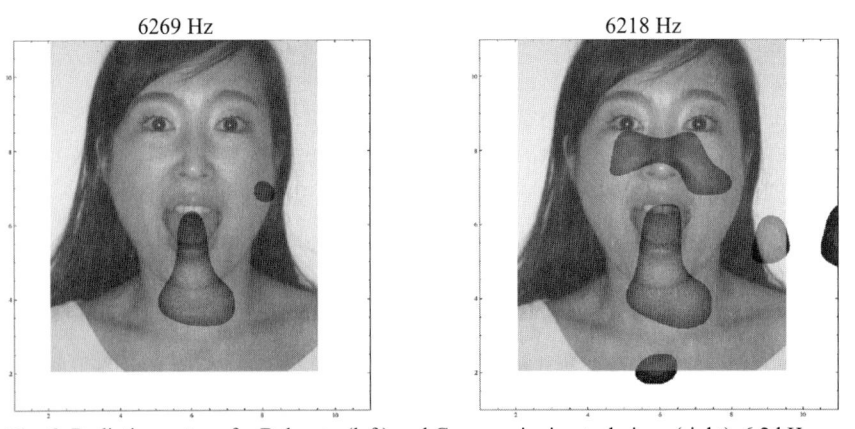

Fig. 6: Radiation pattern for Belcanto (left) and German singing technique (right), 6.2 kHz

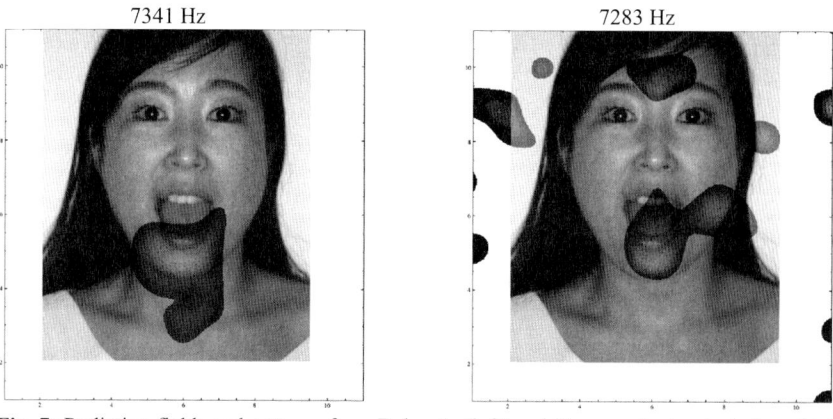

Fig. 7: Radiation fields and patterns from Belcanto (left) and German singing technique (right) in tone B4 at 7.3 kHz

3.2.2. Case study 2: note/tone F5

The fundamentals obtained from both techniques for note/tone F5 look similar not only with respect to their radiation patterns but also when taking their energy values. However, in note/tone F5 the radiated energy of the fundamentals for both conditions (Belcanto, German) shows about ten times as much energy as was observed for the same conditions in note/tone B4. That level halves on the 2nd partial. As already mentioned, data from my study show that in general the voice used according to the Belcanto technique radiates energy somewhat stronger than does the German singing technique, as is obvious in the case of note/tone B4.

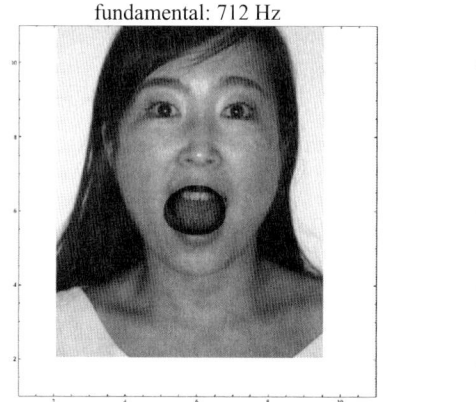

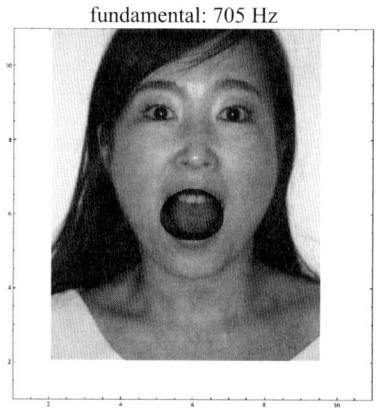

Fig. 8: Radiation of the fundamental from Belcanto (left) and German singing technique (right) in note/tone F5

As yet in this article, only results for the fundamentals and for the high frequency range have been shown. I will now present a finding from the range of around 2 kHz where peculiar radiation patterns occur. As is shown in Fig. 9, it seems as if the radiation for both vocal techniques comes mainly from the mouth, but in fact, there are three radiation points – chin, right and left corner of the mouth – from which energy emanates in different strength. In other words, although also the radiation from the mouth exists, the strongest energy does not originate directly from there.

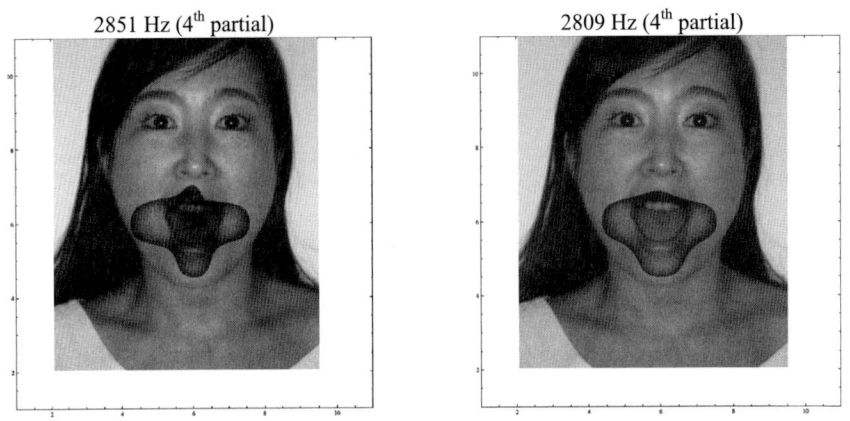

2851 Hz (4th partial)   2809 Hz (4th partial)

Fig. 9: Radiation fields and patterns from Belcanto (left) and German singing technique (right) at around 2.8 kHz (note/tone F5).

In order to find the cause why such a radiation pattern in the mouth area appears, I will state the percentage of the value of the total energy that is radiated at certain frequencies. Energy has been measured at fifteen points at the facial and the chest area (mouth, chin, throat, left and right clavicle, sternum, nose, nasal bone, left and right corners of the mouth, left and right cheek, forehead, left and right lower lid). Fig. 10 shows the results for the Belcanto as an example:

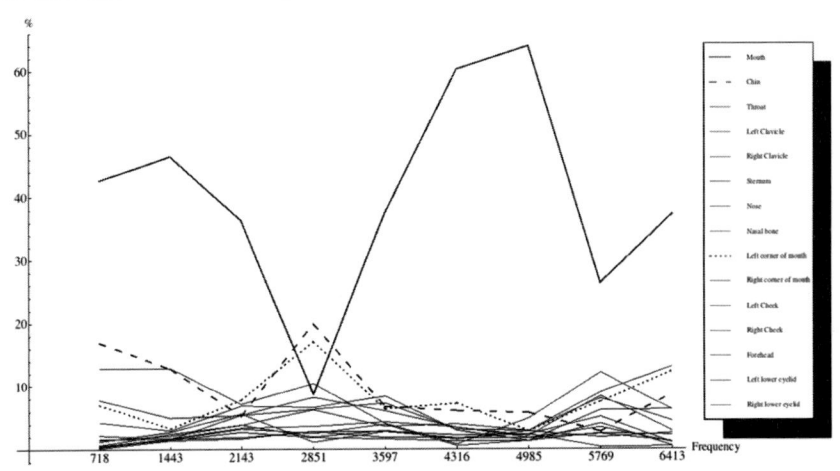

Fig. 10: Percentage (y-axis) of the total energy radiated from the facial and the chest area in note/tone F5 (Belcanto) for frequencies (x-axis) 718 Hz to 6413 Hz

The graphs demonstrate that the radiation energy from the mouth decreases drastically. Instead strong radiation from three other points mentioned above (i.e., chin, right and left corner of the mouth) appears at the 4th partial, around 2800 Hz. Its strong radiation energy exceeds the radiation from the mouth. As Fig. 10 indicates, approx. 20 percent of energy comes from the chin, 17 percent from the left and 10 percent from the right corner of the mouth, respectively. Less than 10 percent of sound energy originates directly from the mouth.

Actually, also at the 5th partial of the tone B4 there is a similar yet not identical visual pattern as is indicated on the respective plots (see Fig. 11). The difference between note/tone F5 and note/tone B4 is that, at the 5th partial of note/tone B4, there is direct radiation neither from the chin nor from the corners of the mouth but only from the mouth. Therefore an energy distribution as documented in Fig.10 does not occur at the 5th partial in note/tone B4.

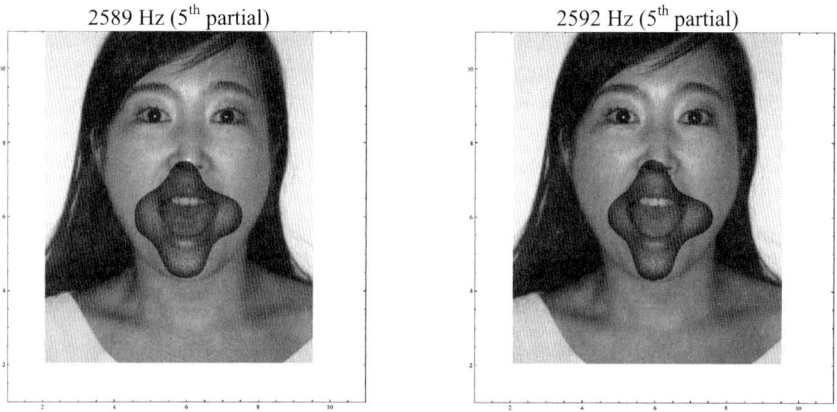

2589 Hz (5th partial)   2592 Hz (5th partial)

Fig. 11: Radiation fields and patterns from Belcanto (left) and German singing technique (right) at around 2500 Hz in note/tone B4

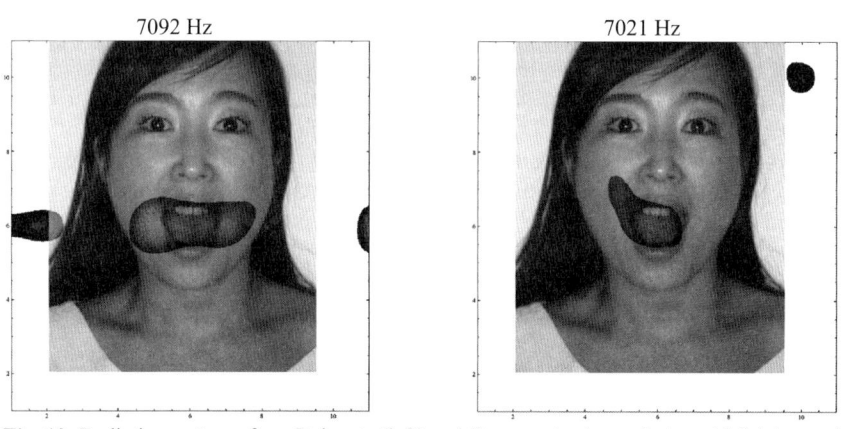

7092 Hz   7021 Hz

Fig. 12: Radiation patterns from Belcanto (left) and German singing technique (right) in note/ tone F5

In addition, radiation from the chin as found for note/tone B4 does not exist for note/tone F5. Most of the radiation comes directly from the mouth or from the mouth area, as is evident in the frequency range between 5 kHz and 7 kHz. This differs significantly from the pattern found for note/tone B4 (cf. Fig. 7).

4. Conclusion

The results of this research show that the radiation patterns of sound energy produced from the singing voice vary considerable depending on the singing voice register (chest or head voice), on singing technique as well as on the pitch to be sung. In principle, there is a correspondence of the singing voice to other musical instruments, which also show changes in radiation patterns according to register and pitch. Looking at the classical singing voice, radiation of sound energy is not restricted to the mouth (as kind of a natural 'point source') but can be effected by parts of the head, neck, and chest as well. In certain cases, especially for partials having rather high frequencies, no radiation of sound from the mouth will be observed whereas radiation from other areas can be measured. For the fundamental frequencies of the notes/tones sung, differences between voice register and singing technique are only slight in regard to radiation patterns and the amount of energy radiated from the mouth, which for fundamentals is the only source of radiation. This schema hence occurs independently of the vocal register and singing technique.

However, as was shown for the note/tone F5 there is an interesting radiation pattern found at around 2800 Hz involving the chin and the left and the right corner of the mouth which can be compared with the pattern at around 2500 Hz for note/tone B4. To explain the similarities in both patterns, I assume a relation with the singer's formant, which occurs at around 3 kHz, because the radiation pattern from both pitches appears close to this formant range, and especially so the pattern measured for note/tone F5. This indicates that the strongest energy (which amounts to almost half of the energy output in this case) comes from the chin and from the left and right corners of the mouth. It seems that radiation of energy from areas other than the mouth in this process helps to prevent a drastic decrease of the energy level and thus ensures to maintain a certain timbre of the singing voice for the note/tone that is produced at a given time.

In any case, a changed configuration of the vocal folds necessary for the change of voice register is certainly one reason for different radiation patterns observed for chest voice and head voice, respectively. The difference in radiation patterns found for Belcanto and German singing technique could also originate, for the most part, from the change of the spatial configuration between the vocal folds and the mouth opening, since the geometrical change of this space, called vocal tract, is central in determining the timbre of the radiated sound (see also Kob 2002, 114, Titze 2009).

5. References

Bader, Rolf 2010. Reconstruction of Radiating Sound Fields using minimum Energy Method. *Jounal Acoust. Soc. Am*. 127, 300-308.

Bader, Rolf, Malte Münster, Jan Richter, Heiko Timm 2009. Microphone Array Measurements of drums and flutes. In R. Bader (ed). 2009. *Musical Acoustics, Neurcognition and Psychology of Music* (=*Hamburger Jahrbuch für Musikwissenschaft* 25). Frankfurt/M.: P. Lang, 15-55.

Kob, Malte 2002. *Physical Modeling of the Singing Voice*, Berlin: Logos-Verlag.

Miller, Richard 1978. *National Schools of Singing: English, French, German, and Italian Techniques of Singing Revisited*. Lanham, Md: The Scarecrow Pr.

Schiller-Institut (Ed.) 1996. *Handbuch der Grundlagen von Stimmung und Register*. Wiesbaden: Dr. Böttiger.

Sundberg, Johan 1987/1997. *The Science of the Singing Voice*. De Kalb: Northern Ill. Univ. Pr. 1987 (German ed.: *Die Wissenschaft von der Singstimme*. Bonn: Orpheus-Verlag 1997).

Titze, Ingo R 2009. Das Saitenblas-Instrument. *Spektrum der Wissenschaft 02/2009*, 54-60.

Andreas Beurmann
Albrecht Schneider

Some Observations on a Stein-Conrad Hammerflügel from 1793

Summary

A Stein-Conrad Hammerflügel from 1793 was studied in regard to hammer/string contact times, repetition times for individual notes/keys and other parameters. Data obtained from acoustical and sonological measurements are reported.

1. Introduction

Concerning the development of the piano from 18th century fortepiano to modern instruments, the invention of the Prellmechanik is considered a major improvement in regard to providing a fast and reliably working action. In particular instruments built by Johann Andreas Stein (1728-1792) including specimens from his shop manufactured after his death are said to offer an extremely light touch and a delicate tone[1]. One such instrument, apparently dating from 1793, and completed by Jacob Fréderic Conrad working in Stein's shop at Augsburg, is in the collection of the first author (Beurmann Nr. 117; for a detailed description of the instrument, see Beurmann 2007, 81-86). It is a beautiful, well-preserved and fully playable Hammerflügel with a compass from F_1 to G_6 (in Helmholtz' designation: F, to g'''), thus spanning five octaves plus one tone, enough to cover the range of notes found in compositions for the fortepiano (predating the term pianoforte by several decades) of Haydn, Mozart and even Beethoven up to opus 49 (1795/1796). As is known from historical sources, Mozart was especially fond of Stein's instruments (see Mozart's letter to his father, October 17th/18th, 1777, in which he praises Stein's instruments. See also Latcham 1998).

In this article, we will in brief report a few experiments carried out on the Stein-Conrad instrument with a focus on hammer/string contact and string excitation. These aspects have been studied in great detail, by Donald Hall, Anders Askenfeld and other researchers in regard to piano acoustics, both theoretically and in modelling as well as in experiments (cf. Hall 1986, 1987a, 1987b, Hall & Clark 1987, Hall & Askenfeld 1988, Askenfeld 1990, Askenfeld & Jansson 1990, 1991, 1993). However, these studies were directed to modern pianos and grand pianos that differ in many respects from the historical Hammerflügel notwithstanding some convergent features. The Hammerflügel as a special type of piano has also been subjected to experimental investigation (cf. Fricke 1996, Gätjen 2003/2008). Given the huge body of research published on piano acoustics (besides the studies already mentioned, see also e.g. Podlesak & Lee 1988, Fletcher & Rossing 1991, ch. 12, Giordano & Korty 1996), basic mechanisms of sound generation are well understood though there are elements that are difficult to model or

---

[1] For a historical overview as well as fundamentals of piano organology, see the article ‚Pianoforte' § I (authors: Edwin Ripin et al.) in Sadie 1984, Vol. III, 71ff.

calculate because of their nonlinear behaviour (as has become evident for hammer mechanics).

Fig. 1: Stein-Conrad Hammerflügel from 1793 (Beurmann Nr. 117).

2. The Stein-Conrad 1793 Hammerflügel: some observations from measurements

As has been stated by piano experts, the action of the Stein instruments is extremely light since the hammers and shanks are so small and have almost no weight. For hammer heads of a Stein 1773 the weights for the lowest hammer has been given as 1 gram, and for the highest as 0.45 gram (compared to 8.4 gram and 4.1 gram in modern instruments; cf. Hauser-Felberbaum & Hauser 2003/2008, 230/231). On the Stein-Conrad 1793 under review, the hammer heads all have their original buckskin (deer hide) cover. However, there have been opinions according to which Stein in the beginning might have employed wooden hammers without any deer hide cover. The thin buckskin covers found in the Stein-Conrad 1793 do not add to the wooden hammer mass in any significant way.

Since the hammer and the shank are so small and light, a weight of 5 grams placed on the F_1 key of the Stein-Conrad 1793 is enough to press it down, and even to produce a tone. By comparison, the static force required to press a key of a modern grand piano is in the range of 0.44 N (equivalent to raising a mass of 45 grams), and 0.48 – 0.49 N for an upright piano of high quality (cf. data from Dijksterhuis [1965] and Lieber [1985] reported in Fletcher & Rossing 1991, 311, 314). In a Steinway D grand piano, the static force needed to press a key is equivalent to applying a weight of ca. 54 grams, however, not resulting in an audible tone.

The string lengths [L] and striking points [l] (both in mm) as well as the ratio of string length to striking point [L/l] are listed in Table 1:

Table 1: String lengths [L], striking points [l], and ratios [L/l]

Note	F_1	C	F	c	f	c^1	f^1	c^2	f^2	c^3	f^3	g^3
L	1695	1540	1360	1065	865	610	432	290	218	148	115	100
l	132	105	96	75	62	45	32	20	18	15	10	9
Ratio	12.84	14.66	14.17	14.2	14.2	13.55	13.5	14.5	12.11	9.87	11.5	11.1

For each note, two strings are provided. The string gauges and other parameter values of the instrument tuned to a^1 = 420 Hz are listed in Table 2 where weight refers to the weight of the string in regard to its actually vibrating length when struck[2].

Table 2: Lengths [mm], Gauges [mm] and other parameters, Stein-Conrad 1793

Note	Length	Diameter	Material	Weight	Tension
F_1	1695	0.8	brass	7,17 g	8,43 kp
F	1360	0.5	brass	2,25 g	8,48 kp
f	865	0.38	iron	0.92 g	9.03 kp
f'	432	0.32	iron	0.27 g	5,18 kp
f''	218	0.28	iron	0.12 g	4,68 kp
f'''	115	0.25	iron	0,07 g	5,93 kp

Using the light string gauges and the corresponding tensions indicated here to tune the instrument to a^1 = 420 Hz, total tension for the 62 notes (each employing a pair of strings) is not more than 942 kp, just a fraction of what is found in a modern grand piano.

We measured the hammer/string contact time for the notes/strings F_1, F, f, f', f'', f''' with a simple setup, in which string and hammer functioned as a switch in an electric circuit that was closed for the contact time, and open otherwise. Technically, a 3 V DC voltage was applied to the string to be measured, and two very thin wires of 0.017 mm diameter were placed across each of the six hammers involved in the measurement. The mass of these thin wires is negligible, hence adding no load to the hammer that was accelerated by pressing the respective key with a force equivalent to dynamic levels either of *p*, *mf*, or *f*.

The voltage resulting from the hammer/string contact was digitized at 32 bit-float/96 kHz sampling and recorded on a computer. The signals obtained are sequences of pulses with voltage peaks proportional to the dynamic force applied to the key (fig. 2). In addition to single pulses, a sequence of such pulses was registered from playing a key as fast as possible in order to determine minimum time between pulses and to check the repetition possible with the kind of Prellmechanik manufactured by Stein-Conrad (see fig. 3, right side)

---

[2] A complete list with values for all 62 notes (F1 to g3) as well as additional data calculated with software developed by the first author will be found in Beurmann 2007, 360-361.

Fig. 2: Twelve hammers of the Stein-Conrad 1793 with thin wires attached to heads

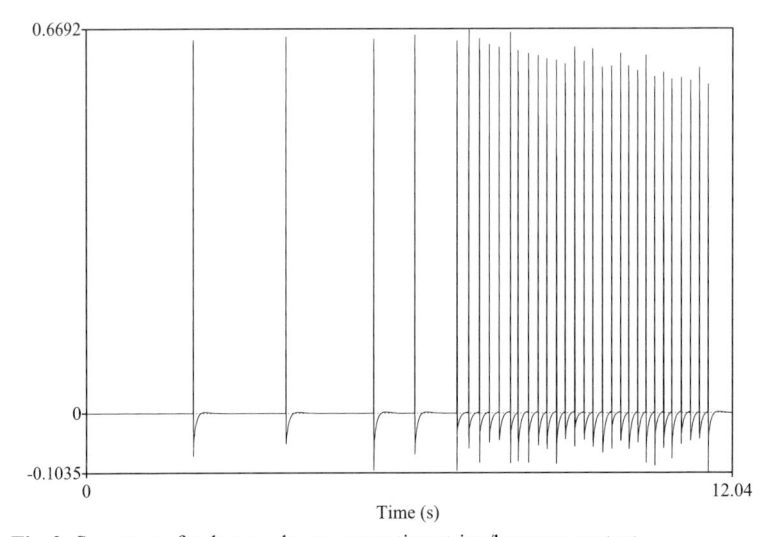

Fig. 3: Sequence of voltage pulses representing string/hammer contacts

The pulses in fact last for only a few ms (see below) and show strong peaks. However, if viewed in detail (fig. 3), one can see that the voltage is not stable over time. Also, multiple string contacts (as discussed in previous publications; see Hall 1987a) can be observed in a number of our recordings. In fact, the same note recorded ten times or more offers some variance not only in regard to the duration of the contact but also concerning its shape(s).

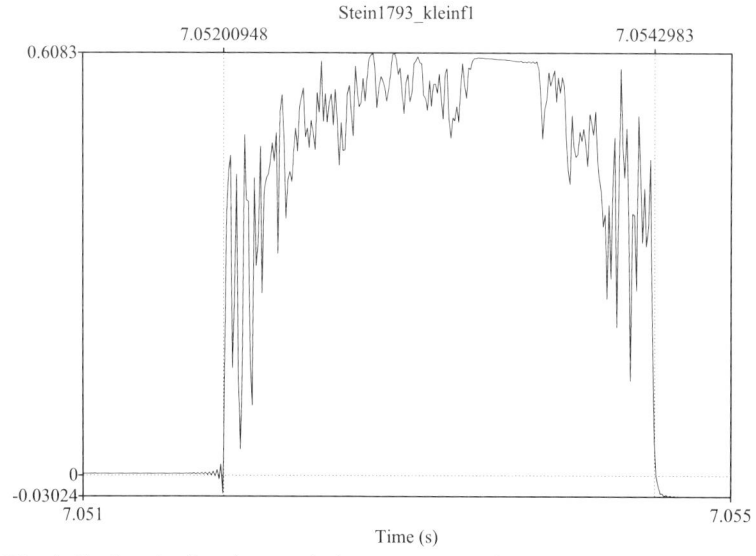

Fig. 4: Single pulse from hammer/string contact, note f', contact time 2.289 ms

For the six notes/keys studied in detail (F_1, F, f, f', f'', f'''), the contact times and the repetition, the latter defined as the time between onsets of notes played (keys pressed) in as fast a sequence as was possible (see fig. 2, right half), are listed in Table 3. The onsets were measured from the string contacts (as shown in fig. 4). Contact and repetition times have been averaged on the basis of a minimum of 10 measurements per note/key; the mean (aM) and the standard deviation (SD) are given for each note/key.

Table 3: Contact time (ms) and repetition (ms) for six notes/keys

Note	Contact Time (aM)	SD	Repetition time	SD
F_1	3.271	0.673	185.42	24.39
F	1.766	0.295	168.026	17.645
f	2.33	0.514	147.482	36.775
f'	1.927	0.146	163.667 (78.322)*	28.64 (13.293)*
f''	1.6108	0.214	190.292	21.885
f'''	1.50636	0.1845	166.06	16.031

The very short repetition times for the f' (in parentheses, marked with an asterisk) were obtained through the most rapid pressing of this key possible; however, the notes recorded in this way lost clear definition and tended to "smear" (resulting in doubling of notes). Taking the mean value for the f' as an extreme that might be realized only at the expense of musical articulation, the other mean values are more realistic, implying that repetition times for the Stein-Conrad 1793 are between, typically, 150 and 200 ms.

Given the tiny size of the hammers and the thin strings used in the Stein-Conrad 1793, the hammer/string contact area is very small; hence one may regard the hammer approximating a point force to thin strings (for which the impedance also is very small).

The disturbance caused from the hammer/string contact travels on the string in both directions. To study the structure of the disturbance more closely, we placed a mini accelerometer (Kistler 8614 A500, mass = 0.7 g) on the bridge next to the pin to record any vibration that would reach the bridge. With 96 kHz sampling, the temporal resolution is about 0.01 ms.

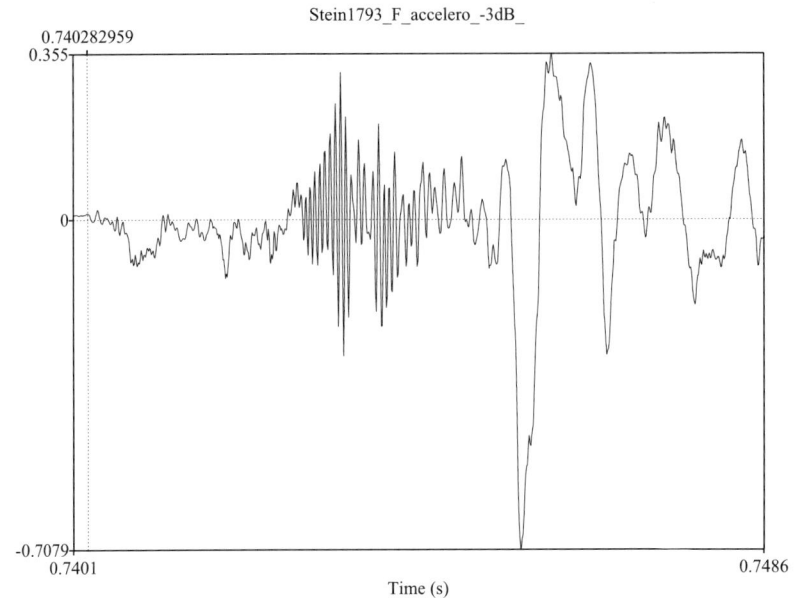

Fig. 5: Note/key F, accelerometer on bridge. The precursor signal (left side) sets in followed by the longitudinal wave (center) and the transversal wave (right side). The length of the time series (oscillogram) displayed is 8.5 ms.

As Fig. 5 demonstrates, the signal (normalized to -3dB) picked up by the accelerometer contains first a precursor, which is a noisy, apparently non-periodic type of vibration that is small in amplitude and lasts for about 2.5 ms. The precursor often has been viewed in connection with the longitudinal vibration of the string (cf. Podlesak & Lee 1988, Giordano & Korty 1996). With sufficiently high sampling and temporal resolution of the signal, the precursor can be clearly distinguished from the longitudinal wave, which is traceable in our sample for less than 2 ms before another very short transient precedes the transversal wave. This of course is much stronger than the longitudinal wave and easier to measure in regard to period length. For the longitudinal wave, the periods (measured by zero crossings in the time series) vary from 0.49 ms to 0.60 ms, corresponding to frequencies of 2040 Hz to 1616 Hz. If subjected to a pitch calculation by means of an autocorrelation algorithm (as available in the Praat software), this turns out 2132 Hz for the short signal segment of 1.8 ms.

From Young's modulus and the density of brass, phase velocity for longitudinal waves on thin brass rods can be calculated as $c_{\text{long}} \approx 3494$ m/s. The actual time measured between the onset of the hammer contact and the onset of longitudinal wave recorded by the accelerometer is ~1.73 ms for the note/key/string of F, where the distance from the striking point to the bridge is ca. 1264 mm, and to the accelerometer was about 1275 mm. The transversal wave occurs in the accelerometer signal only 5.26 ms after the onset of the hammer/string contact. The period of the transversal wave for the F string was found to be 12.058 ms corresponding to 82.93 Hz, that is, the pitch of this string was tuned relative to a' = 420 Hz.

In another session (with the tuning slightly modified), we recorded the string velocity for several strings by measuring the electromotive force (EMF) to reveal the pulse structure (cf. Beurmann & Schneider 2008 for such measurements applied to a harpsichord). Recording was done at 32 bit/192 kHz sampling. For the F-string, inductive measurement of the EMF did yield a period of 11.905 ms ≈ 83.37 Hz, and for the f'-string a period of 3.023 ms ≈ 332.9 Hz.

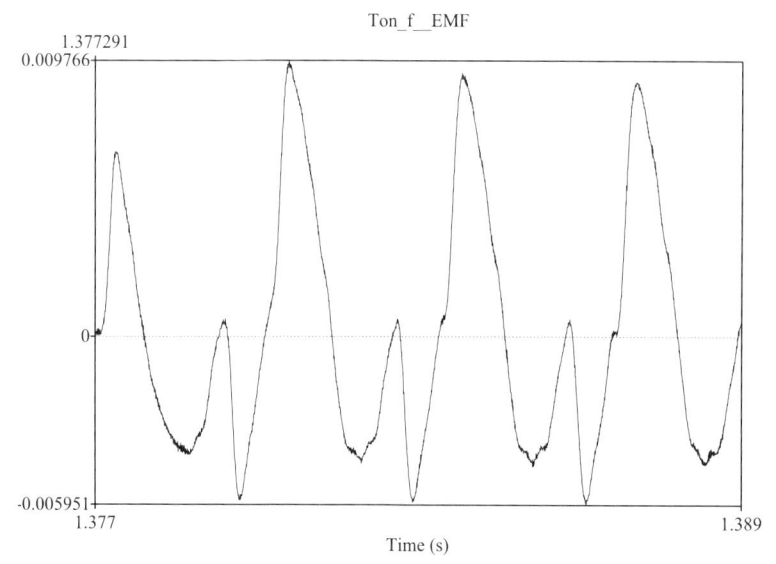

Fig. 6: Stein-Conrad 1793: EMF ./. time for the note/string f', first four pulses on string

The spectrum of the EMF recording of the F-string shows a weak 14th harmonic as can be expected from the *L/l*-ratio that for F is 14.17 (Table 1) causing the hammer to hit near a node. Further, a rather sharp decline of the spectral envelope at harmonic no. 28 (see Fig. 7) occurs due to a number of factors relating to the mass of the hammer and that of the string, the contact time, the force transmitted, etc. (For an analytic treatment of parameters involved, see Hall 1986).

The sound radiated from the strings and the soundboard was recorded with a condenser mic (AKG C414 B-TL) set to cardioid from above the strings and soundboard at a distance of ca. 20 cm. The sound was digitized at 32 bit-float/96 kHz. For a C-major chord comprising the notes c – e – g – c' (C3 – E3 – G3 – C4), the spectral evolution shows the usual fast decay of higher partials. The temporal envelope of this sound can be modelled with the trajectory of the level calculated from the spectrum (Figure 8). If interpreted in terms of an ADSR envelope consisting of four parts (attack, decay, sustain, release), the sound corresponding to the C-major-chord demonstrates a fast attack to a peak level close to 77 dB and also a quite rapid decay by more than 12 dB but then has a long sustain before the release sets in. Hence it can be said that the Stein-Conrad 1793 provides both 'definition' in regard to a fast and clear onset of notes played in articulate fast passages as well as enough sustain to provide for legato-playing even at a very moderate tempo.

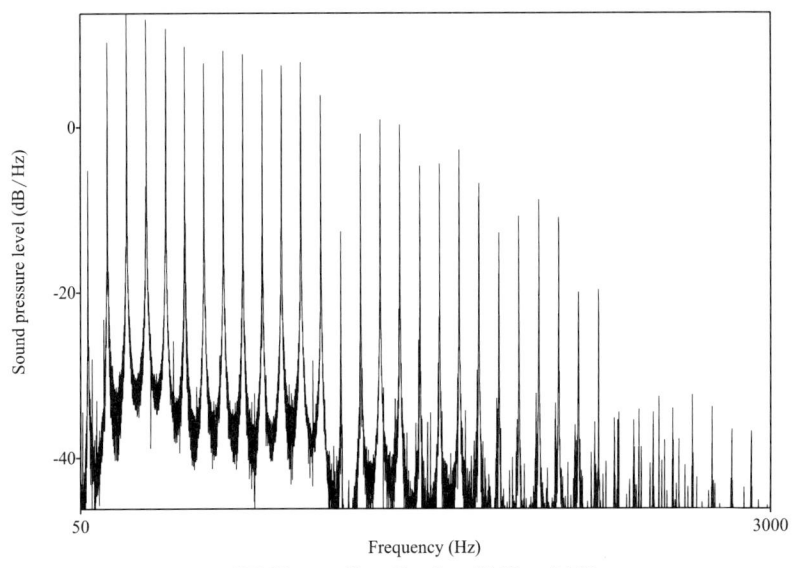

Fig. 7: Power spectrum of EMF recording, F-string, 50 Hz – 3 kHz.

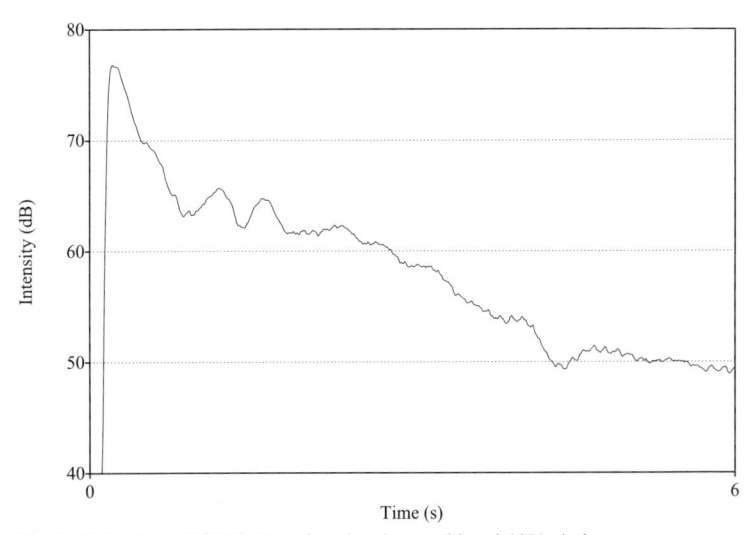

Fig. 8: Stein-Conrad 1793, C-major chord, sound level (dB) ./. time

3. Conclusion

Hammerflügel manufactured in the shop of Johann Andreas Stein have been praised for their excellent craftsmanship and performance capabilities. Since the action of the Stein-Conrad 1793 is extremely light and fast, it was of interest to study actual hammer/string contact times as well as the repetition time for individual notes/keys in this instrument. In addition, some observations relating to wave propagation on strings and string velocity have been reported.

References

Askenfeld, Anders (ed.) 1990. *Five Lectures on the Acoustics of the Piano*. Stockholm: R. Swedish Acad. of Music.

Askenfeld, A., E.V. Jansson 1990. From touch to string vibrations. I. Timing in grand piano action. *Journal Acoust. Soc. Am.* 88, 52–63.

Askenfeld, A., E.V. Jansson 1991. From touch to string vibrations. II: the motion of the key and hammer. *J. Acoust. Soc. Am.* 90, 2383-2393.

Askenfeld, A., E.V. Jansson 1993. From touch to string vibrations. III: String motion and spectra. *Journal Acoust. Soc. Am.* 93, 2181-2196.

Beurmann, Andreas 2007. *Das Buch vom Klavier. Die Sammlung Beurmann im Museum für Kunst und Gewerbe in Hamburg und auf Gut Hasselburg in Ostholstein*. Hildesheim etc.: Olms.

Beurmann, Andreas, Albrecht Schneider 2008. Acoustics of the harpsichord: a case study. In A. Schneider (ed.). *Systematic and Comparative Musicology: Concepts, methods, findings*. (=Hamburger Jahrbuch für Musikwissenschaft, Bd 24), Frankfurt/M. etc.: P. Lang, 241-263.

Fletcher, Neville, Thomas Rossing 1991. *The Physics of musical instruments*. New York: Springer.

Fricke, J. 1996. Die Klangcharakteristik von zwei Hammerflügeln des Musikwissenschaftlichen Instituts der Universität zu Köln. In M. Lustig (Ed.), *Zur Geschichte des Hammerklaviers*. (=*Bericht über das 14. Musikinstrumentenbau-Symposium in Michaelstein ... 1993*), Blankenburg: Stiftung Kloster Michaelstein, 157-170.

Gätjen, Bram 2003/2008. Was macht der Hammer des Hammerflügels mit der Saite? Akustische Untersuchungen zum Verwandtschaftsgrad von Cembalo, Hammerklavier und modernem Klavier. In Klaus W. Niemöller & Bram Gätjen (eds.). *Perspektiven und Methoden einer Systemischen Musikwissenschaft*. Frankfurt/M. etc.: P. Lang (2003, corrected edition 2008), 215-220.

Giordano, N., A.F. Korty 1996. Motion of a piano string: Longitudinal vibrations and the role of the bridge. *Journal Acoust. Soc. Am.* 100, 3899-3908.

Hall, Donald 1986. Piano string excitation in the case of small hammer mass. *Journal Acoust. Soc. Am.* 79, 141-147,

Hall, D. 1987a. Piano string excitation II: General solution for a hard narrow hammer. *Journal Acoust. Soc. Am.* 81, 535-546.

Hall, D. 1987b. Piano string excitation III: General solution for a soft narrow hammer. *Journal Acoust. Soc. Am.* 81, 547-55.

Hall, D., Peter Clark 1987. Piano string excitation IV: The question of missing modes. *Journal Acoust. Soc. Am.* 82, 1913-1918.

Hall, D., A. Askenfeld 1988. Piano string excitation V: Spectra for real hammers and strings. *Journal Acoust. Soc. Am.* 83, 1627-1638.

Hauser-Felberbaum, Annette, Ulrich Hauser 2003/2008. Über die Bedeutung des Hammers im Klavier- und Flügelbau. In Klaus W. Niemöller & Bram Gätjen (eds.). *Perspektiven und Methoden einer Systemischen Musikwissenschaft.* Frankfurt/M. etc.: P. Lang (2003, corrected edition 2008), 229-234.

Latcham, Michael 1998. Mozart and the Pianos of Johann Andreas Stein. *Galpin Soc. Jounal* 51, 114-153.

Podlesak Michael, Anthony Lee 1988. Dispersion of waves in piano strings. *Journal Acoust. Soc. Am.* 83, 305-317.

Ripin, Edwin, Philip Belt, Maribel Meisel et al. 1984. Pianoforte, § 1. In S. Sadie (ed.) *The New Grove Dictionary of Musical Instruments*, Vol. III. London: Grove/Macmillan, 71- 101.

Rolf Bader
Albrecht Schneider

Playing "Live" at the *Star-Club*[1]: Reconstructing the Room Acoustics of a Famous Music Hall

Summary

The *Star-Club* of Hamburg was one of the best-known places for live music that ever existed. Opened in April, 1962, the *Star-Club* saw rock'n'roll greats from the Beatles to Jimi Hendrix, and from Little Richard to The Nice and Yes before the venue was closed as a live music hall on December 31st, 1969. After the building had been badly damaged by a fire in 1983, it was completely torn down in 1986. Musicians who had played the *Star-Club*, and had lauded the venue for its great sound and atmosphere, said that one of the most important places in regard to the history of rock music had been destroyed with no chance ever to reconstruct it. The chance to reconstruct the actual room acoustics came when we talked to musicians who had been on stage in the *Star-Club*, and who gave us valuable information in addition to source material found in archives. We attempted to reconstruct the *Star-Club* in every known detail with the aid of the Odeon Room Acoustics software (version 9.1), where the *Star-Club* was modelled in 3D. Thereby, also reconstruction of sound propagation in the room became possible. At the same time, we recorded some music that had been actually performed in the *Star-Club*, making use of vintage instruments and amplifiers, in a dry (almost reverberation-free) studio environment. The recordings can be played back in the virtual *Star-Club*, which comes close to the original venue in regard of room acoustics. Thereby the sound of the music as it was performed during the heydays of beat and early rock music can be reconstructed within certain limits. The experimental work we did in the field of applied room acoustics and auralisation could be similarly done for other famous rock music venues that are no longer extant (e.g., the original *Cavern Club* of Liverpool).

Zusammenfassung

Der *Star-Club* in Hamburg gilt bis heute als ein Zentrum der Beat- und Rockmusik in den sechziger Jahren. In den Räumen eines vormaligen Kinos wurde der *Star-Club* im April 1962 eröffnet. In den Jahren 1962-64 traten hier Bill Haley, Little Richard, Chuck

---

[1] The name *Star-Club* was indeed employed by the Manfred Weissleder KG in the hyphenated form. Manfred Weissleder (1928-1980) had established his company as a private limited partnership (KG) with the aid of his parents who, according to documents kept in the Hamburgische Staatsarchiv, nominally both became partners (Weissleder's father [Heinrich] died in 1963, and his mother [Antonia] was substituted, in 1964, by Hans Bunkenburg, Weissleder's deputy managing director). Weissleder was the owner of the proprietary name *Star-Club* that became a matter of licencing in the years 1964-1969 when a number of clubs all over West Germany adopted the name on a contractual basis, and consequently had to pay a certain fee per month to Weissleder as well as to share bookings of the bands he had signed (cf. Beckmann & Martens 1980, 137ff.).

Berry, die Everly Brothers, Bo Diddley und sogar Ray Charles auf, aber eben auch die Beatles, Tony Sheridan und zahlreiche andere MusikerInnen und Bands aus Großbritannien, schließlich (ab 1963) deutsche Bands wie die Rattles und die Lords. Nach der Blütezeit 1962-64 geriet der *Star-Club* wirtschaftlich zunehmend unter Druck und wurde trotz einer Vielzahl von Konzerten mit Bands der späteren sechziger Jahre (darunter Jimi Hendrix Experience, Nice, Yes, Spooky Tooth, Vanilla Fudge, Taste) mit Ablauf des Jahres 1969 geschlossen. Anschließend nutzte ein "Erotik-Cabaret" die Räume, die 1983 einem Großbrand zum Opfer fielen. Die Ruine des Gebäudes wurde 1986 abgerissen. Die vorliegende Studie berichtet über eine Rekonstruktion des *Star-Club* mit Hilfe einer Software für raumakustische Modellierungen und über Versuche, den Star-Club mit Verfahren der Auralisation zumindest virtuell wieder "bespielbar" zu machen. Im Zuge der Rekonstruktion wurden die technische Ausstattung des *Star-Club* sowie Sachverhalte, die mit live-Aufnahmen in diesem Club zusammenhängen, in die Untersuchung einbezogen.

1. Introduction: some historical background

The *Star-Club* of Hamburg is considered one of the most famous live music venues in the history of popular music (Beckmann & Martens 1980, Krüger 2010). It opened in April 1962 and saw performances of artists from The Beatles, Tony Sheridan, Bill Haley, Little Richard, Jerry Lee Lewis and Ray Charles in its early days to The Pretty Things and The Spencer Davis Group later on, and then Jimi Hendrix, The Nice, Taste, Yes, Vanilla Fudge and many other important acts of the Sixties. The *Star-Club* was located in the Große Freiheit 39, right in the St. Pauli red light district of Hamburg, in a building that had been a ballroom since about 1900 (see photographs in Zint 1987). By 1948, the ballroom was changed into a cinema that opened in 1949 as the 'Stern-Kino', and was well received by the public during the 1950s. In January 1962, Manfred Weissleder, a young entrepreneur who was running several strip joints and 'erotic bars', had bought the 'Stern-Kino', which was turned from a cinema into a rock music venue within the next two months. By the end of February 1962, Weissleder sought approval from the local authorities to remove the cinema seating, which should be replaced by special boxes each containing several seats, and to build a new dance floor in front of the stage[2]. Permission to change the interior of the 'Stern-Kino' was granted in the beginning of March with the obligation that all wall covering and ceiling lining as well as all other decoration of the interior of the club had to be made from fire-resisting materials according to DIN 4102, the German legal requirements defining standards of construction materials and parts with respect to fire[3]. In addition to the new seating and the new dance floor, the stage area was in part remodelled including the famous 'Manhattan

---

[2] Manfred Weissleder KG, Antrag an Bezirksamt Hamburg-Mitte auf Nutzungsänderung vom 23.2.1962.
[3] Bezirksamt HH-Mitte, Bauamt, Bescheid vom 9.3.1962 an M. Weissleder KG; Betriebserlaubnis Nr. 249/62. German DIN 4102 (Brandverhalten von Baustoffen und Bauteilen) has a parallel in British norm BS 476.

skyline' painting created by Erwin Ross[4]. The *Star-Club* opened on April 13th, 1962, after posters in red had been circulated in the greater Hamburg area announcing that the time of 'village music' was over. On the very first evening, among the bands on stage were The Beatles. They played 48 shows until May 31st and returned in November for another 14 shows (1st to 14th of November). Their third and last stint at the *Star-Club*, from which a collection of (in)famous live recordings remain (see below), was from December 18th to 31st (cf. Rehwagen & Schmidt 1992, 17ff.).

Figure 1: Entrance to the *Star-Club* (viewed from the Große Freiheit) in 1962

The *Star-Club* was a magnet for young people eager to listen to bands playing rock'n'roll and beat music. Such music was hardly available on German radio networks then (where "Schlager" and conventional dance music prevailed in the 'light music' programmes). Also, possession of record players and rock'n'roll recordings was scarce among German teenagers at the beginning of the sixties. Live music venues offering this kind of "wild" music suited to teenagers and twens also could not be found in large number before 1962-63[5]. So Weissleder, and similarly his local competitor, Peter Eckhorn (owner of the *Top Ten* club located on the Reeperbahn; see Rehwagen & Schmidt 1992), rightly saw the demand for 'hot' live music. Weissleder's concept was to present a range of bands every day, that is, at least three bands per evening and well into the night (especially on weekends). The bands followed one after another on stage, each playing for about one hour, and then again after a two hour's break. This scheme

---

[4] Erwin Ross (1926-2010), famous as the "Rubens of the Reeperbahn", was a painter, mostly of 'applied art' (e.g., Pin-up girls). He was a close friend of Weissleder, helping him to decorate the *Star-Club* in March 1962.

[5] For some information concerning the socio-cultural background of 'youth culture' and beat music in Germany in the first half of the 1960s, see Siegfried 2006, Klitsch 2001.

naturally created some competition among bands going on stage since everyone was eager to impress the crowd. However, it was also a situation of mutual benefit as one could ask for help, on the one hand, and offer to help in return, on the other[6]. Most of all, places like the *Star-Club* and the *Top Ten* gave them ample opportunity to practice their respective sets, and to improve their sound and their performance.

The concept of the *Star-Club* to have several bands per evening and night on stage plus offering a more or less regular sequence of "sensational" artists mainly from the U.S. like Bill Haley, Fats Domino, Chuck Berry, Jerry Lee Lewis, Little Richard, the Everly Brothers and even Ray Charles for a couple of weeks, a few days or even a single evening of course was a courageous yet costly enterprise (cf. Beckmann & Martens 1980). In 1962 alone, Weissleder had paid fees to the artists he had contracted to the tune of 436.473,71 DM (Krüger 2010, 100). In addition, he had to cover all the usual expenses as well as to pay tax (again, not a small amount as records show). Apparently, Weissleder had to struggle to make ends meet even in the heydays of beat music in 1964[7], and in later years it was almost impossible to present ever more expensive artists in particular from the U.S. As is well known, popularity of the *Star-Club* was on the wane in the years after 1965, but there were still extraordinary artists like Jimi Hendrix in March 1967 and a whole bunch of first-class bands in the course of the year 1969 (see Zint 1987, 83ff.) that attracted visitors. However, the income generated from a relatively small number of sold-out concerts was not enough to keep the *Star-Club* afloat. On the evening of December 31st, 1969, the *Star-Club* closed with a final show of the power duo Hardin & York.

In the years to follow, the building housed the 'Salambo', a live-sex venue (see Zint 1987). To accommodate the needs of a different business, the interior of the former '*Star-Club*' was remodelled, in particular the stage and dance floor area (where a stage that could be rotated was installed). On February 18th, 1983, a fire not only destroyed the 'Salambo' located in the hall of the former '*Star-Club*' but also the front building on Große Freiheit 39. The ruins of the Star-Club were completely removed in 1987[8], and new buildings were erected on the site where today nothing is left from the once "most famous beat club of the world" (cf. Krüger 2010).

2. "Live" at the *Star-Club*: playing on stage, recordings on site (and elsewhere)

In late summer or early autumn 1962, Adrian Barber, guitarist/vocalist in The Big Three from Liverpool and respected among fellow musicians also for his skills to upgrade amplifiers and to build large speaker cabinets (which went by the name of "coffins"), decided to stay in Hamburg after The Big Three had played the *Star-Club* in July, and to work for Weissleder (himself trained as an electrician and technician) as a stage manager. Barber not only greatly improved the house P.A. system (see below) but also

---

[6] There are some such accounts in Clayson 1997 based on talks with a number of musicians from British bands who had played at Hamburg (*Star-Club* and/or *Top Ten*).
[7] This is evident from files kept in the Hamburgische Staatsarchiv (StAH 442-I, 95-92-15/9). Weissleder in 1964 had a dispute with the tax authorities and apparently had to settle for holdback payment of taxes due for the *Star-Club* even though he had already payed huge sums on taxes.
[8] Well documented in a film by Axel Engstfeld (Bye, bye Star-Club, 1987) that was one of the many sources we used for the reconstruction of the *Star-Club*.

installed some basic recording facilities, which allowed him to cut live performances on tape. According to Adrian Barber (personal communication, 2009), Weissleder even owned a single Neumann U 47 condenser mic, one of the best microphones ever, as well as a small mixing desk besides a range of dynamic mics (AKG D 12, Sennheiser MD 421) that were used on stage for the singers and instrumentalists.

Perhaps due to the favourable response the *Star-Club* had found in the public as well as among rock and beat enthusiasts already in 1962, the idea to record music "live" in the club, with a possible chance of publication by record companies, must have come up soon. As is well known, Bert Kaempfert and some other representatives of the music business (like Alfred Schacht, a lawyer and music publisher from Hamburg) had seen Tony Sheridan and the Beatles perform at the *Top Ten*, in June 1961, and had offered them to record a few songs, among them their now legendary reading of "My bonnie" that (backed by "The Saints") was released as a single by Polydor in October 1961. In the same session, Tony Sheridan and the Beatles recorded some more songs (Why, Take out some insurance, Nobody's child, Ain't she sweet) as well as an instrumental featuring the Beatles (Cry for a shadow). These recordings were made, June 22nd and 23rd, at the Friedrich-Ebert-Halle (Hamburg-Harburg; see Articus et al. 1996, 91ff.) for two reasons: first, this hall was known for its superior acoustics and was available for recordings; second, the *Top Ten* was a rather small venue (compared to the spacey *Star-Club*) and perhaps too narrow to allow live recordings with some control of the sound if a crowd was present screaming and dancing in the room.

As to the *Star-Club*, plans to record live in the venue seem to have been considered by about the autumn of 1962. In fact, Adrian Barber had not only improved the P.A. system greatly, but also recorded many bands on stage of the *Star-Club*, among them The Beatles and King Size Taylor & The Dominoes.

In regard to the P.A. and backline amplification available in the *Star-Club* in 1962-63, the configuration of the original P.A. system (as installed and functioning in April 1962) is not totally clear. First, it is possible that Weissleder continued to use some of the sound equipment installed in the 'Stern-Kino' as part of the P.A. system since cinemas by that time used to have quite powerful sound systems. As an alternative, one can think of a conventional compact P.A. system (German: *Gesangsanlage*, typically comprising an amp and two cabinets as well as a tape echo) as were manufactured in Germany by Dynacord and Echolette. While Echolette offered a small but effective amp (M 40, 4 x EL 84) capable to deliver up to 36 W output power into 8 Ohms, Dynacord had a unit with 45 W output power (Eminent, 2 x EL 34) as well as heavier amps (MV 75 and MV 120, the latter equipped first with 2 x EL 156 and then with 4 x EL 34 to deliver 120 W straight power). Echolette's M40 and Dynacord's Eminent in fact were the backbone of most German beat groups' mobile P.A. systems[9]. Both Echolette and Dynacord offered a combination of their amp with a tape echo machine from their respective production (Echolette NG 51, Dynacord Echocord [Super]) whereby both units were mounted in a frame to protect them when transported from one place to another. There is a possibility that The Beatles and Roy Young had the Echolette combination

---

[9] One can see these units on numerous photos in Klitsch 2001.

(M40/NG 51) on stage in spring 1962 though there is but one photo published that seems to support such an inference[10].

The P.A. system that was available in the *Star-Club* in the summer of 1962, according to Adrian Barber (personal communication, 2009) included two large baffles each containing 15 Telefunken woofers of 25 cm (10") diameter. Since flat loudspeaker baffles lack damping from the back, acoustic short-circuit (depending on wavelength) as well as feedback are likely to occur, especially if the system is driven with high power input. When Adrian Barber took over responsibility for the equipment, he changed the (open) baffles into two large closed loudspeaker cabinets, each still housing 15 woofers. The 15 speakers in each cabinet were combined into two groups of 8 and 7 speakers, respectively. Each loudspeaker group was driven by one of the Telefunken power amps (Adrian Barber, personal communication, 2009). These power amps had 100 V-outputs (the output resistance typically being 400 Ohm, but could have been also 600 Ohm). The nominal amp output can be calculated as

(1) $\quad P = U^2 / Z$, where U is the output voltage, and Z is the output resistance.

The 100 Volt-technology, which implies transformers are needed for each speaker in an array to bring the line voltage down to the level of the signal, was quite common in sound systems of the time, and still in use in the 1980s (cf. Boye & Herrmann 1989, 88-94). Telefunken amps designed for P.A. systems (e.g., the models Ela V 306/1, V 315/1 and V 318) usually had pairs of EL 34 tubes in the power stage; two EL 34 in class AB push-pull wiring typically yield ca. 35 W of power, and can deliver up to 100 W in class B push-pull wiring (Telefunken 1961). According to Adrian Barber the power amps he used were class B wired and the German EL 34 pentodes had been replaced with British KT 88 valves[11]. This would not necessarily have increased the maximum power but could have enhanced the dynamic response of the amp (original KT 88 are known to allow a wide range of undistorted amplification before clipping sets in at maximum power). From the evidence available, it can be assumed that the four power amps could deliver at least 200 Watt power, and possibly up to 400 Watt to the speaker arrays. Compared to compact microphone and instrument amplifiers, most of which were in the range from 32 to 45 W output power fed into 8 Ohm speakers (e.g., Echolette M40, Dynacord Eminent), this was a powerful system indeed. In addition to straight power, the system offered sound effects since Weissleder owned at least one echo machine[12]. However, what is not totally clear and as yet could not be reconstructed with certainty notwithstanding our efforts to interview a range of musicians who played the *Star-Club* in 1962 and 1963, is the connection of the typically three or four microphones used on

---

[10] See the photo in Krüger 2010, 56. Next to George Harrison (playing his Gretsch Duo Jet) on the right side one can see a unit that looks like the Echolette NG 51 mounted on a frame. We like to thank Ulf Krüger for providing a copy of this photo in an enlarged format.

[11] This is possible in principle yet requires some adaption of the amp. The EL 34 can be replaced though quite simply by KT 77 valves (which were produced in Great Britain in the 1960s). For details, see Pittman 1993.

[12] According to Adrian Barber (personal communication 2009), this was a Binson Echorec II from Italy, one of the best echo machines of the 1960s, employing a magnetic disc instead of a tape loop.

stage to the Telefunken amps combined in the P.A. system. One the one hand, these amps all had several microphone inputs to which stage microphones could have been connected. This leaves the question of how the three or four microphones were assigned to the four amps. On the other, Weissleder is said to have owned a small stereo mixing desk into which all microphones could have been plugged, and the output then split into four mono signals feeding the power amps. Several musicians we interviewed told that the amps and other technical devices necessary for stage operation (including the switch to open and close to huge stage curtain) were posited in a recess on the right side of the doorway leading from the backstage dressing rooms to the stage.

The backline amplification available at the 'Star-Club' included two Fender amps, namely a Bandmaster and a Showman Amp, both were new models in 1962. The Bandmaster was a 40 W/8 Ohm amp (preamp: 2 x 7025, power amp: 2 x 5881 or 2 x 6L6 GC), and the Showman had about double output from a power amp consisting of four 6L6 tubes. Both the Bandmaster and the Showman offered a tremolo effect but no reverb in 1962[13]. The Showman 15 amp came with a cabinet that housed a single 15" JBL D 140F Speaker, and this is the configuration shown on many pictures from the *Star-Club*. The Bandmaster used in the *Star-Club* was mostly connected to a standard Fender 2 x 12" cabinet (housing Jensen C12 N speakers), but on some pictures a different, much larger Fender cabinet apparently containing four speakers (might have been a 4 x 10" cabinet) turns up. For the bass, one could have used the Fender cabinet with the 15" JBL speaker. However, the *Star-Club* offered one of Barber's 'Coffins' instead, a large cabinet (approx. 120 x 60 x 60 cm) containing two Goodman 15" bass speakers, which were of a sturdy construction and had heavy magnets and coils to ensure reliability and strong performance. For this bass cabinet, another amp was needed. Ted 'King Size' Taylor suggested it could have been a Leak from England but this is rather uncertain[14].

On a number of pictures from the *Star-Club* also some Echolette B 40N amps can be seen. This amp (3 x ECC 83, 2 x EL 34) was manufactured by Klemt at Munich and was introduced to the market in 1962. Its circuitry was similar to the Fender Bassman, and the B 40N (40 W power output, speaker impedance 5 or 16 Ohms) soon became kind of a workhorse for many bands.

In addition to the P.A. equipment and backline amplification mentioned above, the *Star-Club* in 1962-63 held some equipment in stock in order to replace broken amps or to accommodate artists from abroad who didn't bring their own equipment. The *Star-Club* also had a grand piano on stage and at times seems to have provided a Hammond or similar electronic organ to bands. Also, a Trixon drum set (manufactured at Hamburg) was available to musicians.

---

[13] Specifics of the various Fender models (which changed in many details over the period of production while keeping the model names) are found in, e.g., Pittman 1993, Smith 1995.

[14] Edward Taylor, personal communication, 2009. The Leak TL/25 Plus was a mono amp comprising two EL 34 (or, alternatively, two KT 66) in the power stage. Leak amps were much in use in the EMI Abbey Road studios. Paul McCartney used a Leak TL12 during early recording sessions there as bass amp (Lewisohn 1988, 17).

Figure 2: Fender Band-Master 1962 and Showman Amp 1962 (resting on a 2 x 12" cabinet)

Fig. 3: Goodman 15" bass speaker (16 Ohm) with heavy magnet viewed from the back.

Fig. 4: The Phantom Brothers on stage of the *Star-Club* on December 3rd, 1963[15]. Note the bass 'coffin' cabinet (on the right side of the drums), the grand piano (far right), the organ (left of center), and the 'Manhattan Skyline' painting (E. Ross) in the background of the stage.
Also, a couple of Neumann U47 or U48 are visible (on the left side in front of the organ and to the right over the drums) since the show was (planned to be) recorded live.

Concerning live-recordings in the *Star-Club*, it was apparently Adrian Barber who started to record bands in considerable number beginning in late summer or early autumn of 1962. In fact, recording bands on stage seems to have become kind of routine. According to Adrian Barber (personal communication, 2009), Weissleder owned a semi-professional Telefunken tape recorder as well as a small stereo mixing desk that was used for such recordings[16]. One would think of this equipment also in regard to the (in)famous Beatles recordings that were made during their last stint at the *Star-Club* in December 1962, and were published (after heavy audio processing and editing) in 1977 by Lingasong in the UK and Bellaphon in Germany as well as in many later editions[17]. These recordings however have been made with another tape recorder, which Ted

---

[15] On December 3rd, 1963, the *Star-Club* held its 2nd band competition, in which the Phantom Brothers (from Rendsburg, Germany) had to go on stage as band no. 18 in the final round. They delivered a wild show and came in third in the final ranking.

[16] The machine that comes to mind would be the Telefunken M24, a sturdy all-tube tape recorder that was widely used also by radio stations for mobile recording of small ensembles. The M 24 itself offers four inputs (2 x mic, 2 x line) and a rudimentary on-board mixing facility, however, the M 24 was a mono recorder (available with half-track and full-track heads) so that a stereo mixing desk would not really fit to this machine.

[17] The legal entanglements of these recordings as well as dozens of articles and books published over the years with speculations on the exact date at which this or that song was recorded (or even, in which set it was played on a certain day in December 1962) will not be considered.

Taylor (personal communication, 2009) identified as a four-track mono Philips running at 9.5 cm/sec (3¾ inch/sec). He said that a single AKG D12 (the microphone model used daily by bands on the stage of the *Star-Club*) was put above the stage (where rails were mounted to carry the curtain as well as draperies) and connected to the tape recorder (operated by Barber). Hence a mono mic signal was fed into one track (meaning less than ¼ of a standard tape that is 6.3 mm wide) of the recorder running at a relatively low speed. Such conditions of course are not sufficient to produce high quality recordings but good enough to get live music on tape for personal collection or a similar purpose. Though the exact date of some of the Beatles recordings from the *Star-Club* has been a matter of dispute, there are indications that their show on the 31st of December, 1962, which was the very last evening of their engagement, has been taped (as Ted Taylor confirms)[18]. The recordings (as published in 1977 and later) may lack hifi sound quality, however, they capture the music as presented by the band in a live situation then in an authentic way (including interaction with the crowd) and also demonstrate what the band actually did musically when playing on stage.

Beginning in the early spring of 1963 recordings in the *Star-Club* were made by the German Philips record company (Philips Ton) residing at Hamburg due to activities of one of their young employees, Siegfried ('Siggi') Loch (b. 1940) who took on the job of a producer for such albums as 'Twist im Star-Club Hamburg' (a sampler, Philips P 48 036 L) and the Searchers' "Sweets for my my Sweet. The Searchers at the Star-Club Hamburg" (Philips P 48 052 L), followed by the Rattles' "Twist im Star-Club Hamburg" (Philips P 48 068 L) and by Jerry Lee Lewis (and The Nashville Teens) "Live" at The "Star-Club" Hamburg (Philips P 14 546 L). Not all of these recordings can be called "live" in the sense that the music was played in front of people attending a show. The Searchers were in fact recorded on stage of the *Star-Club* (around March 1st, 1963), however, most if not all songs put on tape by Hans-Georg Dozel of Philips as recording engineer were produced in the afternoon before the club opened to avoid the noise of the crowd (Siegfried Loch, personal communication, 2009). The applause heard on this album (and on others!) was later added to the music. However, on the sampler "Twist im Star-Club Hamburg" (recorded in early spring 1963 and released in September 1963) there are several real live recordings, of which Tony Sheridan's long version of "Skinny Minny" is perhaps the most impressive in regard to musical interpretation and sound[19]. With respect to "Skinny Minny", the singer's voice seems to have been recorded from the house P.A. since there was no second microphone connected directly to a mixing

---

[18] On the published recordings (e.g. Historic Records HIS 10982) preceding the Beatles' "I saw her standing there", there are two announcements to the crowd present in the *Star-Club*, the first of which apparently was made by Manfred Weissleder saying (in a dialect easily identifiable as belonging to the ‚Ruhrgebiet' part of Westfalia) *is genau fünf Minuten vor Zwölf, fünf Minuten vor Zwölf*. This evidently was to point to the circumstance that New Year (1.1.1963) was just 5 minutes ahead. Weissleder's announcement preserved on the recording is followed by Horst Fascher saying (in a clearly identifiable Hamburgese colouring of speech*) und weiter geht's im Star-Club mit unseren Stars aus Liverpool, mit den Beatles.*

[19] For contractual reasons, Sheridan was credited on the record as „Dan Sherry". He was accompanied by his 'Star-Combo' comprising, among other musicians, Roy Young on keyboards and Ricky Barnes on tenor sax.

desk. Tony Sheridan used a Sennheiser MDS 421 dynamic microphone provided on stage as part of the P.A. system when doing this song (Tony Sheridan, personal communication, 2011), that is, the vocal sound heard on this recording (including tape echo) notwithstanding the possibility of equalization and even some dynamic shaping (by means of limiters and/or compression) available to the Philips engineers may be relatively close to the original sound as was audible then in the *Star-Club*. Also some of the numbers the Rattles found on their first album, namely "Mashed Potatoes" and "Hello", were cut during a live performance at the *Star-Club* in 1963 (Achim Reichel, personal communication, 2009). The songs Jerry Lee Lewis and The Nashville Teens have on their magnificent album are all live, however, some apparently were not recorded at the *Star-Club* but (by Peter Kramper, another Philips engineer) during a concert Jerry Lee and the Nahsville Teens played at the Deutschlandhalle of Berlin (March, 1963).

In fact, recordings such as "Skinny Minny" or "Mashed Potatoes" as well as a few other tracks cut at *Star-Club* at least provide an approximate image of the sound as it was projected from the stage to the audience.

P.A. system and backline amplification on stage must have worked nicely since musicians from Liverpool who came to play at Hamburg say that "the sound was absolutely fantastic, I never heard anything like it in my life, you could hear every individual instrument" (Taylor & Frankland 2006). Some musicians we interviewed who had played the *Star-Club* stressed that the drum sound projected well from stage, with no need to mike the drums and that the bass and low mid frequencies that came from bass drum and bass amp were heard prominently even at low sound levels, which was probably due to the construction of the stage that in fact was built on top of a room in the basement (which could have functioned like a resonance chamber). However, the auditorium itself as perceived by musicians when on stage apparently might have been overemphasizing bass and low mid frequencies consequent to textiles on the walls absorbing, most of all, higher frequencies. In addition to textiles covering most of the sidewalls of the auditorium, the stage had a huge drop (curtain) that opened to both sides plus several rows of draperies made from the same textiles above the stage. Also, the back wall of the stage apparently had been covered with waffle board on which Erwin Ross' "Manhattan Skyline" had been painted.

3. Reconstruction of the *Star-Club*

Except for a few planks from the stage that had been saved by some enthusiasts just before the final demolition, there seem to be no material remains of the building or its interior. Hence the motivation for the project presented in this article: to reconstruct the 'Star Club' as a virtual reality music hall that can be "played" in principle, that is, by regaining its acoustical characteristics from reconstructing the geometry as well as the interior and the P.A. system.

The *Star-Club* was established, in 1962, with the intent to showcasing prominent artists as well as upcoming talent to a public that demanded live rock'n'roll as well as (the then new) beat music. The club consisted of an auditorium of ca. 23 x 15 x 9 meter that had been a ballroom in the first decades of the 20th century, and had been remodelled as a cinema in 1949, with balconies on the two sides and the back of the room ca.

3.5 m above the ground floor to offer additional seating to visitors. When the 'Stern-Kino' was transformed into the *Star-Club*, the seats on the ground level were removed and a dance floor in front of the stage as well as two bars at the back of the room created. Otherwise, the room remained much the same though groups of tables and seats were arranged from behind the dance floor to the back of the hall. Also, a drum riser made of wood was added to the stage that consisted of planks mounted across a (hollow) concrete and brick construction, which acoustically must have formed kind of a resonator.

The decoration of the room was changed at least in part by the time the club opened in April 1962 and again in 1964 when the 'Manhattan Skyline' painting at the back of the stage disappeared behind even more curtain-like blue textiles[20]. Also, the room and the stage were remodelled in other aspects then. Our efforts to reconstruct the *Star-Club* relate to the situation as it was in 1962 and 1963.

From various sources, among them architect's drawings, it was possible to reconstruct most of the geometry of the *Star-Club* including the balcony and the stage. For a number of details concerning the interior of the room, the decoration of walls, and in particular the P.A. system and backline amplification as well as actual sound experienced while playing and listening, additional information obtained from experts (most of them musicians who had played the *Star-Club* frequently) was used.

3.1. Room Geometry.

The basic geometry of the *Star-Club* including the balcony and the stage section is shown in figures 5a-c. Figure 5a pictures the stage that was not perfectly in the middle of the back wall and hence asymmetric in its position relative to the left and right side walls of the hall. Fig. 5b and 5c show the back of the *Star-Club* (were two bars were located), the left balcony side with the entrance and the right balcony side with the sidewalk, respectively.

The *Star-Club* for the most part was a brick building reinforced with concrete and iron girders placed across the stage and the auditorium to carry the weight of the ceiling made of plaster as well as the roof construction consisting mainly of timber covered with roofing cardboard[21]. The walls apparently uniformly were covered with plaster. The room had a length of 23.2 m, was 14.8 m wide and had a maximum height of 9.19 m. Taking structures built within the room into account, the volume can be estimated close to 2800 m^3. The global surface area is 1549.18 m^2 including all walls, the ceiling and the floor. The large side-walls to the left and the right of the hall of 137.4 m^2 each and the balustrade of the balcony had been decorated with a textile whose absorption coefficient is assumed similar to those known for cotton, plush, or linen cloth. The floor of the auditorium and the floor of the balcony were made from concrete. The dance floor had been furnished with plastic tiles.

---

[20] The *Star-Club* sold postcards to visitors where bands on stage were pictured. From 1964, there is such a postcard (*Grüsse aus dem Star-Club Hamburg*) showing the Pretty Things on stage (to which an elevation had been added on top of which sat the drum riser as a third level or "floor").

[21] We had access to reports of the fire brigade that was called to fight the fire on February 18th, 1983. One of the reasons the building burnt down so fast was this cardboard roofing.

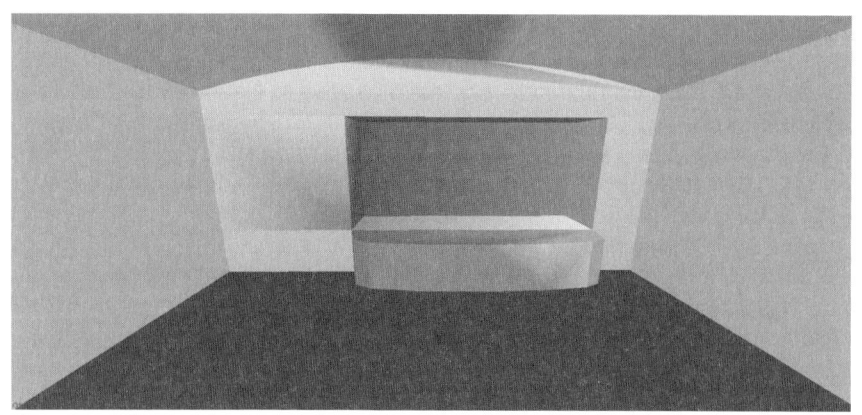

Figure 5a: Model of the *Star-Club*. Stage and dance floor area.

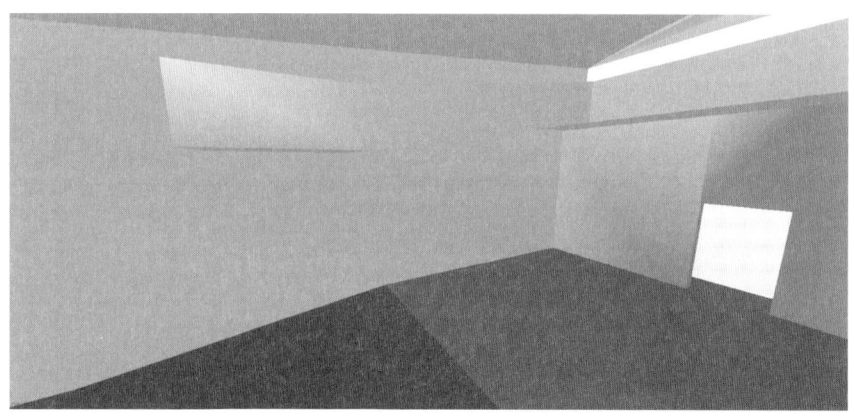

Figure 5b: rear of the *Star-Club* with main entrance to the auditorium. Balcony on left side and across the back of the hall.

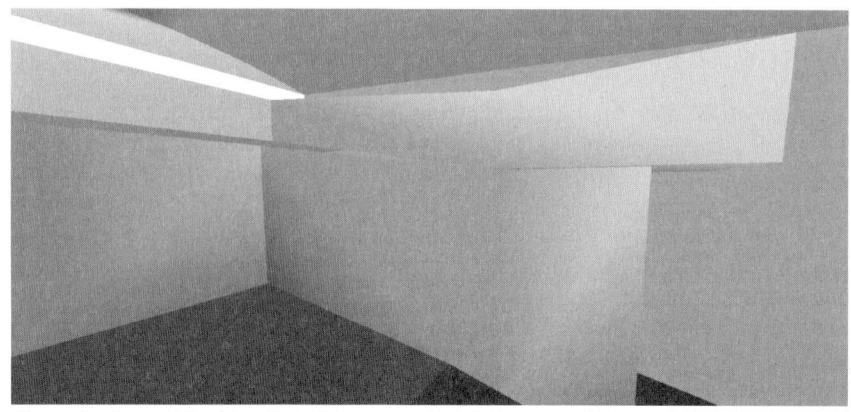

Figure 5c: Rear of the *Star-Club*. Balcony on the left (above a dividing wall) and across the back of the hall

The dimensions of the stage in our model were calculated from original photographs of the *Star-Club* as well as from the "naked" stage left after the fire (shown in the documentary *Bye bye Star-Club* and on various photos). In addition, we asked musicians who had played on this very stage many a night for some details. The stage area (including the portal and the wings as well as the walls to the left and right of the portal) had been covered up with various curtains. The stage floor was made from wooden planks and the ceiling of the stage was a massive construction that apparently had mineral fibre plates and/or plaster as a cover from underneath.

To model sound reflection in the room as well as absorption of energy at walls, absorption coefficients were chosen to match as close as possible the materials used for the historical *Star-Club*. For our calculations, the dance floor is taken as filled with an audience crowd. The frequency-dependent damping parameters as used in the simulation are summed in Table 1. Since the model of the *Star-club* was set up with the room acoustics modelling software, Odeon (Lyngby, Denmark), the values used were taken from the materials library of the software.

Table 1. Frequency-dependent damping coefficients for material used for the *Star-Club* model surfaces and for the audience

Frequency [Hz]	63	125	250	500	1000	2000	4000	8000
Cotton	.09	.09	.29	.35	.41	.43	.55	.55
Plaster	.013	.013	.015	.02	.03	.04	.05	.05
Curtain	.15	.15	.45	.96	.91	1.0	1.0	1.0
Wood	.15	.15	.11	.1	.07	.06	.07	.07
Fibre plate	.13	.13	.13	.49	.86	.99	.94	.94
Audience	.6	.6	.74	.88	.96	.93	.85	.85

Since the *Star-Club* did not have effective air condition, people working their bodies on the dance floor and producing heat and sweat must be taken into account. Therefore, a room temperature of 24° C and a humidity of 70 % were set for the model (corresponding to average conditions in rock venues lacking air-condition).

3.2. P.A. system and backline

The P.A. system of the *Star-Club* available from late summer or early autumn 1962 at least to the end of 1963 (when Adrian Barber left Hamburg) has been described above. It can be assumed that the four power amps could deliver up to 400 Watt to the speaker arrays. For our model, two arrays of 15 speakers each were located on the walls to the right and left side of the stage. Each speaker is designed as a point source with omni directivity. On stage, we assumed a "classical" beat group comprising two electric guitars, a bass guitar, and drums. Hence we have four instruments for which a backline consisting of three amps/cabinets is provided. At the *Star-Club*, thanks to the spacey stage band members could choose their individual position as they liked. Even drummers did not always stick to the drum riser (The Searchers' Chris Curtis used to drum up front standing behind the drum set since he did also much of the lead vocals).

Following a scheme evident from photos, we set up the bass guitar amp on the left side of the stage (taking the musicians' perspective towards the audience) close to the back wall (the default position of Barber's "coffin"). Guitar amp no. 1 is placed to the right side, and guitar amp no. 2 more to the middle. The drums were placed almost in the middle of the stage (where the drum riser had been built). The PA system consists of two times 15 loudspeakers arranged at the left and right side of the stage with source numbers 1 - 15 (left) and 16 - 30 (right).

Two receiver points were defined, one on the dance floor (1) close to the stage, the other (2) at the back of the hall (perhaps a visitor sitting at the bar). The precise source and receiver positions are shown in Fig. 6. In regard to the two loudspeaker arrays of the P.A. system, the sound from 30 loudspeakers radiated towards the listener(s) for each single speaker will have a slightly different travelling time to the receiver points. Hence in the reflectogram multiple impulses appear for the direct sound as well as for all early reflections following thereafter. These multiple reflections, slightly blurred over time, produce a 'fat' sound for instruments being amplified via this PA system, mostly the vocals, but also instruments like the saxophone.

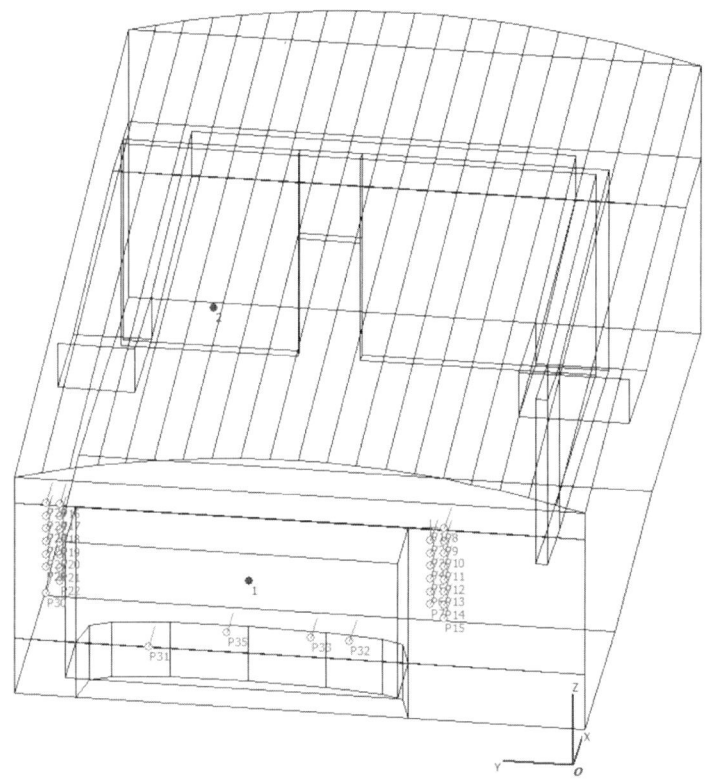

Fig. 6: Model of the *Star-Club*: 34 sources and 2 receiver points (dance floor, bar)

The assumption of omnidirectional radiation of the speakers holds very well up to at least 200 Hz. As we will see in the results section below, the frequency region from about 250 Hz is not very strong. So taking a more detailed radiation pattern for higher frequencies into consideration is not expected to change the sound considerably.

3.3. Ray-Tracing

Ray tracing is an established method for finding the scattering patterns in a given room (conceived as a geometrical construct)[22] and for calculating its impulse response. The ray-tracing algorithm was performed for 5925 rays with a maximum reflection order of 2000. For the walls, a Lambert scattering was used.

3.4. Auralisation

Auralisation is a technique which allows to test the (predicted or, in our case, reconstructed) acoustics by producing the actual sound as it would appear in a real room of given dimensions and properties (cf. Vorländer 2008). For auralisation, two binaural recording points were used, one defined as an audience point about 1 m in front of the stage and one at the back of the hall at the bar (where cocktails and soft drinks were served).

Several methods for auralisation were used according to possibilities offered by the Odeon modelling software:
- 2D Surround sound for a simple two-speaker setup;
- binaural headphone auralisation using HRTF (head-related transfer function);
- ambisonic auralisation;
- 5.1, 6.1, and 7.1 surround sound realisations.

The method of auralisation does not affect the results of the frequency-dependent impulse responses and the calculated echograms. They are only fitting the impulse responses to a specific auralisation setup.

4. Results from measurements

4.1. Frequency-dependent reverberation time

In room acoustics, there are certain factors suited to characterize the acoustic behaviour and quality of a given hall or other geometry (cf. Ando 1985, Beranek 1996). Relevant factors often have an objective basis in that physical properties are measured and expressed in physical units. In addition, psychoacoustic criteria and psychological evaluation made by individuals play an important role in the assessment of concert halls, opera houses, etc.

Perhaps the most widely used factor to characterize a given room structure is its reverberation time. The reverberation time (RT) was calculated as Early-Decay Time (EDT) and as so-called T_{30} to determine the decay from the maximum energy level down to -60 dB in eight frequency bands ranging in octaves from 63 Hz to 8 kHz (as are mostly used in room acoustics simulations). Both, the T_{30} and the EDT are two views on the RT. When plotted on a dB scale, the impulse response decay of a closed space is very close to a linear decay. The RT is defined as the time of an impulse response lasting

---

[22] Ray tracing algorithms are also used since long in 3D computer graphics.

until it can no longer be heard, which corresponds to a drop of the initial level to -60 dB. Still this is difficult to measure because of measurement noise. Therefore only the beginning of the decay or a portion in the middle is used to calculate the RT as its linear slope allows to reconstruct or extrapolate its decay further. Here, the EDT algorithm calculates RT as a least square fit to the drop from the start of the impulse to a drop of -10 dB, the T_{30} uses the section starting from -5 dB down to -35 dB. So the EDT algorithm takes the very beginning into consideration which may be stronger and therefore often results in longer RT times. We calculated RTs for all combinations of source and receiver points listed in Tab. 2. The case of the PA system as heard at the dance floor is shown in Fig. 7 as a typical example.

Table 2: Calculated RT (as EDT) for different sources with respect to two receiver positions (a) on the dance floor in front of the stage, (b) at the back of the hall (at the bar) in seconds.

Frequency [Hz]	63	125	250	500	1000	2000	4000	8000
Dance Floor								
PA	1.56	1.78	0.79	0.42	0.26	0.25	0.21	0.19
Drums	1.44	1.61	0.71	0.37	0.16	0.15	0.14	0.13
Bass	1.53	1.73	0.77	0.41	0.26	0.25	0.22	0.18
Guitar 1	1.36	1.69	0.72	0.37	0.20	0.19	0.16	0.14
Guitar 2	1.48	1.63	0.68	0.29	0.17	0.15	0.13	0.12
Cocktail Bar								
PA	1.79	1.81	0.87	0.45	0.32	0.31	0.28	0.26
Drums	1.56	1.83	0.87	0.48	0.32	0.30	0.27	0.25
Bass	1.53	1.65	0.87	0.42	0.29	0.27	0.24	0.22
Guitar 1	1.63	1.74	0.85	0.44	0.29	0.29	0.25	0.22
Guitar 2	1.73	1.74	0.85	0.49	0.32	0.31	0.26	0.23

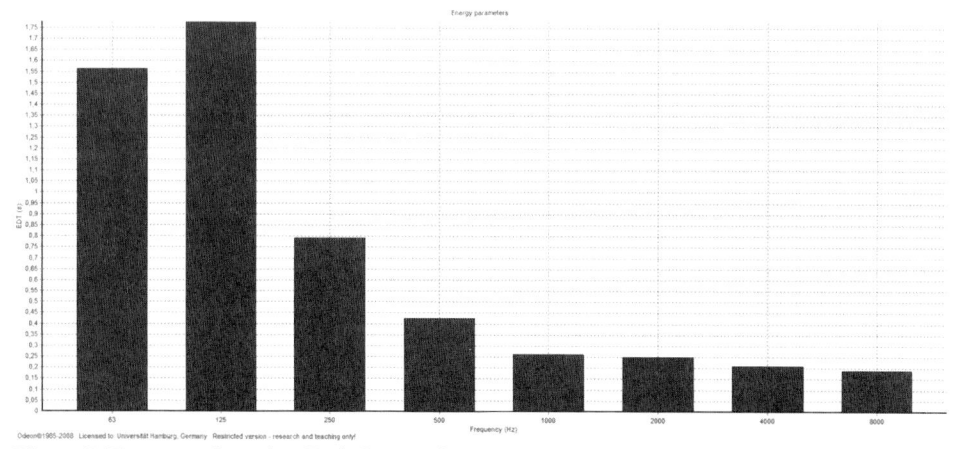

Figure 7: Frequency-dependent Early Decay Time (EDT) of the PA speakers (sources 1 – 30) relative to the dance floor (receiver point 1) in seconds. Most of the energy is found within the frequency range from 63 Hz to 250 Hz.

201

Not surprisingly, for all calculated RTs most energy is concentrated in the bass frequency region between 63 Hz and 250 Hz. This corresponds to the reports of musicians having played the *Star-Club* (see above) who said the room emphasized (or even overemphasized) bass and low mid sound.

4.2. Clarity factors

In addition to the reverberation time, which correlates with the perceived 'liveliness' of a hall (very short RT makes a room appear "dry" or even "dead", while sufficient RT goes along with a sensation that the room "responds" to sound radiated from a source or from several sources), there are factors concerning the perceived clarity of the sound in terms of understanding speech or musical textures. In German room acoustics, it is customary to distinguish between the distinctness (*Deutlichkeit*) and the clarity (*Klarheit*) of a given sound perceived at a certain spot (cf. Fasold et al. 1987, 251-258, Ahnert & Steffen 1993, 38-39). There are two algorithms to calculate either distinctness or clarity, which are very similar since both are based on the ratio of "early" energy (calculated from the square of the pressure amplitude of the impulse response) to "late" energy, whereby "early" means energy measured within the first 50 ms (C_{50}) after onset or within the first 80 ms (C_{80}), and "late" points to energy measured after 50 ms or 80 ms (up to, in practice, 3 seconds after onset). Energy within intervals thus is determined from integration. While C_{50} typically is regarded relevant to speech intelligibility (of speech presented in large rooms or halls to an audience), C_{80} relates to music (Fasold et al. 1987, 257)

$$(2) \quad C_{50} = 10 \log \left(\frac{\int_{t=0\,ms}^{t=50\,ms} p(t)^2 \, dt}{\int_{t=50}^{t=\infty\,ms} p(t)^2 \, dt} \right)$$

$$(3) \quad C_{80} = 10 \log \left(\frac{\int_{t=0\,ms}^{t=80\,ms} p(t)^2 \, dt}{\int_{t=80}^{t=\infty\,ms} p(t)^2 \, dt} \right)$$

C_{50} and C_{80} values from 0 dB to +4 dB are considered optimal, however, this depends somewhat on the type of signals under consideration. Whereas for speech a high degree of claritiy seems necessary to ensure intelligibility, music listeners would perhaps demand also a ‚lively' (somewhat reverberant) and ‚spaceous' sound. However, if C_{50} or C_{80} is too low the sound in the room may be too blurred. In fact, claritiy and liveness are basically contradictory acoustical qualities so that a compromise must be found for many concert rooms to allow both performance of polyphonic as well as homophonic orchestral works (cf. Beranek 1996).

In addition (or as an alternative) to 'claritiy', in particular for speech signals but also for music the so-called degree of distinctiveness (*Deutlichkeitsgrad*) or 'definition' (Meyer & Thiele 1956, Schroeder et al. 1974) can be calculated like

(4) $$D = \left(\frac{\int_{t=0}^{t=50\,\text{ms}} p(t)^2 \, dt}{\int_{t=0}^{t=\infty\,\text{ms}} p(t)^2 \, dt} \right)$$

The 'definition' D_{50} represents the amount of energy within the first 50 ms of the impulse response divided by the total energy in a logarithmic way. Hence $D_{50} = 1$ means the total energy of the response occurs within the first 50 ms. D_{50} is often used as a parameter for the clarity of speech, where a high value points to a good acoustic for speech. In general, 'clarity' and 'definition' are high if the fraction of energy contained in the direct sound signal and in early reflections is high. Taking into account the speed of sound ($c \approx$ 330-340 m/sec) and a temporal limit of 50 ms (known as the threshold for echo), this means that sound rays send from a source, and reflected from walls or ceiling, should not exceed a length of 17 m relative to the perceiver point and to the distance the direct sound travels to ensure optimal conditions for speech intelligibility. For music (depending though on the genre), energy arriving within an interval of 80 ms is important in regard to direct sound and early reflections contributing to distinctness and clarity while sound reflections arriving later than 80 ms contribute to a parameter defined as 'spaciousness'. Since the bands playing the *Star-Club* offered a mix of vocals and instrumental sounds, one could consider C_{50}, C_{80} and/or D as relevant parameters. For the purpose of this article, it is sufficient to consider D_{50} values, which are listed for all combinations of source and receiver points and for the eight frequency bands in Table 3.

Table 3: D_{50} calculated for different sources with respect to two listening room positions (on the dance floor in front of the stage and at the cocktail bar).

Frequency [Hz]	63	125	250	500	1000	2000	4000	8000
Dance Floor								
PA	0.52	0.48	0.71	0.87	0.92	0.92	0.94	0.96
Drums	0.56	0.53	0.71	0.88	0.93	0.94	0.96	0.97
Bass	0.51	0.49	0.69	0.87	0.92	0.93	0.95	0.96
Guitar 1	0.55	0.54	0.73	0.89	0.93	0.94	0.96	0.97
Guitar 2	0.57	0.55	0.75	0.91	0.95	0.95	0.97	0.97
Cocktail Bar								
PA	0.44	0.41	0.68	0.84	0.91	0.91	0.93	0.94
Drums	0.39	0.37	0.62	0.82	0.89	0.90	0.92	0.94
Bass	0.39	0.37	0.63	0.84	0.91	0.92	0.93	0.95
Guitar 1	0.42	0.39	0.66	0.84	0.91	0.91	0.93	0.95
Guitar 2	0.39	0.36	0.62	0.82	0.89	0.90	0.92	0.94

Clearly the RT cause the lower frequency bands to also have lower D_{50} values, while above 1 kHz nearly all energy is within the first 50 ms. Thus, the *Star-Club* had good definition in bands of higher frequencies.

To show the amount and the pattern of reflections per time unit, three reflectograms are displayed in figure 8a-c. Fig. 8a and 8b show the early reflections of the bass amp sound as it arrives at the dance floor and at the cocktail bar, respectively. The dance floor receives only a few reflections at the beginning, whereas the receiver point near the bar shows a more wide spread pattern. The polar plots on the right of fig. 8a/8b clearly indicate a more spatially distributed reflection pattern at the bar receiver point compared to the dance floor. The reflectogram of the P.A. system with respect to the bar receiver point as displayed in fig. 8c shows a much more dense field of reflections. As discussed above, this pattern results from the multiple loudspeakers, all of which have a slightly different distance to the bar receiver point, to the effect that waves radiated from different loudspeaker contained in the two arrays arrive at slightly different points in time. In regard to listeners, this leads to a 'chorus' effect perceived as a dense or even 'fat' sound.

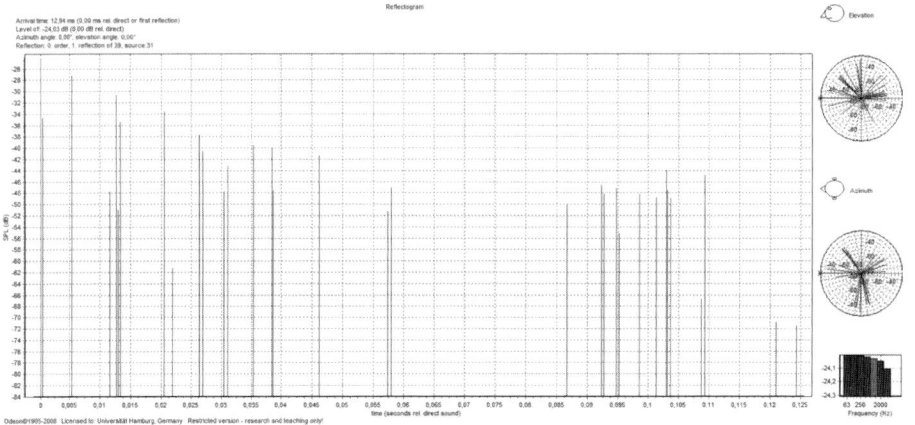

Fig. 8a: Reflectogram: bass amp sound received at the dance floor close to the stage

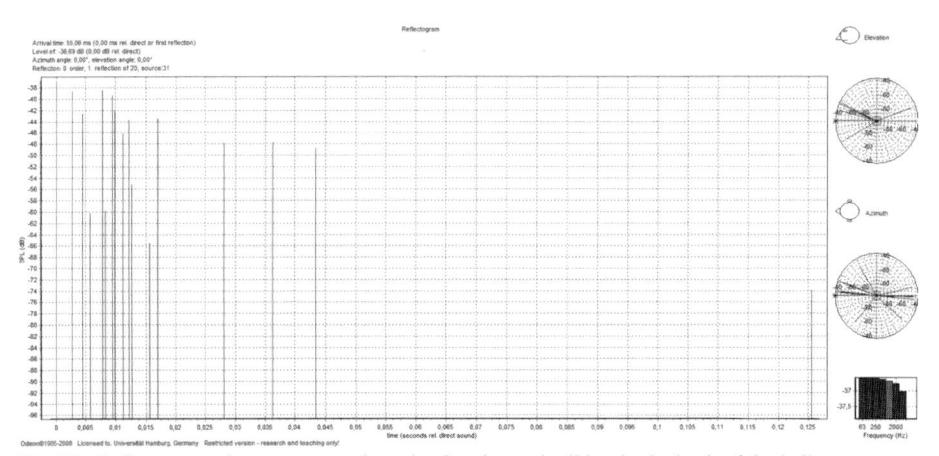

Fig. 8b: Reflectogram: bass amp sound received at the cocktail bar in the back of the hall

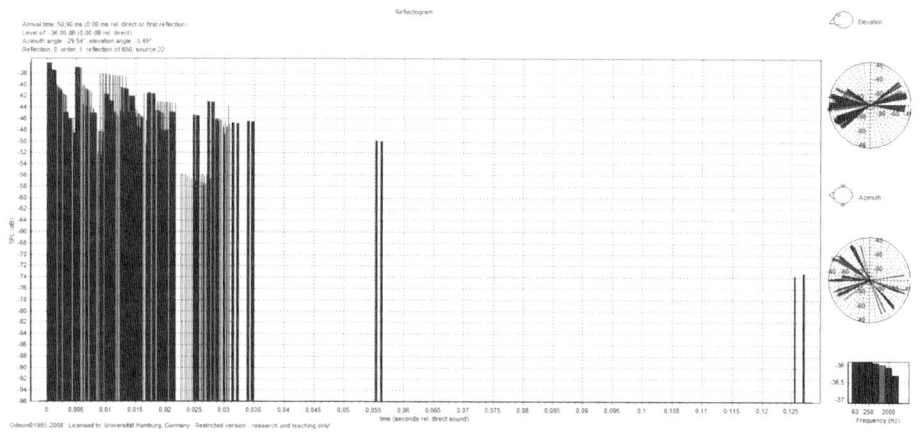

Fig. 8c: Reflectogram: P.A. sound as received at the bar in the back of the *Star-Club*

4.3. Lateral Energy Fraction LF_{80}

As a binaural parameter, the lateral energy fraction was also calculated. This parameter is mostly associated with the spaciousness or sound envelopment. It is defined as the ratio of lateral energy received within a time span from 5 ms to 80 ms after onset of sound to the total energy that occurs within the first 80 ms. Technically, the output of a figure-of-eight microphone is taken to represent the lateral energy, and the output of a non-directional microphone to represent the total early energy up to t = 80 ms.

$$(5) \quad LF_{80} = \left(\frac{\int_{t=5}^{t=80 \, ms} p_8^2(t)dt}{\int_{t=0}^{t=80 \, ms} p^2(t)dt} \right)$$

Table 4: LF_{80} calculated for instruments and P.A. with respect to two receiver positions

Frequency [Hz]	63	125	250	500	1000	2000	4000	8000
Dance Floor								
PA	0.214	0.212	0.189	0.148	0.125	0.112	0.110	0.106
Drums	0.193	0.193	0.168	0.093	0.056	0.042	0.031	0.027
Bass	0.319	0.321	0.315	0.331	0.311	0.296	0.256	0.242
Guitar 1	0.178	0.173	0.152	0.072	0.045	0.038	0.030	0.027
Guitar 2	0.158	0.156	0.131	0.066	0.042	0.035	0.026	0.023
Cocktail Bar								
PA	0.281	0.277	0.251	0.234	0.211	0.199	0.170	0.162
Drums	0.228	0.221	0.185	0.146	0.126	0.122	0.109	0.102
Bass	0.212	0.212	0.170	0.140	0.115	0.104	0.090	0.085
Guitar 1	0.245	0.245	0.218	0.212	0.198	0.196	0.165	0.158
Guitar 2	0.243	0.242	0.215	0.207	0.189	0.182	0.157	0.150

Table 4 summarizes the values calculated for the four instruments and the P.A. relative to two receiver points. Most fractions are around 20 % of lateral energy. Hence the binaural spatial perception of the Star Club was reasonably low (perhaps due to damping and absorption of sound effected from side wall and balcony decorations). As expected, the cocktail bar values are higher than those for the dance floor area as the bar was in the back of the club, which means there are more possible reflection points from the source to the receiver during the early reflection time. The only exception is the bass amp sound as sensed at the dance floor. It has the highest value of $LF_{80} = 0.319$ at 63 Hz and is still high at 250 Hz with $LF_{80} = 0.315$. Although the reason for such high LF_{80} values is not perfectly clear, they may be caused by the location of the bass amp on stage, which is behind the other stage sources used here, the drums and both guitar amps. As the floor and the ceiling of the stage (and to some degree also its back wall) functioned as hard reflective walls, strong standing waves may appear on stage when the sound has the opportunity to travel some way within the stage area. As the drums and the guitars were located more to the stage front (and are also located this way in our model), their sound leaves the stage into the direction of the dance floor without much interference with the ceiling, the portal or the rear wall of the stage. The bass amp sound coming from the depth of the stage probably is projected to some extent against structural elements of the stage and reflected from there resulting in a higher fraction of lateral energy as compared to the other instrument sources.

5. Discussion: from model data to virtual 'live' music

The parameter values determined from the model of the *Star-Club* and the subsequent auralisation are well in line with reports from musicians who had played in this hall, their opinion being that it had good acoustics. T_{30} averaged over eight octave bands from 63 Hz to 8 kHz comes close to 0.7 seconds. According to a study of halls used for rock music concerts in Denmark (Larsen et al. 2004), those venues that were rated best by experts (musicians, sound engineers) all had a frequency-averaged T_{30} in the range from 0.8 to 1 second, and not too much bass response below 100 Hz (with a preferable T_{30} at 100 Hz of less than 1.5 seconds). Further, the D_{50} obtained from the P.A. for the audience (taken as a group to represent the receiver area) in the best rock music halls was around 0.6 - 0.7. For the *Star-Club*, the D_{50} at the dance floor receiver point would be 0.8 when averaged over five sources (P.A., drums, bass, guitar 1, guitar 2) and eight frequency bands from 63 Hz to 8 kHz, and would yield 0.79, 0.81, 0.79, 0.814, 0.827 for the individual sources, respectively. Hence the 'definition' of the sound radiated from all source types for listeners perceiving beat music in front of the stage of the Star-Club must have been quite high, while at a distance (closer to the back of the hall) the reverberation of course took greater effect. Since, however, T_{30} apparently was less than 1.5 seconds for the deep bass (63 Hz), above 1.5 seconds for low mid frequencies at 125 Hz, and short for frequencies from 0.5 to 8 kHz (see figure 7), the Star-Club sound was not muddy in the deep bass while it had some 'warmth' (another parameter relevant for room acoustics, cf. Beranek 1996) in the midrange, and a fairly crisp high mid and treble range. All in all, this must have resulted in a reasonable balance between 'liveness' and 'definition'.

In order to test our model and the auralisation further, we recorded the song "I saw her standing there", which Paul McCartney wrote in 1962, and which the Beatles have played live at the *Star-Club*, as it seems on the very last evening of their last stint (31.12.1962) when it was recorded on tape. Their version in fact is the opener on the (in)famous 1977 Lingasong (and Bellaphon, etc.) album (see above). Our version was recorded on eight track analogue with vintage instruments and amps as well as vintage recording gear[23]. Drums, instruments and vocals were recorded under unechoic conditions on a small Fostex 80, from which the eight original analogue tracks were transferred to digital on a computer disc by means of a Fireface 800. These tracks then have been used to produce a virtual "live" performance in our *Star-Club* model where tracks 1-8 were assigned to their proper sound sources and then processed making use of the model data. Finally, the sound radiated from the P.A., drums, bass amp, and two guitar amps has been recorded in stereo at the two receiver points (dance floor, bar area) in a mix that resembles the (not too polished) 'live' sound of a beat group playing in a club around 1962 or 1963. Due to the fact that the two receiver points have different characteristics in regard to several acoustic parameters (see above), the two versions recorded on the dance floor and in the back of the hall sound quite differently. For legal reasons, we have made only brief excerpts of our recording (representing two different mixes and sound images) available for listening on our home page (www.systmuwi.de). So, almost 50 years after the Beatles and other greats played the *Star-Club*, the two versions of "I saw her standing there" as realized with our model at last may help to convey what the sound in this famous venue was like.

6. Conclusion

This article reports work directed to the reconstruction of the acoustics of a famous music hall by means of a geometrical model of the original venue that served to create the impulse response of the room. For this purpose, a specific ray tracing method available in the Odeon software package was employed. Subsequently, auralisation has been carried out to yield relevant parameter data characteristic of this room. Finally, a piece of music closely connected to the history of the *Star-Club* has been recorded with vintage instruments and equipment that was used to create a virtual 'live' performance making use of the P.A. and backline sound sources in the *Star-Club* model. The music produced in this way was recorded at two receiver points (on the dance floor and at the bar in the back of the hall). The sound material thus gained seems to 'emulate' the original sound known (at least approximately) from earlier recordings made in the *Star-Club* in a realistic way. The approach chosen for this experiment could be used similarly to reconstruct the acoustics of other once famous yet long extinct music halls and clubs.

---

[23] Instruments: Gibson ES 330 (1966), Höfner 185 bass (1963), Sonor drums (mostly from 1965, modern cymbals), Echolette Showstar and B 40N amps (1963, 1962) with vintage cabinet (ET 80 equipped with 3 vintage Celestion 12" speakers); recording: Neumann U 67, Sennheiser MKH 405 and MDS 421 mics. Studiomaster 16/8/2 and TAC 16/8/2 mixing desks, Telefunken and TAB preamps, compressors and filters.
The recording was made by A.S. (guitars, bass, vocals) and Norman Schleicher (drums) in October 2010.

7. Acknowledgements

This project would not have materialized without the help of musicians who have played on stage of the *Star-Club*, or have worked there as producer, technician, or photographer. We'd like to express our thanks to (in alphabetical order) Adrian Barber, Frank Dostal, Gibson Kemp, Siegfried Loch, Achim Reichel, Tony Sheridan, Ted ‚King Size' Taylor, Günter Zint.

8. References

Ahnert, Wolfgang, Frank Steffen 1993. *Beschallungstechnik. Grundlagen und Praxis.* Stuttgart: Hirzel.

Ando, Yoichi 1985. *Concert Hall Acoustics.* Berlin etc.: Springer

Articus, Rüdiger, Gerhard Beier, Lothar Krüger, Ulf Krüger, Klaus-Christian Schulze-Schlichtegroll 1996. *Die Beatles in Harburg* (Ausstellungskatalog, Helms-Mueseum). Hamburg: Christians.

Beckmann, Dieter, Klaus Martens 1980. *Star-Club.* Reinbek/Hamburg: Rowohlt.

Beranek, Leo 1996. *Concert and Opera Halls. How they sound.* Woodbury, N.Y.: Acoustical Soc. of America.

Boye, Günther, Urbi Herrmann 1989. *Handbuch der Elektroakustik.* 3rd ed. Heidelberg: Hüthig.

Clayson, Alan 1997. *Hamburg. The Cradle of British Rock.* London: Sanctuary Publ.

Fasold, Wolfgang, Ernst. Sonntag, Helgo Winkler 1987. *Bau- und Raumakustik.* Berlin: Verlag für Bauwesen (und Köln: Müller).

Klitsch, Hans-Jürgen 2001. Shakin' all over. *Die Beatmusik in der Bundesrepublik Deutschland 1963-1967.* 2nd ed. Erkrath: High Castle.

Krüger, Ulf 2010. *Star-Club Hamburg. Der bekannteste Beat-Club der Welt.* Höfen: Hannibal.

Larsen, Niels, Esteban Olmos, Anders Gade 2004. Acoustics in halls for rock music. *Proc. of the Joint Baltic-Nordic Acoustics Meeting 2004* (BNAM 2004, Mariehamn, Åland).

Lewisohn, Mark 1988. *The Complete Beatles recording sessions.* London: EMI/Hamlyn Publ.

Meyer, Erwin, Rolf Thiele 1956. Raumakustische Untersuchungen in zahlreichen Konzertsälen und Rundfunkstudios unter Anwendung neuerer Messverfahren. *Acustica* 6, 424-444.

Pittman, Aspen 1993. *The Tube Amp Book.* 4th ed. Sylmar, CA: Groove Tubes.

Rehwagen, Thomas, Thorsten Schmidt 1992. *„Mach Schau!" Die Beatles in Hamburg.* Braunschweig: EinfallsReich Verlagsges.

Schroeder, Manfred, D. Gottlob, K.F. Siebrasse 1974. Compartive Study of European concert halls: correlation of subjective preference with geometric and acoustic parameters. *Journal Acoust. Soc. Am.* 56, 1195-1201.

Siegfried, Detlef 2006. *Time is on my side. Konsum und Politik in der westdeutschen Jugendkultur der 60er Jahre.* Göttingen: Wallstein.

Smith, Richard 1995. *Fender - the sound heard 'round the world.* Fullerton, CA: Garfish Publ.

Taylor, Edward, Frankland, John 2006. We could not believe the sound (Interview). In: Ulf Krüger and Ortwin Pelc (eds.). *The Hamburg Sound. Beatles, Beat, und Große Freiheit*. Hamburg: Ellert & Richter, 112-119.

Telefunken 1960. *Telefunken Taschenbuch Röhren und Halbleiter* (1961 edition). Ulm: Telefunken.

Vorländer, Michael 2008. *Auralization. Fundamentals of Acoustics, Modelling, Simulation, Algorithms and Acoustics Virtual Reality*. Berlin, New York: Springer.

Zint, Günter 1987. *Große Freiheit 39. Vom Beat zum Bums. Vom »Star-Club« zum »Salambo«*. München: Heyne.

Till Strauf

"You Don't See the Stitching" – Some Comments on Stylistic Diversity in Rock Using the Example of Jethro Tull

Summary

This paper is based on my Master's thesis (2010), which deals with stylistic devices and influences in the music of British Rock band *Jethro Tull*. The group serves as a good example for the popular music of the 1970s and 1980s in displaying a wide diversity of musical styles in their output that is difficult to allocate to a single genre. Since its formation as a Blues band in the heyday of the Psychedelic era, the group subsequently went through different stylistic phases blending mainly Hardrock, British Folk, Jazz and elements of Art music. While this could be cited common practice in the sphere of Progressive Rock, *Jethro Tull* are more distinctive for putting a focus on certain musical styles on different records in order to form an entity of lyrics, music and image that can be easily varied on subsequent records or songs. The following examination of *Minstrel in the Gallery* (1975) and *Velvet Green* (1977) should reveal certain musical influences and how they are embodied into a framework of musical intertextuality referring to a musical past, whereas the later song *Budapest* (1987) could be seen as an example of a less conceptionally-driven fusion of different styles the group showcased in the late 1980s.

1. Introduction

Since the mid-1990s there has been a growing interest in the musical and sociological impact of British and American Progressive Rock in Musicology (see, for example, Covach 1997, Macan 1997, Moore 2001, Holm-Hudson 2002). For most of these authors, Progressive Rock emerges from the fragmentation of the Psychedelic era around 1970 (Macan 1997, 26) as a style distinctive to other forms of contemporary popular music in its *surface and structural affinities for and connections to "classical" music* (Steinbaum 2002, 28).

Some of the musical and stylistic characteristics of "mature" Progressive Rock, arguably represented through major British groups like *Yes, Genesis* and *ELP* (Macan 1997), are detectable through every stage of *Jethro Tull's* career. Although one hears irregular rhythms, shifting meters, an extended instrumentation incorporating instruments that were "in the beginning" uncommon in the context of Rock or the juxtaposition of acoustic and electric sections, in the eyes of most Progressive Rock scholars the group remained somehow distant from the "movement". Perhaps mostly because only on two records, namely *Thick As A Brick* and *Passion Play* (1972 and 1973), a deeper "structural affinity" to classical music becomes unambiguously apparent.

The work of *Jethro Tull* is undoubtedly determined by its frontman, main songwriter, producer and centre of media attention, Ian Anderson, who has been in control of all artistic issues since 1969. Over the years he showed great interest in developing in terms of musical style, instrumental skills and production techniques. This approach seemed not only to suit his urge to keep the music challenging for the musicians but also enabled him to incorporate stylistic idioms that dominated the contemporary popular music of the time. Even in his pre-Tull days Anderson moved seamlessly from Rock´n´Roll and Mersey Beat (with his first band *The Blades* 1963-1965) to R´n´B and Soul in the style of the *Graham Bond Organisation* (*John Evans Band* 1965-1967). With *Jethro Tull,* he switched from Blues Rock (early years) to Hard, Progressive and Folk Rock (1970s), to Synthesizer Rock (1980s), and on to "World Music" in the 1990s (note especially his solo album *Divinities,* 1995). At the same time, this could only be accomplished by working with different kinds of musicians who were able and willing to follow Anderson's changing artistic directions. As a result, there have been over 30 musicians, forming 19 different *Jethro Tull* line-ups over the years. Remarkably, the band suffered no loss of image, with Anderson becoming more and more synonymous with the band. Or as *The Virgin Illustrated Encyclopedia Rock* (1998, 199) has put it: *For many spectators, Jethro Tull was the name of the extrovert frontman Anderson – the other musicians were merely his underlings. This impression gained credence through the bands internal ructions.*

In a chapter of his book *The Primary Text - Developing a Musicology of Rock* (2001), that takes account of Progressive Rock, Allan F. Moore has examined some of *Jethro Tull's* stylistic practice and used the band as a example of modern aesthetic in mass-culture (Moore 2003). Especially his *ideolect* concept seems to be the most profound effort so far to define the changes that took place in British popular music culture during the late 1960s and early 1970s. Moore has argued that Progressive Rock should be less considered in terms of a genre or a style but more of as *the moment within the history of modern Anglophone popular music which actualizes the insubordination of ideolect to style* [...] (Moore 2007, 2). While being in accordance with most of Moore`s observations, I am more concerned with analysing the components of *Jethro Tull's* eclectic practice, in detail referring to influences that are used for different purposes within the music.

2. Becoming Jethro Tull

Jethro Tull formed in early 1968 consisting of former members of the *John Evan Smash* (formerly known as *John Evan Band*) and the Luton-based blues band, *Mc Gregor's Engine*. Arguably due to Ian Anderson´s expressive style of flute playing – a newcomer to the Blues rock context but apparently influenced by Jazz multi-instrumentalist Roland Kirk by incorporating "massive" overblowing and a scat-singing technique to gain a better pitch control (Anderson 2009) – and his "manic" stage performance[1] the band rapidly gained some initial success on the London club scene.

While their debut record *This Was* (here already hinting at musical changes yet to come) is mostly made up of blues compositions allowing Anderson to test and improve

---

[1] See for example the review of a live concert in Rolling Stone magazine July 1971, where Anderson is described as *grimacing, twitching, gasping, lurching along the apron of the stage, rolling his eyes, para diddling his arms, feigning flinging snot from his nose, exchanging the guitar for a flute, gnawing on the flute like a baton, gibbering dementedly.*

his soloing skills on the flute in a pentatonic framework, the 1969's release of their second album marks a stylistic turning point.

On *Stand Up* an expanded instrumentation (mandoline, balalaika, tabla etc.) leads the way to a broader eclecticism mixing elements of Blues, Folk and Jazz with allusions to Indian and quotes from West European Art music. The latter represented by an arrangement of Bach's *Bourrée* where the primary voice and harmonic progression of its first eight bars are placed in a jazz context. The theme is played with a triplet-feeling accompanied by a walking bass and a shuffle beat functioning as an A section to the succeeding extended soloing in the vein of contemporary Blues Rock rather than containing any aspects of the baroque style.

In addition, new lead guitarist Martin Barre's (besides Anderson the only permanent member of *Jethro Tull* since 1969) riff and power chord-based style – later reworked into a more distinctive technique often replacing the fifth in "standard" power chords with thirds, fourths, or sixths (Strauf 2010) – coined more heavily by contemporary Hard Rock idioms than the Blues, sets the stage for two essential stylistic devices in *Jethro Tull's* music. Namely the trading of short phrases (riffs) between flute, guitar and other instruments (Anderson 2009) and the compositional juxtaposition of acoustic and electric sections, that become not only central to the music of *Jethro Tull* (Moore 2003, 160), but to the whole "genre" of Progressive Rock (Macan 1997).

The album can be seen as a forerunner to *Jethro Tull's* subsequent output in the 1970s and 1980s, both in terms of stylistic diversity and orientation towards current musical trends (for example, the "Indian allusion" in *Fat Man,* an obligatory reference in the Psychedelic era) not to mention the commercial success in being the band's first number one album.

In the course of the 1970s, *Jethro Tull* released a number of very successful albums enabling the band to play arenas and stadiums, especially in the United States. The album *Aqualung* (1971), containing the all-time fan favourite *Locomotive Breath,* marks another important point of stylistic arrival for a stronger emphasis on modal "folk-flavoured" arrangements (often contrasted with Martin Barre's hard rock riffs) based on Anderson's acoustic guitar playing. Deriving from traditional Country & Western and Blues flatpicking techniques, he developed a relatively complex way of mixing variable strumming patterns with arpeggios, short riff-like phrases and picked notes (also discussed by Roger Anderson 1988) in order to allude to the vocal melody and compensate for his missing fingerstyle, best heard on tracks like *Wondering Aloud* (1971, Fig. 1).

Rhythmically the song rests upon a five-beat pattern (with the first beat accented) that takes up each half bar of the underlying 6/8 pulse (best articulated in the second bar, fig. 1). Anderson uses the tonal range of F-Mixolydian following a bVII – v – IV – I - bVII – I – IV – II – I harmonic progression that echoes remains of traditional Folk songs through the prominence of the lowered seventh degree in the double tonic pattern of bar 12/13 (fig. 1). Such pendular patterns often occur in Scottish and Irish music (Middleton, 1990, 588). At the same time the use of the bVII degree had already been established – perhaps also filtered through the second British Folk revival - as a compositional resource of Rock music by *The Beatles* and others (Tillekens 2006) in the late 1960s. Another aspect of Anderson's technique shows up in the harmonic static sections resting on the F chord, where he constantly switches between alternate voicings by lifting or adding one or two fingers producing suspended 2 and 4 chords. Sometimes these alternations give rise to short motifs like in bar 9 and 11 through playing a F - F6 - Fsus2/4 - F progression. A similar approach can be found in the work of the contemporary British singer-songwriter Roy Harper (for example in songs like *Goodbye* (1970)), which Anderson calls a major influence (Anderson, 2000).

Figure 1: *Wondering Alound* 0:00-0:48

After *Aqualung,* the band made their two most "progressive" efforts with the release of *Thick As A Brick* and *A Passion Play* (1972 and 1973). In each case a single, over 40-minute long composition spanning over both sides of the vinyl record displays a new level a complexity by employing shifting meters, irregular rhythms, and constant key changes (though common in the sphere of Progressive Rock). Whereas in particular *Thick As A Brick* establishes a musical coherence through the reoccurrence, development and variation of motifs, progressions and patterns in the harmonic, melodic and rhythmical domain (cf. Strauf 2010 and Josephson, who labels *Thick As A Brick the most impressive variation cycle in progressive rock* 1992, 75).

In the mid 1970s Anderson's artistic vision surfaces to its full extent, in staging himself as a mythological figure on record covers and in live performances, mirrored in the historical "archetypes" (Moore 2001, 102) he creates as pegs for several concept albums the band releases in the second half of the 1970s. All these characters, starting from the "urban outlaw" *Aqualung* (Anderson 2008), that appeared to have an impact on the following generation of punk musicians (Anderson 1993b), to the old "sea salt" on the cover of 1979s album *Stormwatch*, are seemingly incapable of finding their place in a fully industrialized, fast changing society, reflecting Anderson's own distrust in modernity (c.f. Moore 2003, 169). This seems not only embedded in his apparent countercultural socialization and an early developed consciousness of ecological matters, but in his own unease in becoming a "rock star" (Anderson, 2009). Which is among other things expressed in his demonstrative disinterest for "hard drugs" and promiscuity (Anderson 1971, 1977). Thematically this "distrust" channels itself in a recourse to mythological and historical content (cf. Caswell 1993), or what Stump (1997, 157) has called a *fascination with the rustic* [that] *often reflects a view of the countryside inherited through the refracting lenses of a century of popular, mass-cultural idealisation of rural life.*

This applies to most *Jethro Tull* records made during the 1970s and most notably to their "Folk Rock phase" starting with *Songs from the Wood* (1977). Musically we find sections that in many cases seem to be directly related to the particular lyrical subject of the respective song. A technique that is referred to by Moore as *modernist eclecticism* as opposed to *postmodern relativism* (Moore 2003, 171). A rather obvious example of this manifestation can be found in the 1974s piece *The Third Hoorah.* The lyrics refer to a "Warchild", who dances *the days and nights away.* In the music this "dance" is represented through a 6/8 keyboard line reflecting melodic features similar to those in dance forms widespread in Ireland and Scotland, in this case arguably a blending of the single and double jig. Later on bagpipes, underlined with a march-like staccato pattern played on a snare, recall an association with a Scottish military band.

Instead of that, other songs from the same period already reveal a more "loose" fusion of styles. Like in the song *Ladies,* starting as an orchestrated guitar ballad that later develops into a polymetric R´n´B tune.

On subsequent records of the 1970s the rework of elements from the British Folk music tradition and the *closely aligned Elizabethan art-music* (Macan 1992, 101) become more central. As in most of British Rock of the 1970s, the music serves as a auxiliary source of inspiration in establishing a distinctive expression in order to distinguish itself from its (Afro-)American blueprints that were boldly "copied" throughout the 1960s. Of course this becomes even more articulated in the music of contemporary Electric Folk groups. Not surprising as the music had been commonplace in not only British everyday life, but also in concert hall music since the beginning of the 20th century, traceable from the works of British Folk revivalist Vaughan Williams to early Maxwell Davies (Macan 1992, 100). Thus paving not only the way for the revival of early music led by lutenist Julian Bream (and others) in the 1950s, but to some extent also for what some observers have seen as *the final decisive conformation of that English musical Renaissance [...]*(Kerman 1985, 24), namely the formation of British Rock in second half of 1960s. Contrary to many of the Electric Folk and Folk Rock groups, Anderson seemed never interested in providing an "authentic, archaic" musical statement. In an interview 1977 he explained: *In Songs From The Wood we did go back to the roots of what our music was about, at the same time avoiding what had become the clichés of blues as spawned by the Americans. It's a peculiarly British sounding album, but is in no way a traditional, academic interpretation of old folk song; I mean it's not a Steeleye Span number at all. It's something else ... it's still my songs* (Anderson 1977).

The following two examples should reveal how the styles mentioned before are embodied into the overall framework and mixed with stylistic idioms stemming from contemporary forms of popular music.

3. *The Minstrel In The Gallery*

By the release of *Minstrel In The Gallery* (1975), the band enjoyed one of its more stable line-ups (apart from alternating bass players), lasting from 1972 to 1979. The line-up consisted of Anderson (vocals, flute, acoustic guitar), Martin Barre (electric guitar), Barriemoore Barlow (drums), John Evan (keys). Also worth mentioning is David Palmer (string and brass arranger and conductor), who was involved with every *Jethro Tull* record until 1979 and became an "official" band member between 1977 and 1979.

The title track of the album gives a rather apt hint at the conceptionally-driven eclecticism mentioned earlier. In the lyrics Anderson stages himself as a modern minstrel who "polarizes", "titillates" and "pacifies" the crowd, providing at least an artistic distance to the rock star image he disclaimed in interviews over the years. The over eight minute long piece can be broken down roughly into three distinctive sections, starting with a two-minute long intro. Later a guitar interlude, dominated by shifting meters and chromatic scale runs leads into the proper song. Represented through a four minute section, whose ABCABCA- structure, coined by power chords and short riffs played over a constant 4/4-meter, this could be labelled as contemporary Hard Rock, disregarding some of Barre's typical rhythm displacements.

The section that I´m concerned with here is the intro, which consists mostly of Anderson´s singing and guitar playing, sometimes supplemented by overdubbed voices and flute-phrases.

In contrast to Wondering Aloud, Anderson is not using "his" picking technique to allude to the vocal melody but only alternates between strumming and arpeggios. Furthermore, the constant meter is abandoned in favor of constantly changing vocal patterns composed of uneven verse lengths. Albeit the rhythmic division shown in figure 2/3 may not be the only interpretation possible, it clarifies the rhythmic and metric irregularity of this passage. Here the guitar accompaniment seems to be degraded, functioning only as an attachment (cf. Moore 2001, 103) for the vocals recited in a declamatory fashion instead of providing a rhythmical and harmonic framework. Anderson's melodic line uses a modal outline in B-Aeolian with short excursions to the Dorian mode, while the guitar accents are often placed between two successive vocal notes. The only periodic feature lies in the rapid chord changes underlying the last two syllables of a melodic phrase. Thereby Anderson uses his typical voicings, one time switching from a Esus4 to a "reversed" A5 and from the slash chord Bsus479 (by playing open strings with a capo on second fret) to Bmaj, maybe unconsciously incorporating a feature common in Renaissance music using the major I in a Dorian context.

Figure 2: Intro *Minstrel In The Gallery* 0:19-0:37

Figure 3: Intro *Minstrel In The Gallery* 0:38-0:48

217

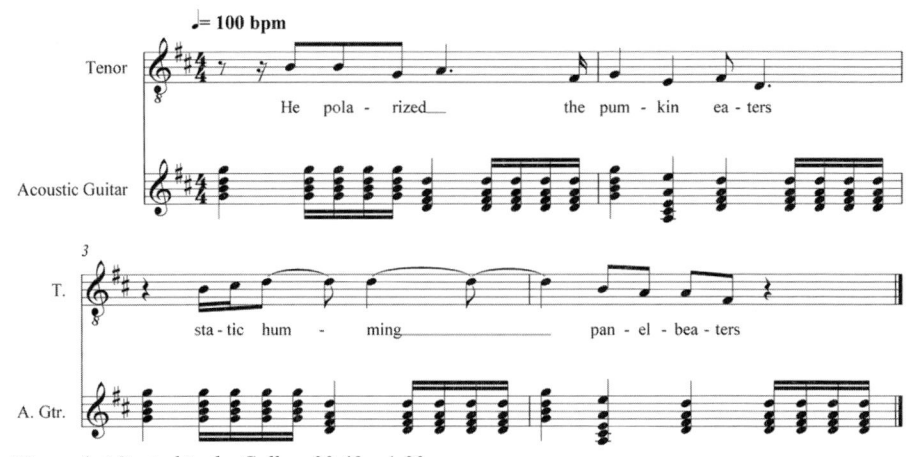

Figure 4: *Minstrel in the Gallery* 00:49 – 1:00

Succeeding another short excursion into D-Ionian (bar 5, fig. 2), the harmonic progression is repeated in a different rhythmical form. Here the flute adds counterpunctual lines that also double the vocal line at the end of a verse. After 14 bars a conventional IV – I – IV – V – I progression is established (fig. 4). In the use of the "regular cadence" underlying the chorus, now played over a rather stable 4/4 pulse, lies a stylistic device of *Jethro Tull:* harmonic or rhythmic complex sections are juxtaposed with simple ones, often displaying "standardized" Pop or Rock song idioms. In the intro of *Minstrel In The Gallery* the complexity arises through the rhythmic and metric shape and the counter-accentuation of the guitar. This independency from a regular pulse is an often described characteristic of the vocal British Folk tradition (see also Sharp 1908, 142) as Van der Merwe notes: *The loner singer, untrammeled by any accompaniment, is free to play with the rhythm as much as he likes. Notes can be added to or removed from a phrase, dwelt or shortened. When such liberties are taken to extremes, the result is complete absence of a bar* (Van der Merwe 1992, 22).

Analogue characteristics can be assumed about the performance practice of Minstrels and Troubadours (Aubrey 1996, 240-254), where a prose-centered presentation led to similar irregularities. Even if "such extremes" are not detectable here, it seems clear that Anderson tries to evoke a certain allusion by adopting such techniques to suit his conceptional archetype. Arguably, this is represented through the recitative form, the modal outline and the spare lute-like strumming pattern mixed with "modern" elements of Rock like the muted slash chords in bar 9.

4. *Walking On Velvet Green*

On the 1977's *Songs From The Wood*, the allusions to traditional British music become more profound. This time Anderson "incarnates" the escapist outdoorsman, often referring to an archaic, pagan living environment in the lyrics (note especially songs like *Cup Of Wonder* or the obvious *Beltane*).

The title track employs a similarity to *Minstrel In Gallery* in starting with an irregular four-part a-cappella section. While the first and fourth bar are due to some performance deviations elongated by a semiquaver, and therefore almost fall into a regular 4/4 pulse, the other bars show no hint of a regular rhythm or meter. Anderson´s main voice (labelled no. 3 in fig. 5) serves as a "cantus firmus" accompanied by lines in parallel fourths, fifths and octaves. A practice assumably common in rural British singing since the medieval times (c.f. Sweers 2005, 158). Probably also heard by Anderson in the arrangements of contemporary Folk Rock groups like Fairport Convention or Steeleye Span (Sweers 2005, 160) on collective tours. Later in the song the verse section is reworked in a more clearly arranged fashion, build on additive meters (cf. Moore 2001, 105), that are "countable" for the drummer, alternating between 4, 3 and 5 beats per bar.

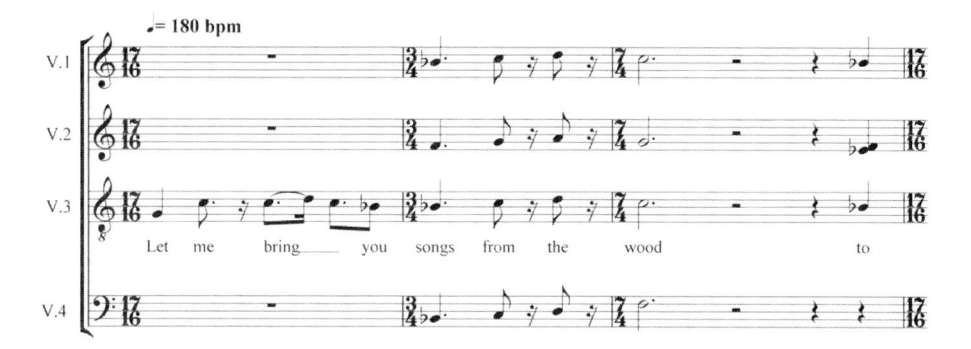

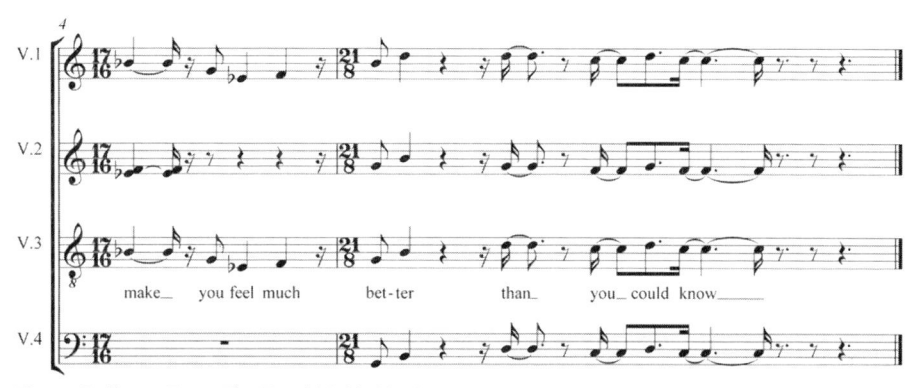

Figure 5: *Songs From The Wood* 00:00-00:10

Moore (2001, 107) has pointed out that from the mid-1970s onwards the band periodically starts to exchange the block-structured harmony of Rock with *contrapuntal textures*. Thereby Moore refers to sections that proceed harmonically through independent melodical lines. A technique that can also be found in the work of other "progressive" peers (most notably *Gentle Giant*). This appears to be an expression of Anderson´s interest *in avoiding American cliches* (Anderson 1977). Opposed to that intention, Anderson has often stated his ignorance of musical history, emphasizing his disinterest in what he calls a *Smithsonian approach* to Folk music (Anderson 1977, 1996). Regarding Elizabethan music, he admits, that *some of the musical things might have just slipped in*, without him having an exact conception of the music (Anderson 2004). Perhaps in this context the joining of David Palmer as an official band member is worth mentioning as Palmer is the only "classical trained" musician working with Anderson throughout the 1970s. In an interview from 2004 he notes: *With Jethro Tull, Ian was taking all of the loose ends of the English rock movement, going back to The Kinks and The Beatles, and embraced the freedom of the blues people. What we [Anderson and Palmer] did was pick up all the loose strings of the English canon of music writing and put them together. What came out were the jagged rhythms and the harmonies. All of it came from English music heritage. Some of it came emphatically because I don't think Ian knew the difference between Bach and Beethoven. I am sure he knows it now but then he would not have known how one evolved from the other* (Palmer 2004).

In *Velvet Green* (1977) this becomes especially articulate. Here the reminiscence of a British past is embodied in the music through some stylistic allusions. In addition to that, the scenery evoked in the lyrics seem to settle in a rural environment. For Caswell (1993) the mixture of sexual overtones with rather "poetic" descriptions of nature are similar to the vein of traditional "erotic folk-ballads" (see also Lloyd, 1967, 194). It's to assume, however, that some of these descriptions found on *Songs From The Wood* and the subsequent album *Heavy Horses* (1978) are inspired by 18th century Scottish national poet Robert Burns, openly quoted in the song *One Brown Mouse* from the latter album.

Common for *Jethro Tull* the song Velvet Green falls into two distinctive verse strains, each preceded by elaborate instrumental sections with no recognizable chorus. However the often repeated "leitmotif" (fig. 6) seems to function in a similar manner.

Figure 6: *Velvet Green* motif

The intro of *Velvet Green* is arguably played by David Palmer whose first 8 bars are shown in Figure 7[2]. Palmer uses a synthesizer sound with a timbre that recalls both harpsichord and pipe organ, a device often displayed by Progressive Rock groups to imitate "classical" or symphonic timbres (Macan 1992, 102). The beginning of the pieces moves from G-Dorian to D-Mixolydian mode. Starting with a I-VI change in the

---

[2] The following transcriptions are oriented towards the original, handwritten score of *Velvet Green* (containing the first 20 bars) that can be seen on www.jehtrotull.com.

first bar, the "open" I-IV-V progression in the second bar is completed on the first beat of the following bar. Interesting here is the F-sharp in the melodic line also played by the guitar forming the "dominant" Dmaj. This inflection of the major/minor-tonality in a modal framework seems to be an allusion to songs of the late Renaissance (a similarity can be found in *Greensleeves*, when played in Dorian mode) that generated before the primacy of the former was fully constituted. Here assumably used with the intention to create some sort of "archaic" character. Furthermore, the overall rhythmic shape of the melodic line played with the harpsichord timbre is redolent of late renaissance pieces like those that can be found in collections like the *Fitzwilliam Virginal Book*. Even if the level of originality in terms of polyphonic part-writing is not reached here, the way in which the stylistic reference points seems rather obvious.

Figure 7: *Velvet Green* 00:00-00:12

As typical for the band's rhythmical practice, the intro consists of no stable meter but is constantly switching between different numbers of beats. In the fourth bar (fig. 7) the guitar dissolves from its function of underlying a harmonic background and doubles the harpsichord line in parallel thirds. In the subsequent bar the guitar starts to add ornamenting notes to the melodic line, which is also briefly imitated by the bass (bar 5). With these rather subtle contrapuntal elements the band seems to deliberately contrast the often occurring unison lines. In the tenth bar (fig. 8, b. 1) follows a short passage rather reminiscent of a baroque sequence in ascending seconds than the Elizabethan style. Here the song "returns" to G (-Dorian) through a prominent descending fifth in bar 4/5 (fig. 8). In the seventh bar the *Velvet Green* "motif" is heard for the first time, but interrupted by an unison run in 5/8 with material taken from the previous section. Thereafter the leitmotif is repeated seven times with the drums joining after four times. Drummer Barriemore Barlow counters the shifting meter with a pattern that dubs the melodic outline. To reinforce the "folkish" effect he replaces the regular snare drum with the more low-frequent, "medieval" tabor (in live performances integrated in a second little drum kit), while the added marimbaphone is merely acting as an timbral enrichment for the arrangement and therefore more likely to comprehend as an expression of the band's non-dogmatic eclecticism.

Figure 8: *Velvet Green* 00:13-00:23

In the first verse section (fig. 9) Anderson earlier mentioned guitar technique reveals a further facet. Now triads are avoided in favour of two-tone quaver and semiquaver lines alluding to the vocal melody through unison and contrapuntal runs accompanied by bourdon-like use of open strings (similar to the intro section moving between G-Dorian and D-Mixolydian mode). Again the verse is constructed in an additive manner, alternating between 5, 3 and 6 beats per bar. The second verse section employs a similarity already noticed in *Minstrel In The Gallery*. Anderson resides on a static pattern I-bVII in B-Aeolian while the underlying 4/4 meter is shrouded by a syncopated, variable strumming pattern. Every line ends on a bIII-IV-I sequence, a progression derived from the (Hard)-Rock idiom of moving power chords along the fret board. The impression that "we are" now in a rather modern context is additionally gained by other stylistic devices contrasting the "natural" timbres of the previous sections, that were mostly dominated by acoustic instruments. Anderson acoustic guitar is now supplied with an intense reverb. Furthermore, the tremolo effect used by Martin Barre to overdub the first chord of every respective sequence could be interpreted as a reference to American popular music for its frequent occurrence in styles like Rock´n Roll and Surf Rock. Not surprisingly, at this point Anderson is referring to *the civilisation raging afar*, the only contemporary hint the can be found in the lyrics. A detailed examination of the following instrumental interlude (discussed more deeply in Strauf 2010) would go beyond the scope of this paper and should only be regarded shortly: The section is based on patterns in parallel fourths, played on a portative organ by Palmer that is in the course of its development transposed from E-Flat-Mixolydian mode to C-Mixolydian further on to D-Mixolydian, reminiscent of medieval dance music (or the band's idea of it). Notably the intro section with its IV -V - I cadence occurs again now reworked in a more "ancient" fashion using the double tonic progression I – bVII – I – V. The melodic lines, that dominate the rest of the interlude, bring to mind examples from traditional British dance music. These lines are played in shifting meters over harmonic static patterns (including numerous I-bVII) that are, notwithstanding the acoustic instrumentation, rather typical for block harmony structures of Rock. After a short baroque like bass-driven sequence in ascending seconds, accompanied by short imitations of the leading voice from guitar and keyboard, the song returns to the second verse strand.

Figure 9: *Velvet Green* verse 0:52-1:07

5. *Budapest*

In 1987 the band released their sixteenth album *Crest Of A Knave*. In between the ten years span the band went through several line-ups changes particularly in 1980 when Anderson´s fellow musicians from the 1970s (apart from Martin Barre) were replaced by those participating in the recordings of material originally intended for a solo album by Anderson but released as a regular *Jethro Tull* record (Russo 2000, 117). The Folk Rock approach of the late 1970s is still present in some pieces but retreated into the background to benefit a more synthesizer-driven style providing a basis for lyrics often dealing with "cold war thematics". Though such a development is in no way uncommon for "former" Progressive Rock bands that existed throughout the 1980s (prominent examples may be *Genesis,* turning from artistically ambitious albums into a comercially successful major pop-act, and *King Crimson*, arguably the aesthetically most convincing transformation of Progressive Rock in an 1980s context), the overall stylistic variability showcased by Anderson and his musicians is more comparable to the constant stylistic "conversions" of solo artists like David Bowie and Elvis Costello (for a discussion of the latter see Brackett, David 1995). On *Jethro Tull's* fifteenth album, *Under Wraps* (1984), acoustic instruments are hardly present and the conventional drumkit is exchanged by a programmable beat machine. In this context *Crest Of The Knave* has been seen as some sort of stylistic return for the band for compromising more acoustic sections again (Russo 2000, 140). It is also their most successful release of the 1980s, winning a Grammy for *Best Hardrock/ Metal Performance, Vocal or Instrumental* in 1988 (Russo 2000, 141). While not distinctively "heavy" (at least compared to the also nominated *Metallica*), this categorization perhaps reflects the elusive stylistic eclecticism that dominates parts of the album. My treatment of the song *Budapest* (1987) should reveal how some of the "old" *Jethro Tull* techniques have changed in the light of current musical trends and how different styles are incorporated in one single piece. Even if the consideration of other songs from *Jehtro Tull's* 1980s output may be better examples to show how synthesizers and sequencers are embedded in the music, *Budapest* lends itself for a closer examination. Mostly because Anderson often brings the song up when asked about his favourite composition. In an interview dating from 1999 he stated: *Budapest is the kind of song I like to write because it embodies a lot of different nuances which I think are subtly joined together. It sort of moves from classical to slightly bluesy to folk, and it just slips between them and you don't see the stitching. The song is like a really good Elton John hairpiece: you can't see the seams too obviously* (Anderson 1999). The excerpt not only gives an example of Andersons's typical, humour but a clue to his conception of a felicitous song.

As opposed to many older pieces, *Budapest* (with a duration of more than 10 minutes) follows a conventional intro – verse – chorus - bridge – verse – chorus sequence that is later interrupted by an over three minute long instrumental interlude, before the song assembles again for another verse – chorus succession. The structure of this kind can be traced back to the performance practice of late 1960s Psychedelic Rock, where conventional songs are often elongated through extended soloing and improvisation (especially in the live context), with the difference that here we find a carefully constructed middle section that can be divided into five distinctive parts.

Most of the song settles in D-Aeolian except for the interlude sections that are all in different keys/modes. Contrary to many compositions from the 1970s most of the sections are underlied with a standard Rock beat and the 4/4 meter shifts only two times within the whole song, while the typical rhythm displacements occur more often. For example, in the intro (fig. 10) that consists of a syncopated keyboard motif played over a pedal point-like I – VI – VII succession. After two bars Anderson starts with an ornamenting flute line that always ends on the downbeat of the reconvening keyboard pattern.

Verse and bridges are based on Anderson's acoustic guitar. His approach to build non-periodic harmonic progressions (shown in fig. 11) via underlying nearly every verse line with a different chord succession draws a parallel to some of his older arrangements, but the technique referred to above has nearly vanished since he is now restricted to strumming only.

Figure 10: *Budapest* intro 00:00-00:12

Text section	Progression
1. *I think she was...*	I-IV-VII-I-VII
2. *The translation...*	V-IV-I-VII
3. *Could be...*	V-VI-IV
4. *International...*	V- III-V
5.& 6. = 1.& 2.	I-IV-VII-I-VII - V-IV-I-VII
7. *While she...*	V-VI-VII
8. *And she...*	III-VII-IV (VII4-IV-VII)

Figure 11: *Budapest* verse 1

As Anderson has mentioned, this self-reduction was a deliberate step he took in the 1980s in order not to cut the other musicians *out of action* (Anderson 2000). Here the available space is filled out by Martin Barre's licks based on the pentatonic scale. Beside these stylistic shifts regarding composition we find production techniques that were so common in the 1980s. Both the synthesizer and a reverb effect put on several instruments are used to produce a timbral backdrop that solidifies the overall texture. Another noticeable aspect is Andersons lowered singing voice. His limited vocal range is a result of a vocal cord damage he suffered from in the mid-1980s. Therefore critics accused Anderson of copying the singing style of *Dire Straits's* leadsinger, Mark Knopfler (Russo 2000, 140). Even if this specific charge is not worthy to be commented on here, the first part of the instrumental interlude in *Budapest* reveals a commonality to a section from the Knopfler composition *Private Investigation* (1982). In both sections the bass plays a pedal point on E (in the case of *Jethro Tull* in quarter notes whereas the *Dire Straits* part stresses the first and third beat of the 4/4 meter) providing the backdrop for scale runs in e-minor played by the lead guitarists imitating gestures of Flamenco style.

Figure 12: *Budapest* interlude 1, 3:40-3:50

While the *Jethro Tull* section can be probably labelled as "inspired by" the former, it is also an example of incorporating a stylistic device that has not been present in *Jethro Tull's* output before, but that is also influenced by current musical trends. In this case the adoption of the "Flamenco guitar-style" could be cited as fashionable among guitarist in the 1980s promoted mostly by the worldwide success of Spanish guitarist, Paco de Lucia.

The second interlude section settles in g-minor making short excursions to harmonic minor. This passage is presumably the one Anderson referred to as "classical" in the quote above for its semiquaver line played in unison by guitar and flute reminiscent of baroque string figuration accompanied by a harmonic progression that could be described in terms of common practice tonality as tonic – subdominant – dominant – tonic. After some faster chord changes compromising i – iv – V and a pedal point intersection on E-flat the third interlude section (fig. 13) occurs in a different fashion. Now the keyboard interlaces modal block chord voicing in B-Aeolian, that are typical in Jazz rather than in the Baroque style.

Figure 13: *Budapest* interlude 3, 4:55-5:03

A few bars further ahead the flute line shown in figure 13 is taken up by the guitar. Disregarding the distorted sound of the guitar the progression produced now via a changed bass line seems relatively uncommon for the sphere of Rock.

A similarity can be found in the affiliated solo passage where flute and violin trade phrases on the background of Martin Barre's riff based on G-flat-Ionian. As in other songs, Barre occasionally plays thirds and fourths instead of the regular fifth in power chords.

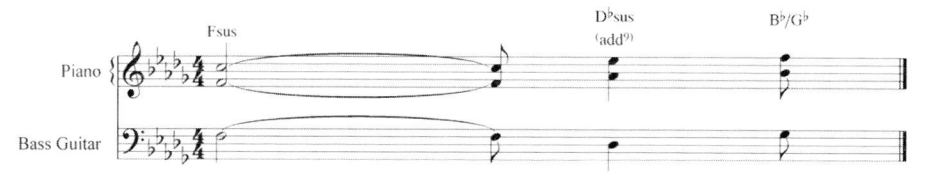

Figure 14: *Budapest* interlude 3, from 5:10

Figure 15: *Budapest* interlude 3, guitar riffs

The fourth interlude section on the other hand rests upon a keyboard motif in F-Aeolian. In a typical rhythmical fashion the motif starts on the last beat of the proceeding repeated bridge section in 4/4. The next bar only consists of three beats functioning as a pickup for the pattern now reinterpreted in 7/4.

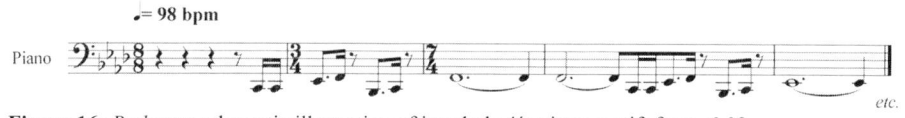

Figure 16: *Budapest* schematic illustration of interlude 4´s piano motif, from 6:02

The gaps between two succeeding notes of the keyboard line are filled with other instruments: here an improvisational character results in the absence of a constant drum beat. This impression is gained by off-beat scale runs on the acoustic guitar, short flute phrases and drum fills, that at times appear like they would neglect the underlying pulse. In addition, the percussion instruments used in the passage seem a reference to a not otherwise specified exoticism.

The last section of the interlude lasts only for five bars. Anderson plays a line of semiquavers in c-minor spanning the compass of an octave. The 18 notes are grouped in an off-beat fashion (3+3+2+2+3+3+2+2/16) placing the accents in between the regular beats of the 10/8 pulse, another typical rhythmical device of Anderson's practice.

Figure 17: *Budapest* interlude 5 motif, from 07:09

227

The rest of the song contains only sections that have been already noted, therefore there is no need to discuss these to any further extent.

6. Conclusion

The preceding analysis of the three pieces should suffice to outline some of the stylistic diversity that can be found in the music of *Jethro Tull*. As is typical of Progressive Rock, elements of different styles, such as (Hard) Rock, Blues, Folk, Jazz and Flamenco, sometimes occur within one single piece. In the case of Art music we find what Covach (1997, 23) has labeled *stylistic references on the surface*, namely passages that recall certain Art music styles like Baroque or Elizabethan music in terms of melodic and harmonic shapes, and are sometimes played with "archaic" instruments like the portative organ or otherwise imitated by synthesizer timbres. As mentioned above, structural affinities to "classical" composition techniques are very rare in the music of the group except for the two very long (duration more than 40 minutes) pieces *Thick as a Brick* and *Passion Play*. In their ambition these records should be regarded as to be geared towards a current musical trend of the early 1970s. In fact Anderson has often stated that *Thick As A Brick* was initially intended as a joke, making fun of Progressive Rock's pretension to foster a fusion of Rock and Art music (Anderson, 1997).

In the second half of the 1970s the stylistic references to British Folk and Elizabethan music are used to transport Anderson's countercultural critique of contemporary society. Influenced by contemporary Folk Rock groups like *Fairport Convention* and *Steeleye Span* (this point is more deeply discussed in Strauf 2010), he tapped into a fascination with rustic and mythological topics. Musically mostly signified by a modal outline, often stressing bVII-I progressions and a rhythmical practice uncommon in Rock. Notwithstanding Anderson's statements concerning his ignorance of musical history, these references could not been made without a certain competence in regard to the styles mentioned. On the one hand, these allusions seem to function as a vehicle for Anderson's lyrical concerns, while on the other they are used to create a specific British form of Rock intended to be different from American forerunners. Neither their reactionary and in some ways nationalistic approach (for further reading on this topic taking into account British Progressive Rock in general, see Macan, 1997), nor the overall eclecticism seems suited to distinguish *Jethro Tull* from several other contemporary British artists. Rather, *Jethro Tull* appears identifiable for the stylistic and technical variation employed in order to establish a form of connectional entity that involves lyrics, music and image, but is varied within different records or songs (note for example Anderson's profoundly "varied" guitar playing in different contexts). As said before, these "changes" are often orientated on current trends. This accounts for *Jethro Tull's* "progressive phase" of the early 1970s as much as for the stylistic shift in the early 1980s, where the lyrics and the music are more in accordance with the current zeitgeist, embodying "new" electronic instruments like sequencers and samplers. In the second half of the 1980s this approach becomes less explicit, while overall concepts are not so apparent. Later compositions like *Budapest* reveal that Anderson's interest lies not in the fusion of art and rock music, respectively in the revaluation of the latter as a form of "high" art, but merely in the display of a musical diversity that is challenging and entertaining for the musicians and the audience. As has been pointed out in the present article, *Jethro Tull* provides a fitting example within popular music for an 'intertextual' stylistic approach where allusions to the West European Art music tradition are merely used as one component among others. As indicated above, this intertextuality could only be accomplished technically through the use of extended instrumentation and a willingness to develop in terms of musical skills and production. Or, as Anderson puts it: *The reason Jethro Tull has been so eclectic, that's the polite term, 'confusing' might be the more realistic one, is because 22 guys have been in the band at different times. In one double digit, that's both the strength and the failing of Jethro Tull* (Anderson 1993a).

Artistically, as Moore has argued, this was only possible through a consistency of an ideolect. The often used rhythm displacements, the juxtaposition of acoustic and electric sections (Moore 2003, 160), as well as Anderson´s flute and guitar playing technique, his recitative singing lines and the overall basis of the style described by Anderson as *the trading of phrases between flute and guitar*, are reoccurring stylistic devices in the music of *Jethro Tull*. Of course none of these techniques developed completely independent of each other, but rather as the result of the combining and reworking of several influences (some are shown in the analyses) integrated in the stylistic context of Rock. For example, songs like *Minstrel In The Gallery* show how rhythmical features of a recitative performance practice are joined with techniques of Rock in a way not comparable with the rhythmical "looseness" occurring in improvisational passages common to music of the Psychedelic era. In regard to the eclecticism found in the music of *Jethro Tull*, one may point to a statement of John Brackett who recently noted, *that the development of any artist or group's individual style necessarily involves the ability to assimilate and transform pre-existing musical features* (Brackett 2008, 53).

In this respect, a further examination of eclectic practice coining subsequent popular styles from the 1980s till today could prove worthwhile in terms of enabling us to gain a better understanding of how features stemming from different sources and traditions are integrated into the music of certain artists, on the one hand, and how they become part of the overall vocabulary of popular music, on the other. A close example would be the adoption of the Afrobeat-style, already an eclectic "genre" of its own, by New Wave bands like *Talking Heads*. This stylistic feature is hardly present in the sphere of 1970s Progressive Rock, but traceable to a certain extent in more recent "progressive" styles like the awkwardly labeled "Math Rock" and others. Evidently, in popular music, as in many other art forms of the 20th century, "new" artistic expressions are only gained through the embodiment of "different nuances subtly joined together", namely the eclectic assembly of styles before unrelated, or as Anderson quips, a seamless "Elton John hairpiece".

7. References

Amon, Reinhard 2005. *Lexikon der Harmonielehre*. Wien: Doblinger.

Anderson, Roger L. 1988. Ian Anderson´s acoustic guitar style in the early recordings of Jethro Tull. In *Tracking: Popular Music Studies* Vol.1. http://www.icce.rug.nl/~soundscapes/DATABASES/TRA/Ian_Andersons_acoustic_guitar.shtml. Accessed June 4 2011.

Aubrey, Elizabeth 1996. *The Music of the Troubadours*. Bloomington: Indiana Univ. Press.

Brackett, David 1995. *Interpreting Popular Music*. London: Cambridge Univ. Press.

Brackett, John 2008. Examining Rhythmic and Metric Practices in Led Zeppelin's Style. *Popular Music*, Vol. 27/1, 53-76.

Brocken, Michael 2003. *The British Folk Revival*. Aldershot: Ashgate Publishing.

Burns, Robert 2004. British Folk songs in popular music settings. In I. Russel, D. Atkinson (eds.). *Folk Song – Tradition, Revival and Re-Creation*. Aberdeen: Elphinstone Institute, 115-130.

Caswell, Judson C. 1993. Minstrel In The Gallery: History in the music of Jethro Tull. *The St. Cleve Chronicle: The Jethro Tull Mailing List 7* Vol. 4. http://www.cupofwonder.com/essays3.html. Accessed June 4 2011

Covach, John 1997. Progressive Rock, "Close to the edge", and the boundaries of style. In J. Covach (ed.). *Understanding Rock Music*. New York: Oxford University Press, 3-31.

Frith, Simon 1996. *Performing Rites: On the Value of Popular Music*. Cambridge: Harvard Univ. Press.

Hicks, Michael 1999. *Sixties Rock: Garage, Psychedelic and other satisfactions*. Chicago: Univ. of Illinois Press.

Holm-Hudson, Kevin 2002. *Progressive Rock Reconsidered*. New York/ London: Routledge.

Josephson, Nors S. 1992. Bach meets Liszt: Traditional Formal Structures and Performance Practices in Progressive Rock. *The Musical Quarterly* Vol. 76/1, 67-92.

Kerman, Joseph 1985. *Contemplating Music: Challenges to Musicology*. Cambridge: Harvard Univ. Press.

Larkin, Colin (Ed.) 1998. *The Virgin Illustrated Encyclopedia of Rock*. London: Virgin Publishing Ltd.

Lloyd, Albert Lancaster 1967. *Folk Song in England*. New York: Lawrence & W.

Macan, Edward 1992. "The spirit of Albion" in twentieth-century English popular music: VaughanWilliams, Holst and the progressive rock movement. *The Music Review*, Vol. 53/2, 100-125.

Macan, Edward 1997. *Rocking the classics. English Progressive Rock and the counterculture*. New York: Oxford Univ. Press.

Middleton, Richard 1990. Review of "Origins of the Popular Style: the Antecedents of Twentieth-Century Popular Music". By Peter van der Merwe. *Music & Letters*, Vol. 71/4, 586-589.

Moore, Allan F. 2001. *Rock: The Primary Text - Developing a Musicology of Rock*. Cambridge: Ashgate Publ. Co.

Moore, Allan F. 2003. Jethro Tull and the case for modernism in mass culture. In Allan F. Moore (ed.). *Analyzing Popular Music*. New York: Cambridge Univ. Press.

Moore, Allan F. 2007: Gentle Giant´s Octopus. In *Philomusica on-line: Composition And Experimentation In British Rock 1967-1976.* http://www.unipv.it/britishrock1966-1976/testien/moo1en.htm. Accessed June 4 2011.

Russo, Greg 2000. *Flying Colours: The Jethro Tull Reference Manual.* New York: Crossfire Publications.

Sharp, Cecil; Broadwood, Lucy E. Some 1908. Some Characteristics of English Folk Music. *Folklore* Vol.19/ 2, 132- 152.

Steinbaum, John J. 2002. The inversion of musical values. In K. Holm-Hudson (ed.). *Progressive Rock Reconsidered*. New York/ London: Routledge, 21-42.

Strauf, Till 2010. *Eklektizismus in der Rockmusik der 1970er Jahre am Beispiel von Einflüssen und Stilmitteln in der Musik von Jethro Tull.* (Unpublished master´s thesis). Universität Hamburg.

Sweers, Britta 2005. *Electric folk: the changing face of English traditional music.* New York: Oxford Univ. Press.

Tillekens, Ger 2006. A flood of flat-sevenths Or, what are all those flat-sevenths doing in the Beatles' Revolver ? In *Soundscapes – Journal on media culture* Vol. 9. http://www.icce.rug.nl/~soundscapes/VOLUME09/A_flood_of_flat-sevenths.shtml. Accessed June 4 2011.

Van der Merwe, Peter 1992. *Origins of the Popular Style: The Antecedents of Twentieth-Century Popular Music*. New York: Oxford Univ. Press.

Interviews cited

All Urls accessed on June 4, 2011.

Anderson, Ian 1971. In *Crawdaddy* July 18th. http://www.tullpress.com/cd18jul71.htm.

Anderson, Ian 1977. In *National Rock Star* February 5th. http://www.tullpress.com/rst5feb77.htm.

Anderson, Ian 1977. In *Circus* April 14th. http://www.tullpress.com/c14apr77.htm.

Anderson, Ian 1993a. In october´s edition of *Rolling Stone*. http://www.tullpress.com/rsoct93.htm.

Anderson, Ian 1993b. Talking Tull. In *Jethro Tull* Songbook. Schramm, Karl (eds.). Heidelberg: Palmyra.

Anderson, Ian 1995. In *Dirty Linen* issue no. 61. http://www.tullpress.com/dl95.htm.

Anderson, Ian 1997. In *Guitar Legends* issue no. 22. http://www.tullpress.com/gljun97.htm.

Anderson, Ian 1999. In september´s edition of *Guitar World*. http://www.tullpress.com/gwsept99.htm.

Anderson, Ian 2000. In november´s edition of *Acoustic Guitar*. http://www.tullpress.com/agnov00.htm.

Anderson, Ian 2004. In"Ian Answers Fan Questions". http://www.j-tull.com/fans/media/questions/index.html.

Anderson, Ian 2008. In *The Sun*, November 21th.
http://www.thesun.co.uk/sol/homepage/showbiz/sftw/article1954597.ece.

Anderson, Ian 2009. In *"Ian Anderson's equipment"*.
http://www.jethrotull.com/musicians/iananderson/equipment.html#playing.

Palmer, Dee 2004. In an interview with *Classicrockrevisited.com*.
http://www.classicrockrevisited.com/Interviews04/DeePalmer.htm.

Discography (selection)

Dire Straits (2005). *Private Investigations- Best Of*. Mercury Records 0602498744758.

Jethro Tull (1968). *This Was*. Digital Remaster 2001. Chrysalis Records 724353545935.

Jethro Tull (1969). *Stand Up*. Digital Remaster 2001. Chrysalis Records 724353545826.

Jethro Tull (1971). *Aqualung*. Digital Remaster 1996. Chrysalis Records 724385221323.

Jethro Tull (1972). *Thick As A Brick*. Digital Remaster 1998. Chrysalis Records 724349540026.

Jethro Tull (1973). *A Passion Play*. Digital Remaster 2003. Chrysalis Records 724358156904.

Jethro Tull (1974). *Warchild*. Digital Remaster 2002. Chrysalis Records 724354157127.

Jethro Tull (1975). *Minstrel In The Gallery*. Digital Remaster 2002. Chrysalis Records 72435415726.

Jethro Tull (1977). *Songs From The Wood*. Digital Remaster 2003. Chrysalis Records 724358157024.

Jethro Tull (1978). *Heavy Horses*. Digital Remaster 2003. Chrysalis Records 724358157123.

Jethro Tull (1979). *Stormwatch*. Digital Remaster 2004. Chrysalis Records 724359339924.

Jethro Tull (1984). *Under Wraps*. Digital Remaster 2005. Chrysalis Records 724347341502.

Jethro Tull (1987). *Crest Of A Knave*. Digital Remaster 2005. Chrysalis Records 724347341328 .

Jan Clemens Moeller

Comments about Joni Mitchell's Composing Techniques and Guitar Style

Summary

The article (written to expand on findings reported in Moeller 2011) explores some of the musical and instrumental features found in songs of Joni Mitchell. Peculiar guitar tunings as well as chord structures that in part seem to have been derived from such tunings, are given special attention. Two songs, one from an early phase of her career (*The Circle Game*, 1969) and another (*Refuge of the Road*) from one of Mitchell's "classic" albums of the 1970s (*Hejira*, 1976) are analyzed. Transcriptions of parts of the songs are provided to illustrate features and textures of these songs.

1. Introduction

Joni Mitchell (born November 7, 1943) no doubt is one of the most respected and at the same time perhaps the most underrated singer and songwriter of the last century. The "Rolling Stone" magazine even called her one of the greatest and most influential songwriters ever. She received countless awards, such like the Billboard Century Award and the Grammy Lifetime Achievement Award, and she also was inducted into the Rock and Roll Hall of Fame.

Nevertheless, there is a great difference between the early years of her career and the reception she found (or, rather, missed) in later years. While her song "Both sides, now" (1969) was covered more than 640 times, her album "Mingus" (1979) failed to attract the attention of a wider public and did not even see significant radio airplay. In regard to musical concepts and instrumental techniques, Mitchell always was the artist that explored the world of non-standard tunigs like no other. Starting in the mid-60s, when she began to compose songs in conventional open tunings such as open G (DGDGBD) or D (DADF#AD), she also developed a number of quite unusual tunings. Joel Bernstein, who in a way is her "tuning-archivist" said that *while (she was) tuning her guitar from one open tuning to another she came upon unlooked – for intermediate chords whose tone-color immediately resonated with her. She thus began to compose in tunings that had never even explored before*. Mitchell herself commented: *For years everybody said 'Joni's weird chords' and I thought, how can they be weird chords? Chords are depictions of emotion. These chords that I was getting by twisting the knobs on the guitar until I could get the chords that I heard inside that suited mm – they feel like my feelings. You know – I called them-not knowing (technical names) – 'chords of inquiry' – they have a question mark in them. There were so many unresolved things...... those chords suited me, and .... I'd stay in unresolved emotionality for days and days.*[1]

---

[1] A comment she made in a DVD-documentary of her's *Woman of heart and mind: A life story* (2003; the passage is found at time code position 23:11).

In the 135 songs that she wrote for guitar she used more than forty different tunings. So-called conventional open tunings (open G, open D, or D modal) she uses in less than 19% of her songs. There are tunings that she employs for just one or two songs. To remember all these different tunings Joni Mitchell doesn't use the note names for each string. She just writes the name of the lowest string and then numbers which represent the fret numbers at which one plays one string to tune the next open string. The standard tuning EADGBE becomes E55545, and an open G tuning she notates D57543.

A tuning like F#BEAC#F# she would notate F#55545. So what is important is the relative tuning of the strings and it's easy to recognize that E55545 and F#55545 have the same relative tuning of the strings and just the root note is different. So when I mention that there are more than forty tunings this means there are forty different tunings of strings.

2. Analyses

In what follows, I'm going to show some aspects of her guitar style and her harmonic perception. The first example is from her third album *Ladies of the canyon* released in 1970.

Example 1 is the transcription of the guitar intro of the song *The circle game*. The guitar is tuned to open G (DGDGBD / D57543), and the capo is on the fourth fret, so it is sounding B^2.

The song offers a straightforward fingerpicked accompaniment, harmonies that are quite simple, all the typical aspects for urban Folk style. Also, we see a regular verse-chorus form, each composed of four four-bar phrases. However, the intro has 5 bars and provides a little tension to the clear structured song and it does not start with the tonic triad as could be expected in a conventional folksong.

The chord changes are I Bm Am7 I Bm Am7 I Bm Am7I G C G I G I. Starting with a Bm (b6)/chord and followed by a Am7-chord. This movement B-A is repeated three times until finally the tonic triad G is introduced.

---

[2] The capo is on the 4th fret. Therefore a G chord played sounds at the pitch B. To make reading easier, I transcribed the piece in question in G-major.

Example 1: Joni Mitchell: *The Circle Game*, Intro

The circle game

Joni Mitchell

Guitar

Guitar tuning
DGDGBD

Git.

Git.

Mitchell often uses the same fingering to create chords or sonorities and just moves it along the neck of the guitar, like in bars 1-3.

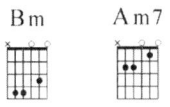

Bm   Am7

(the same fingering in the intro)

These fingerings which let open strings ring is another stylistic feature of Joni Mitchell`s guitar style. Here it is the G which rings throughout all chords and it gives a special character to the Bm-chord (b6), which almost sounds like a B/Gmj7-chord, and in the Am7-chord the open G is the 7th. This example is quite easy to understand.

Example 2 is much more sophisticated but it employs similar composition techniques, for example parallel chord movements. This song is from the album *Hejira* released in 1976 and is called *Refuge of the Roads*. The main theme of this album is traveling and being on the road. The songs were for the most part written by Mitchell while traveling by car from Maine to Los Angeles. The album title is a transliteration of the Arabic word 'hijra', which means "journey".

The tuning that she developed for this song is unique. As it seems it was only used for this song. The guitar is tuned CACFAC (C93533), apparently a F-major-Chord. The third string is tuned to the root note F, with the sixth, fourth and first string tuned to C (as 5th) this tuning is slightly different from a conventional open tuning, where, like in the example above (open G = DGDGBD), the root note is much more present. Here we have 3 times the 5th (C) and 2 times the 3rd (A) and only one root note (F), which however is not the lowest note in the tuning. If this were the case, the tuning might at least give a stronger tonal perception of a F-major triad. But here it is the fourth string (viewed from bottom) that is tuned to F. On the recording, Mitchell is doubling her guitar playing though not exactly in regard to onsets of notes, which gives a kind of small delay effect besides the chorus effect that has been added to the guitar tracks to yield a brighter sound. As Mitchell explained: *On Hejira I doubled the guitar and I doubled it in a way that Wayne Shorter and Miles double on Nefertiti. It's like silk-screening – it's not tight doubling. I'm playing the part twice but there's some variations on it so they're not perfectly tight - they're shadowing each other in some places.*[3]

The song starts with this chord

which is far beyond a so called slash-chord, because it is a mixture of at least three chords. In fact it contains essential notes of an E-minor, an A-minor and a C-major chord, all at the same time, but it sounds more like a Gsus4 chord, even with the lack of the 5th. This seems a clever choice, because the resulting complex chord is harmonically far away from the F-tuning, and like in *The circle game* she does not start this song with the tonic chord. But here Mitchell goes much further. While in the intro of "The circle game" she starts with a Bmb6-chord, which is a chord that is normal for a song in a G-major scale, she decided in this instance to place a chord with notes that are not in the F-scale. Here it is the B (sharp) which is the diminished 5th.

The next chord is a kind of a Bbmaj9 chord

which is followed by a strong C-major triad

---

[3] Interview with Chip Stern, Musician, January/February 1995

which is soon altered with the ninth and eleventh (D and F#)

the same movement is repeated two steps down and

just with beginning of the vocal the key is settled and becomes F-major.

With the refrain the key changes to C-major with this strong C-major triad.

Followed by the this F-major chord (2nd invention)

How ambivalent the function of the same chords can be becomes clear in bar 25. Here the same chord that in bar 1 sounds like a Gsus4, in the C-major context sounds more like a Em7. The commentary that Wayne Shorter (famous American jazz saxophonist) made about Joni Mitchell's chords underlines this: *Joni didn't play the guitar with an academic or clinical approach. It was like she was going where her vocabulary guitar-wise took her. And there was variation. They put the music in front of me, and then I'd start play and close my eyes instead of looking at a B or D7 chord, because it wasn't actually those chords anyway. It was the inversion of something, and the chord would*

sound like it was from Asia. Some other chords sounded minor-ish, or besides minor, you could say melancholy, sentimental, questioning. Some harmonic chords you'd hear in Stravinsky, Bartók, those kinds of chords.[4]

The bass lines played by Jaco Pastorius (famous jazz/fusion bass player, b. 1951, d. 1987) on this recording does not have an importance for the perception of the harmonies. The transcription shows that he almost only plays melodic figures (even though his playing is great and the sound of his fretless bass really fits to the song). Maybe it is because the songs on which he played were already recorded and finished by the time that Joni Mitchell asked him to join. The function that his bassplaying had in groups like Weather Report, his divinely rhythmic playing combined with his virtuosity, the way he used "chime tones" (flageolets, harmonics) that has influenced thousands of bass players is absolute worth to be studied more closely, however, this would be beyond the scope of this article. In "Refuge of the road", being the first work of Mitchell and Pastorius recording together, his playing is more melodic and subtle than in recordings he did before.[5]

He does not play in the intro of the song, he just starts when the key becomes clear (bar 11, F-major, he antedates the F in bar 10). Only in the refrain when the key evidently becomes C-major he adds some rhythmic phrases (bar 21) but as soon as the intro is repeated he switches again to melodic phrases (bar 28 to 33).[6]

Joni Mitchell describes her perception of harmonies like this: *I think because men need to solve things and to come to conclusions – the "sus" chord – there's a law that Wayne Shorter told me: never stay on a sus chord too long; never go from one sus chord to a sus chord. Well, I know I'm going from a sus chord to a sus chord to sus chord- you know, chords of inquiry, because my life was full of questions: When are they gonna drop the big one?" "Where is my daughter?" You know there are so many unresolved things....those chords suited me, and......I'd stay in unresolved emotionality for days and days... so here's a depiction – why can't you just go three chords unresolved like that, and then when you hit a major, or even minor, in a progression – boom – you know, it's quite a dramatic change coming out of that into a resolution.*[7]

Refuge of the Road is exactly structured like this. First, we have an intro where a defined mode (major or minor) is not present, then the verse seems to be in F-major, but a lot of Joni's "inquiry"-chords are used (bar 13 and 15). However, when the refrain is introduced (bar 21) there is this strong C-major-chord (bar 21) and the second inversion of

---

[4] Mercer 2009, 109.
[5] *The album was already finished at that time. And then Jaco came out and added bass on four tracks.....And more melodic than he was playing before that* (A conversation with Ingrid Pastorius by Wally Breese, 1998. Retrieved from www.jonimitchell.com).
[6] There is definitely a difference in the way he plays between this album and the albums that he participated afterwards. On the next album "Don Juan reckless daughter" he is playing much more basic rhythms while he continues to add melodic elements. This is due to the fact that he was not involved in the basic recordings of the 4 "Hejira"-songs. He just added his bass on already finished songs. So his genius was restricted. But exactly this made him invent a different way to play his bass that he afterwards used for different projects, too.
[7] See DVD-documentary on Mitchell titled *Woman of heart and mind: A life story* (2003).

the F-chord which give this dramatic change and resolution that even the "inquiry"-chord in bar 25 sounds like Em7 in this context.

After looking into some of the harmonic textures, let us now redirect attention to Joni Mitchell´s guitar style. The interesting thing is that Joni Mitchell always uses only a few fingerings. For "Refuge of the road", she uses only four fingerings. But because of the open string tuning totally different chords are created with the first fingering.

The first fingering is played in 7th, the 10th and the 5th fret.

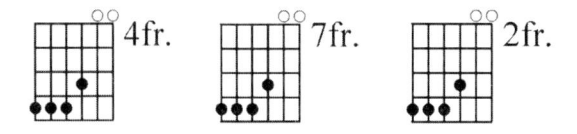

The resulting notes/tones are

GEGB   AC
BbGBbD AC
FDFA   AC

The 1st and 2nd string ring open (A and C). And what the 9th and the sus4 is for a G is the major 7th and the 9st for Bb, and the 3rd and 5th for the F.

The second fingering is simply a full Barré.

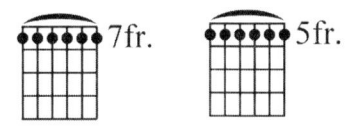

The chords resulting are

GEGCEG
FDFBbDF

The third fingering:

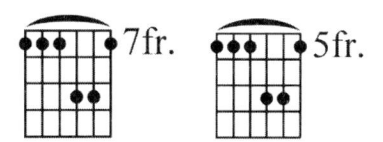

The notes/tones resulting are

GEGDF#G
FDFCEF

Finally, the fourth fingering is

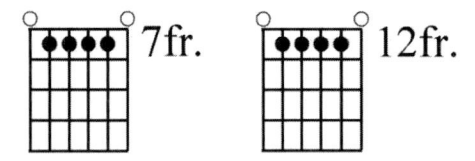

[chord diagram: 7fr.] [chord diagram: 12fr.]

resulting in the chords

CEGCEC
CACFAC

As to the method of finding fingerings resulting in chords and sonorities, Joni Mitchell gives this account: *There are certain simple fingerings that were difficult in standard tunings. My left hand is not very facil; my right hand is extremely articulate. At the time that I began to write my own music, Eric Andersen showed me open G and D modal, dropping down the bass string, I had always heard beautiful melodies in my head, so I just tuned the guitar to those chords, or slipped into a tuning so that the shapes made by the left hand were simplified.*[8]

Pragmatically this explains the way she creates: simple fingerings for the left hand while the right hand that is playing accentuated and sometimes intricate rhythms.[9]

---

[8] Hinton 1996, 89.
[9] See also Moeller 2011, 119.

Example 2: Joni Mitchell: *Refuge of the Roads*

Refuge of the Roads

Refuge of the Roads

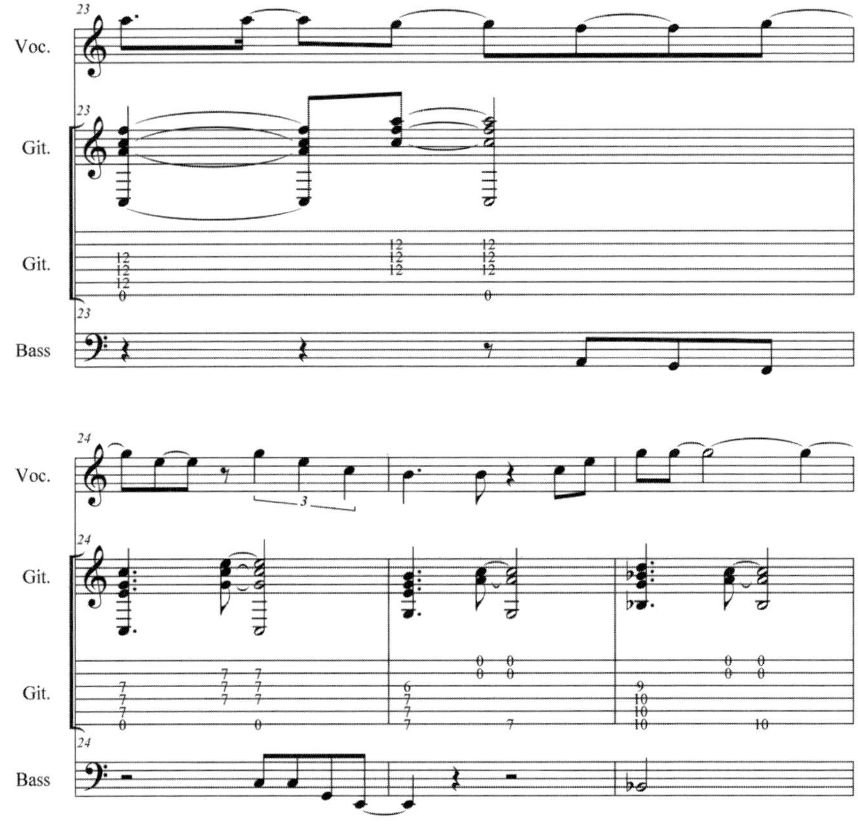
Voc.
Git.
Git.
Bass
Voc.
3
Git.
Git.
Bass

Refuge of the Roads

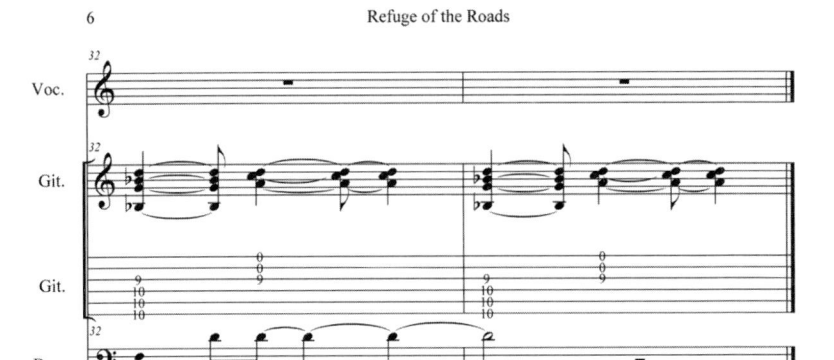

3. Conclusion

There are several techniques that determine Joni Mitchell´s style of guitar compositions. Firstly, she is using (with only one exception) open tunings. When she started to compose her own music in the sixties she used more conventional open tunings (like drop D-DADGBD used for "Free Man in Paris" 1974 or open G-DGDGBD used for "The Circle Game"1970) but with the years she became more and more radical. Some tunings like CGEbFBbD that she uses for "The wolf that lives in Lindsey" (from the 'Mingus' album 1979) are besides being considered as a tuned slash-chord (here Cm with Bb or Cm11), and are certainly a challenge for any guitar. The strings are tuned so low that the C she often strucks percussively rattles and clatters, but she managed to make this sound an integral part of the composition.

Secondly, we should mention her parallel motion of fingerings. She often moves the same fingering along the neck and fretboard of the guitar, thereby keeping the relative positions of the fingers of the left hand in a certain configuration. Quite often, some of the strings are played "open" (no finger used on these strings). The open strings that ring well in resonance with the guitar (especially in open tunings, cf. Schneider 2011) are another reason for molding these special chords that lack a clear mode.

Thirdly, there is the recurrent feature of simple fingerings. Maybe it is just because of her weak left hand, but the fingerings Mitchell uses are simple. Some fingerings she even employed in different tunings (the first fingering she uses in "Refuge of the roads" occurs also in the song "Amelia" on the same album though with a different tuning). Fourthly, the right hand's playing is done percussively. Over the years, a progress in the use of the right hand could be observed. When Mitchell started to play guitar in the 1960s she was picking the strings much more like folk musicians usually do (that is, mostly in regular patterns according to the meter of a particular song), but then she developed her own style, which makes use of the thumb and the fingers nearly independently, creating almost polyrhythmic patterns, slapping with the heel of the hands on the strings.

This article considers only exemplary aspects of Joni Mitchell's music which is complex in many respects, and moreover has undergone changes in the course of her long career spanning several decades. However, there are some persistent features in particular in her use of the guitar both in regard of the chords and sonorities she creates as well as her unique style of playing.

References

Hinton, Brian 1996. *Joni Mitchell. Both sides now – The biography*. London: Sanctuary Publishing.

Mercer, Michelle 2009. *Will you take me as I am: Joni Mitchell's Blue Period*. New York: Simon & Schuster.

Moeller, Jan 2011. Anmerkungen zur Musik Joni Mitchells. In Friedrich Geiger & Frank Hentschel (eds.). *Zwischen "U" und "E". Grenzüberschreitungen in der Musik nach 1950*. Frankfurt/M. Etc.: P. Lang, 119-123.

Schneider, Albrecht 2011. Analytische Notiz zu Joni Mitchell: "In France they kiss on main street". In Friedrich Geiger & Frank Hentschel (eds.). *Zwischen "U" und "E". Grenzüberschreitungen in der Musik nach 1950*. Frankfurt/M. Etc.: P. Lang, 125-134.

Ulrich Morgenstern

Egalitarianism and Elitism in Ethnomusicology and Folk Music Scholarship[1]

Vsiakii spliashet, da ne kak skomorokh.
Everyone can dance – just not like a minstrel.

Russian proverb

Summary

In ethnomusicology and folk music scholarship concepts of equality and elitist thought are both reflected in most different ways. Social-romanticist as well as collectivist and totalitarian approaches highlight simplicity and accessibility as characteristics of traditional music while numerous researchers, in contrast, emphasise the emergence of musical elites in traditional cultures. The cultural criticism in ethnomusicology frequently comes in conflict with the guiding principles of a society. Therefore musicology is exposed to the danger of ideological usurpation and functionalisation.

Zusammenfassung

In Ethnomusikologie und Volksmusikforschung spiegeln sich auf unterschiedlichste Weise Vorstellung von Gleichheit und elitäre Denkweisen. Sozialromantische, aber auch kollektivistische und totalitäre Konzepte sehen Simplizität und allgemeine Zugänglichkeit als bestimmende Eigenschaft traditioneller Musikformen an, während nicht wenige Forscher im Gegenzug auf Leistungseliten auch in Volksmusikkulturen verweisen. Ethnomusikologische Kulturkritik gerät häufig in Konflikt mit gesellschaftlichen Leitbildern. Hierbei ist Musikwissenschaft vielfach der Gefahr der ideologischen Vereinnahmung und Funktionalisierung ausgesetzt.

Introduction

Concepts of egalitarianism and elitism are both fundamental to Western civilisation. They shaped intellectual discourses and powerful political movements up to our days. The Judaeo-Christian confession of equality of human beings before God is the precondition for our secularised ideal of equality before the law, born in the Age of Enlightenment. But surely, in broad historical periods this ideal in political practice was not extended to all members of a society. But it still existed as a continuous claim, at least starting with the French Revolution, when Olympe de Gouges put forward the *Déclaration des droits de la femme et de la citoyenne*. Even in the period of early modernity when European colonial rulers established their own system of slavery in Africa

---

[1] I would like to express my gratitude to Antje Steward (Weisendorf) for careful proofreading of the largest part of this text.

and America, Western societies immediately mobilised intrinsic intellectual resources for resistance. It is hard to deny that the abolition movements were strongly inspired by ideals of Christianity and later by the philosophy of Enlightenment.

Notwithstanding this deeply rooted egalitarianism the very notion of *culture* in Europe and North America is frequently linked to an elitist thought. The upper class in the Roman Empire defined the *humanitas* largely by contrast to the despised *vulgus*. In modern times, habits of the social elite became extremely attractive beyond their primary social borders. The aristocratic ideals, be it the British *gentlemen* or *lady*, the Polish *pan* or *pani*, to some extent the notion of *kul'turnost'* in Russia, became a basic idea for large parts of the society. This is not a superficial adaptation of status symbols but a much deeper process than Hans Naumann's "gesunkenes Kulturgut" may suggest. And, after all, one of the main goals in the cultural policy of the socialist labour movement – emerged as a reaction to a most dramatic material inequality – was by no means the subversion of the bourgeois culture but a better access to its standards for the lower classes[2].

The political and cultural history of Europe is often characterised as shaped by a tension-filled balance of power. A similar state of tension also exists between the concepts of egalitarianism and elitism in the history of European intellectual thought. This configuration could not remain without consequences for the social sciences and the humanities. To some extent egalitarianism lies at the basis of anthropology and comparative musicology. Considerations of universals in human music making and reception presuppose that human beings are fundamentally equal (Walter Graf's 'biological substructure'). Nevertheless their talent and the propensity for musical activities are not equally distributed. In most societies a considerable amount of meaningful music making is delegated to performers with special skills and experience. These groups are of particular interest for ethnomusicology.

In the following article I would like to outline issues of egalitarianism and elitism in folk music discourse and scholarship as well as in ethnomusicology. It will be necessary also to speak about the relation between scholarship and political ideology.

Folksong as 'simple songs' (Egalitarianism I)

Gotthold Ephraim Lessing in his *Literarian letters* commented on a collection of *dainas* in Ruhig's *Lithuanian dictionary* with remarkable enthusiasm: "What a naive wit! What a charming simplicity!"[3] This estimation is highly ambiguous. On one hand Lessing insists "that in each climate there are born poets, and vivid sentiments are not a privilege of civilised peoples"[4], on the other hand he could not characterise the artistic accomplishments of the 'non-civilised' peoples other than 'simple' and 'naive'. The notions of 'simplicity' and "nature", crucial for the contemporaneous Philhellenism, became fundamental to the folk song concept of Johann Gottfried Herder as well. Some time later, one of the first Russian folk song collections (published in 1776 by Vasilii Trutovskii) was

---

[2] This was a leading idea even for the early British cultural studies, as represented by the works of Richard Hoggart.
[3] „Welch ein naiver Witz ! welche reizende Einfalt", (Lessing 1759, 242).
[4] „daß unter jedem Himmelsstriche Dichter geboren werden, und daß lebhafte Empfindungen kein Vorrecht gesitteter Völker sind" (ibid.).

labelled *Compilation of Russian Simple Songs with Musical Notation*. (Herder's term *Volkslied* was translated only in 1790 by Nikolai Lvov in his famous collection.) The 19th century Russian folk music discourse created the hybrid term *prostonarodnyi* ('belonging to the simple folk'), relating most of all to traditional peasant repertoire.

The idea of peasant songs and music as 'simple' is closely interlinked with a naive underestimation of the artistic and cognitive efforts of "illiterate singers". Cecil J. Sharp claimed folk songs to be "the product of spontaneous and intuitive exercise of untrained faculties" (Sharp 1907, 17). The paradigm of simplicity corresponds with the idea of a common availability of local styles and repertoires. It is not at all restricted to the 18th century or to the area of national romanticism: Albert L. Lloyd was convinced that "what he [the illiterate folksinger] was singing, he knew many of his neighbours could sing as well" (Lloyd 1944, 12). It falls short to explain Lloyd's egalitarianism only with his orthodox communist convictions. Still the former director of the German Folksong Archive in Freiburg, Otto Holzapfel[5], claimed that "real folk songs are songs everyone can sing". Such down-levelling judgements, including Ernst Klusen's "irrelevance of aesthetics" (1967, 39), can arise only in ignorance of the results of fieldwork in European folk music scholarship over of at least the last hundred years[6]. In all traditional music cultures[7] we find genres, including highly artificial ones, and performing situations demanding special and even exceptional musical skills. The egalitarian concept of folk music as 'simple songs', thus accessible more or less to each member of a society, is one of the most persistent myths in folk music discourse.

Totalitarian Concepts: Folk Music as the Expression of 'Volksgemeinschaft' and
'massovaia kul'tura' (Egalitarianism II)

It is well-known that the "romantic amateurism" (Marin Marian-Bălașa 2007), and also parts of professional folk music scholarship, can exhibit a certain propensity to nationalistic and collectivistic ideologies, using – or perverting – the socially integrative potential of musical activity and experience (Karbusicky 1973, Turino 2008). In totalitarian movements, egalitarianism is an ideological corner stone. To be sure, the most prominent and most far-reaching aspect of the National Socialist's ideology was the postulate of a fundamental *inequality* of human beings according to their ethnic origin, eventually leading to the Holocaust. However, in respect to the members of the *Herrenrasse* – regardless of the strong hierarchical structure of the state – it is the equality of the *Volksgenossen* (national comrades) that constitutes the guiding ideology in Hitler's *national socialism* (Götz Aly). The *völkische* egalitarianism finds expression in the never seen before generous social policy of the NSDAP as well as in a radical abolition of aristocratic privileges and class boundaries (Aly 2005). Not accidentally, in his diary

---

[5] „Echte Volkslieder sind Lieder, die alle singen." Broadcasting of the „Süddeutscher Rundfunk", 13. Jan. 1994.
[6] It would be insightful to compare these superficial statements with Ivan Turgenev's impressive description of a singing competition in a Russian village inn. See: his "Singers" from "Sketches from a Hunter's Album". I am indebted to Alexander Romodin for communicating this source.
[7] Towards a general, relative delimitation of this frequently disputed term from popular music (including folk music revival), see Morgenstern 2010b.

Adolf Eichmann wrote that Communism and National Socialism are "sort of like sibling children" (ibid. 15).

In folk music scholarship in the spirit of the German *Volksgemeinschaft* egalitarianism is a central concept for an imagination of the past. So Josef Pommer (1845-1918) believed that "in the times of Walther von der Vogelweide and earlier (...) education, outlook, the whole thinking, feeling, willing of almost all *Volksgenossen* was equal."[8]

For the Marxist ideology equality is the final goal – requiring in Lenin's reading the violent extinction of the former leading classes and other categories of persons. In political practice, however, above the faceless collective there rises the figure of the 'Leader of the world proletariat', 'Father of the peoples', 'Sun of Communist future', 'Máximo Líder' and so forth. The combination of brutality and ridiculousness is one of the most vulnerable points of totalitarianism in power. The inevitable sarcastic reactions of the subjects, creating a large repertoire of political folklore, demand an additional control over everyday language use by the regime.

Totalitarian systems, besides political obedience, require also changes of the private live and the inner feelings of their subjects. Thus it is not surprising that musical activities are of high concern for pedagogical as well as repressive efforts of the state. In the National Socialist educational ideology collective singing played a fundamental role. Their music policy definitely borrowed substantial ideas from the romantic German *Jugendbewegung*. This refers to the emphasis on group singing, musical simplicity, and broad accessibility of the repertoire. However, Adorno's accusation that the *Wandervogel* had prepared the subjugation of the youth under the NSDAP is highly questionable (Karbusicky 1973, 189, 190). Because for a considerable part of the *Jugendbewegung* attending the concerts of Serge Jaroff's 'Don Cossack Choir', the illegal singing of the extremely popular Russian songs was a sign of mental resistance (Schepping 2005). Most of the National Socialist song repertoire is rooted in other social settings. As Vladimir Karbusicky (1973) has shown, its musical idiom, as well as essential textual patterns, are closely related to soldiers' songs of the Wilhelmine era as well as – perhaps not accidentally – with battle songs of the German communists.

Unfortunately, the ultra-nationalistic collectivism with its mistrust toward individual creativity was also influential for politicised folk music discourse in Eastern Europe. In Ceausescu's Romania, nationalism became the official ideology (Marian-Bălaşa 2007) while in late Soviet period it appeared more as a traditionalistic counterculture (not without a certain support from some officials), generally linked with an aggressive anti-Semitism. The former professor of the St. Petersburg Conservatory, Anatoly Mekhnetsov (1936-2008), a highly influential person in nationalistic folklore circles, propagandised a total re-education of contemporary Russian society as a whole:

> "A Committee for traditional culture is further called upon to provide a complex restoration of folk traditions: in land use, house building, in clothing and nutrition, in education and handicrafts, in dance and martial arts. It's a matter of the ecology of culture, of the salvation of Russia, if you will."[9]

---

[8] "Zur Zeit Walthers von der Vogelweide und früher [...], da war Bildung, Anschauungsweise, das ganze Denken, Fühlen und Wollen fast aller Volksgenossen gleich" (Pommer 1901, 115).
[9] From an interview with Mekhnetsov in the journal *Russkii stil'. Boevye iskusstva* [Russian style. Martial arts], Moscow 1992 (without numeration), p. 8. See also Morgenstern 2007, 371 f., 2006, 152.

Mekhnetsov's quasi-totalitarian claim is reflected in his dismissal of individual expression in revival performance. Laura J. Olson locates one of the main lines of conflict in Russian folk music revival in the issue of self-expression:

> "One of the defining characteristics of the liberal camp of the folklore revival movement is their facilitation of individual expression within the group. Whereas Mekhnetsov argued that he does not 'display himself', that is precisely what these performers are trying to do: 'show themselves' on stage." (Olson 2004, 24)[10]

Anyone acquainted with traditional Russian music and dance can only wonder why a most experienced fieldworker could overlook the enormous potential for individual creativity in Russian peasant culture.

The Soviet cultural policy appealed to Lenin's normative dictum that "the art belongs to the people". From there arises the popular pedagogical ambition of the regime as well as its repressive politics. The enormous educational efforts after the Bolshevik Coup d'Etat were directed towards the creation of a thoroughly politicised 'proletarian culture'. This did not include a renunciation of the European music of the classic and romantic epoch, even in the heyday of the *proletkult*. In contrast, Anatoly Lunacharskii's vision was the adoption of the musical heritage by the 'common people': "Probably there will be a time when the symphonic orchestra, the piano, and other forms of music will gush out to the villages" (Lunacharskii 1928, ct. after Blagodatov 1960, 106). Realistically, the Soviet commissar for culture preferred another pedagogical tool: "the musical impact on the masses, and peculiarly in the villages, through the accordion [*garmonika*]". Being aware of the most prestigious and influential status of the young male accordion player in the village, the Ministry of culture and especially the *komsomol* expressed concern that the accordion, because of its high price, "gets in the hands of our class enemy" (A. Sergeev in *Muzyka i revoliutsiia*, 1929, ct. after Blagodatov 1960, 98, 99). The result was an enormous production of cheap button accordions and balalaikas (the latter prepared already under the Ancient Regime by the educational policy of Vasilii Andreev, the founder of the Great Russian Orchestra). Of course, most of the village musicians did not follow slogans like "The accordion into service of the *komsomol*!" (ibid. 99) or proclamations for a "decisive struggle against apoliticism on the musical front" (*Krasnaia gazeta*, 15.06.1931, ct. after Vertkov 1975, 226). Their basic repertoire of this period comprised most of all traditional local tunes, played earlier on home-made balalaikas, hornpipes, flutes and probably bagpipes, along with some ballroom and contemporary dances. Nevertheless, the popularity of Soviet 'mass songs' is – up to our days – much higher than the classical regional collections (oriented on archaic repertory and highly elaborated lyrical songs) of Soviet/Russian ethnomusicologists may suggest.

The repressive side of the Soviet cultural policy is generally associated with Stalin's persecution of writers and composers. However, it is already rooted in Lenin's resentment against contemporaneous avant-garde literature. The total functionalisation of literature ("Down with non-partisan writers! Down with literary supermen!" Lenin 1967

---

[10] Unfortunately Olson disregards the "Chamber folklore ensemble" of Igor' Matsievskii, the first revival formation in Leningrad/Saint Petersburg (1977) as well as a programmatic article of its former participant Aleksandr Romodin (1984), another representative of the "liberal camp".

[1905], 100) is initially hostile to any concept of individual creativity[11]. Musicians, in the first years of the regime, generally experienced less pressure than writers. It was Lunacharskii who maintained a certain pluralism of composition techniques. In 1934, on the eve of Stalin's Great Terror, Zhdanov proclaimed the Socialist Realism as the official guideline for artists. With its egalitarian concepts of *massovost'* (mass participation), *narodnost'* (folkishness) and *dostupnost'* (accessibility) it stayed in place until 1991.

True, the very construction of *narodnost'* in Soviet 'mass songs', promoted in the framework of the organised *kudozhestvennaia samodeiatel'nost'* ('amateur artistic activity') was a world apart from local musical traditions. And of course, the national-romantic phraseology of the regime did not at all protect the traditional musicians from repression. The mass execution of hurdy-gurdy players by the NKWD in the Ukraine is only the most dramatic example. Kazakh epic singers and also traditional song competitions were repressed (*aitys*; cf. Zemtsovsky/Kunanbaeva 1997, 20). In Russian villages, performing the very melody of the *Semenovna* (sometimes associated with a paramour of one of the Bolshevist leaders) could entail a person five years of imprisonment (Pskov and Tver' region, fieldwork 2005). In the kolkhozes, seven day working weeks without holidays and the ban of religious feasts and village fairs under Stalin and Khrushchev did not stimulate the musical activity of the 'masses'. The professional manufacturing of accordions in the villages was also prohibited (along with other types of peasant secondary occupation), so that for example the production of the famous *Novorzhevskaia garmonika* in the Pskov region came to an end in the early thirties (Morgenstern 2007, 116).

Folklore against High Culture: The Social Romanticism of Folk Music Revival
(Egalitarianism III)

The folk music revival in the USA was – from its very beginnings – founded both on the aesthetical appreciation of young middle-class musicians of traditional styles and repertoires, as well as on the understanding of folk music as a counterculture to the American ideal of individual economic success. Representatives of the revival movement were clearly associated with left wing convictions, idealising – sometimes in a highly selective way – songs of underrepresented groups such as workers, blacks, hoboes. Even more, the activism of the Anglo-American revivalists is initially connected to the directives of radical organisations. R. Serge Denisoff has convincingly shown the early folk music revival in the USA as a part of Stalinist policy[12]. In Great Britain as well the post-war revival was strongly promoted and controlled by the Communist party

---

[11] In his famous reply to Maxim Gorky's protest in September 1919 (not the first and not the last one) towards repressions against intellectuals ("we are destroying the [people's] brain"), Lenin stated that "in fact it's not the brain but its crap" (*Polnoe sobranie sochinenii, 5. izd.,* Moskva 1978, p. 48)

[12] Denisoff explains the dependence of North American 'folk consciousness' from directives of Soviet cultural policy. Unfortunately, following the Soviet folklorist Jurii Sokolov, he overestimates the folk origins of Soviet propaganda songs (1971, 10, 11). This repertoire definitely took much more from military marches, 19th century romances, and urban 'folk orchestras' than from the by far more sophisticated traditional peasant style. So the image of Stalin as "a folk music enthusiast" (1971, 15) is founded solely on doubtful stereotypes.

(Harker 1985, 236). In contrast to the pedagogical efforts of the 19th and early 20th century revival, associated with the name of Cecil Sharp, the identity of left wing revivalists rests on the conviction that it is "coming from below now" (Albert L. Lloyd, cited after Harker 1985, 236). This notion is not only – as Harker remarks – contrary to the organisational basis of the British revival, but most of all to the social basis of the folk music revival as a middle class phenomenon (Livingstone 1999).

Regardless to the obvious ideological interweaving of the Anglo-American revival movement it would be unjust not to consider essential differences in the approach to traditional music cultures. Soviet style stage folklorism presented itself from the very beginning as a caricature of local folk music, while peasant traditions were largely ignored by mass media up to the 1970's. Woody Guthrie, Pete Seeger, Albert A. Lloyd experienced a passionate devotion to traditional singers and musicians and – due to their artistic sensitivity – acquired much of the expressive qualities of their inspiring paragons. Their enthusiasm is worlds away from the aesthetics of Soviet *fakelore* and corresponding directives. One should only imagine a Bolshevist cultural worker hitchhiking with his guitar (or anything else) half a year and more all over his land, spending time with rural musicians, playing in bars, looking what is going on in the country. It's just ridiculous. It's just as hard to imagine Guthrie and Seeger working under Soviet rule, let's say – as censors of recording companies or concert agencies, or as rigid instructors of rural culture houses. There is something very tragic about the Stalinist aberrations of these and other Western 'folksters'.

Pete Seeger, Joan Baez and other American protest singers had a far-reaching influence on the left wing of the German *Jugendbewegung*. The Newport festival gave birth to the festival on the *Burg Waldeck* (1964-1968) in Western Germany (Kröher 1969, Schneider 2005, Kleff 2008). Sharing with the pre-war *Wandervogel* a romantic interest in history, progressive singer-songwriters searched for musical manifestations of social conflicts in the past. This led to a misinterpretation of musical history according to the current idea of 'counterculture'. Songs of the German peasant wars (mostly fakes), of the 1848 Revolution, antimilitaristic 'leaflet songs', and others were supposed to set a counterpoint to the school repertoire, perceived as sentimental and reactionary (or at best apolitical)[13]. As an additional point of identification, the medieval minstrels (*Spielleute*) served as imagined agents of the riotous 'folk'. Their real role as entertainers in most different social classes appears to be much more pragmatic (Salmen 1960, 1983). Generally, the widespread imagination of folk music as expressing a persistent counterculture does not take into account the largely fruitful interaction of *europäische Volksmusik* und *abendländische Tonkunst* (Wiora 1957).

A conflict between egalitarian claims and the exposed position of the singer-songwriter pervades the Waldeck festival as a whole. The festival concept initially involved a certain renunciation of the musical collectivism of the pre-war *Jugendbewegung* (the very name of the first three festivals refers to a solo genre – the *chanson*). Adherents of the conservative 'Nerother Wandervogel', the owner of the very castle ruin where the Waldeck festivals were staged, generally dismissed the program and even more so the

---

[13] Especially noteworthy is the reception of Wolfgang Steinitz's *Deutsche Volkslieder demokratischen Charakters aus sechs Jahrhunderten* (1954, 1962, s. John 2006), popularised first of all by Peter Rohland (1933-1977).

political orientation of the festival. Their supposed responsibility for the incendiary attacks and further sabotage in 1967 could never been proved. Ironically, one year later it was again collectivism, now in its leftist version, that turned against the festival's idea: members of the SDS (Socialist German Student Union) with Vietcong flags drove away musicians from the stage, pressing for common discussions on actual political issues. This was the end of the 'German Woodstock'. Only some years later the 'Adornian time of silence' ('adornitische Schweigezeit', cf. Mossmann/Schleuning 1978, 337) drew to a close. It was the German folk music revival of the early seventies, essentially influenced by contemporary Irish folk style, which established a new era of freedom for music making without direct political purpose. The recovery of instrumental folk music (Irish, German medieval, Russian, Balkan) is a strong indicator for the emancipation of musical activities from political functionalisation and ideological pressure in left wing settings. Nevertheless the imagination of a peasant counterculture in the past still remained to be influential[14].

In the selective view on folk music's social history as well as in its own musical activities, egalitarianism appears as a basic concept of folk music revival. Emotional expression (taken as a universal human quality) as well as a social topicality of music making (often merely imagined) were regarded higher values than was artificial accomplishment. The structure of most musical settings was ostensibly democratic. In *folk sessions* and open stage events typically – at least as a claim – every musician sharing essential requirements of style and repertoire was welcomed, regardless to his performance skills. In concert situations, folk musicians usually tried to break the hierarchy between the stage and the audience, including a broad participation by singing, dancing, and the like. The 'stars' of the folk song revival (Pete Seeger, Joan Baez) as well as the German 'Liedermacher'[15] felt themselves most of all as parts of a movement or a social milieu. In clothing and lifestyle they tried not to stand out too much from their audience. Airs and graces of the contemporaneous rock musicians (not to speak of *schlager* singers) were profoundly alien to them[16].

Revivalist musicians preferred instruments, requiring – at least on a basic level – less technical training, such as the guitar, the mandolin, the banjo. Folk fiddlers frequently made use of their former experience as middle class educated violinists. More sophisticated instruments such as the bagpipe and the hurdy-gurdy came in use as well.

---

[14] Tellef Kvifte (2001) emphasises the priority of ideology in the Scandinavian 'Progressive Music Movement': "But when the folk musicians of the PMM went to see old fiddlers, it was not because they looked for the music of the peasants. Instead, they demonstrated an act of solidarity with the oppressed – the proletarian. The more oppressed people were, the better; the more oppressed a musical genre was, the more important was solidarity".

[15] Literally: "song maker". This curious social romantic expression was coined by Wolf Biermann, following Brecht's hardly translatable self-image as a 'Stückeschreiber'. In contemporary German culture the term "Liedermacher" has been largely replaced by the English "singer/songwriter".

[16] James Porter has aptly characterised Pete Seeger's modesty as an essential protestant trait: "Ideology alone […] did not hold his interest; the puritan instinct to preach, to embrace moral purity, to maintain a certain emotional aloofness […] have all been a marked part of the Seeger character (1991, 124). It would be promising to investigate the significance of Puritanism and Protestantism for the modest and almost ascetic habits of folk music revivalists in North America and Western Europe.

However, musicians playing such instruments and instrument makers established more 'elite' circles, often distinguishing themselves from the average 'folkies'.

Egalitarian ideals and participatory concepts shaped the sceptical attitude of the folk revivalists' environment towards the classical and romantic repertoire and the 'bourgeois' concert life. Hierarchies between the conductor and the orchestra, as well as within the orchestra, strict rules for the behaviour on stage and in the audience – all this stood in sharp contrast to the overall cultural concepts of the alternative folk movement. How strongly anti-elitism could influence careers becomes evident in the biography of Walter Mossmann (b. 1941). At the Waldeck festival 1966 the German singer-songwriter was met with a "grandiose response by the media" (Kleff 2008, 161). What followed, however, were not lucrative recording contracts, big concert halls, international tours through the German speaking countries but Mossmann's growing concern with his exclusive position apart from the audience. In 1969 he stopped public performances until 1974 when the ecological movement gave new perspectives for a singer to be directly involved in political processes (Steinbiß 1984, 77). The idea of maximal accessibility of his art is crucial for Mossmann's understanding of a singer-songwriter:

"Here is indeed a connection to what once was folk music. Actually, I always use rather simple techniques, so others also can be encouraged to make things like this on their part. The opposite of this is the artistry of the bourgeois concert where you need ten years of special training to produce such sounds. Here as a normal person you can just squat down, admire and clap your hands" (interview with Mossmann 1982; Steinbiß 1984, 89).

Within the folk music movement, such attitudes were expressed more in internal discussions and less in cover texts or other public manifestations. A dispute in 1984 between Kaarel Siniveer, a singer-songwriter and radio journalist, and members of the North German folk group 'Liederjan' gives interesting insights in the elitism/egalitarianism issue of the contemporaneous folk music discourse:

> Kaarel (tearing his hair): "What - actually, do you have an understanding of art? Liederjan in the concert hall. Isn't that a total reproduction of the bourgeois concert situation?
> Anselm [Noffke]: Well, there are various areas that are clearly different than in a bourgeois symphonic concert or in the opera. Firstly, we want to communicate something. We don't just want to uplift (…).
> Jörg [Ermisch]: What indeed I miss about Karajan is that he turns around from time to time shortly performing the next choral singing that has to happen on stage so that the other people in the hall could also sing along. (Frey / Siniveer 1987, 242)

Folk music seemed to be most of all an expression of personal freedom, solidarity and a refuge of spontaneity. Thus, the ambivalent relationship of personal creativity and strongly regulated performing situations in traditional music cultures was frequently overlooked. However, sometimes it was a certain culture of subtlety in traditional music settings that impressed the young folk music enthusiasts, tired of the eccentric habits of rock concerts and disco dancing. Rainer Prüss from 'Liederjan' emphasises the *aesthetic collectivism* of the traditional dancing events in his homeland Dithmarschen in Schleswig-Holstein: "Much of the [revivalist] dancing is really important for our time – not to rattle again toward this disco dancing. But if in a dance genre you cut back your wishes a bit in favour of a common expression, I think that's indeed a basic attitude we should encourage a bit more today" (Steinbiß 1984, 123).

Generally speaking, the resentment against Western art music in the revival movement was less rigid as in higher politicised settings. When the *Kommunistische Volkszeitung* (issued by the *Kommunistischer Bund Westdeutschlands* with a paid circulation of several ten thousands) called for "criticising bourgeoisie music" (Kühn 2007, 159) this was directed not only against 20th century avant-garde composers (as in Soviet cultural policy) but against the repertoire of the classic and romantic epoch too – as well as against other 'non-proletarian' styles[17]. The career of the German cellist Frank Wolff (born in 1945) is most insightful in this regard. In 1966 he gave up his musical education for studying sociology with Adorno and joining the SDS where soon he was elected as a federal chairman. Comparing his teacher's attitude toward music with that of his own social environment Wolff remarks:

> "He allowed himself much of what in the student movement was believed to be proscribed. He liked to play the piano, he played it well, he played Schubert whenever he wanted." (Wolff 1989, 83)[18]

Anyway, in the early seventies Wolff continued his musical career – much to the disgust of his comrades:

> "In 1971/72 I began again to play string quartets as well, which I had done from my childhood. This was an important political break, as the whole scene I come from did not understand this at all, and many therefore shunned me, considering this to be a betrayal." (ibid., 88)[19]

Against such musical fundamentalism the typical folk revivalist practiced his cultural criticism more as a personal attitude without general claims to what other people have or have not to play or to listen to.

Participation and Accessibility in Folk Music Cultures (Egalitarianism IV)

The ability of experiencing and producing music as a "cultural and human universal" (Nettl 2005, 173) is given to any physically and mentally healthy human being. A considerable part of musical practice around the world appears as participatory music, when most or all attendants of a social event are encouraged or expected to take part in music making or dancing. Thomas Turino has described performing situations in which the maximal engagement of the participants is evaluated higher than the quality of the

---

[17] In Germany members of some Maoist sects were not allowed to listen to Rock music (Kühn 2007, 161).
[18] „Er hat sich vieles gestattet und bei sich vieles zugelassen, was man in der Studentenbewegung als geächtet wähnte. Er hat gerne und gut Klavier gespielt, er hat Schubert gespielt, wann er wollte".
[19] „1971/72 habe ich auch wieder angefangen Streichquartette zu spielen, was ich seit meiner Kindheit getan habe. Das war ein wichtiger politischer Bruch, weil die ganze Szene, aus der ich komme, das überhaupt nicht verstanden hat, und viele haben mich auch deswegen gemieden, die fanden das Verrat."

musical result (2008, 33-35)[20]. As Turino notes, this not at all means that all participatory music must be uniformly simple like campfire songs in societies dominated by presentative music (2008, 30).

In European folk music traditions participatory music was widespread in different genres. Among others these are working songs, religious chants, and female round dances, accompanied by the singing dancers, frequently without support of instrumentalists. However, a broad engagement in music making of a large part of a society is not necessarily linked to participatory performing situation. Irish céilí are a well-known example for presentative performance, requiring the (successive) participation of all attendants, regardless of their talent (Glassie 1982, 99-100). In the 18th century, Jakob von Stählin observed an extreme popularity of the Russian balalaika: "hardly a house in Russia can be found where there would be no young servant who could play for the maidens his tune on it" (Stählin 1770, 68). Johann Joachim Bellermann reports that "only few peasants live without it" (1788, 363). At the turn of the 20th century in many North Russian villages nearly every young man who was going to marry was expected to play the accordion. As we can see, in folk instrumental practice the number of musicians can be much higher than the traditional performing situations (weddings, spinning rooms, dancing events) would require – even more so in Russian folk instrumental music where soloist performance prevails. It's hard to explain this picture without the significance of aesthetic enjoyment. The equal access of young men to instrumental performance in these communities at the same time heightens the incentive for an elaborated individual performing style. The result is an enormous variability of local instrumental tunes (more probably – of individual versions) within a range of seldom more than two or three traditional patterns in any village, at least in the first decades of 20th century (Morgenstern 2007).

Peasant art as High Culture. The Folk Music Discourse in the Counterculture of the Intelligentsia under Communist Rule (Elitism I)

When Bruno Nettl asserts that ethnomusicologist "have a passion for showing that the music of the oppressed people of the world […] is something worthy of attention and respect" (2005, 15) this holds true by no means only for the postcolonial discourse of the West. Ethnomusicologists and folklorists working under communist rule were tacitly but constantly engaged in similar struggles. Klyment Kvitka's works on the last Ukrainian *lirniki* (hurdy-gurdy players with religious repertoire), countless secret studies of forbidden or totally destroyed genres as Central Asian epics, shamanistic performance, apocryphal religious songs, carols, speak of a strong however hidden scholarly counterculture in Soviet folkloristics and ethnomusicology. Some of these studies concerned highly elitist traditions of music making and poetry. When the censorship was abolished,

---

[20] Issues of participation are also central to Ernst Klusen's theory of singing, established more than twenty years before Turino's concept, however based on a more narrow geographical area. Klusen outlines different types of social interaction in musical situations: inner-directedness (*Innensteuerung*), inner/outer-directed substitution (*innen-/außengesteuerte Stellvertretung*), outer-directedness (*Außensteuerung*). It is, nevertheless, hard to agree with Klusen's historical implications in the sense of a general development from participatory inner-directedness to presentative outer-directedness (Klusen 1989, 179-183).

numerous post-Soviet scholars opened their poison chests, dangerous not only within the disciplinary framework. They also began to publish narratives from oral history on Stalin's cultural revolution and other repressive campaigns (Razumovskaia 1991, Ivleva/ Romodin 1998 [1989]).

When the Bolsheviks came to power long ago, 'romantic amateurism' was dominated by 'academic professionalism' in Russian folk music discourse (to use again Marian-Bălaşa's terms). It is due to the ideological pressure that the anthropologically grounded *muzykal'naia ?tnografia* was reduced to a more philological *muzykal'naia fol'kloristika* (Zemtsovsky/Kunanbaeva 1997, 20; Pashina 2005, 438-441). Leading scholars such as Evgeniia Linëva, the founder of comparative folk song research in Russia, the abovementioned Kvitka, Evgenii Gippius and many others were representatives of the intellectual elite. Gippius, the son of the well-known poet and literary scholar Vladimir Gippius, attended the most advanced Tenishev School in St. Petersburg together with Vladimir Nabokov. As a relative of the poet Zinaida Gippius who had to flee from the Bolsheviks, he was under observation of the NKWD.

It is noteworthy that still in the late Soviet period the intellectual criticism against the totalitarian system was fundamentally inspired by elitist, almost aristocratic attitudes. The axiological concept of culture in the writings of Dmitrii Likhachëv (1906-1999) largely corresponds with Matthew Arnold's understanding ("the best that has been thought and said"). It was only after the perestroika when Likhachëv – who was held from 1928 to 1932 in the concentration camp Solovki for joining a religious literature circle – could express his concern about the levelling down strategies: "Mass culture, that's nonsense. Culture is always to a certain degree elitist" (Likhachëv 2006 [1998]).

Typically, in Likhachëv's concept 'elitist culture' is not restricted to the social elites. The scholar was particularly interested in peasant culture, especially in newly discovered Russian peasant literature of the 18th and 19th centuries. A non-egalitarian understanding of peasant culture is not accidentally widespread in Eastern and Central European ethnomusicology. There is a strong tendency to operate with notions, traditionally associated with 'high culture', such as 'professionalism', 'theory' and, finally, 'elitism'. Yet Nikolai Onchukov characterises North-Russian epic singers and storytellers as the "intelligentsiia of the village" and even its "mental aristocracy" (Onchukov 1908, cit. after Ivanova 2009, 186f.). When Gippius asserted that "folklore is the art of an elite"[21] this sharpened statement is based particularly on observations of musical performance and experience in the Russian North. Ludwik Bielawski calls the Polish folk musicians "the cultural elite" of the village (Bielawski 1981, 17). Igor' Matsievskii who belonged to the closest circle around Gippius speaks in his profound study *Folk instrumental music as a phenomenon of culture* (2007) of professionalism as of "a cardinal attribute of folk instrumental music" (2007, 96), appearing on a psychological, functional, social-demographic, structural-stylistic level (180, see also: 179-232). In a special study "Towards the artistic views of traditional Polish musicians in the western Białystok district" (2009), he demonstrates a huge corpus of knowledge – not only practical – required from village musicians. Matsievskii analyses discourses of rural musicians, freely operating with notions traditionally restricted to the academic sphere like "theory", "theoretics", "thinkers", "oral music scholarship", "folk musicology" (142). In a similar

---

[21] I refer to manifold mentions by Igor' Matsievskii (St. Petersburg).

way, Gippius' disciple Inna Nazina (in print) explored the artistic concepts of "Byelorussian folk musicians and thinkers". Aleksandr Romodin, a conservatory-taught pianist and an ethnomusicologist and revival musician as well, emphasises the outstanding role a few accordion players have achieved in the southern Kun'ia rayon of the Pskov region. In the 1990's were indeed many musicians in the rayon, "But the truly talented (as in any sphere of activity) are a few" (Romodin 1999, 8). Romodin's aesthetic scepticism strongly reminds one of Herder's preface to his folk song collection. Referring to the popularity of singing in the Middle Ages, Herder supposes a considerable difference in performance quality: "However, everywhere and always the good is rare" (Herder 1779).[22] In Romodin's studies on North Byelorussian musicians issues of professionalism play an important part.

The concept of professionalism with regard to Middle and East European village musicians is however not undisputed. Bálint Sárosi (1981, 12), as well as Bielawski (1981,17), prefer to speak of semi-professional musicians, arguing that in Hungarian and Polish rural society it was impossible to make a normal living entirely from musical performance. In a special investigation on the economics of Polish and Ukrainian village music, William Noll asserts that the peasant instrumental musician

> "was not engaged in music full time, but only occasionally. He was not an outsider to the village group as a whole, but an integral part of the social fabric of the village. His activities as a specialist were both supplemental to his labours as a farmer and vital to village ritual life. The peasant musician was not a professional any more than was the local smith, carpenter or wheelwright" (Noll 1991, 355).

Nevertheless it would be inadequate to examine the social significance of instrumental music making and the exposed status of the artist only in terms of economics. At least I have never heard village people discussing the peculiarities of blacksmithing, wheelwrighting or other craftsmanship in a way comparable to the enthusiasm they can speak about the accomplishments of their local musicians.

Without any doubt the emphasis on professionalism, elaborated aesthetic concepts and artistic accomplishment in oral traditions has to be understood as a contribution to the rehabilitation of a musical culture formerly disdained, oppressed and at large purposefully destroyed (Ivleva/Romodin 1998 [1989]). Implicitly, Russian ethnomusicologists in the tradition of the liberal intelligentsia contested not only the repressive but also the pedagogical orientation of communist cultural policy. They mistrust the patronising concept of "heightening the cultural level of the folk", popular still in the late 19th century's folk music discourse. After years of extensive fieldwork they claimed that the local traditions are 'high enough' and any centralised re-education could only spoil their local diversity and artistic quality. The ardent attacks against soviet-style 'fakelore' (Boiko 1984, Zemtsovskii 1989) do not only emphasise the striking contrast between local peasant art and state-promoted kitsch. They were essentially aimed

---

[22] "Allerdings ist überall und allezeit das Gute selten" (Herder 1779, 20). It is noteworthy that Herder not at all believed in a quasi homogenous "folk culture". When Alain Finkielkraut opposes Herders seemingly collectivistic idea of a *Volksgeist* regarding the individuality, Finkielkraut definitely underestimates "the comprehensive valorization of individuality in the writings of Herder" ("die umfassende Aufwertung der Individualität bei Herder", see: Heinz 1996, 104).

against the very idea of cultural egalitarianism. From a purely aesthetical perspective, of course, engagement in amateur art without higher artificial claims can be criticised. In cultural policy, however, such elitism would appear extremely short-sighted. Nevertheless, in contemporary Russian language *samodeiatel'nost'* (literally: 'self-making') became an abusive word, a synonym for botching and incompetence. The inhabitants of the USSR were every day aware of the fact that political servility and personal connections had priority over professionalism. Not only in dissident circles the end of the first verse of the Russian *International* – "Kto byl nichem, tot stanet vsem" (He who was nothing will become everything) was frequently quoted with outright sarcasm: "That's exactly what has happened to us!"

In this context it cannot surprise that proponents of Eastern European folklore revival, largely associated with a liberal intellectual environment, did not share the scepticism of many Anglo-American and especially German revivalists against Western art music. As a matter of fact, many of them were professional musicians and composers with an excellent education. Therefore, attending a concert with the music of Mozart, Haydn or Schumann for many representatives of the intelligentsia was regarded as a possibility to escape the everyday life of totalitarianism. Vladimir Spivakov only takes up a widespread sentiment when saying that "here [in Saint Petersburg] we went to the philharmonic hall as if it was a church: When the churches were closed we got purification just there" (Spivakov 2005). So the affinity with European high culture – widely supported by the educational policy of the regime – could become an implicit manifestation of elitist counterculture against this very regime.

Musical Elites in Folk Music Cultures (Elitism II)

Ethnomusicologists frequently deal with highly elitist music cultures, divided from average musical practice and sometimes representing borders between social classes. For example, one may point to Indian and Middle East court music, many spheres of religious music making, shamanistic practice and increasingly also to art music of the West (Nettl 1989, Shelemay 2001). It is a peculiarity of European art music that the social boundaries with regard to performing activity were systematically broken, at least in the last two hundred years.

This does not mean that within European traditional cultures music making should be generally participatory or even egalitarian. As we have seen, performing wedding music in Polish or Ukrainian villages was a typical occupation for (semi)professional ensemble musicians. The same holds true for female wedding singers in Byelorussia. North-Russian epic singers and mourners were also semi- or full professionals.

This exposed status of musicians and singers corresponds with the complexity of the repertoire in question and with possible extra musical skills required in different social settings. However, different levels of performance quality can also be observed within a common, broadly accessible repertoire, as well as the different social prestige of the musicians. Some decades ago, nearly everybody in traditional Russian villages was capable to perform *chastushki* (epigrammatic short songs). Certain individual singers, mostly female *chastushechnitsy* enjoyed particular popularity for composing trenchant verses about current events in the village, or at least for picking them out in accordance to the actual situation. In many villages most of the young men or adults were able to play the balalaika or the accordion (*garmon'*). However, not everyone who was able to play the instrument on a certain level was worthy to be called a *garmonist*: "I'm not a *garmonist*. I can play the *garmon'* a bit, but I don't call myself a *garmonist*." (Vasilii Iakovlevich Ermakov, born in 1939, Solovianovka, Riazan' region; notes from my fieldwork 1990). This statement clearly reveals acknowledged hierarchies among different local musicians.

In Russian villages skillful musicians were highly respected as artists and extraordinary personalities.[23] Male as well as female musicians and singers are remembered as socially active members of the local community. A lot of the male adult musicians correspond in a special way to the patriarchal ideal of the *khoziain*, including authority, responsibility, and economical prosperity. (The happy-go-lucky, exuberant, rarely sober Russian balalaika player is a romantic imagination, bearing little relation to reality.) For these musicians their art is the adornment of successful living. This social appreciation of outstanding music seems to be typical in social settings with less developed professional or semi-professional music making. As in European rural societies it was rarely possible to feed a family basically by making music, professional musicians generally belonged to the lower classes of the community (Bielawski 1981) or to separate ethnic groups (Roma, Jews)[24].

Dancing is generally not a professional activity in rural Russia, except in the past from gypsy dancers and *skomorokhi* (minstrels). However, outstanding dancers gained no less prestige than skilful musicians. Entering the circle of the attendants of a dancing event for a soloist *pliaska* was a highly responsible decision. An evening's dancing was definitely not the right place for 'learning by doing'. There is evidence from the Smolensk region that even for the highly participatory couple dances (waltz, polka, krakowiak, foxtrot) dancers were expected to be well prepared. Otherwise they could be easily expelled from the dance floor. Thus, while in the participatory dance events of the Peruvian Aymara signs of impatience towards incompetent dancers "are generally considered bad manners" (Turino 2008, 34), in Russian villages, by contrast, a violation of good manners consists in an incompetent performance.

Ethnomusicologists as Cultural Critics and Cultural Warriors (Egalitarianism V)

As Philip Bohlman has pointed out, ethnomusicological thought, beginning with the early ethnography in the 18th century, is closely linked to cultural criticism: "Cultural critique at some moments in ethnomusicology's history may have been an even more compelling promise than it has been for anthropology because of the explicit aesthetic availability of another music" (Bohlman 1991, 143).

The aesthetic availability of other music refers to experience as well as to performance. Yet in 18th century Russia, foreign visitors with very limited language skills enthusiastically performed Russian songs (Morgenstern 2010a, 277f.). In the salons of the 19th century it was highly fashionable to sing "exotic" melodies. Here are the roots of

---

[23] Aleksandr Romodin (2005) has published impressive narratives on North Byelorussian musicians, demonstrating their appreciation within the local communities.
[24] The North Byelorussian professional accordion players, gaining a solid income as wedding musicians (Romodina/Romodin 1990, Romodin 2005) seem to be an exceptional phenomenon that is not yet studied in the context of the very special economics of rural society in Soviet times.

bi-musicality or *intermusability* (Baily 2008) in ethnomusicology, appearing as a scholarly tool as well as a personal passion. Other than with most ethnographic experience (dress, habits, rituals), it's the prerogative of music and maybe dance, that the modern time ethnographer is accepted to include his knowledge of other expressive culture in everyday practice at home.

In the Age of Enlightenment Western travellers sometimes regarded folk music and dance of other peoples as superior to their own cultural environment, at least in its aesthetical perception. The Scottish biologist Matthew Guthrie in his well known Russian ethnography writes: "The balalaika [...] is the favoured instrument of the Russian peasant, on whom it has a much greater effect than the best orchestra has on the town inhabitants whose sensitivity are blunted from exorbitance of pleasures".[25]

The enthusiastic appreciation of the "natural language" (*Natursprache*) of Russian dances by the German music teacher Johann Joachim Bellermann also reveals certain scepticism against his own cultural experience: "It's always only two people dancing with each other, but not nearly as monotonously as in the stiff minuet".[26]

This cultural self-criticism, clearly influenced by the aesthetics of Rousseau and Herder, can be understood against the background of European and North American political and cultural history. The historian Egon Flaig asserts that "the Western culture was subjected to continuous pressure by criticising elites [...]. All other cultures conduct their self-criticism comparing themselves with an ideal past, against which they define themselves as decadent. On the contrary, The Western [cultures] – or at least a large part of their intellectual elites – compare themselves to universal standards, necessary to be complied to" (Flaig 2007, 252-253). Of course, one may argue that the same holds true at least for many of the Old Testament prophets. Nonetheless, Flaig's writings (far from being free of exaggerations and unnecessary polemic) can act as a counterbalance to a popular understanding of history that associates the West solely with colonial exploitation and oppression, while the communities under study can appear as a "social and musical utopia and an image of egalitarianism" (Kisliuk 2000, 25).

The ties between cultural criticism and ethnomusicology, which increased in postcolonial discourses, are not always harmless. In an extreme form they are able to compromise ethnomusicology as a field of academic scholarship. A particularly sad example of its ideological instrumentalisation is Deborah Wong's diatribe "Ethnomusicology and Difference" (2006) – as far as I know, yet without a critical response.

In a retrospect to the last two decades of US-American ethnomusicology, Wong emphasises the "arrival of multiculturalism in the academy, and the ascendance of cultural studies in the humanities" (259), especially against the background of the "cultural wars". It is easy to recognise Wong's position in the canon debates and her particular hostility to what she calls WEAM (Western European art music), at least in regard to its weight in musical departments. She also considers interviews with female ethnomusicologists in the academy and some personal experience of the "intersection of

---

[25] La balalaika [...] est l'instrument favori de paysans Russes, sur lesquels sa simple musique produit plus d'effect que l'orchestre le mieux fourni n'en peut produire sur les habitants des grandes villes, dont les sensations sont, pour ainsi dire, émoussés par l'exces de plaisirs (Guthrie 1795, 29, 30).

[26] „Immer tanzen nur zwei Personen mit einander, aber bei weitem nicht so einförmig, wie in der steifen Menuet" (Bellermann 1788, 359).

discipline, gender, and race in my own person" (260). Surprisingly, Wong regards these categories as "a pedagogical tool" (ibid.).

Wong's most furious passages are directed against an article by Edward Rothstein in *The New Republic* (1991). The author, a music critic and composer, sharply comments on the role of political multiculturalism in the "cultural wars" concerning also ethnomusicological issues of social stratification in music cultures. Ethnomusicologists can argue about Rothstein's assertion that "musical culture as a whole is ethnically divided" (1991, I). They would also not share his scepticism toward bi-musicality. Rothstein's obvious misgivings against the idea of equity of musical cultures are problematic as well. One could refer to the "ethnomusicological rule of thumb that the aesthetical parameters of listening were incorrectly chosen by the researcher if another music style in its concepts seems to be plain and simple" (Brandl 2005, 24). But generally Rothstein's objection is not directed against ethnomusicology. His appreciation for most different musical styles available due to the efforts of ethnomusicologists is not at all rhetorical. Rothstein insists, following Nettl, on certain hierarchies of repertoires in most of the world's musical cultures. He primarily objects to the multiculturalists' claim for equal representation of *any* musics in education, media and funding with its obviously destructive implications: "The tremendous energy, of multiculturalism, which now reigns in universities, on public television stations and in art organisations, comes not from its noisy enthusiasm for other cultures, but from a frightened response to, and an animus against, the West" (1991, III). One mustn't necessarily share Rothstein's choice of words to recognize that his concern is not far from what generations of ethnomusicologist were doing – the advocacy of musical traditions experiencing pressure from hegemonial ideologies. The scandal consists in the fact that Rothstein speaks about Western compositional tradition.

To a large extent Wong's text bears resemblance rather to a speech to the members of a radical organisation than to an essay or even a scholarly article. Particularly striking is her strong propensity to an imagery of violence: reading "riotous and provoking" texts of Stuart Hall and others "was like discovering guerrilla warfare" (2002, 236). The "death of the canon" is celebrated, the "foxhole politics of multiculturalism" (268), ethnomusicologists "were drawn into the fray and put in center ring" (261). Of special curiosity is the subheading "The View from the Trenches. When Ethnomusicologists Talk". It would seem more appropriate to analyse Wong's texts in the context with other radical manifestations. Her rallying cries reveal all components of a battle song, as singled out by Vladimir Karbusicky (1973, 48-51), based on examples from the era of the Reformation and the repertoire of 20th centuries totalitarianism. Below I will juxtapose the elements of Karbusicky's "four-act scheme", which gives a structural description of the "mythological method" applied to battle song, with Wong's citations.

Act I: Reduction of reality to the situation of struggle:

"Ethnomusicologists' social location is essentially ideological and political" (Wong, 263)

Act II: Meditation. Recognition of our emergency and weakness. Ethically founded appeal for assembly:

"the discipline has tended to resist an openly politicized reading of its institutional location" (268-69)
"Ethnomusicoloists (…) have been mightily distracted by (neocapitalist [sic!]) arguments of relative "worth" (275)
"We have been slower to explore critical race theory" (266)
"We have been disastrously slow to acknowledge that our discipline is ideologically threatening to the very foundations of most musical departments" (266)

Act III: Logic foundation of the struggle through dramatisation of the enemy and his outrages:

"Edward Rothstein's infamous column" (261)
"Ethnomusicologists often experience the kinds of institutional discrimination and isolation similar to those experienced by ethnic minorities and women" (274)
"A significant percentage of North American Ethnomusicologists are women or scholars of color – or both – so it is important to take seriously the impact of the doubled or tripled minoritarian position" (273)
"Perhaps my shift from writing about ethnomusicology to writing about hate speech and racism seems abrupt" (273).

In fact, it's less abrupt than absurd. Hardly "hate speech and racism" are rampant in the musicological departments of the United States, as Wong instead of citing even a single example resorts to Judith Butler's most general considerations on the discomfort of being injured by speech.

Act IV: Directives, future, promise of salvation:

"Expect trouble", "Get involved in the life of your institution", "Stay on top of broader institutional initiatives", "When things go wrong, seek help immediately", "Find mentors". (274)[27]
"Marxist theory is alive and well". (263)
"The challenges of the early twenty-first century (…) make it necessary for intellectuals to speak, teach, and organize" (Actually, I'm not sure didn't they do so in the centuries before as well). "Our work, whether research or teaching, is inherently progressive but only as proactive as we insist that is be." (276)

Involuntarily but effectively Wong confirms Rothstein's thesis about the ideology of cultural disintegration. Her claim for "ethnomusicology as a politicized project" (275) is essentially totalitarian. Ethnomusicology, and folk music scholarship as well, have never been entirely part of a political agenda. In the era of national romanticism ethnomusicologists like Evgeniia Linëva, Béla Bartók, Constantin Brăiloiu and many others established a reasonable scholarly approach. And even in the darkest years of totalitarian dictatorship there were scholars such as Klyment Kvitka, Evgeny Gippius, John Meier, Ernst Klusen who tried to resist the ideological pressure to save a minimum of intellect-

---

[27] Here Wong refers to tactics offered by "more than one of the ethnomusicologists I interviewed" (274). Such an extensive paraphrasing of field data (17 lines) seems to be unusual in modern ethnography.

tual autonomy. Why should Western ethnomusicologists, working under conditions of a liberal society, abandon this autonomy voluntarily?

As Wong does not seem to take up an entirely isolated position I would like to shortly address two concepts central to her argumentation, having much in common: the cultural studies and the so-called gender theory.

Imagined Comrades: The Cultural Studies

The British cultural studies, as represented by the Birmingham school, are initially a politicised enterprise. Their central issue is definitely not "the whole way of life of a society" (Raymond Williams), but the examination of cultural expressions according to their "subversive potential" in capitalist societies. In the neo-Marxist imagination the hopelessly outdated Marxist-Leninist category of class is replaced with "the people". Stuart Hall, a most influential exponent of cultural studies, seriously claims that "[p]opular culture, especially, is organized around the contradiction: the popular forces versus the power-bloc (Hall 1981[sic!], 238). Consequently, popular culture "is one of the places where socialism might be constituted. That is why 'popular culture' matters. Otherwise, to tell you the truth, I don't give a damn about it" (Hall 1981, 466). Rarely, at least in a free society, the political instrumentalisation of culture and the academy, not to say the ideological corruption of scholarship, was expressed more bluntly.

The key feature of the cultural studies – though not from the very beginning (Gibson 2007) – is the obsessive preoccupation with power and power relations, seemingly pervading and determining all aspects of the cultural live of a society. The overestimation of power and violence rests upon Marxist ideas of "history as history of class struggle" but also in the negativistic image of man in the works of the late Nietzsche, who was not able to think the sovereign human being without contempt, the memory "without blood, torture and sacrifices" Nietzsche (1989 [1887], 61) and the culture without violence. Power relations, finally, are crucial in Foucault's concept of culture, whatsoever with less alarmist undertones as there usually can be found among his adepts.

Regardless to its obvious ideological foundations, the British cultural studies do not share the Marxist-Leninist concept of culture as a reflection of "objective reality". Antonio Gramsci regarded culture as the place where a revolutionary movement has to gain power. While the notion hegemony/hegemonic in the cultural studies is connoted negatively, Gramsci himself called for the conquest of hegemony as a means for takeover[28]. The celebration of an everlasting "counterculture" in post-war cultural studies[29] has to be understood against the background of a stabilised civil society whose

---

[28] In contrast to Lenin, Trotskii and later Mao with their insistence on military power and mass terror (*massovyi terror*), Gramsci emphasised the appeal to the majority. Nevertheless, his final purpose, especially concerning the role assigned to the intellectuals after the victory, is not free of totalitarian traits as well.

[29] The idea of a persistent "counterculture" was theoretically revaluated by the adoption of Mikhail Bakhtin's highly speculative concept of carnival culture. As Dietz-Rüdiger Moser has convincingly shown, the carnival, invented in the late Middle Ages, was initially not at all a participatory "folk festivity" or even an expression of opposition, not to speak of pre-Christian paganism, but an essentially Catholic celebration "most closely interlinked with the educational goals of the church" (Moser 1990, 98).

destruction – from a neo-Marxist perspective – has ceased being realistic or even desirable. Cultural studies at best underestimate the significance of "shared feelings" for the normal functioning of a society as expressed in the writings of the German sociologist Karl-Otto Hondrich (1937-2007). The problem is yet that for many exponents of cultural studies (and of Western sociology as well) a normally functioning society seems to be something highly suspicious.

Western subcultures and minorities (ethnic, sexual, etc.), any cultures of the „periphery" were scrutinised for their (mostly imagined) suitability in terms of political overthrow or at least maximal disintegration of the liberal democracy[30]. It is really a strange picture when scholars, near to retirement or after, spend many years examining and celebrating the "subversive" potential of cultural practices. Stuart Hall's backward pupils, John Fiskes' wrestlers, tabloid press readers, and female quiz show audience, Ian Taylor's football hooligans are all united in an imaginative "counterculture". One might raise the question, how low the intellectual left can go looking for auxiliaries like these? To be sure, all these social phenomena can appear as an object of sociology, cultural anthropology (and partly of criminology as well). It would be just desirable to preserve some basic distinctions between political activism and scholarship.

The cultural studies – however affiliated to academic institutions – are essentially part of a political agenda and leftist ideology rather than a matter of scholarship or even anthropology[31]. The adherents of Hall and Fiske do not seem to be disturbed by the irony that their explorations of "resistance potentials" against "the system" are more or less generously maintained by "the system" itself.

I am not sure that in the long term "the whole way of life" can be fruitfully investigated under the traditional directives of those cultural studies. Even more so as an examination of their intellectual originality leads to sobering results: "While adopting to long-debated anthropological concepts, theories and methods and presenting them as their own, there is no doubt that in the process they [cultural studies] are repackaging them very seductively" (Howell 1997, 104). The same seems to hold true for the study of literature: "From a theoretical and methodical point of view, British cultural studies have not proved to be original or innovative. They muddle trough – more bad than good – imitating expensive branded goods"[32]. Long before, issues frequently linked with the Birmingham school became topics of research in musicology and in folkloristics as well – albeit with an entirely different epistemological background. Studying audiences was a general topic in Russian folklore research up to the beginning Soviet period[33]. The

---

[30] See Stuart Halls phrase: "Unsettling the Foundations of the Liberal-Constitutional State" (2000, 227), his hopes at "a third transruptive effect of 'the multi-cultural question'" (ibid.), and suchlike leaflet rhetoric.

[31] Fiske remakes that "the human universal I can dispose of in a couple of paragraphs." (Müller 1992). I don't think that it would take up more space to appraise the relevance of such studies for cultural anthropology.

[32] „British cultural studies haben sich, theoretisch und methodisch betrachtet, bislang gerade nicht als originell oder innovativ erwiesen; sie schlagen sich vielmehr – mehr schlecht als recht – mit der Nachahmung teurer Markenartikel durch" (Bode 1996, 318).

[33] This socio-anthropological trend in Russian scholarship was mentioned by Pëtr Bogatyrëv and Roman Jakobson: "The contemporary collector tries, within his powers, to shine a light on the individ-

valorisation of the "recipient's" active role in the creation of meaning that is so often ascribed to Stuart Hall's "encoding/decoding model" was a crucial point in Boris Asaf'ev's *The Musical Form as Process* (Asaf'ev 1930, 1947)[34] and ten years later in Jan Mukařovský's poetics, challenging the "mechanistically stiffened Hegelian 'dialectic' of form and content" (Karbusicky 1990, 64). It was Mukařovský's disciple Vladimir Karbusicky who applied the concepts of aesthetic structuralism – and to some extent Asaf'ev's "gestalt theory" (Karbusicky 1986, 281, 1990, 45) – to his musical semiotics. Even within musicology the innovative potential of the cultural studies sometimes is grossly overestimated. So Kevin Dawe, curiously, believes that in organology "ethnography and material culture studies" are "new perspectives offered by the cultural study of music" (2002, 276). These perspectives can be new only for one who takes the risk of writing an article named "The Cultural Study of Musical Instruments" unfamiliar with the works of Ernst Emsheimer, Erich Stockmann, and Oskár Elschek.

It would be unfair not to mention that the doctrinaire positions of the Birmingham school have evoked manifold criticism within the field of cultural studies. Andy Bennett expressed concern with the cultural studies' highly selective approach to musical youth cultures according to their "potential for counter-hegemonic action" (1999, 604). Jim Collins has questioned "the continuing obsession with marginality as the only legitimate subject matter for cultural studies (2002, 16)"[35].

Unfortunately the enthusiasm for "resistance" and "subversion" was for a long time also fundamental for popular music research. A more realistic view, questioning "the constant misreading of the mainstream as the margins" (Frith 1992, 180) as well as Hall's "myth of resistance through ritual" (179), still does not express an emancipation from the political claims to popular music. Such ideological misinterpretations are extensively examined in Gabriele Klein's study of the techno culture (1999). Recently Bruce Johnson and Martin Cloonan in their groundbreaking study on the destructive dimensions of popular music critically addressed the "radical background" of the founders of popular music studies (2009, 11)[36].

Beyond any doubt, popular music and folklore can really play a big part in social struggles. Programmatic poems and – maybe more important – satirical verses and jokes can accompany political and religious movements, as in ancient times (Wiora 1957). A large repertoire of struggle songs was created during the Reformation. The totalitarian

---

uality of the storyteller and to characterise the milieu of its listeners and its aesthetic propensities (1923, 626, cf. Ivanova 2009, 186).

[34] "It seems that Asaf'ev is interested in performative aspects of the music and perception, in its aurality, not simply the music as "text." [...] For Asaf'ev, there was always a balance between the listener's perception and the musical work. *Intonatsiia* is therefore a broad and contextual embodiment of a sound idea rooted in historical time" (Titus 2006, 30). One could also mention Fritz Winckel's concern about the adoption of a simplified communication model in musicology: "the information-bearing source gains its properties only through the perceptive properties of the recipient" ([daß] die informationsträchtige Quelle ihre Eigenschaften erst durch die perzeptiven Eigenschaften des Empfängers erhält, cf. Winckel 1964, 12).

[35] See also Jean Burges's study on chamber music in Brisbane (2004). Unfortunately the author does not make use of the ethnomusicological study of Western art music (s. below).

[36] "The founders of IASPM were from radical backgrounds and were often attracted to popular music precisely because of its potential role in counter-hegemonic struggles. But popular music is itself the instrument of macro- and micro-hegemonies". (Johnson/Cloonan 2009, 11)

systems of the 20th century unintentionally gave birth to an enormous corpus of protest folklore in the form of jokes and satirical poetry. Even rather apolitical musical genres, under conditions of illegality, became a symbol of mental opposition or resistance, e.g. swing in Germany during the Second World War and in the USSR after. In Pinochet's Chile the *charango* – largely associated with famous leftist agitation groups – was banned. Today Cuban hip hoppers are a serious challenge to the regime. All these phenomena would be an interesting topic for an unbiased comparative study. Music and resistance is too serious a field for scholarship to leave it explicitly or implicitly for ideological projects.

It's hard to overlook the parallels between the cultural studies' obsession with power and the impact of "postcolonial" discourses on anthropology and ethnomusicology. Concern with the "colonialist past" and the vociferous appeals for "decolonising ethnomusicology" ignore the simple fact that the discipline has never been colonialist through and through. Leading representatives, especially in Central Eastern Europe, worked in countries not engaged in any colonial ventures. And even if many of the satellite states of the Soviet Union experienced severe exploitation of their industrial resources, this had little impact on ethnomusicological thought[37]. Another critical point uniting postcolonial, "engaged" ethnomusicology with cultural studies is their illusionary social romanticism. Our sympathy for the "powerless" seems to rest on hopes (we do not know what they will do if they will actually gain power).

Excursus: Music and Power Relations in 20th Century Rural Russia

Rejecting the overestimation of power relations in cultural anthropology and ethnomusicology, I am far from denying the occurrence of such interrelations in musical practice. Based on my own field of research, I would like to outline the significance of this interrelationship in the traditional rural music practice in Northwest Russia (basically the Pskov region).

Wedding ceremonies in patriarchal societies are initially related to economic and power relations between two families. They also organise the transfer of power over the young women from the bride's father to the groom. A considerable part of Russian wedding songs represent the process from the perspective of the bride. Psychologically they are designed to accustom her to the dramatic changes in her life. Many wedding songs also serve to remind the bride as well as the groom of their obligations to each other according to the patriarchal standards.

Traditional *see-off ceremonies* for recruits show striking parallels to wedding laments of the bride and her girlfriends. In countless short songs (corresponding to the meter of the *chastushka*) the young soldiers complained about their impending separation from their families and their beloved, about the hardship and danger of the military service,

---

[37] One should remember that the concept of *muzykal'naia ètnografiia* (Maslov 1904) and *etnomuzykologia* (Łucjan Kamieński 1934, cf. Stęszewski 1992, 529) was introduced in the academy unaffected by colonial or postcolonial discourses. The same holds true for Nikolai Serov's concept for an interdisciplinary musical anthropology, including what he metaphorically called *muzykal'naia èmbriologiia* (1870, cf. Vul'fius 1979, 127).

and the severity of the commanders[38]. Decades after the abandonment of this custom, male musicians, when asked to demonstrate the most typical local tune, frequently choose these recruits' texts, usually with a special manner of vocal and instrumental articulation. This way I have heard maybe hundreds of such recruit *chastushki* without a single text of heroic character. So, while the musical dramaturgy of the wedding ritual is supposed to lead to a harmonic ending and an acceptance of the new power relations, in recruit songs the expression of individual protest prevails.

Due to changing power relations the above-mentioned activities became pedagogical as well as repressive means of the *Soviet cultural policy*. Considerable changes of the traditional repertoires are a result of the electrification of the villages in the sixties, when radio, television and records gained great popularity.

In many different ways *chastushki* are interlinked with power relations. An enormous number of texts sharply comment on actual political processes in most different ways. Some celebrate the invention of the civil marriage by the Bolsheviks, later widespread issues are Stalin's extinction of free peasantry, sufferings during the war, inefficiency, corruption and nearly unpaid work in the kolkhozes, as well as Gorbachëv's anti-alcohol campaign and the dubious "privatisation" in the El'tsin era. A lot of satirical *chastushki* scoff at exponents of the (former) clerical and political power: popes, monks, leaders and henchmen of the party, policemen.

The most remarkable and most direct intersection of music and power in large parts of Russia is the *igra pod draku* (music for brawl), geared for inciting fights between young men from neighbouring villages at parish fairs[39]. In contrast to the "classical" armless Russian fist-fighting (*kulachnyi boi*), with its sportive ethos and strong regalement, these rather ferocious confrontations (sometimes – particularly in post-war periods – including fence posts, stones, knives, plummets) required a special cause. So, at village fairs wrongs and misconducts on the part of the neighbours or general rivalries were actualised and fought out in a socially accepted frame, limited in time and space. A strong stimulus for the young fighters was the dominating position (or even the exclusive right of participation) at the local dance event in the evening. In Pskov region the *igra pod draku* is one of the most prominent instrumental genres, enthusiastically remembered both by men and women of the old generation.

The case of village fights refers less to institutionalised power relations existing beyond the ritualised situation of the parish fair. (Here the configuration of power can totally change at another fair a week later.) Of highest importance in social interaction, accompanied or shaped by musical activities, is not the political or economical power of a person or a group but their social prestige. At weddings a central function of songs and (in formerly Polish rayons of the Pskov region) instrumental music is the celebration of the most important participants of the ritual. Dancing events were regarded as the place where young men and women could display their personal expressive qualities and gain social prestige (Romodina 1990, Romodin/Romodina 1991). Besides the exposed position of skilful dancers and musicians, the possibility of dealing with conflicts by

---

[38] On the performative function of recruit *chastushki* cf. Adon'eva (2006, 29-32). For video examples see Morgenstern 2008, chapter III.

[39] For more information and relevant publications see Adon'eva 2006, 16. The musical aspects are discussed in Mekhnetsov 2007, Morgenstern 2007, 143-55, 353-59.

performing *chastushki* in a public place was until recently crucial to negotiating social relations in Russian villages (Adon'eva 2006).

In general, the personal prestige of the musician or other individuals, involved in musically relevant situations, in Russian traditional culture is of much more significance than representations of institutionalised power relations in music.

From Class Struggle to Gender Trouble

The preoccupation with power is not a prerogative of the neo-Marxist cultural studies. In a very similar way it has predetermined the post-feminist "gender" paradigm. Doubtlessly the feminist movement with its commitment for equal rights and campaigns to increase sensitivity in regard to physical and verbal violence has done a lot for women as well as for (mostly) Western societies as a whole. In the academy, however, political activism and scholarship are even more confused as in the case of cultural studies.

The concept of "gender" was introduced in 1955 by John Money in the context of sexual developmental disorders. Money's theory, based on experiments on human beings (Bruce/Brenda Reimer case), rests on the assumption that any difference between man and women ,except physical characteristics, is "socially constructed". Radical genderists[40], following Judith Butler, insist on the social constructiveness even of the biological differences. In political practice however, the concept of "gender mainstreaming", adopted by the European Union in the Amsterdam treaty 1997/1999 as a binding directive, emphasises an ubiquitous diversity of "gender" roles. Thus the German Federal Ministry of Family Affairs, Senior Citizens, Women and Youth (Bundesministerium für Familie, Senioren, Frauen und Jugend) tries to explain the hardly translatable and to most Germans rather incomprehensible term as follows:

> "Gender Mainstreaming means to take into account beforehand and regularly with all projects of society the different situations and interests of women and men, because there is no such thing as a gender neutral reality."[41]

The paradox of simultaneously denying and overemphasising diversity resembles, to some extent, contradictions of the "race" discourse:

> "Struggling through the praise of difference against the neoracism that gives praise to difference: here is the paradox, laden with consequences, that demands to be seriously interrogated" (Taguieff 2001, 80 [1988, 107])

It is really hard to take seriously a "theory" dealing with the relationship of men and women that ignores the obvious fact of their mutual attraction or defames it as "compulsory heterosexuality" (Butler). The genderist ideology runs contrary to elementary human experience. No one having children or observing their behaviour attentively can seriously claim that there are no notable differences between the two sexes. Nevertheless

---

[40] Following Diamond and Moisala (2000, 3) I use the term genderism (genderist) in analogy to feminism, Marxism, Catholicism etc. and not analogous to sexism, racism, as it is sometimes used in North American political contexts.

[41] http://www.gendermainstreaming.net/tlp/english/agora_part_bpb.htm.

the ideology became a political force on governmental and even supranational level. Recently the German criminologist Michael Bock has singled out some common features between gender politics and totalitarian ideologies: "The claim for bringing a society this way 'into line', using a uniform design principle comprehensively, we know from the totalitarian 20th century. The idea is not only to bring effectively on track the respective innovation policy of the whole state apparatus but also associations, societies and further social groups" (Bock 2009)

It's not only the practices of political power Bock refers to that resembles totalitarianism. The selective perception of social reality in the past and present, as well as intellectual, rhetorical and political strategies reveal striking parallels between genderism and Marxism, especially Marxism-Leninism:

- the perception of social reality as struggle (Karbusicky)
- the demonisation of a (largely imagined) mighty enemy (the "patriarchate")
- the vision of the (gender-neutral or multiple gendered?) "New man"
- the imposition of a new nomenclature for old phenomena (Mamardashvili 1992, Zemtsovsky 2002), the creation of *word-idols* (Karbusicky), as essential to any ideology
- a system of administrative control (especially language control)
- a widespread pressure to adapt to the new standards of language use and every day behaviour

These parallels are less but surprising, as for a long time both ideologies shared a common social and intellectual environment. Whereas Alexandra Kollontai's utopian feminism was a rather isolated phenomenon in Bolshevik Russia, in the left wing student milieu of the seventies and eighties in the Western World feminism and Marxism were closely related to each other. Frequently they are united in the biography of their intellectual leaders and political activists.

I am not pretending to offer any new insights to gender ideology. The criticism is widespread – however less in the academy than in other discursive fields. At least in Germany references to "political correctness" for the last ten years are found most of all in polemical or satirical columns as well as in the repertoire of comedians. Genderism is continuously contested by journalists of most different political orientation.

Only recently some basic assumptions of gender studies were questioned within the field. So the German philosopher Hilge Landweer, a representative of feminist studies, insists on "the human duality of sex as an anthropological condition" (2005, 30). It is difficult to dispute the following statement as well: "even if what is experienced as erotically and sexually stimulating is or could be highly individual, it is still hard to imagine that all this should be completely independent of the sexed morphology of the body one approaches" (2005, 42). Ultimately, considerations like these seem dangerous for the very foundations of genderist ideology.

In ethnomusicology, the gender concept is of high priority in numerous publications of the last two decades. In an anthology of the ICTM Study Group on Music and Gender Marcia Herndon (1941-1997) emphasises that the "study of music and gender is not simply a matter of describing the domains, styles, and performance types typical of male or female musicians in particular social settings" (Herndon1999, 11). However this is actually the main point in the articles by Anna Johnson, Anna Czekanowska, Ankica Petrović, Susanne Ziegler, Ursula Reinhard and many others contributors. The book presents valuable insights in male and female roles in different music cultures but very few contributions to the "gender theory" which is largely ignored.

Some more emphasis on theory we find in *Music and Gender* edited by Pirkko Moisala and Beverley Diamond (2000). As usual in postmodern writing we find a lot of vociferous attacks against "essentialism" without mentioning or even citing a single incarnate essentialist. In this volume the name of Judith Butler appears after all three times on 376 pages. For instance, Michelle Kisliuk refers to the hip-swinging movement of the dance "Elamba" as a "crystal-clear example of a BaAka construction of the feminine" (Kisliuk 2000, 37), in the sense of Butler's "stylized repetition of acts", constituting "gender identity". However the episode Kisliuk describes shows nothing more, nothing less than that the "stylized act" is meaningful for the given community and is accepted to be displayed in the public sphere. The significance of the hip-swinging itself is anything but "socially constructed". Similar acts can occur all over the world, even without any stylisation, due to the obvious fact that under certain conditions they are sexually stimulating for women (and for men as well). A BaAka women is not a woman because of repetitive Elamba dancing, but for the reason that she was born as a girl.

A strong constructivist stance is expressed (among others) in Helmi Järviluoma's article on Finnish folk music formations („Thus, Anna constructs herself as a part of an important activity"; Järviluoma 2000, 69). Somewhat surprising is Järviluoma's conclusion: „I hope that I have managed to interrupt the discourse of music researchers who tend to put all forms of folk music into a homogeneous category" (2000, 71). It corresponds with the hardly more original statement of the editors: "the contributors to this anthology [...] have assumed that culture is not a static and rigid phenomenon but a fluid and relational one" (Diamond / Moisala 2000, 1). Fighting positions no one has seriously argued for is a rather cheap intellectual trick. Other contributors to this volume as Ursula Reinhard and Ingrid Rüütel do not depend in their ethnography of the "gender roles" in Turkey and Estonia on the ideological framework of genderism. The same holds true for Naila Ceribašić's in-depth analysis of female and male images in Croatian popular music in the context of the Yugoslavian war.

Tullia Magrini (1950-2005) in the introduction to her famous anthology *Music and Gender: Perspectives from the Mediterranean* (2003) emphasises that "the gender roles of a given social group may be examined through a study of its musical practices" (ibid., 5). Considering "the views of the feminine and the masculine" as "cultural constructs" (ibid., 6), Magrini however unintentionally comes into conflict with the gender concept, according to which the feminine and the masculine themselves are culturally constructed. Most convincing are Magrini's references to the northern Italian ballad as a basically female genre. Here she finds expressed particularily "the danger coming from men (abduction, rape, murder, betrayal, mistreatment, abandonment)" (ibid., 4)[42]. It seems that these dark sides of man-woman relationship (especially the classical ballad topic of the young single mother, left alone) can not be related solely to cultural

---

[42] One can only regret that Tullia Magrini was not familiar with Zinaida Èvald's article "The social reinterpretation of harvest songs in the Byelorussian Polesie" (1937 [germ. transl. 1967]).

constructions, as the danger arises from the unequal distribution of physical strength and from the different roles of women and men in the reproductive process (and the varying degree of responsibility among the latters).

Valuable contributions to women in music are to be found in Gerlinde Haid's and Ursula Hemetek's *Die Frau als Mitte in traditionellen Kulturen. Beiträge zu Musik und Gender* (2005). Though some articles in this volume refer to patriarchal discrimination (Elschek and others) and to redefining female roles (Haid, Bohlman), the volume contains very little reference, if any, to the gender theory. In contrast, numerous articles operate with notions and concepts unacceptable from a constructivist "gender perspective": "the women" (book title), "biological differences between female and male singing" (Haid, 28) and even (horribile dictu) the "two-sex nature of man" (Moser, 107).

Particularly interesting is Gerlinde Haid's observation that in the Alps women frequently sing songs with lyrics from a male perspective (Haid, 46), while the opposite is rare. The striking parallels in European folk music cultures would be an important topic for an unbiased anthropology of music.

Conclusion

Ethnomusicologists frequently come in conflict with leading concepts of their societies. In liberal societies with their intrinsic and unavoidable acceptance of a certain inequality of the economic status of people (however criticised in political discourses and regulated by social politics), ethnomusicologists tend to be adherents of egalitarianism. In the reign of communism with its initial claim to equality, in contrast, concepts of elitism are wide spread within the discipline. In both cases the emancipatory potential of ethnomusicological scholarship is being revealed.

Emancipation is generally regarded as the struggle for freedom and equality of disfranchised individuals or social groups. History knows numerous examples when political movements, claiming to defend man from oppression, turn out to be no less – and in the intellectual and artistic sphere even more – repressive than the systems they had challenged, as in France 1789, Russia 1917, and Iran 1979. For the postcolonial history Alain Finkielkraut (1987) convincingly explained the authoritarian turns of the new national states with the initial adoption of European nationalism.

In the Western world cultural critique for centuries became a mighty stimulus for the study of the world's cultures. Nevertheless, ethnomusicology and folk music scholarship had never proved to be intellectually productive when wedged into an ideological framework or shared only by the adherents of a particular doctrine (be it national-romantic, social-romantic, Marxist, genderist or anything else). Perhaps we should become more critical about the preoccupation of ethnomusicology with political ideologies having lost their emancipatory potential since long, and having turned into new power blocks with corresponding pseudo-scholarly disciplines. It's time to think about the emergence of ethnomusicology from ideological barriers that, in more than one case, have constraint our discipline, and have caused unfortunate effects largely due to *self-imposed immaturity*.

References

Adon'eva, Svetlana Borisovna 2006. *Derevenskaia chastushka XX veka* [The rural *chastushka* of 20th century]. Sankt-Peterburg: Izd. Sankt-Peterburgskogo universiteta.

Aly, Götz 2005. *Hitlers Volksstaat. Raub, Rassenkrieg und nationaler Sozialismus.* Frankfurt a. M.: S. Fischer.

Asaf'ev, Boris Vladimirovich 1930, 1947 *Muzykal'naia forma kak protsess* [Music Form as a Process], 2 vols. Moskva: Gos. muz. izd. Engl. transl.: Tull, James R. *B. V. Asaf'ev's Musical Form as a Process*. Translation and Commentary. Dissertation. The Ohio State University, 1976 (Microfilmxerography, Ann Arbor, Michigan, U.S.A., London, England: University Microfilms International 1979).

Baily, John 2008. Ethnomusicology, intermusability, and performance practice. In H. Stobart (ed.). *The New (Ethno)musicologies*. Lanham: Scarecrow Press, 117–134.

Bellermann, Johann Joachim 1788. *Bemerkungen über Rußland in Rücksicht auf Wissenschaft, Kunst, Religion und andere merkwürdige Verhältnisse*, T. 1. Erfurt: Keyser.

Bennett, Andy 1999. Subcultures or neo-tribes? Rethinking the relationship between youth, style and musical taste. *Sociology* 33 (3), 599–617.

Bielawski, Ludwik 1981. Musiker und Musiksituationen. *Studia instrumentorum musicae popularis* VII, 17–22.

Blagodatov, Georgii Ivanovich 1960. *Russkaia garmonika. Ocherk istorii instrumenta i ego roli v russkoi narodnoi muzykal'noi kul'ture* [The Russian button accordion. A survey on the history of the instrument and its role in the Russian folk music culture]. Leningrad: Gos. muz. izd.

Bock, Michael 2009. Gender-Mainstreaming als totalitäre Steigerung von Frauenpolitik http://www.kellmann-stiftung.de/index.html?/beitrag/Bock_Gender.htm.

Bode, Christoph 1996. Anglistische Literaturwissenschaft und/oder Cultural Studies? *Anglia. Zeitschrift für englische Philologie* 114 (3), 396–424.

Bogatyrëv, Pëtr, Roman Jakobson 1921. Slavianskaia filologia v Rossii za gg. 1914–1921 [Slavic philology in Russia for the years 1914–1921]. *Slavia. Časopis pro slovanskou filologii* 4, 171–184.

Bohlman, Philip V. 1991. Representation and Cultural Critique in the History of Ethnomusicology. In B. Nettl and Philip V. Bohlman (eds.). *Comparative Musicology and Anthropology of Music: Essays on the History of Ethnomusicology*. Chicago: University of Chicago Press, 131–48.

Boiko, Iurii Evgen'evich 1984. Russkie narodnye instrumenty i orkestr russkikh narodnykh instrumentov [Russian folk instruments and the orchestra of Russian folk instruments]. In I. I. Zemtsovskii (ed.). *Traditsionnyi fol'klor v sovremennoi khudozhestvennoi zhizni*. Leningrad: Len. gos. in-t. teatra muzyki i kinematografii, 87–96.

Brandl, Rudolf M. 2005. Universale Basis-Definitionen von Mehrstimmigkeit, Polyphonie und Heterophonie (= multiple Abläufe) aus Sicht der Vergleichenden Musikwissenschaft. In G. Gruber, A. Schmidhofer, M. Weber (eds.). *Mehrstimmigkeit und Heterophonie. Festschrift für Franz Foedermayr zum 65.Geburtstag* (= Vergleichende Musikwissenschaft Bd.4). Peter Lang: Frankfurt/M. et alii, 9–35.

Burgess, Jean 2004. *High Culture as Subculture: Brisbane's contemporary chamber music scene*. Ph.D. Diss, School of English, Media Studies and Art History at the University of Queensland, http://eprints.qut.edu.au/28527/1/28527.pdf.

Collins, Jim 2002. High-Pop: An Introduction. In Jim Collins (ed.). *High-Pop: Making Culture into Popular Entertainment*. Malden, MA: Blackwell, 1–31.

Dawe, Kevin 2002. The Cultural Study of Musical Instruments. In M. Clayton, T. Herbert, and R. Middleton (eds.). *The Cultural Study of Music. A Critical Introduction*. London: Routledge, 274–283.

Denisoff, R. Serge 1971. *Great Day* Coming. *Folk Music and the American Left*. Urbana, London: University of Illinois Press.

Ėval'd, Zinaida 1934. Sotsial'noe pereosmyslenie zhnivnykh pesen belorusskogo Poles'ia [The social reinterpretation of harvest songs in the Byelorussian Poles'e]. *Sovetskaia ėtnografiia* 5, 17–39. Germ. trans.: Zinaida V. Ewald. Die soziale *Umdeutung* von Ernteliedern im belorussischen Poles'e. In E. Stockmann, H. Strobach (eds.). *Sowjetische Volkslied- und Volksmusikforschung. Ausgewählte Studien* (= Veröffentlichungen des Instituts für deutsche Volkskunde, Band 37). Berlin: Deutsche Akademie der Wissenschaften zu Berlin. 1967, 259–291.

Finkielkraut, Alain 1987. *La defaite de la pensée*. Paris: Gallimard. Engl. trans: *The Defeat of the Mind*. New York: Columbia University Press, 1995.

Flaig, Egon 2007. Levi-Strauss im anti-universalistischen Gefängnis. Zum Verenden des Multikulturalismus. *Zeitschrift für Kulturphilosophie* 2, 325–353.

Frey, Jürgen, Kaarel Siniveer 1978. *Eine Geschichte der Folkmusik*. Reinbek: Rowohlt.

Frith, Simon 1992. *The Cultural Study of Popular Music*. In L. Grossberg, C. Nelson, P. A. Treichler (eds.) *Cultural studies* 6 (2). New York: Routledge, 174–181.

Gibson, Mark 2007. *Culture and Power. A History of Cultural Studies*. Oxford: Berg Publishers.

Glassie, Henry 1982. *Passing the Time in Ballymenone: Culture and History of an Ulster* Community. Philadelphia: University of Pennsylvania Press.

Haid, Gerlinde 2005. Frauen gestalten. Zur Rolle der Frau in der Volksmusik Österreichs und der Alpen. In: Haid, Hemetek (eds.), 25–52.

Haid, G., U. Hemetek (eds.) 2005. *Die Frau als Mitte in traditionellen Kulturen. Beiträge zu Musik und Gender* (Beiträge des Internationalen Symposiums „Die Frau als Mitte in traditionellen Kulturen", das anläßlich des 60. Geburtstages von Gerlinde Haid im April 2003 in Wien stattfand, Klanglese 3). Wien: Institut für Volksmusikforschung und Ethnomusikologie.

Hall, Stuart 1981. Notes on Deconstructing 'The Popular'. In R. Samuel (ed.). *People's History and Socialist Theory*. London: Routledge, 227–240.

Hall, S.2000. Conclusion: the Multi-cultural Question. In Barnor Hesse (ed). *Un/Settled Multiculturalisms: Diasporas, Entanglements, "Transruptions"*. London: Zed Books, 209–41.

Harker, Dave 1985. Fakesong: *The Manufacture of British "Folksong" 1700 to the Present*. Milton Keynes: Open University Press.

Heinz, Jutta 1996. *Wissen vom Menschen und Erzählen vom Einzelfall. Untersuchungen zum anthropologischen Roman der Spätaufklärung*. Berlin, New York: de Gruyter.

Herder, Johann Gottfried 1779. *Volkslieder. Nebst untermischten andern Stücken. Zweiter Theil.* Leipzig: Weygandsche Buchhandlung.

Herndon, Marcia 1990. Biology and Culture: Music, Gender, Power, and Ambiguity. In M. Herndon, S. Ziegler (eds.), 11–26.

Hondrich, Karl Otto 2006. Geteilte Gefühle. http://www.protosociology.de/Download/KarlOttoHondrich-GeteilteGefuehle.pdf. First publication: *Frankfurter Allgemeine Zeitung*, 29. Jul. 2006 (174), 8.

Howell, Signe Lise 1997. Cultural Studies and Social Anthropology: Contesting or Complementary Discourses? In S. Nugent, C. Shore (eds.). *Anthropology and cultural studies*. London Pluto Press, 103–124.

Ivanova, Tatiana Grigor'evna 2009. *Istoria russkoi fol'kloristiki XX veka: 1900 – pervaia polovina 1941 g.* [The history of Russian folkloristics of the 20th century. 1900 – *first half of the year 1941*]. Sankt-Peterburg: Dmitrii Bulanin.

Ivleva, Larisa Michailovna, Aleksandr Vadimovich Romodin 1998 [1989]. "Ran'she starinushka ne nuzhna byla, a seichas prishli za nei" [„Once nobody cared about the good old times, and now they come to bring them back."] In V. Ken (ed.). *Sud'by traditsionnoi kul'tury. Sbornik statei i materialov pamiati Larisy Ivlevoi*. Sankt-Peterburg: Dmitrii Bulanin 1998 [written in 1989], 19–24.

Järviluoma, Helmi 2000. Local Constructions of Gender in a Finnish Pelimanni Musicians Group. In P. Moisala, B. Diamond (eds.) 2000, 51–79.

John, Eckhard 2006. *Die Entdeckung des sozialkritischen Liedes. Steinitz als Wegbereiter eines neuen »Volkslied«-Verständnisses.* In E. John (ed.). Die Entdeckung des sozialkritischen Liedes. Zum 100. Geburtstag von Wolfgang Steinitz. Münster et alii: Waxmann, S. 13–24.

Johnson, Bruce, Martin Cloonan 2009. *Dark Side of the Tune: Popular Music and Violence* (Ashgate Popular and Folk Music Series). Aldershot et alii: Ashgate.

Karbusicky, Vladimir 1973. *Ideologie im Lied – Lied in der Ideologie. Kulturanthropologische Strukturanalysen* (= Musikalische Volkskunde. Materialien und Analysen, Bd. 2). Köln: Gerig.

Karbusicky, V. 1986. *Grundriß der musikalischen Semantik*. Darmstadt: Wiss. Buchgesellschaft.

Karbusicky, V. 1990. *Kosmos – Mensch – Musik. Strukturalistische Anthropologie des Musikalischen.* Hamburg: Dr. R. Kraemer.

Kisliuk, Michelle 2000. Performance and Modernity among BaAka. Pygmies: A Closer Look at the Mystique of Egalitarian Foragers in the Rain Forest. In Moisala, Diamond (eds.) 2000, 25–50.

Kleff, Michael 2008. *Die Burg Waldeck Festivals 1964–1969. Chansons Folklore International.* Mit Beiträgen von Günter Zint (with 10 CDs). Hambergen: Bear Family Records.

Klein, Gabriele 2004. *„Electronic Vibration". Pop, Kultur, Theorie*. Wiesbaden: VS-Verlag.

Klusen, Ernst 1967. Das Gruppenlied als Gegenstand. *Jahrbuch für Volksliedforschung* 12, 21–41.

Klusen, E. 1989. *Singen. Materialien zu einer Theorie*. Regensburg: Bosse.

Kröher Hein, Oss Kröher 1969. *Rotgraue Raben. Vom Volkslied zum Folksong.* Heidenheim/Brenz: Südmarkverlag.

Kühn, Andreas: Musik in der Lebenswelt der maoistischen K-Gruppen. In A. Jacobshagen, M. Leniger (eds.). *Rebellische* Musik. *Gesellschaftlicher Protest und kultureller Wandel um 1968*. Köln: Dohr.

Kvifte, Tellef 2001. Hunting for the Gold at the end of the Rainbow: Identity and Global Romanticism. On the Roots of Ethnic Music. *Popular Musicology Online*. http://www.popular-musicology-online.com/issues/04/kvifte.html

Landweer, Hilge 2005. Anthropological, Social, and Moral Limitations of the Multiplicity of Genders. *Hypatia. A Journal of Feminist Philosophy* 20 (2), 27–47.

Lenin, Vladimir Il'ich 1967 [1905]. Partiinaia organizatsiia i partiinaia rabota [Party organisation and party literature]. *Polnoe sobranie sochinenii*, 5. izd., tom 12. Moskva: Izd. polit. lit. 99–105. Originally published in *Novaia Zhizn'* 12, Nov. 13, 1905.

Lessing, Gotthold Ephraim 1759. *Briefe die neueste Litteratur betreffend*, vol. 2, Berlin.

Likhachëv Dmitrii Sergeevich 2006 [1998]. *Universitetskie vstrechi. 16 tekstov* [University encounters. 16 texts]. Sankt-Peterburg: Izd. Sankt-Peterburgskogo Gumanitarnogo universiteta profsoiuzov. Republished in: *Studencheskii meridian* 11.2006 (http://www.stm.ru/archive/475/).

Livingston, Tamara E. (1999) Music Revivals: Towards a General Theory. *Ethnomusicology* 43 (1), 66–85.

Lloyd, Albert L. 1944. *The Singing Englishman. An Introduction to Folk Song*. London: Workers' Music Association.

Magrini, Tullia 2003. *Introduction*: Studying Gender in Mediterranean Musical Cultures. In T. Magrini (ed.), 1-23.

Magrini, T. 2003 (ed.). *Music and Gender: Perspectives from the Mediterranean*. Chicago: University of Chicago Press.

Mamardashvili, Merab 1992. Mysl' pod zapretom (besedy s A. Ė Ėpel'buėn). Per. s fr. [Thought under prohibition (Talks with Annie Epelboin), transl. from french. *Voprosy filosofii* 4, 70–78; 5, 100–115.

Marian-Bălașa, Marin 2007. On the Political Contribution of Ethnomusicology: From Fascist Nationalism to Communist Ethnocentrism. *Journal of Musicological Research* 26 (2, 3), 193-213.

Maslov, Aleksandr Leont'evich 1904. Zadachi muzykal'noi ėtnografii [The tasks of musical ethnography]. *Russkaia muzykal'naia gazeta* 40, 872–873; 45, 1046–1048.

Matsievskii, Igor' Vladimirovich 2007. *Narodnaia instrumental'naia muzyka kak fenomen kul'tury* [Folk instrumental music as a phenomenon of culture]. Almaty: Daik-Press.

Matsievskii, I.V. 2009. O khudozhestvennykh vozzreniiakh traditsionnykh pol'skikh muzykantov Zapadnoi Belostochiny (k problemam kognitivnoi muzykologii [On the artistic views of traditional Polish musicians in the western Białystok district (towards the problems of cognitive musicology)]. In L. Savvina (ed.). Muzykal'noe iskusstvo i sovremennost'. Sbornik nauchnykh stat'ei k 40-letiiu Astrakhanskoi gosudarstvennoi konservatorii. Astrakhan: Astr. gos. kons., 142–145.

Mekhnetsov, Aleksei Anatol'evich 2007. Derevenskaia draka: Vzgliad ėtnomuzykologa [Village brawl. A perspective of an ethnomuzikologist]. *Muzhskoi sbornik*, vyp. 3. Moskva: Indrik, 146–157.

Moisala, Pirkko, Beverley Diamond 2000. Introduction: Music and Gender – Negotiating Shifting worlds. In Moisala, Diamond (eds.) 2000, 1–19.

Moisala, P., B. Diamond (eds.) 2000. *Music and gender* (foreword by Ellen Koskoff). Urbana: University of Illinois Press.

Morgenstern, Ulrich 2006. Concepts of the National in Russian Ethnoorganology. *Tautosakos darbai,* XXXII (= Studia instrumentorum musicae popularis XVI), Vilnius, 148–160.

Morgenstern, U. 2007. *Die Musik der Skobari. Studien zu lokalen Traditionen instrumentaler Volksmusik im Gebiet Pskov (Nordwestrußland).* Göttingen: Cuvillier, Bd. 1.

Morgenstern, U. 2008. *Traditional Russian Instrumental Music* (DVD). Hamburg: Systemata Musika.

Morgenstern, U. 2010a. "Musicae subtilioris ignari sunt" – "einen beinahe auch liebreicheren Ton" The Western Reception of Russian Folk Instrumental Music and Dance in the 16th to the 18th Centuries. In S. Ziegler (ed.). *Historical Sources and Source Criticism.* (ICTM Study Group on Historical Sources: Proceedings from the 17th International Conference in Stockholm, Sweden, May 21–25, 2008). Stockholm: Svenskt visarkiv, 169–188.

Morgenstern, U. 2010b. „Aber was ist Rock 'n' Roll? Davon hatten wir keine Ahnung." Populargattungen und mündliche Tradition in der russischen Dorfmusik. In M. Bröcker (ed.). *Berichte aus dem Nationalkomitee der Bundesrepublik Deutschland im International Council for Traditional Music (ICTM/UNESCO)* XVIII: Musik in urbanen Kulturen / XIX: Musik und Gewalt, Bamberg: Universitätsbibliothek, 43–67.

Moser, Dietz-Rüdiger 1991. Lachkultur des Mittelalters? Michael Bachtin und die Folgen seiner Theorie. *Euphorion* 85, 423–429.

Moser, D.-R. 2005. Die Frau im Zentrum närrischer Musik. In Haid, Hemetek (eds.), 107–133.

Mossmann, Walter, Peter Schleuning 1978. *Alte und neue politische Lieder* Reinbek: Rowohlt.

Müller, Eggo (1992): From "Ideology" to "Knowledge" and "Power". Interview with John Fiske, Madison 09/17/1991, authorised version April 1992. http://www.hum.uu.nl/medewerkers/e.mueller/publications/interview-fiske.htm

Nazina, Inna Dmitr'evna (in print). Belorusskie narodnye muzykanty-mysliteli [Byelorussian folk musicians and thinkers]. In N. Almeeva, A. Nekrylova, A. Romodin (eds.). *Fol'klor i my: Traditsionnaia kul'tura v zerkale eë vozpriiatii. Sbornik nauchnykh statei, posviashchennyi 70-letiiu I.I. Zemtsovskogo,* ch. II. Sankt-Peterburg: Rossiiskii institut istorii iskusstv.

Nettl, Bruno 2005. *The study of ethnomusicology: Thirty-one issues and concepts.* Urbana, IL: University of Illinois Press.

Nettl, B. 1989. Mozart and the Ethnomusicological Study of Western Culture (an essay in four movements). *Yearbook for Traditional Music,* 1–16

Noll, William 1991. Economics of Music Patronage among Polish and Ukrainian Peasants to 1939. *Ethnomusicology* 35 (3), 349–379.

Nietzsche, Friedrich 1989 [1887]. *On the Genealogy of Morals,* trans. by Walter Kauffman and R.J. Hollingdale. New York: Random House. Originally published as: *Zur Genealogie der Moral, Eine Streitschrift.* Leipzig: C. G. Naumann.

Olson Laura J. 2004. *Performing Russia: Folk Revival and Russian Identity*. New York et alii: RoutledgeCurzon (Routledge Curzon Series on Russian and East European Studies).

Onchukov, Nikolai Evgen'evich: *Severnye skazki (Arkhangel'skaia i Olonetskaia gg.)* [Northern tales (Arkhangel'sk and Olonets gouv.], Sankt-Peterburg: IRGO: 1908.

Pashina, Olga Alekseevna et alii 2005. *Narodnoe muzykal'noe tvorchestvo. Uchebnik dlia vuzov* [Folk music creativity. Textbook for higher educational institutions]. Sankt-Peterburg: Kompozitor.

Pommer, Josef 1901. Was ist das Volkslied? Ein Wort der Entgegnung und Abwehr von Dr. Josef Pommer, III. *Das deutsche Volkslied. Zeitschrift für seine Kenntnis und Pflege*, H. 7, 115–118, repr. from *Lyra*, 15.03.1901.

Porter, James 1991. Muddying the Crystal Spring: From Idealism and Realism to Marxism in the Study of English and American Folk Song. In Bruno Nettl and Philip V. Bohlman (eds.). *Comparative Musicology and Anthropology of Music: Essays on the History of Ethnomusicology*. Chicago: University of Chicago Press, 113–130.

Razumovskaia, Elena Nikolaevna 1991. 60 let kolkhoznoi zhizni glazami krest'ian [60 years of kolkhoz live in the eyes of the peasants]. *Zven'ia. Istoricheskii almanakh* 1. Moskva, 113–162.

Romodin, Aleksandr Vadimovich 1999. Narodnye muzykanty iuga Pskovshchiny [Folk musicians of the southern Pskov region]. *Zhivaia starina* 4 (24), 8–10.

Romodin, A.V. 2005. Traditsionnye rasskazy o severobelorusskikh muzykantakh-instrumentalistakh [Traditional stories on north Byelorussian folk instrumental musicians]. In A. Timoshenko (ed.). *Muzykant v kul'ture: kontseptsiia i deiatel'nost'*. Sankt-Peterburg: Rossiiskii institut istorii iskusstv, 102–120.

Romodin, A.V., Irina Aleksandrovna Romodina 1991. Vzaimodeistvie instrumental'noi muzyki i khoreografii v narodnych èsteticheskikh predstavleniiakh [The interaction of instrumental music and dance in folk aesthetics]. In A. Sololov-Kaminskii (ed.). *Narodnyi tanets. Problemy izucheniia*. Sankt-Peterburg: Rossiiskii institut istorii iskusstv, 77–85.

Romodina, I.A. 1990. Molodëzhnye sobraniia Poozer'ia. Trud – obriad – igra [Traditional youth gatherings of the Poozer'e. Work – custom – play]. In L. Ivleva (ed.) *Zrelishchno-igrovye formy narodnoi kul'tury*. Leningrad: Len. gos. in-t. teatra muzyki i kinematografii, 46–52.

Rothstein, Edward 1991. Roll Over Beethoven: The New Musical Correctness and its Mistakes. *The New Republic* (4 Feb.).

Salmen, Walter 1960. *Der fahrende Musiker im europäischen Mittelalter*. Kassel: Hinnenthal.

Salmen, W. 1983. *Der Spielmann im Mittelalter*. Innsbruck: Helbling.

Sárosi, Bálint 1981. Professionelle und nichtprofessionelle Volksmusikanten in Ungarn. *Studia instrumentorum musicae popularis* VII, 10–16.

Schepping, Wilhelm 2005. Deutsche Jugendbünde in der ersten Hälfte des 20. Jahrhunderts als Sammler und Vermittler russisch-slawischen Liedgutes im politischen Kontext der NS-Epoche. In H. Müns (ed.). *Musik und Migration in Ostmitteleuropa*. München: Oldenbourg, 183–241.

Schneider, Hotte: *Die Waldeck – Lieder Fahrten Abenteuer. Die Geschichte der Burg Waldeck von 1911 bis heute*. Potsdam: Verlag für Berlin-Brandenburg.

Sharp, Cecil James 1907. *English Folk-Song: Some Conclusions*. 4th rev. ed. London 1965.

Spivakov, Vladimir 2005. Interview with V. Spivakov by Anna Vetkhova. *Vremia Novostei* 27 (17. Feb). http://www.vremya.ru/print/118537.html.

Shelemay, Kay Kaufman. 2001. Toward an Ethnomusicology of the Early Music Movement: Thoughts on Bridging Disciplines and Musical Worlds. *Ethnomusicology* 45 (1), 1–29.

Steinbiß, Florian 1984. *Deutsch-Folk: Auf der Suche nach der verlorenen Tradition. Die Wiederkehr des Volksliedes.* Frankfurt: Fischer Taschenbuch Verlag.

Steinitz, Wolfgang 1954, 1962. Deutsche Volkslieder demokratischen Charakters aus sechs Jahrhunderten, Bd. 1, 2. Berlin: Akademie-Verlag. Reprint: *Der große Steinitz. Deutsche Volkslieder demokratischen Charakters aus sechs Jahrhunderten.* Frankfurt: Zweitausendeins 1983.

Stęszewski, Jan 1992. Zur Geschichte des Terminus „ethnomusicology". In R. Schumacher (ed.). *Von der Vielfalt musikalischer Kultur. Festschrift für Josef Kuckertz zur Vollendung des 60. Lebensjahres.* Anif/Salzburg: Müller-Speiser, 527–534.

Taguieff, Pierre-André 2001 [1988]: *The Force of Prejudice: Racism and its Doubles.* Minneapolis: University of Minnesota Press, trans.: Hassan Melehy. Originally published as: *La force du prejuge: essai sur le racisme et ses doubles.* Paris: La Decouverte.

Titus, Joan Marie 2006. *Modernism, socialist realism, and identity in the early film music of Dmitry Shostakovich*, 1929-1932. Ph.D. Diss., Graduate School of the Ohio State University http://etd.ohiolink.edu/send-pdf.cgi/Titus%20Joan%20Marie.pdf?osu1164752307

Turino, Thomas 2008. *Music as Social Life: The Politics of Participation.* Chicago: University of Chicago Press.

Vertkov, Konstantin Aleksandrovich 1975. *Russkie narodnye muzykal'nye Instrumenty.* Moskva: Muzyka 1975

Vul'fius, Pavel' Aleksandrovich 1979. *Russkaia mysl' o muzykal'nom fol'klore. Materialy i dokumenty* [Russian thought on musical folklore. Materials and documents]. Moskva: Muzyka 1979

Winckel, Fritz 1964. Die informationstheoretische Analyse musikalischer Strukturen. *Die Musikforschung* 17, 1–14.

Wiora, Walter 1957. *Europäische Volksmusik und abendländische Tonkunst.* Kassel: Hinnenthal.

Wolff, Frank 1989. Der *Musiker* Frank Wolff im Gespräch mit Ruth Fühner und Peter Noller, In R. Erd et alii (eds.). *Kritische Theorie und Kultur.* Frankfurt a. M.: Suhrkamp, 82–94.

Wong, Deborah 2006. Ethnomusicology and Difference. *Ethnomusicology* 50 (2), 259–279.

Zemtsovskii, Izalii Iosivovich 1989. Ot narodnoi pesni k narodnomu khoru: igra slov ili problema? [From folk song to folk choir: a play on words or a problem?] In V.A. Lapin, I.I. Zemtsovsky, L.M. Ivleva (eds.). *Traditsionnyi fol'klor i sovremennye narodnye khory i ansambli.* Leningrad: Len. gos. in-t. teatra muzyki i kinematografii, 6-19.

Zemtsovsky, Izaly, Alma Kunanbaeva 1997. Communism and Folklore. In J. Porter (ed.) *Folklore and Traditional Music in the Former Soviet Union and Eastern Europe.* Los Angeles: Department of Ethnomusicology, 3–23.

Zemtsovsky, I. 2002. Musicological Memoirs on Marxism. In R. Burckhardt Qureshi (ed.). *Music and Marx: Ideas, Practice, Politics.* New York: Routledge, 167–189.

Rolf Bader

Buddhism, Animism, and Entertainment in Cambodian Melismatic Chanting *smot* – History and Tonal System

Introduction

The Cambodian Buddhist Chanting style *smot* is highly elaborated in terms of melismas and therefore unique to this area of Southeast Asia. As the style in its most sophisticated form needs extensive vocal training and precise knowledge of the correct ornaments to present, monasteries give *smot* training courses running over years with final exams finding the best singers. The musical parameters like the tonal system or performance style is discussed in relation between measurements and the musical concepts of informants. Here both, the pure tone Western and the equal Cambodian tuning exist side-by-side even within one piece. The melodies and melismas of *smot* are fixed and therefore little improvisation is normally done which is different from most chanting styles where the pitches and length of sections may be caused by semantic reference e.g. to mental visualizations (Chong 2011). Still in the follow of *dharma*, the Buddhist doctrine, this chanting is for enlightening and healing the minds of listeners and therefore can also and indeed is often sung by layman people, too. As literature about the existence of *smot* is known from times before the Red Khmer regime from 1975-1978 and only a few sources are available today, a fieldwork in 2010 was to determine if this chanting is still used. Indeed it was found to be vividly alive and recordings could be done in several monasteries. Cambodian Buddhism is known to have strong elements from Hindu and animistic traditions and also the Khmer Rouge seem to have taken over not only practices of Buddhist performances but also of musical and lyrical styles. This could explain the survival of *smot* as a musical form rather than a Buddhist doctrine. As the style is not often performed in public but rather at monastic ceremonies or in private healing or cremation contexts it is much less known to the Western world compared to other chanting styles.

Chanting and Literature in Cambodian Buddhism

The Hinayana Buddhism of Cambodia has two main monastery traditions, the older Mahanikay and the younger Thommayut being introduced to Cambodia in the mid 19th century from Thailand (Harris 2005). According to Brunet (1967) both have different chanting styles. Where Mahanikay monks chant phrases without any interruption, Thommayut singers pause after each syllable. As Brunet is not mentioning *smot* with this practice explicitly this seams to refer to other Buddhist chanting in Cambodia (see below) staying mainly on one pitch with only using a half tone or a semitone step up or down at the beginning or the end of phrases.

Hai (1980) in the *Grove Dictionary* calls *smot* the 'basic Buddhist prayers', where melismas are only taught after ten years of syllabic recitation. He then distinguishes syllabic chanting staying on two to three notes from melismatic performance using 'tritonic, tetratonic or pentatonic scales'. In the later edition of the *Grove Dictionary* Sam-Ang Sam does not mention *smot* anymore (Sam 2000).

Interestingly, dealing with Khmer literature, Khing (1990) sorts *smot* among *lpaen* (secular) rather than *ghambir* (religious) texts. His reasoning follows the appearance of Buddhist stories all along the Khmer literature, also in Cambodian novels (*riong lpaen*) which often repeat texts of the *paññāsajātaka* of the *jākata* text collection dealing with the former lives of the Buddha. He also mentions that *smot* needs many years of training.

Another important Cambodian chanting style is *badschawat*, which is used for performing the *vissakh boca*, also the name of a text collection. *Vissakh* is the sixth month of the Buddhist calendar in which the Buddha has died, and *boca* means a sacrafice. Here the chanting takes place at full moon. It is closely related to *miakh boca*, where *miakh* is the 15th day of the third month of the Buddhist lunar calendar, when the Buddha announces his death in front of 1250 monks, a scene often found as drawings in today's Cambodian monasteries. The style was first introduced by King Rama II around 1817 in Thailand. Maha Pan, founder of the Thommayut order brought it to Cambodia in 1855. *Vissakh boca* was then taken over by the Mahanikay order during the times of king Sisowath (Harris 2005). It reminds on the birth, enlightenment, and death of the Buddha. This style is not a melismatic one which it cannot reasonably be as it is mostly sung by many monks making elaborated performance difficult (still also *smot* may be sung by more and one monk). The last great performance of *vissakh boca* took place at the yearly general meeting of Southeast Asia monks which happened to be in Siem Reap, Cambodia, at April 28th 2010 where many thousand monks chanted the texts which took about a whole day. All lines of the *vissakh boca* texts have seven syllables which is also different from *smot* texts. The style is publicly known very well, each morning the Cambodian state radio station is broadcasting chanted excerpts of *vissakh boca*.

Figure 1: Buddha announcing his death in front of 1250 followers. Contemporary painting in the *vihara* (main hall) of Wat Muni Sala Prek, Sihanoukville. The painting style is common throughout today's Cambodia and canonized by the Cambodian Ministry of Culture leaving the painters little space for individual ideas.

Another Cambodian singing style is *no koriech*, meaning a small world reigned by a king, in which a similar vocal style is used as found in *vissakh boca*. Also before the *desnah*, the Cambodian story telling, songs of this kind may be sung. Chu Nath, the most prominent figure of 20th century Cambodian Buddhism which took decisive part in finishing the first Khmer dictionary and who was a supporter of a renewed Khmer Buddhism and nationalism is also known of having composed songs performed today. One of those is the 'Buddhist flag raising song' with the text and maybe also the melody written by him. More important may be the composition Bat Sara Phanh, a song very well known in Cambodia performed in the *smot* style which is often reported to have been composed by Chu Nath.

Figure 2: Left: Advertisement of a sound system in a village near Sihanoukville to attract customers to purchase this system for their own private feasts in the future. The very loud performance lasts the whole day without people around. Right: Excerpt from top image through the right gate displaying the sound system speakers.

Smot may also be performed by laypersons, and often the best performers are not monks. Also women (*srei*) sing *smot* then called *smot srei*. As with all Southeast Asian countries, popular music, media, and sound systems are all around (Mamula 2008). Sound systems are used today for wedding parties (where still often the traditional *mohori* band plays), birthdays and many other celebrations. It is often cheaper to rent a sound system and play cassettes than to rent a band and therefore at celebration days in villages from the very early morning on a mostly heavily distorted sound system is playing pre-recorded traditional music. Here, *smot* music is also played via these sound systems, where people buy cassettes in Phnom Penh of *smot* and *smot srei* recorded by professsional performers. These cassettes do not have a commercial market, the recordings, copying, and the distribution are all done privately. There are also famous *smot* singers e.g. Di Ballad On, a monk who lived before the civil war.

Buddhism and Animism Performance

The coexistence and mixing of Buddhism and Animism in Cambodia has often been pointed out, maybe most prominently by Bizot (1980, 1976). Cambodian Buddhism is very liberate in terms of becoming a monk and leaving the monastery for a secular live again. Cambodians may become monks for ten years, one year or even only a day. Former monks which have been in the monastery for many years leading a secular live again are then *ajars* which are highly respected and asked to perform rituals in the monastery e.g. the dedication of a new monastery. Here with the *sima* (Buddhist *sanga* border) stones blood and musical instruments are buried clearly pointing to animistic traditions. Bizot also reports rebirthing rituals performed by monks in caves, where the cave is viewed as an uterus and where chanting is performed.

Arak, the music played and sung during trance rituals is performed by an *ajar* and monks chanting at the beginning of the ritual. The *ajar* is highly respected for knowing the performance ritual details often much better than younger monks. Still, when in the *arak* ritual people start drinking alcohol the monks leave the place. The *arak* music itself is not similar to *smot* chanting. The spirits in Cambodia are called *boramey*, which are possessing people. They can be religious and mythological figures as well as animals, historical figures, or *neak ta*, lit. 'old people' mostly old local people (Bertrand 2001). A medium is assigned to one *boramey* for his/her hole life. Another important figure is the *preah go*, the holy bull which also has a temple at the king's palace in Phnom Penh. Here many Brahmans, Hindu priests take over old rituals. During the funeral rites of King Monivong 1941 the king's body was dived into mercury, clearly no Buddhist ritual (Cravath 1986). In two of the analyzed *smot* chanting below, the *chey teous* and the *Bat Sara Phanh*, the *devata*, Hindu celestial figuresd or angles are called for help.

Figure 3a: *Preah go* (holy bull) temple in the king's palace in Phnom Penh.

Figure 3b: Fortune telling of Brahman priest (middle) to laymen (right) in the temple. The text was chosen by the layman by cutting a knife in the bundle of text palm leaves, the Brahman is then citing the text.

Smot during the Khmer Rouge

The devastation of the Khmer culture by the Khmer Rouge during their regime 1975-1978 and the civil war lasting until the UNESCO lead election in 1993 also made Buddhist tradition suffer tremendously (Harris 2007). Although many figures cannot be trusted, the amount of about 60.000 monks present in Cambodia before the Khmer Rouge times ended in a handful of about 10 monks left, most of the others were forced into marriage, flew to Thailand or further abroad or were murdered. Still, according to Harris, no really systematic destruction of temples took place. Bizot (2000), himself captured by the Red Khmer and present in the French embassy during the last days of the evacuation of Phnom Penh had the chance to personally discuss the ideology and study the performance of the Khmer Rouge. His main point is the parallel nature of Buddhist with Red Khmer practices. He remembers Douch, the main responsible at the infamous torture prison Tuol Sleng in Phnem Penh interrogating Bizot to report that in the town he was born "...the monks are also mediums and the fishermen consult them. The spirit of the dead speaks through their mouths. Others are called *lok angkouy* because their bodies remain 'seated' while they take leave of them to inspect the surroundings of the village..." (Bizot 2003, 58). The parallels also include similar naming. The Red Khmer called their rules *vinaya*, as the Buddhist call their 'discipline'. The Buddhist abstentions *sila* became the Khmer Rouge moral commandments. He continues with giving up family ties, renouncing material possessions, giving new names, ect. (ibid. 110). Not a surprise he reports the performance of Chinese revolutionary songs. Still Harris, quoting Bizot also reports that "...parallels may also be found even in the way they intone their respective litanies, all the way down to the incorporation of similar trills at the end of each stanza." (Harris 2005, 187). He also reports that the same songs were sung, where *sanga*, the Buddhist community was simply substituted by *angkar*, the Red Khmer community which should substitute all family ties and state institutions. The trills may point to *smot* singing, and therefore we may find one of the reasons for the survival of *smot* in Cambodia in the fact that the Khmer Rouge took over the singing style maybe changing the words. Informants also report that the Khmer Roughe, although they systematically killed intellectuals, court dancers, and musicians, still enjoyed when laypersons played traditional musical instruments like the *roneat deik*, a metal plate instrument similar to the xylophones *roneat ek* and *roneat tung* for entertainment.

Smot Lyrics and Performance

Smot is music of sorrow and comfort and therefore often performed at *sok mon* (funerals). The singing is often performed at the death bed during the death feast *pchum vay* or *pchum benn* (Sam 1991) in September. The main attempt is to teach the Buddhist view as expressed maybe most prominent in the first of Four Noble Truths of the Buddha, namely that all life is suffering. Overcoming of this suffering may be done living a life according to the Buddhist path of virtues, still suffering will always be present and therefore the acceptance of this fact and a life in according to the Noble Path of virtues will give release.

According to the informants Bung Sopheap and the *ajar* and professional musician So Tia, *smot* is also often sung by monks and laypersons in private without a feast. Bung Sopheap remembers that when his father had health problems with his eyes a monk had come along and sung *bat kiriminon*, a song also recorded during the fieldwork at Wat Chan Boryvong by three monks, among those Samdeck Preah Venarat Noy Chrek, the third highest monk in the hierarchy of the Mahanikay order. The songs lyrics are about eyes thickness, describing them and advising the sufferer that nothing can be done about it and he has to cope with the thickness by simply accepting it as part of becoming older. The monk then taught Bung Sopheap, then a child, the song and from then on he sung the song to his father often later on. Kiriminon is said to be the name of a student of the Buddha who became ill. The Buddha asked another student, Annan to sing this text to Kiriminon. The lyrics are about *sengadod* which are the ten points of the illness and *sosanga*, the senses which do not work properly at age anymore.

Other *smot* songs often performed are *antrai*, texts from the *tripitaka*, *thamchak kabavathanka soth* in which the Buddha explains five of his students how enlightenment can be achieved. *Preah kun mer* (*kun* = good deeds, *mer* = mother) is a song about the love of a mother to her children although she suffered during giving birth. *Viyo'k* (weeping) describes the sadness of Buddha about the death of his mother. *Tom nunh anan* is the sadness of the Buddhas student Annan about the death of the Buddha. *Sovansam* describes a former life of Buddha as Sovansam. In *sang phnous* the Buddha tells his wife and children that he will leave for the forest. So indeed, *smot* is about suffering and sadness.

Nevertheless, as discussed above, Hindu ideas are also present in this chanting style, e.g. *thor bort*, the blessing songs of the Buddha. The lyrics below are from a performance of Phen Sophaf, right secretary of the monastery Moni Prosity Vong near Phnom Penh recorded in the *vihara* by the author in march 2010[1]. Phen Sophaf performed this *smot* as asked by the author to perform a typical *smot* and so gave additional information about the song: "The *thor bort* was invented in pre-Buddhist times. Hindu scriptures divide the *thor bort* into three songs called *chey*." The three songs are *chey tes, chey preah puth*, and *chey dorb brokah*. He further explains:

> **CHEY ONE** is called "**CHEY TES**" meaning "Directions Blessings". It describes the ten blessings of the Buddha appearing from the eight directions[2].
>
> **CHEY TWO** is called "**CHEY PREAH PUTH**". It explains all the blessings of the Buddha dedicated to all Buddhist people.
>
> **CHEY THREE** is called "**CHEY DORB BROKAH**". It means the ten kinds of blessings of the Buddha starting from number one and running to number ten. These blessings have been offered by Ey Sou (Superior Silva) or Ey Sey (Hermit or Holy man).
>
> So on this occasion I would like to chant or sing loudly and harmoniously in each Chey in the following sections. But before I start to chant all of them, I would like to apologize to all Buddhist people that there are little differences of the ways of singing, it can be rough and up and down in sound.

The difference between 'rough and up' and 'down' Phen Sophaf mentions in the last paragraph refers to two different performance practices, a public and a private one. His performance following this explanation is loud and public. Below is the translation of this performance.

> **CHEY TES**
> (Pali) Heh Teh Pheh Sorh Pakavear. …Preah Ratanak Tray
> (Khmer)…Hey…please get Chey from Buddha gods (*devata*) in the east come to bless all people on the precious stone freely
> ….Heh…Eryh…..please get Chey form gods (*devata*) in the south-east come together and give blessing to all people free and happy
> …Hey…Eryh…please get Chey from gods in the south coming quickly and blessing to all people on our wonderful world freely
> …Hey…Eryh….All of these called "Chey Tes".

---

[1] As there was no written text source known the lyrics are transcribed and translated from the performance by Im Phana, Sihanoukville 2010.
[2] Next to the four main directions, the four middle directions (south-east, north-west, etc.) are added.

289

CHEY PREAH PUTH
(Pali) Chey Chey Preah Puth Thomearh
(Khmer) is a great blessing from the Buddha gods to the Royal power
....Ery...Chey...Chey...overwhelming glory is coming to protect all people to get rid of enemies
....Ery...Chey...Chey...please live in happiness and harmony more than hundred years.
This is called Chey Preah Puth in summary.

CHEY DORB BROKAH
(Kmher) All blessing come from the Buddha gods (*devata*), they are really great happiness, harmony, and long lifes. It is given by the hermit or the holy man named Kah Sorb
...Ery...Preah Moni....Ery.....All these called Chey borb Brokah.

As can be seen from the transcription of the lyrics, the texts are sung in Pali and Khmer alike. It can be one line in Pali followed by one in Khmer, first sung entirely in Pali then entirely in Khmer or only the first line is in Pali, the rest is in Khmer.

Another example is the *smot Bat Sara Phanh* which is also analysed below in terms of its tuning system. The song describes the main Buddhist doctrine (*dharma*) with the three jewels (*Buddha, dharma, sanga*) and the blessing coming to people praying to it. Again the *devata* are mentioned coming from Hinduism and a direct reference to the Khmer people is mentioned in the last phrase.

1.
Honouring the Buddha	*Som Thway Bág-kum Preah Sám-put*
Is the best to do.	*Práh-seur Bam-phot Khnong Look-ka*
Master of all angles (*devata*) and mankind	*Chea Kru Ney Monus Neng Tewada*
The sublime is praying to all beings.	*Trung Tras Tesna Práh-dau Shàtt.*

2.
He shows us the Middle Path	*Cháng-ol Aoy Deur Phlow Kán-dal*
As best way of liberation.	*Mea-kea Trá-kal Ach Kam-chàtt*
Fear and sorrow disappear.	*Tuk Phey Cháng-raiy Aoy Khchay-bàtt*
Suffering can be released.	*Ach Kàtt Sángsa-ràk Tuk Ban*

3.
The wisdom of the Buddha stays until today	*Sasna Preah-áng Now Sáph Thgaiy*
In sympathy since long ago.	*Shàtt Mean Ni-saiy Pi Bo-ran*
Learn and hear constantly, remember and understand,	*Breung Rean Breung Sdàb Ches Cham Ban*
Follow the way, live happily.	*Kànn Tam Lum-an Ban Kdey Sok.*

4.
There is no better than inner peace.	*Eit Mean Sok Na Smeu Khdey Sgáb*
End in happiness, free from suffering.	*Bánh Cháb Treum Sok Khleat Chak Tuk*
In this world and in eternity.	*Taing Pi Look Nich Tá Tao Muk*
Welfare through the holy *dhamma*.	*Khdey Sok Neung Mean Prurs Thoir Sgáb*

5.
I bow before dhamma

And the precious sangha of all worlds.
To admire the Three Juwels highly
Is welfare of the universe.

Khgom Som Báng-kum Chhpurs Preah Thoir
Preah Sáng Bá wár Teang Krub Sáb
Rurm Chea Traiy Roath Kur Kor-rub
Chea Mlub Trá-cheak Ney Looka

6.
To honour the enlighted
As true master and example.
The Three Jewels protect the Khmer people
In peace and happiness forever.

Preah Roub Preah Theat Ney Preah Put
Wi-soth Tang Áng Preah Sa-sda
Som Kun Traiy Roath Chuy Khemara
Aoy Ban So-kha Tá Reang Tao.

When asked why melismata are used at all the *ajar* So Tia and the performing monk at Moni Prosity Vong, Kai Sokmean both clearly stated that this attracts listeners much more than when only chanting around one pitch. As mentioned above, *smot* is part of the secular text canon in Cambodia and therefore coming from a religious tradition but meant to become popular to fulfil its healing role, although not from a commercial standpoint.

Musical Parameters

Contemporary Cambodian society of course knows Western Popular music and – maybe much more – Indian film music, so Western concepts of music theory are well known to musicians and instrument builders. An *roneat tung* (xylophone) and *gong vong* (tuned gong instrument) builder near Phnom Penh explained that he is changing the pitches of his instruments from when performing in the Khmer traditional music style with its equal tuning to a Western tuning when playing with classical Western musicians which became quite popular in recent years in Cambodia. Then he changes the tuning of his instruments by adding wax to the xylophone or metal bars, a common technique with these instruments throughout Southeast Asia. So both tunings, the seven-tone equal tempered and the seven-tone major and minor tuning, are well known to musicians in Cambodia. So Tia explains that *smot* is pentatonic using the Western solmization Do-Re-Mi-So-La leaving out the fourth step (Fa) and the seventh step (Ti). Still although the western solmization is used, he insists that the tuning is Cambodian with its equal temperment of 171 cent per step. Cambodian music theory also knows the measure of cent and divides a semitone into 100 cent. The Cambodian notion for cent is *go ma* which literally means a child denoting someone small. As many Western notions become part of Cambodian language it may be a misunderstanding of the important notion of a comma in the theory of tonality and therefore may be transformed simply because sounding similar from 'comma' to *go ma*. So Tia finds the Re to be nearly the same in both tuning systems but describes the Fa to be higher (or 'harder' as he literally states) in Cambodian tuning. Below we discuss the micro tuning in the singing performance of the song *Bat Sara Phahn* in detail. The music theory also states that *smot* melodies either start and stop at Do or start and stop at So. Combinations may be possible but seldom. So when looking at *smot* as being modal, authentic and plagal cases are possible.

Smot is performed in a 4/4 meter where the fourth beat is punctuated. Accenting the last beat is known from other styles, too, most prominent maybe from Indonesian *gamelan* music. The tempo is around 60 BPM and therefore pretty slow as expected from a lament style.

The melismas are all learned precisely in terms of their occasion in the piece and in terms of the amount and shape of pitch jumps and slurs. This makes the style so complex to learn and difficult to perform and tells a good performer from a minor one. The precise shape of these melismas appears from the microtonal analysis example below where the main elements are discussed.

Performance of *Bat Sara Phanh*

Above we discussed the music theory used in Cambodia. Still to decide about the tuning system really performed with *smot*, whether the Cambodian equal or the Western pure tone is used we want to take a closer look at the performance of *Bat Sara Phahn*, one of the most popular *smot* broadcasted via the national radio station every morning in the performance of Kai Sokmean, a young monk at Wat Moni Prosity Wong near Phnom Penh. Fig. 4 a-p[3] show the sixteen phrases of the song. Using an autocorrelation method the fundamental was calculated and plotted on a logarithmic frequency axis vs. time (the consonants are omitted). The two tuning systems are shown, the Western system has solid the Cambodian dashed lines.

The melismatic character of the style can clearly be seen. Certain elements appear throughout the performance (also of other songs):

- Vibrato around the sung pitch which is mostly pretty close around the mean pitch and never really exceeds a 50 cent distance between the extremes. So it is not touching or even crossing other pitches and is therefore limited in character although still prominent.
- Sudden fast jumps between two pitches like e.g. in Phrase 4 in the first second between fourth and fifth, in Phrase 8 around 4 seconds between fundamental and second, or in Phrase 10 around second five between fifth and seventh. Other occasions can easily be found, where the jump direction is down like in Phrase 16 after second three.
- Sudden fast upper jumps at the end of the phrase from a medium pitch up to a higher pitch to then end in the lower one performed in Phrases 1, 3, 4, 6, 7, 8, 9, 10, 14, 15.
- Slurs up and down, most prominent at the end Phrase 16 but also e.g. in Phrase 1, second five, Phrase3 after second three etc.
- A jump in the throat register very strongly at the end of Phrase 4, slightly at Phrase 6, 7, 9, and 10. This can also be heard with other song performances.

---

[3] See appendix for figures 4 a-p and figure 5.

The sudden jumps are often performed very precisely between two pitches and may be repetitive like in Phrase 8 from second four, where two jumps down from the second to the fundamental is followed by one up from the second to the third and back again. These 'jumps' are not really infinitesimally small but show a clear trajectory which can also be heard. So the idea is one of gradually change although very fast.

Tuning System

To decide whether Kai Sokmean uses pure Western tuning or the Cambodian equal tuning the calculated pitches were accumulated as shown in Fig. 5. Again, the Western tuning is indicated with solid, the Cambodian tuning has dashed lines. It is interesting to note that often double peaks occur in the plots caused by the vibrato and allowing the determination of a middle pitch and the vibrato amplitude. Still not always two pitches occur as in Fig. 5 c) where the higher end is sung. So we need to discuss all three cases, the mean pitch and the upper and lower pitches. In Fig. 5 a) a mean pitch of 190 Hz was used, b) shows a fundamental at 188 Hz, and c) the relations for 192 Hz. The range of 188 – 192 Hz means 36 cent and is a reasonable mean for the vibrato amplitude.

Different integration times were used for the three plots. This was done because from the 10th phrase on Kai Sokmean is slowly overall decreasing in pitch. This is not the case for the first 9 phrases and so Fig. 5 a) is integrated over the first 9 phrases. To better be able to discuss the three fundamental pitch cases Fig. 5 b) was integrated over phrases 1 and 2 only, while Fig. 5 c) was taken between 5 – 7 (although the plot does not look much different if integrated over phrases 5 – 9).

From Fig. 5 a) we clearly see that the relations between the third (second peak), fourth, fifth, are clearly Western. Such a global fitting can not be achieved with equal tuning no matter where the fundamental frequency as placed with this tuning the third and fourth are above, but the fifth is below the Western one. So simply shifting the peaks would not lead to a match of the peaks to Cambodian tuning. Still when examining Fig. 5 b) with a fundamental of 188 Hz for this lower fundamental peak we find a very good fit of the Cambodian tuning for the third and fourth. Still the fifth is not met with both of the tunings. In a similar manner, when using a fundamental of 192 Hz like in Fig. 5 c) this fundamental is in very good agreement with the Cambodian equal fifth. Here we need to keep in mind that these plots do not display between which pitches the melody changes and therefore which pitch steps are indeed performed. So the fitting between single pitches may be caused by the choice of a pitch distance between these two which would not necessarily hold for the whole tuning.

Now the use of different integration times may become more clear when interpreting these results. It seems to be that the performer changes his performance between the Cambodian and the Western tuning according to the phrase to sing. So e.g. when going from the fourth to the fifth or vice versa the pure tone distance is used, when changing from the fourth to the third the equal or pure temperament is taken. Going from the fundamental to the third and fourth the pitches meet the Cambodian tuning very well in the cases the lower fundamental is used. When a jump from the fundamental to the fifth is performed the Cambodian distance is present in these cases. As we need enough data to perform a reasonable mean it is not always easy to perform this analysis with two notes only and therefore make a precise decision when which distance is used. Nevertheless the accumulated mean cannot simply be interpreted with respect to one tuning system only. It is furthermore interesting to see that the mean vibrato amplitude mainly causing the double peaks in Fig. 5 a) are clearly in the range of the difference between Western and equal tuning. So here the performer may play with this uncertainty of vibrato to meet this ambiguity, too.

A very interesting example of this change of the tuning system is found in Phrase 14 around the first second. There, starting from the fifth three jumps up are performed. The first arrives perfectly at the pure tone seventh (actually the natural seventh, *Naturseptime* 4/7), the third arrives perfectly at the equal tuning seventh. Still the middle one arrives a bit above the Cambodian sixth. This phrase is also sounding very distinct and within this very short time span perfectly reminds one once of a Western and once of a Southeast Asian tuning.

Conclusions

The survival of *smot* in Cambodian society through the Khmer Rouge times seems to come from several sources. Most important is probably the popular nature of the style where laymen and –women sing the songs often much better than monks. This again arises from Cambodian Buddhism which allows temporary entry in a monastery for years or days. Also the teaching of *smot* to laymen or children for healing purpose plays an important role. The fact that the melismas are used to attract people rather than to have any semantic or religious function is pointing in the same direction. Still, the survival of this chanting style through times of nearly complete destruction of Cambodian traditional music and dance seems also to be enhanced by the Khmer Rouge taking over many habits and styles of Cambodian Buddhism which they were naturally raised in. So singing not only Chinese revolutionary but also the old Buddhist *smot* songs while substituting Buddhist words by those supported by the *ankar* seems to have made this style survive these times after which in Cambodia only a handful of monks were left. Of course, Khmer in exile, especially at the Thailand border or in California, USA, were able to maintain this singing style. Traditional *mohori* music mostly used at weddings or other secular feasts or the *phen pheat* music used at the Cambodian traditional court survived abroad, too.

The influence of Hindu or animistic traditions on Cambodian culture is also found in *smot* singing which the performers are aware of and even the performing monks do not find problematic in any way. Still, any kind of inner or esoteric meaning or semantics is strictly rejected by monks and professional performers pointing to the Theravada Buddhism doctrine of healing people's minds by making them intellectually aware of the Buddhist *dharma*. So the lyrics of *smot* is for education, the melismas are for entertainment.

The fusion of Western and Cambodian culture is clearly present in the performance of the *smot* analyzed above. If the performer is aware of these tuning changes is hard to say as much of it is in his practice and in theory the singing should clearly be in equal tuning. Still we find obvious cases of Western influences with some tonal relations. It is also remarkable that these often small deviations are not only heard but performed in such a precision. The fact that musicians clearly mention both systems and are perfectly aware of them when it comes to tuning their instruments is also pointing to a fusion of

Cambodian and Western style in the performed tuning system, and makes it reasonable to appear even within one performed song.

Acknowledgement

My thanks go to the performing monks and their monasteries, Samdech Preah Venarat Noy Chrek, Phen Sophaf (Seerefary), Kai Sokmean, Chin Hin, Chhoan Rithy, Horng Seng Houth (Choa Atikar), Soun Bunchorng (Seerefary), and many others, my informants, among them the *ajar* So Tia, Bung Sophean, Im Phana, Savuth Prum, and Chanbo Tan for translation and many comments and suggestions. Also many thanks to Anton Isselhardt in Phnom Penh, whos excellent work and engangement in music, organization of music festivals, and musical exchange between Cambodia and Germany for many years enriches the musical scene in Cambodia a lot, and was a great help for the research, and to my dear colleague Dieter Mack for his links and support. Many thanks also to Christian Köhn joining from Thailand for his professional ethnomusicological support, help, and ideas.

References

Bertrand, Didier 2001. The Names and Identities of the "Boramey" Spirits Possessing Cambodian Mediums. *Asian Folklore Studies*, 60(1), 31-47.

Bizot, Francois 2000. *Le portail.* Table Ronde : Paris. (translation: *The Gate*, Vintage 2003).

Bizot, Francois 1980. La grotte de la naissance. *Bulletin de l'École Française d'Extrême-Orient* 67, 221-273.

Bizot, Francois 1976. *Le figuier à cinq branches: Recherche sur le bouddhisme khmer.* Paris: École Française d'Extrême-Orient.

Brunet, Jacques 1979. L'Orchestre de mariage Cambodgien et ses instruments. *Bulletin de l'Ecole francaise d'Exrême-Orient* 66, 203-254.

Chong, Lee-Suan 2011. Tibetan Buddhist Vocal Music: Analysis of the Phet in Chod Dbyangs. *Asian Music* 42(1), 54-84.

Cravath, Paul 1986. The Ritual Origins of the Classical Dance Drama of Cambodia. *Asian Theatre Journal* Vol. 3, No. 2, 179-203. 1986.

Dorivan, Keo, Theara, Yun, Lina, Y, & Lenna, Mao 2004. *Traditional Musical Instruments of Cambodia.* Phnom Penh: Royal University of Fine Arts, UNESCO.

Hai, Trân Quang: Kampuchea 1980. In: Sadie, Stanley (ed.) *The New Grove Dictionary of Music and Musicians.* Vol. 9, 789-792.

Harris, Ian 2005. *Combodian Buddhism. History and Practise.* Honolulu: University of Hawai'i Press.

Harris, Ian 2007. *Buddhism under Pol Pot.* Documentation Series No. 13, Documentation Center of Cambodia 2007.

Heywood, Denise 2008. *Cambodian Dance. Celebration of the Goda.* River Books.

Jacobi, Moritz 2008. *Buddhismus in Kambodscha.* Studienarbeit. Grin-Verlag für akademische Texte.

Mamula, Stephen 2008. Starting from Nowhere? Popular Music in Cambodia after the Khmer Rouge. *Asian Music* Vol. 39, No. 1, 26-41.

Narom, Keo 2005. *Cambodian Music*. Phnom Penh.

Sam, Sam-Ang & Campbell, Patricia Shehan 1991. *Silent Temples, Songful Hearts. Traditional Music of Cambodia*. World Music Press.

Sam, Sam-Ang 2001. Cambodia. In: Stanley Sadie (ed.): *The New Grove Dictionary of Music and Musicians*. New York, London: Macmillan Publ., 861-864.

Schumann, Hans Wolfgang 2005. *Buddhismus. Stifter, Schulen und Systeme*. Diederichs Gelbe Reihe. Kreuzlingen, München: Hugendubel.

Snellgrove, David L. 2001. *Khmer Civilization and Angkor*. Orchid Guides.

Zangpo, Shenphen (Stephen Powell) & Huang, Francis (Huang Pao-ling) 2000. *Sangha Talk. Advanced Level. A Dharma English Textbook*. The Corporate Body of the Buddha Educational Foundation, 2000.

Discography

Khmer Traditional Music. Musician and Recorded by handicap's Group of Neak Pean Temple in Siemreap Province. Vol-05. Victims of Landmines. Erworben: 2010.

Classical music from Cambodia. Homrong chum Ngek. Celestial Harmonies, Tucson, Arizona 2004.

Cambodia – Music of the Exile. The Orchestra of the Khmer Classical Dance Troupe. Archives Internationales de Musique Populaire. Musée d'ethaographie, 1205 Genéve, 1992.

Music of Cambodia. Big Drum Music. Pern Peat Music. Real World 2000.

Musique Khmére. Mélodies populaires pour instruments à vent. Sous sumaly. Reyum Production, Phnom Penh 1999.

The Music of Cambodia. 9 Gong Gamelan, Royal Court Music, Solo Instrumental Music. 3 CD Box. David Parsons (Producer). Celestial Harmonies, Tucson, Arizona 1993.

Cambodia. Folk and Ceremonial Music. Alain Daniélou, International Institute for Comparative Music Studies and Documentation (IICMSD) Berlin, UNESCO Collection.

Figures

In the following section, figures 4a – 4p and 5 are presented. For technical reasons, figure 5 precedes figures 4a – 4p.

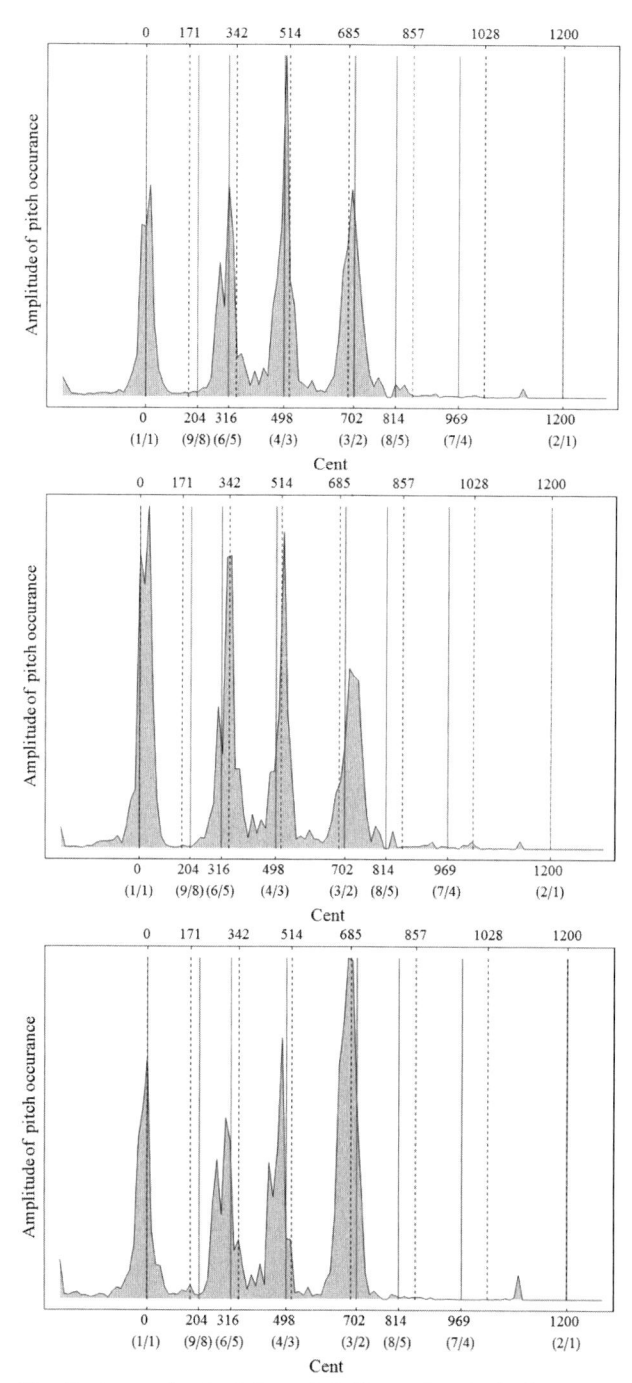

Fig. 5: Accumulated pitches of a) Phrase 1 – 9, fundamental taken as 190 Hz, b) Phrase 1 – 2, fundamental taken as 188 Hz, c) Phrase 5 – 7, fundamental taken as 192 Hz.

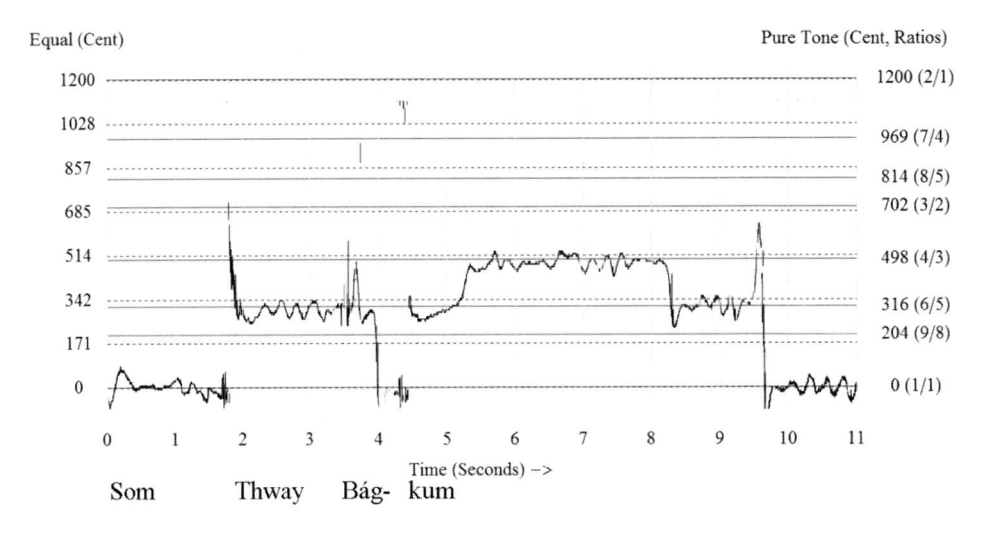

Equal (Cent)   Pure Tone (Cent, Ratios)
1200 ─────────────────────────────────── 1200 (2/1)
1028
                                                        969 (7/4)
857
                                                        814 (8/5)
685   702 (3/2)
514   498 (4/3)
342   316 (6/5)
171   204 (9/8)
0   0 (1/1)

0   1   2   3   4   5   6   7   8   9   10   11
                        Time (Seconds) –>
   Som   Thway   Bág- kum

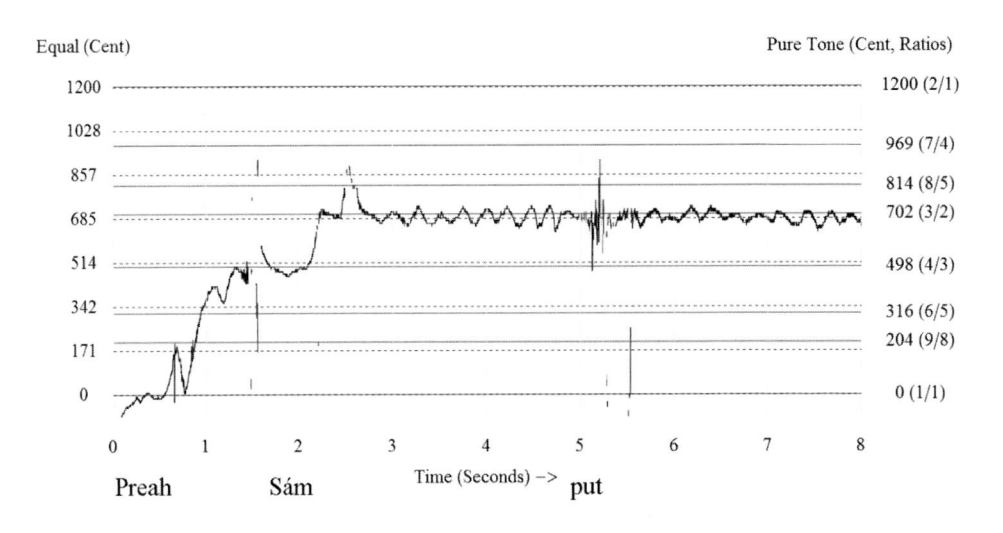

Equal (Cent)   Pure Tone (Cent, Ratios)
1200 ─────────────────────────────────── 1200 (2/1)
1028
                                                        969 (7/4)
857
                                                        814 (8/5)
685   702 (3/2)
514   498 (4/3)
342   316 (6/5)
171   204 (9/8)
0   0 (1/1)

0   1   2   3   4   5   6   7   8
                 Time (Seconds) –>
  Preah   Sám   put

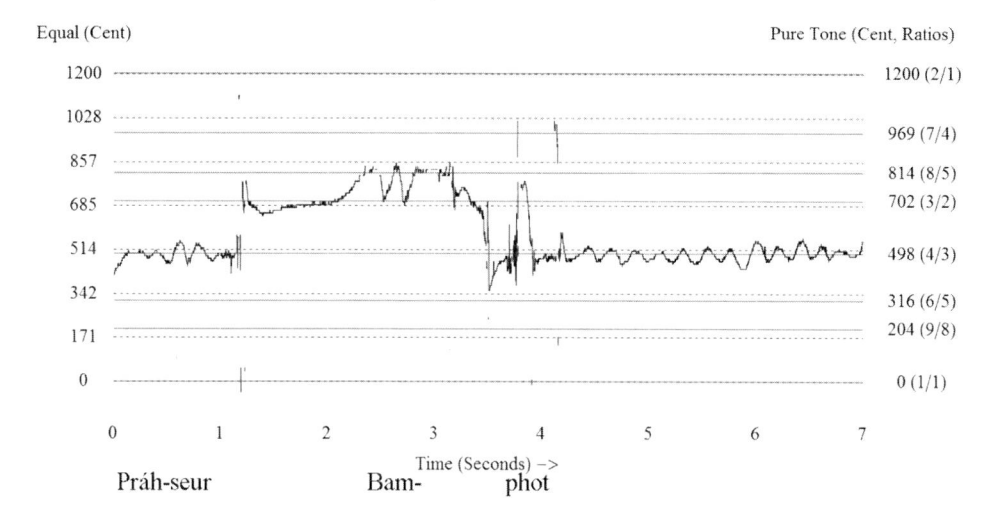

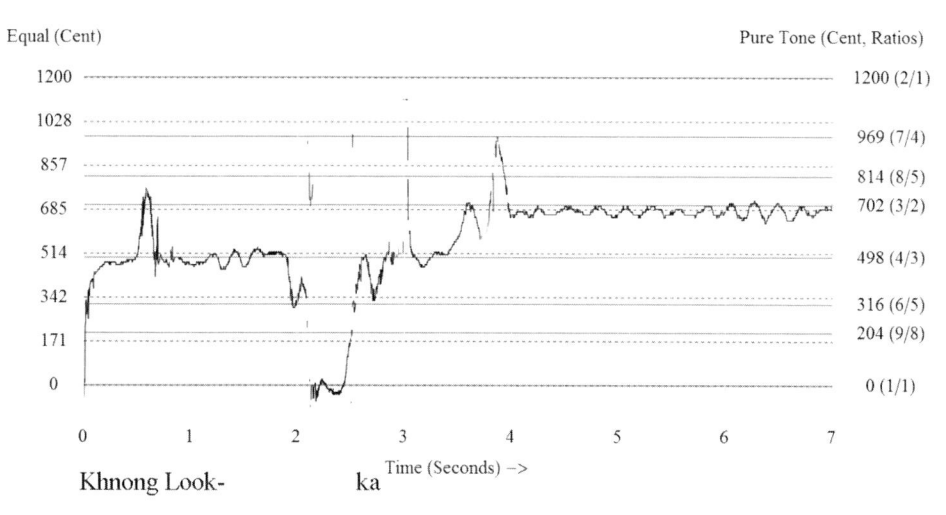

Fig. 4 a) – d): First four phrases of *Bat Sara Phanh* performance of Kai Sokmean, pitch fundamental shown. Solid lines: Western pure tone, dashed lines: Cambodian equal tuning.

299

300

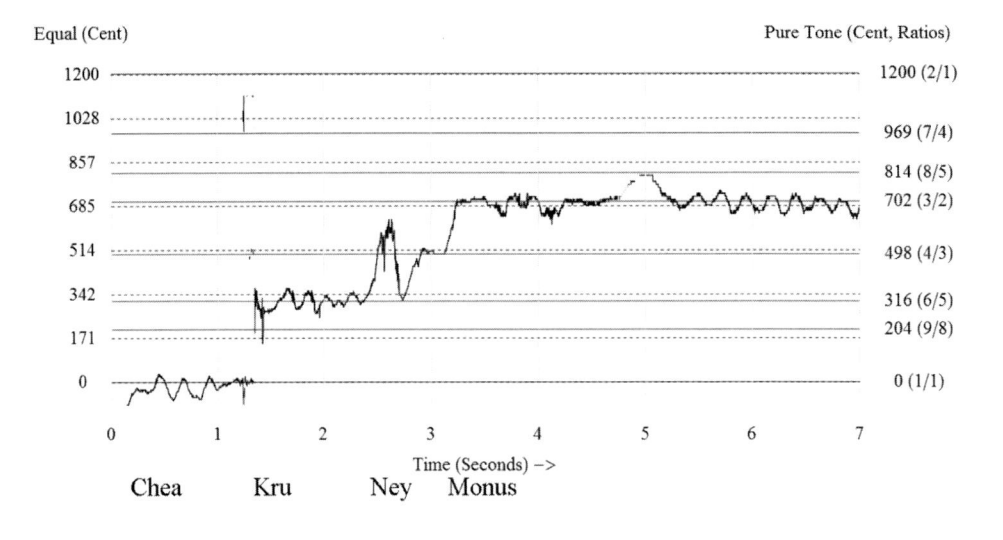

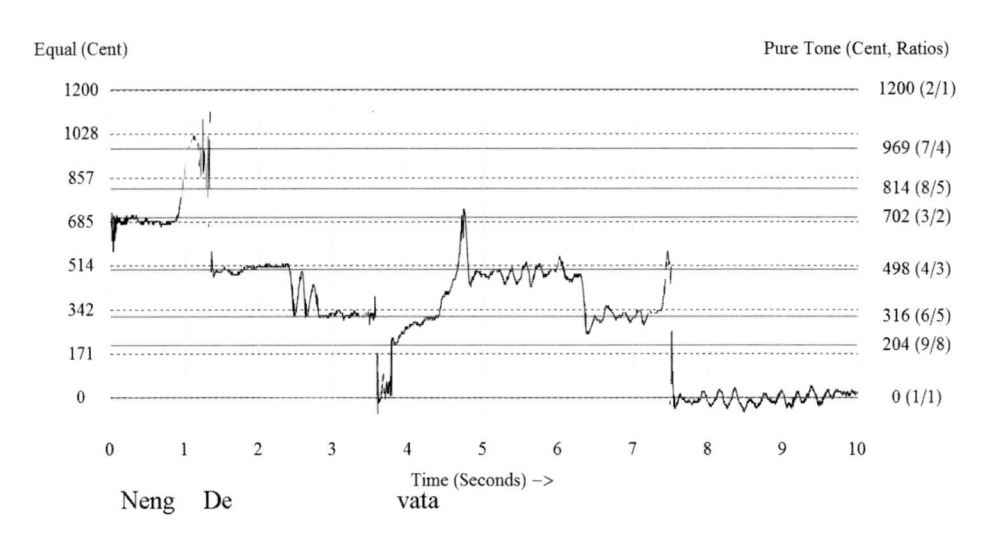

Fig. 4 e) – h) Phrase 5 – 8

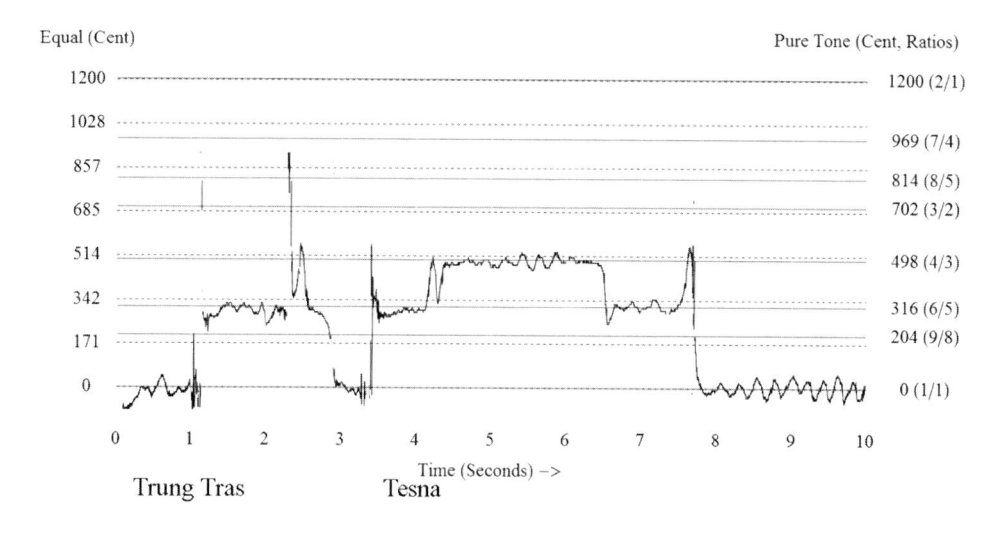

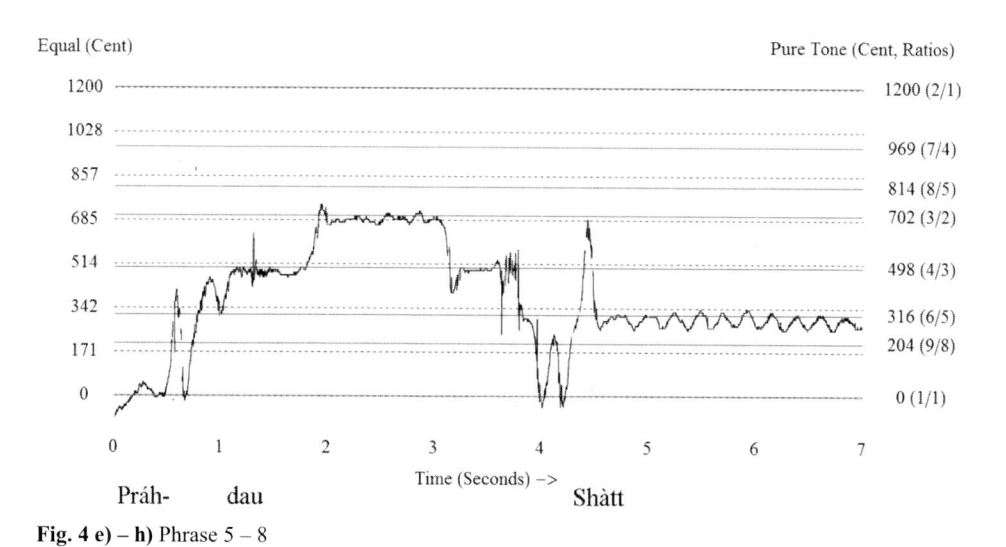

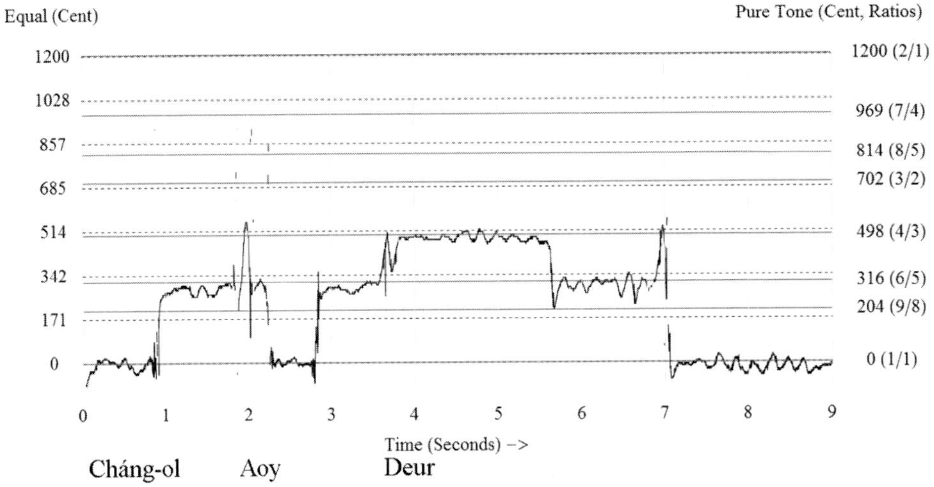

Equal (Cent)
Pure Tone (Cent, Ratios)
1200
1028
857
685
514
342
171
0
1200 (2/1)
969 (7/4)
814 (8/5)
702 (3/2)
498 (4/3)
316 (6/5)
204 (9/8)
0 (1/1)
0 1 2 3 4 5 6 7 8 9
Time (Seconds) ->
Cháng-ol Aoy Deur

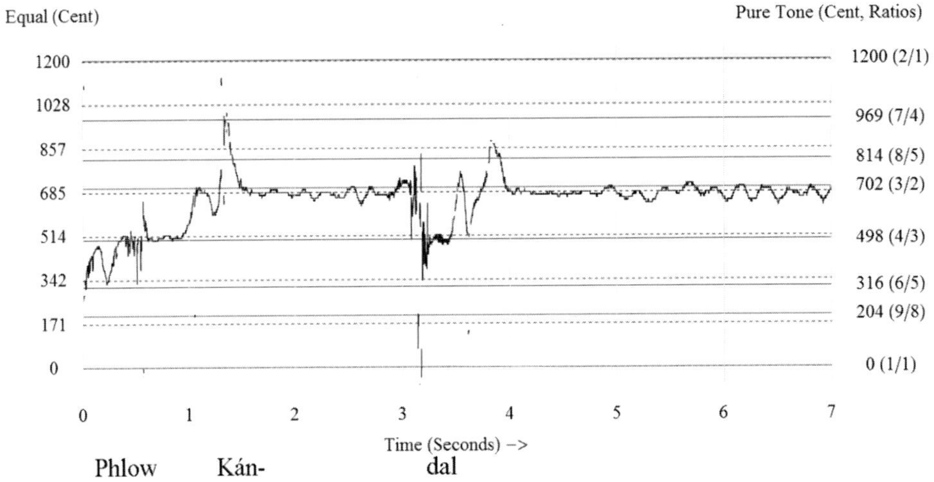

Equal (Cent)
Pure Tone (Cent, Ratios)
1200
1028
857
685
514
342
171
0
1200 (2/1)
969 (7/4)
814 (8/5)
702 (3/2)
498 (4/3)
316 (6/5)
204 (9/8)
0 (1/1)
0 1 2 3 4 5 6 7
Time (Seconds) ->
Phlow Kán- dal

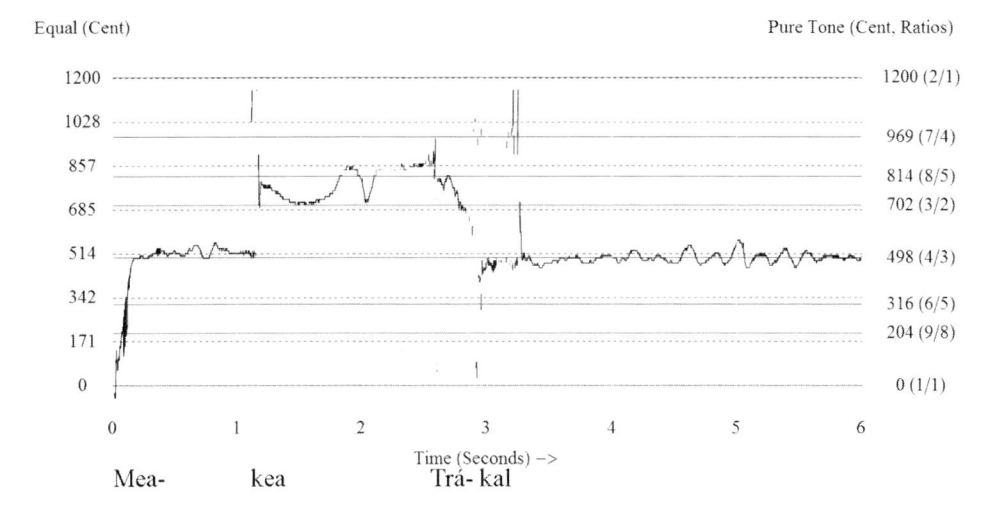

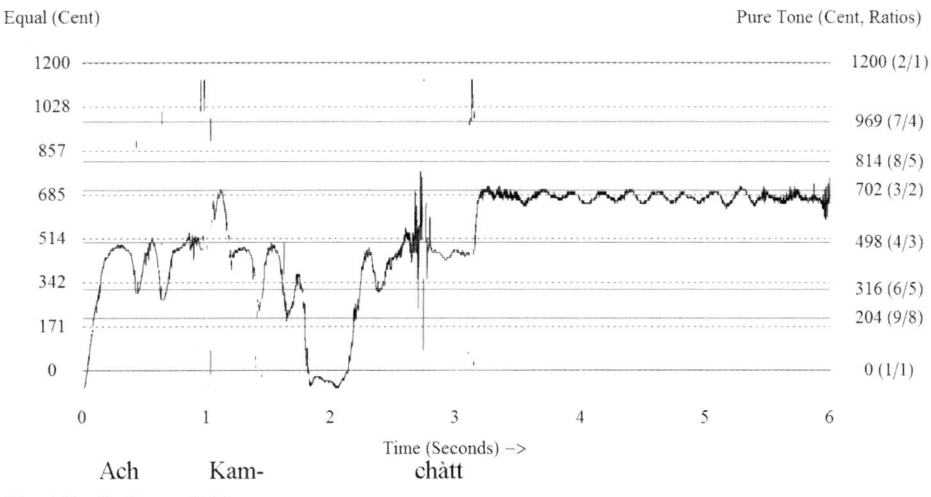

Fig. 4 i) – l): Phrase 9-12

304

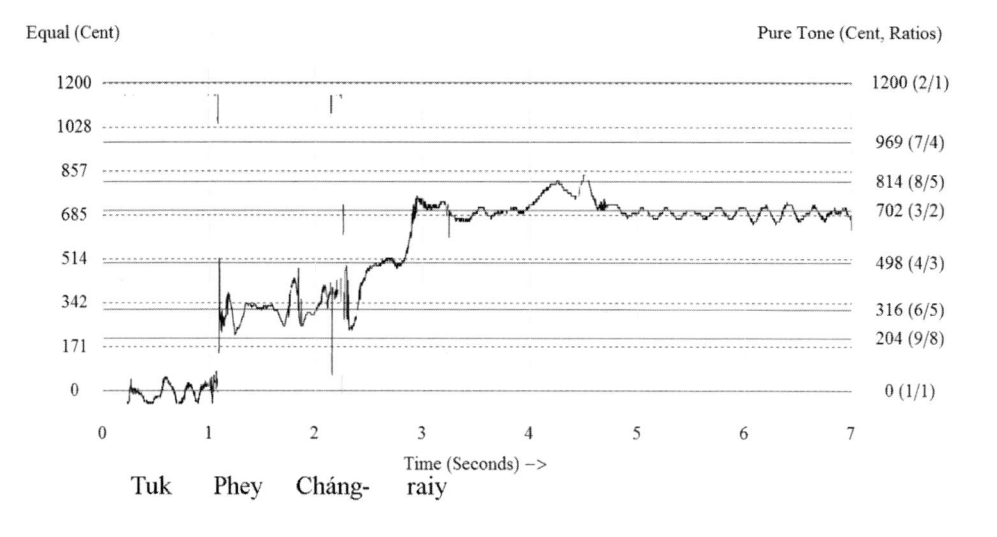

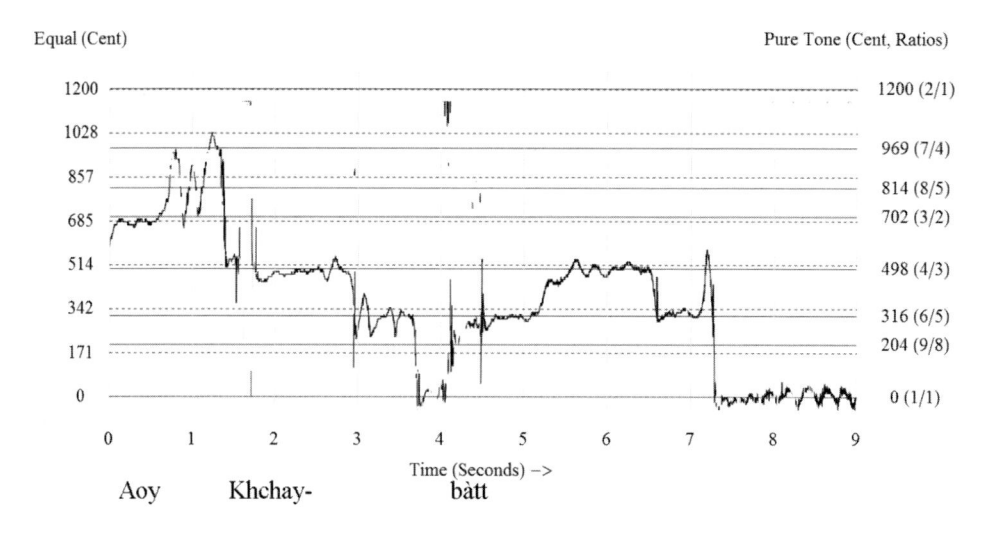

Fig. 4 m) – p): Phrase 13-16

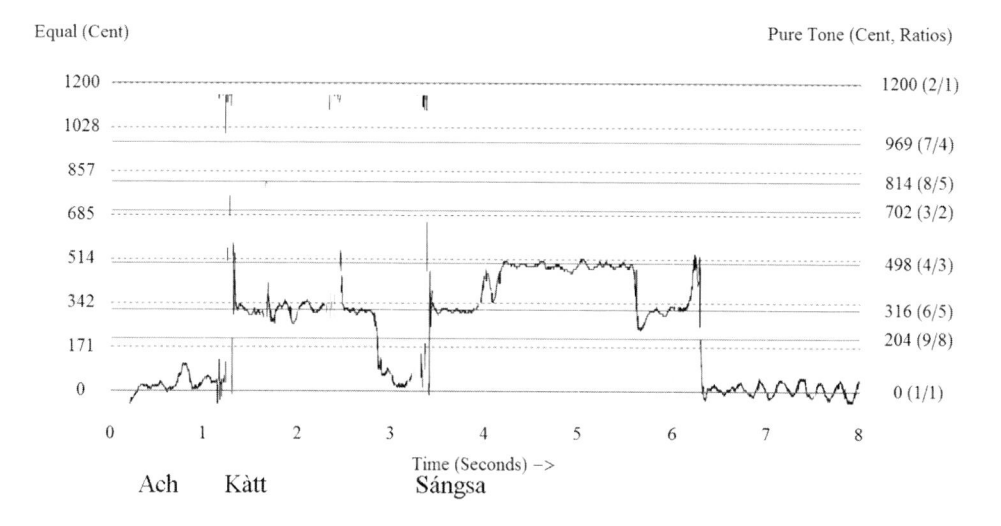

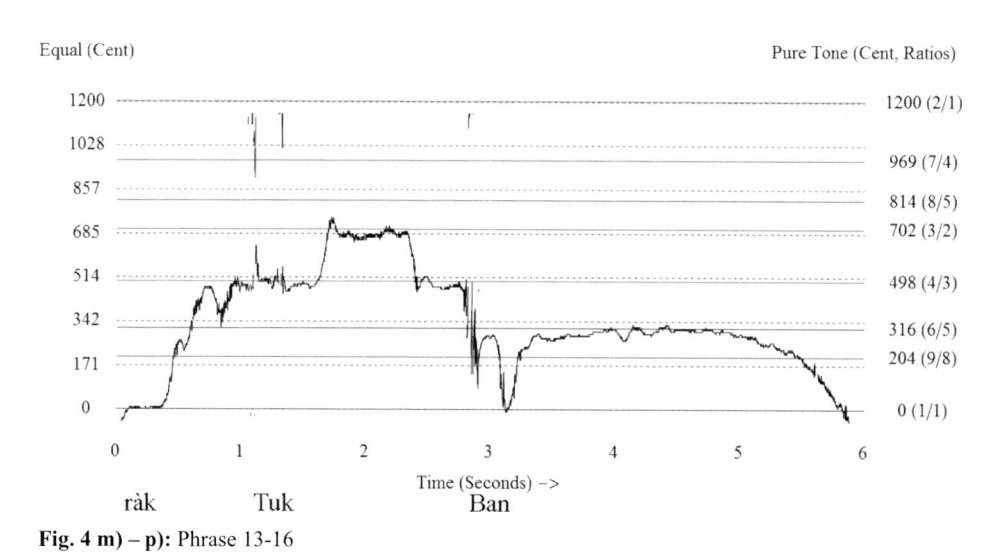

Rytis Ambrazevičius

Concerning the Question of "Loosely-Knit" Roughly Equidistant Scale in Traditional Music[1]

Abstract

It is widely accepted that asymmetries in intervals of the musical scale (i.e., inequalities of the interval steps) serve as "orientation points so that we can know 'where' we are in the scale" (Krumhansl, Snyder). This feature is often treated as universal (Dowling, Harwood, Trehub, etc.). At the same time, there is evidence of equitonics (equidistant scales) in various world musics.

Examples of equitonics can be found, *inter alia*, in European folk music (Grainger, Sachs, Sevåg, etc.). Often such scales are anchored on a framework of a fourth or fifth (i.e. the strongest consonances) and filled in with "loosely-knit" (Grainger) intermediate tones. The result is "anhemitonic heptatonism" (Sevåg). Measurements of the musical scales in Lithuanian songs (71 examples) show intermediate cases between equitonics and 12ET-diatonics, however, the principle of equitonicism predominates. Their transcribers and authors of numerous theoretical notes, however, misinterpret the scales as "Ancient Greek" and/or characteristic of "chromaticisms".

Equitonics may be more widespread throughout the world than presumed. Often diatonic "Ancient Greek" scales and scales with chromaticisms are mere misinterpretations of "anhemitonic heptatonism". Equitonics can be regarded as a "more ancient" universal characteristic of the early stages of musical phylogenesis (Alexeyev) and ontogenesis (Zurcher).

I. Introduction

The notion of "loosely-knit" equidistant scale is explained in the first part of this paper. The second part is an analysis of musical scales in Lithuanian traditional singing. Three sample repertoires containing 71 songs are employed. The results of the acoustical measurements and statistical generalizations show that the scales under investigation can be considered to be based on equitonic principles. Third, similar phenomena in other musics (centering on some European examples) are discussed. The discussion raises questions about the place of equitonics in the system of musical universals.

II. Definition of "Loosely-Knit" Equidistant Scale

To avoid any objections and misunderstandings, we should agree in the very beginning that the "equidistant scale" as considered here does not mean the sequence of sounds separated by mathematically equal intervals. First, even if the exact equidistance was intended by the performers (first of all, singers), it could never be produced because of limited jnd of pitch perception. In other words, if we measure intervals between neigh-

---

[1] This paper is reworked and supplemented version of earlier conference paper (Ambrazevičius, 2009).

boring scale steps in a hypothetical vocal performance and we find that they differ in some 10 cents, we can nevertheless safely conclude that we register a case of **exact** equitonics. Second, if the measurements show quite large and perceivable differences between the intervals, yet those intervals do not cluster into separate categories, we still can guess about possible **rough** equitonics. This presumption is especially valid if intonations of the scale steps fluctuate considerably in the course of a performance, and therefore the inter-step intervals can be defined only roughly (e.g., their averages and standard deviations can be estimated). Namely with this kind of "loosely-knit" equidistant scale we are dealing in the study.

To make it more visual, let's generate some examples. Say, we measure a sequence of intervals and get the following results (in cents): 181+162+190–184–170–167. We can safely conclude that we encounter what may be called a "loosely-knit" roughly equidistant scale (e.g., steps from the first to the fourth and back). Now imagine a different sequence: 192+204+115–104–209–205. In this case, we register the manifesttation of a non-equidistant scale as the intervals clearly cluster into two groups: narrow (104 and 115 cents) and wide (192, 204, 205, and 209 cents). Specifically, here we deal with the case of ordinary diatonics (e.g., with the first four steps of a major scale). We should not confuse that the whole tones (~200 cents) are not equal in this performance; the same can be stated about the semitones (~100 cents). First, they are never equal in a free-intoned performance. Second, remember that even, for instance, in a diatonic set of the theoretical Just intonation, the whole tones are not equal, and still this scale can be considered as diatonic, of course.

III. Analysis of Musical Scales

The present study applies the data of acoustical measurements already described in my previous papers (Ambrazevičius, 2006, etc.). Here I briefly repeat the information about the samples discussed and the acoustical methods applied.

Samples and methods

Samples of three repertoires of Lithuanian traditional singing were chosen. All three repertoires include examples of solo singing.[2] Two repertoires represent two male idiolects of the *Dzūkai* (Southern Lithuanian) vocal tradition. Both singers – Jonas Jakubauskas (henceforth Sample JJ) and Petras Zalanskas (henceforth Sample PZ) – were outstanding representatives of the tradition. Most of the recordings were made in the last three decades of the 20th century. The third repertoire group reflects the dialect of *Suvalkiečiai* (Southwestern Lithuania; henceforth Sample S) vocal tradition. The recordings of various singers were made in the 1930s.

The statistical samples of the three repertoires contain, correspondingly, 26, 20, and 25 songs.

Since the recordings of the songs were relatively long (most of the songs contained from 10 to 20 melostrophes), only one (the second) melostrophe of every song was chosen for the investigation.

---

[2] See also analysis of the sample containing polyphonic *Sutartinės* in Ambrazevičius, 2009.

For the acoustical measurements, the software programs Speech Analyzer and, later, Praat, were applied. Perceived (integral) pitches of tones were estimated from continuous tracks of log frequency automatically transcribed by the software (refer to Ambrazevičius, 2005-2006, p. 66–67, for details).

Results

Generally, certain scale notes have more than one occurrence in a melostrophe. The pitches of these occurrences differ somewhat. For the investigation presented below, the pitches were averaged, i.e., the averaged scales were considered. Then relative scales were calculated normalized to tonics, for instance, 0 (tonic), 1.88 (the second; in 12ET[3] semitones), 3.43 (the third), 4.84 (the fourth), and so on (Example PZ1). Finally, the deviations from the 12ET major scale were calculated: 1.88–2.00 = –0.12 (the second), 3.43–4.00 = –0.57 (the third), 4.84–5.00 = –0.16 (the fourth), etc. Fig. 1 shows the results for Sample JJ. It becomes clear that the scale notes acquire quite different pitch versions. Nevertheless, there is no reason to conclude that the versions differentiate into categories. For instance, the versions of the third cannot be treated as minor and major thirds as the range of the third is quite homogeneous, there are quite a few instances of various "neutral" thirds, and no clusters corresponding to minor (deviation –1) and major (deviation 0) thirds are seen.

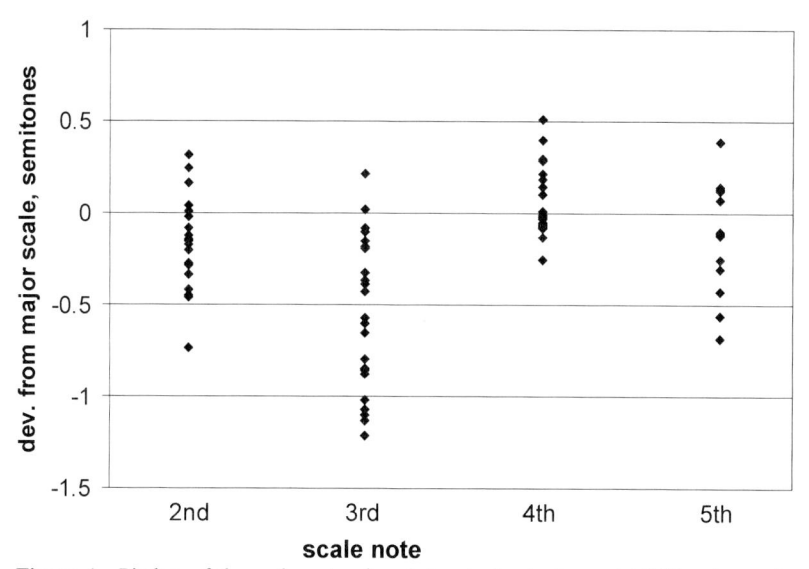

Figure 1. Pitches of the scale notes, in relation to the tonics and 12ET major scale. All songs from Sample JJ. The scale notes with few occurrences are omitted

The conclusion on homogeneity can be made for the remaining samples as well. For easier comprehension, the cumulative results are presented in simplified form: only

---

[3] twelve-tone equal temperament

medians and interquartiles are shown (Fig. 2).[4] The second is found to be generally a bit flat in comparison with the 12ET major second, the third is very flat, the fourth is a bit sharp, the fifth is more or less "normal", the sixth is noticeably flat, and the subsecond is extremely flat. The third shows the largest flexibility; its versions cover a large range of pitches.

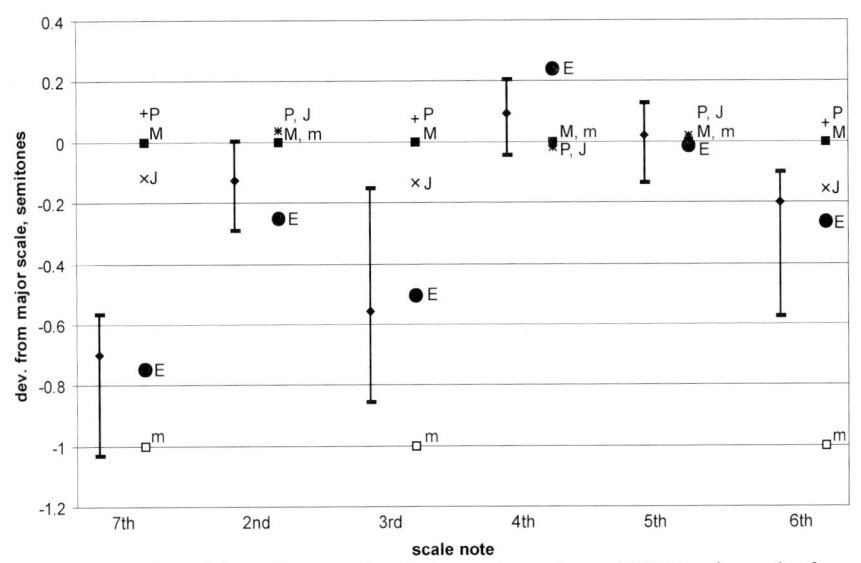

Figure 2. Pitches of the scale notes, in relation to the tonics and 12ET major scale; for cumulative Sample of performances (JJ+PZ+S). (7th scale note – subsecond – below tonic.) Medians (diamonds) and interquartiles (vertical bars) are depicted. Also values for theoretical scales are shown: M – 12ET major, m – 12ET minor, P – Pythagorean (major), J – Just intonation (major), E – equitonics with the step of 175 cents

It can be safely concluded that the samples, in general, do not resemble twelve-tone equal temperament, i.e., its diatonic subsets including the minor and major versions and other diatonic scales (e.g., so-called Ancient Greek or Gregorian modes). Possibly, the scales of some songs correspond to the abovementioned theoretical diatonic scales, i.e. they can be treated as diatonic scales with small deviations arising from the tolerable categorical zones of intonation, pitch performance rules, possible mistakes and imperfections, etc. However, the prevailing deviations are too large to be explained by such inconsistencies.

Some may speculate that not 12ET diatonics, but other theoretical diatonic scales (for instance, Pythagorean or Just intonation) are at work. To examine this possibility Figure 2 includes additional marks showing deviations of Pythagorean tuning and Just intonation from the 12ET major scale.

---

[4] See Ambrazevičius, 2009; for more detailed discussion on separate Samples.

From Fig. 2 it is clear that Pythagorean tuning and Just intonation do not provide a viable explanation. The discrepancies between these scales and the actual scales in the performances under investigation are still very large.

However, deeper examination reveals that the scales in the traditional singing discussed correspond roughly to the theoretical non-diatonic equidistant scales (equitonics). The thick dots in Fig. 2 show the equitonics with the step (the constructive interval between two neighboring scale notes) of 175 cents. The correspondence between this scale and the actual scales seems to be quite reasonable.

The hypothesis regarding the equitonal nature of the scales discussed can be verified by a supplementary technique. Majority of intervals in the melody contours under investigation are seconds or, to be precise, step-by-step movements (and not leaps) prevail. Let's measure these intervals. Figs. 3–5 show the results for the Samples (results for steps up and down are pooled).

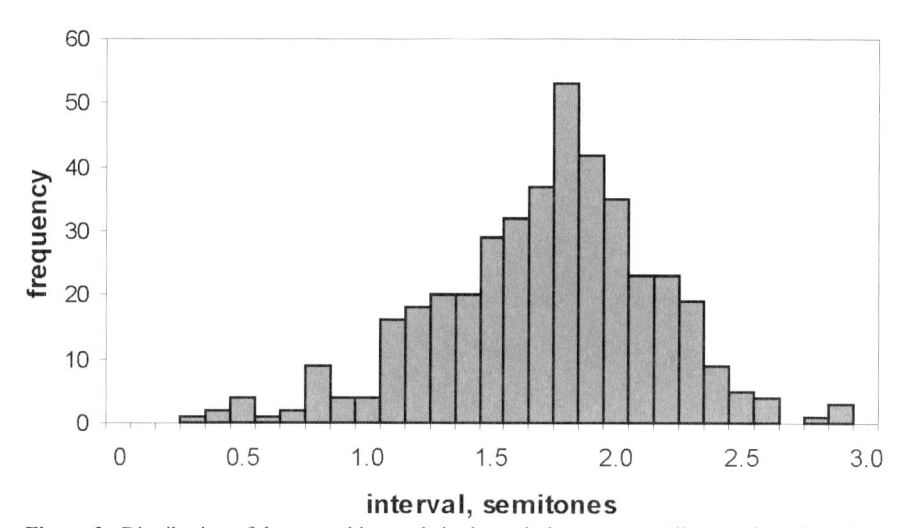

Figure 3. Distribution of the second intervals in the melody contours. All songs from Sample JJ.

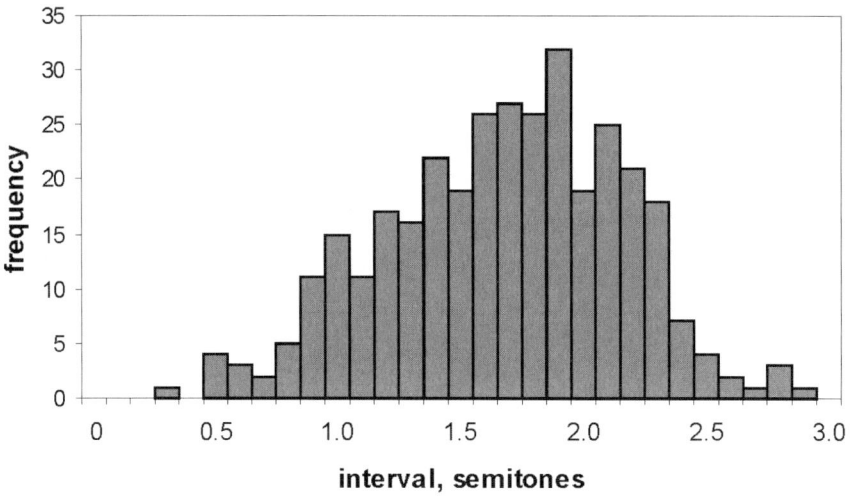

Figure 4. The same as in Fig. 3, for Sample PZ.

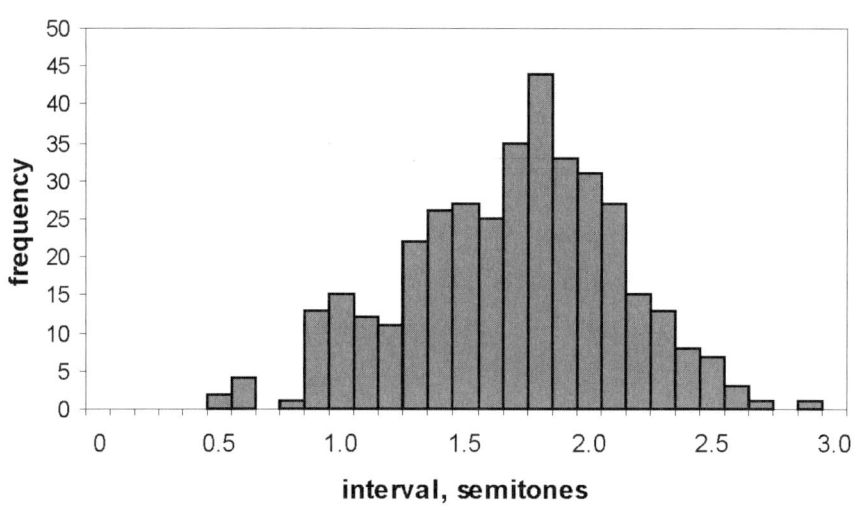

Figure 5. The same as in Fig. 3, for Sample S.

The distributions are skewed to the left. Their means are at 172, 169, and 170 cents (for the Samples JJ, PZ, and S, correspondingly). Most importantly, the distributions are quite homogeneous. It means that the seconds do not split into narrow and wide (minor and major) versions. They can be regarded as versions (though quite different) of one interval. More precisely, possibly some songs in the samples have structures close to theoretical diatonics, but cases with equitonics predominate.

The small peaks around 100 cents (most clearly standing out for the sample S) might result from partial diatonization. Even so, there is no reason to believe that the distribution clusters into two classes of intervals (semitones and whole tones) would mean the prevailing of diatonics. On the other hand, these and other obscure peaks could result from moderate sizes of the Samples.

Of course, it would be naïve to expect the scales discussed to follow an exact scheme of equidistant notes. First, as already mentioned, equitonics in practice does not mean an ideally equidistant scale; the deviations from the latter theoretical (mathematical) structure can be quite significant (see below Alexeyev's γ-intonation). Second, there can be influences of the modified (rationalized) version of equitonics, i.e. a structure based on the anchored framework of consonant notes (predominantly separated by the pure fourth or fifth) filled in with more flexibly intoned intermediate notes (also see more in the next chapter). From the ethnomusicological perspective, it can be concluded that the samples discussed contain mostly "quarttonic" and "quinttonic" tonal structures (i.e., based on tonal anchors separated by the fourth or fifth), in various proportions. Thus, the summarized graph in Fig. 2 reflects an "effective" scale which is intermediate between the 4th- and 5th-based scales. The steps in the two ideal tonal structures equal 166 cents (498/3; 4th-based structure) and 176 cents (702/4; 5th-based structure). In reference to those values, after the calculations of the corresponding values for certain scale notes, the tendencies of "sharpening" and "flattening" in Fig. 2 can be explained.

Possibly, the widest range of versions of the third results from the fact that on average the third is the most distant note from the tonal anchors: although in the 4th-based structure, it neighbours with the anchored fourth, but in the 5th-based structure, it is separated from both anchors by additional notes. Due to the significant impact of linear (horizontal) thinking, the additive strategy of the scale design is most probably quite important (as opposed to the divisive strategy in vertical thinking). In summary, the more the intermediate note is distant from the tonal anchors, the more flexible its intonation, since, in a sense, the "flexibilities" are summarized when receding from the tonal anchor.

More details describing the regularities in the scales could be adduced. However, the most important issue has been discussed: scales found in various examples of Lithuanian traditional vocal music are predominantly "loosely-knit" roughly equidistant (i.e., of equitonic-type) and in most of the cases under review cannot be treated as diatonic.[5]

IV. Discussion

The starting point of the discussion rests on the contradiction between the origin of musical scales and their ethnomusicological interpretations. In Lithuanian ethnomusicological studies, the scales discussed in the previous chapter are never referred to as equidistant, and always are treated as examples of diatonics. This is because of our 12ET-biased perception: perceptually we successfully force the musical material we hear into the 12ET-frame. From my personal experience with students, even artificially synthesized exactly equidistant pentatonics (i.e., with 240 cents in between the scale notes) tends to be perceived as "normal" pentatonics consisting of major seconds and minor thirds, though accompanied by remarks about some "mistuning".

---

[5] The closeness of the certain musical scale to diatonics or equitonics can also be quantitatively evaluated with the help of the "coefficient of diatonic contrast", see Ambrazevičius, 2006.

It is even easier with scales such as the ones analyzed in this paper. It was demonstrated that these scales are (mis)perceived as so-called Ancient Greek or Gregorian scales (Ambrazevičius, 2006) and how fictitious "chromatic changes" appear as the result of slight deviations caused by pitch performance rules (Ambrazevičius & Wiśniewska, 2008). Of course, the problem is closely connected with the transcriptional means provided by the standard Western five-lined staff, which reflects and presupposes diatonical thinking unless special modifications of the orthography are used.

The abovementioned studies dealt with Lithuanian traditional music, but what about other European musical traditions? Contrary to the Lithuanian convention, the phenomenon of equidistant scales was noted, though not often. For instance, Reidar Sevåg found "anhemitonic heptatonics" in the scales of Norwegian *langeleik* (1974)[6] and Percy Grainger has reported "one single loosely-knit modal folksong scale" in Lincolnshire (as cited in Powers & Cowdery, 2001, p. 824).

Russian ethnomusicologist Eduard Alexeyev argues that "tonal subordination" ("t-intonation") corresponding to the modern perception of mode was preceded by "tonal coordination" ("γ-intonation") characteristic of roughly proportional steps between "wandering tones" (Alexeyev 1976, 1986). He found the relics of "γ-intonation" in Yakut vocal tradition as well as in various Eastern European traditions. If we apply Haeckel's "biogenetical law", Alexeyev's and similar conceptions on phylogenesis of musical scales are in fair agreement with the observations on ontogenesis of the scales: at a certain stage of development, young children sing "roughly equidistant" scales, i.e., they do not differentiate between the semitone and whole tone, and the tones are "wandering", i.e., the intonation is not fixed. Only later does the intonation stabilize and the contrast of semitone and whole tone appears (Zurcher, 1994, etc.).[7]

Sometimes indirect notes tell us about the probable manifestations of equitonics. For instance, Nettl wrote, "One interval widely used in primitive music but foreign to Western is the so-called neutral third, which is roughly between the tempered major and minor thirds" (1972, p. 47). If we relate this statement with the results in the previous chapter, it becomes clear that most probably we are dealing with equidistant scales: the third is noticed specifically because of its largest deviation from 12ET while the other intervals deviate less and thus remain acceptable as "normal" (for that point see also Ambrazevičius, 2006).

To summarize, it seems that equidistant scales are found nowadays (or in the not too distant past) in European musical traditions.[8] However, because of the 12ET-biased

---

[6] I would like to quote him again: "...out of the great amount of *langeleik* scales can be abstracted a superimposed scale structure which is heptatonic and has a fixed framework of fundamental, fifth and octave. The other intervals are variable over a spectrum of a little more than a quarter tone... (Sevåg, 1974, p. 210).

[7] I shorten the comprehensive description of the phylogenetical and ontogenetical parallels. It should be stressed that there is fair agreement between not mentioned elements of both geneses as well. Also, see the explanation of the methodological discrepancies in the studies of production and perception (e.g., the studies by Trehub and colleagues) of musical scales by little children (Zurcher, 1994).

[8] I intentionally omit the discussion on the presumably equidistant scales in exotic musical cultures produced by idiophones (Indonesian gamelan, African xylophones, etc.). These scales should be considered taking into account the phenomenon of pitch perception in the case of inharmonic sounds (Schneider, 2001, 2002, etc.).

perception, the latter cases tend to be considered as a manifestation of diatonics. Even the idea that a certain musical scale can be other than diatonic is rarely considered.

It is widely accepted that asymmetries in the intervals of the musical scale (i.e., inequalities of the interval steps) serve as "orientation points so that we can know 'where' we are in the scale" (Rosch, 1975, Krumhansl, 1979, Sloboda, 1989, etc.). This feature is often treated as universal (for instance, Dowling & Harwood, p. 101).

We must consider whether statements regarding the universality of asymmetry are based on a vast array of seemingly diatonic examples that are actually not diatonic at all. It is true that the asymmetries work as reference or orientation points, but maybe they are not that necessary for the perception characteristics of earlier stages of mode development. There may be other means for "finding where we are in the scale" (such as melodic and metrorhythmic markers or pitch performance rules, etc.)? Anyway, it seems that the universal of scale asymmetry works, primarily in contemporary musical thinking, but then it is not clear whether it can be treated as a true universal. The principle of rough equidistance can probably be regarded as a "more ancient" universal characteristic of the early stages of musical phylogenesis and ontogenesis. Thus we can probably think about types of quasiuniversals that sometimes work in different domains, and sometimes overlap.

References

Alexeyev, E. (1976). *Problemy formirovanija lada*. Moscow: Muzyka.

Alexeyev, E. (1986). *Rannefol'klornoe intonirovanie. Zvukovysotnyj aspekt*. Moscow: Sovetskij kompozitor.

Ambrazevičius, R. (2005-2006). Modeling of scales in traditional solo singing. *Musicae Scientiae, Special Issue "Interdisciplinary Musicology"*, 65–87.

Ambrazevičius, R. (2006). Pseudo-Greek modes in traditional music as result of misperception. In M. Baroni, A. R. Addessi, R. Caterina, & M. Costa (Eds.), *ICMPC9. Proceedings of the 9th International Conference on Music Perception and Cognition. 6th Triennial Conference of the European Society for the Cognitive Sciences of Music. Alma Mater Studiorum University of Bologna, Italy, August 22–26, 2006* (pp. 1817–1822) [CD]. Bologna: Bononia University Press.

Ambrazevičius, R., & Wiśniewska, I. (2008). Chromaticisms or performance rules? Evidence from traditional singing. *Journal of Interdisciplinary Music Studies, 2 (1&2)*, 19–31.

Ambrazevičius, R. (2009). Returning to musical universals: Question of equidistant scale. In J. Louhivuori, S. Saarikallio, T. Himberg, & P.-S. Eerola (Eds.), *ICMPC9. Proceedings of the 7th Triennial Conference of the European Society for the Cognitive Sciences of Music (ESCOM 2009). Jyväskylä, Finland*. Retrieved June 22, 2011, from: https://jyx.jyu.fi/dspace/bitstream/ handle/ 123456789/20847/urn_nbn_fi_jyu-2009411231.pdf

Dowling, J., & Harwood, D. (1986). *Music cognition*. Orlando: Academic Press.

Krumhansl, C. (1979). The psychological representation of musical pitch in a tonal context. *Cognitive Psychology, 11*, 346–374.

Nettl, B. (1972). *Music in primitive culture*. Cambridge: Harvard University Press.

Powers, H. S., & Cowdery, J. (2001). Mode, $IV, 2. Modal scales and melody types in Anglo-American folksong. In S. Sadie (Ed.), *The New Grove dictionary of music and musicians* (pp. 823-829). London: Macmillan Publishers Limited.

Rosch, E. (1975). Cognitive reference points. *Cognitive Psychology, 7*, 532–547.

Schneider, A. (2001). Sound, pitch, and scale: From "tone measurements" to sonological analysis in ethnomusicology. *Ethnomusicology, 45 (3)*, 489–519.

Schneider, A. (2002). On tonometrical and sonological analyses of "exotic" instruments: From Stumpf's measurements to the present. In G. Berlin & A. Simon (Eds.), *Music archiving in the world. Papers presented at the Conference on the occasion of the 100th anniversary of the Berlin Phonogramm-Archiv* (pp. 247–257). Berlin: Verlag für Wissenschaft und Bildung Staatliche Museen Berlin.

Sloboda, J. A. (1989). *The musical mind. The cognitive psychoogy of music* (reprint from 1985). Oxford: Clarendon Press.

Sevåg, R. (1974). Neutral tones and the problem of mode in Norwegian folk music. In G. Hilleström (Ed.), *Studia Instrumentorum Musicae Popularis III* (pp. 207-213). Stockholm: Musikhistoriska Museet.

Zurcher, P. (1994). *The path of the ant.* Retrieved April 28, 2009, from http://musicweb.hmt-hannover.de/escom/english/Newsletter/NL9e/ZurcherE.html

List of contributors to this volume

Ambrazevičius, Rytis (rytisam@delfi.lt), Faculty of the Humanities, Kaunas University of Technologies, Lithuania

Bader, Rolf (R_Bader@t-online.de), Institute of Musicology, University of Hamburg

Beurmann, Andreas (ABeurmann@aol.com), Institute of Musicology, University of Hamburg

Frieler, Klaus (klaus.frieler@uni-hamburg.de), Institute of Musicology, University of Hamburg

Höger, Frank (frankhoeger@alice-dsl.de), Hamburg

Korries, Jörg (korries@omniversum.de), Hamburg

Moeller, Jan Clemens (JCMDIGITON@aol.com), Hamburg

Mores, Robert (mores@mit.haw-hamburg.de), Department Medientechnik, Hamburg University of Applied Science

Morgenstern, Ulrich (ulrich.morgenstern@t-online.de), Institute of Musicology, Johann Wolfgang Goethe-University, Frankfurt/Main

Müllensiefen, Daniel (d.mullensiefen@gold.ac.uk), Department of Psychology, Goldsmiths, University of London, United Kingdom

Pfeifle, Florian (Florian.Pfeifle@haw-hamburg.de), Institute of Musicology, University of Hamburg

Schneider, Albrecht (aschneid@uni-hamburg.de), Institute of Musicology, University of Hamburg

Strauf, Till (strauf@gmx.net), Hamburg

Takada, Orie (orie_deutschland@hotmail.com), Institute of Musicology, University of Hamburg

von Ruschkowski, Arne (arne.von.ruschkowski@uni-hamburg.de), Institute of Musicology, University of Hamburg

Tsatsishvili, Valeri (valeri.oberon@gmail.com), Institute of Musicology, University of Jyväskylä, Finland

Wiggins, Geraint (g.wiggins@gold.ac.uk), Department of Computing, Goldsmiths, University of London, United Kingdom

Ziemer, Tim (T.Ziemer1@gmx.de), Institute of Musicology, University of Hamburg

HAMBURGER JAHRBUCH FÜR MUSIKWISSENSCHAFT

Herausgegeben vom Musikwissenschaftlichen Institut
der Universität Hamburg

Das *Hamburger Jahrbuch für Musikwissenschaft* besteht seit 1974. Jeder Band ist thematisch gebunden, wobei wechselweise musikalische Gattungen, Epochen der europäischen Musikgeschichte, bedeutende Komponistenpersönlichkeiten oder fachsystematische Grundsatzfragen ins Zentrum treten.

Die Bände 1-13 sind im Laaber-Verlag, 93164 Laaber, erschienen.

Ab Band 14 erscheint diese Reihe im Verlag Peter Lang, Internationaler Verlag der Wissenschaften, Frankfurt am Main.

Band 14 Peter Petersen/Hans-Gerd Winter (Hrsg.): Büchner-Opern. Georg Büchner in der Musik des 20. Jahrhunderts. 1996.

Band 15 Annette Kreutziger-Herr (Hrsg.): Das Andere. Eine Spurensuche in der Musikgeschichte des 19. und 20. Jahrhunderts. 1998.

Band 16 Peter Petersen/Helmut Rösing (Hrsg.): 50 Jahre Musikwissenschaftliches Institut in Hamburg. Bestandsaufnahme – aktuelle Forschung – Ausblick. 1999.

Band 17 Constantin Floros/Friedrich Geiger/Thomas Schäfer (Hrsg.): Komposition als Kommunikation. Zur Musik des 20. Jahrhunderts. 2000.

Band 18 Hans Joachim Marx (Hrsg.): Beiträge zur Musikgeschichte Hamburgs vom Mittelalter bis in die Neuzeit. 2001.

Band 19 Helmut Rösing / Albrecht Schneider / Martin Pfleiderer (Hrsg.): Musikwissenschaft und populäre Musik. Versuch einer Bestandsaufnahme. 2002.

Band 20 Peter Petersen (Hrsg.): Hans Werner Henze. Die Vorträge des internationalen Henze-Symposions am Musikwissenschaftlichen Institut der Universität Hamburg. 28. bis 30. Juni 2001. 2003.

Band 21 Claudia Maurer Zenck (Hrsg.): Der Orpheus-Mythos von der Antike bis zur Gegenwart. Die Vorträge der interdisziplinären Ringvorlesung an der Universität Hamburg, Sommersemester 2003. 2004.

Band 22 Claudia Maurer Zenck (Hrsg.): Musiktheater in Hamburg um 1800. 2005.

Band 23 Beatrix Borchard / Claudia Maurer Zenck (Hrsg.): Alkestis: Opfertod und Wiederkehr. Interpretationen. 2007.

Band 24 Albrecht Schneider (ed.): Systematic and Comparative Musicology: Concepts, Methods, Findings. 2008.

Band 25 Rolf Bader (ed./Hrsg.): Musical Acoustics, Neurocognition and Psychology of Music. Musikalische Akustik, Neurokognition und Musikpsychologie. Current Research in Systematic Musicology at the Institute of Musicology, University of Hamburg. Aktuelle Forschung der Systematischen Musikwissenschaft am Institut für Musikwissenschaft, Universität Hamburg. 2009.

Band 26 Friedrich Geiger (Hrsg.): Musikkulturgeschichte heute. Historische Musikwissenschaft an der Universität Hamburg. 2009.

Band 27 Friedrich Geiger / Frank Hentschel (Hrsg.): Zwischen „U" und „E". Grenzüberschreitungen in der Musik nach 1950. 2011.

Band 28 Albrecht Schneider / Arne von Ruschkowski (eds.): Systematic Musicology: Empirical and Theoretical Studies. 2011.

Albrecht Schneider (ed.)

Systematic and Comparative Musicology: Concepts, Methods, Findings

Frankfurt am Main, Berlin, Bern, Bruxelles, New York, Oxford, Wien, 2008.
446 pp., num. fig., tab. and graph.
Hamburger Jahrbuch für Musikwissenschaft.
Editor: Musikwissenschaftliches Institut der Universität Hamburg. Vol. 24
ISBN 978-3-631-57953-4 · pb. € 43,80*

This volume presents essays on the theory, methodology, and disciplinary history of Systematic and Comparative Musicology as well as on concepts of current empirical research. Part 1 is devoted to Systematic Musicology which is viewed as a transdiciplinary approach to fundamental music research, on the one hand, and as a field of learning which is offered as an academic subject in universities, on the other. Part 1 also includes articles which illustrate modern research concepts many of which are based on experimental and other empirical methods as well as on computational and modelling approaches. The articles concern problems which range from acoustics and psychoacoustics to neuromusicology and music cognition. Part 2 addresses issues in Comparative Musicology and Ethnomusicology, for instance the relevance of comparative methods as applied to the study of non-western musical phenomena. Further, sound analysis combined with fieldwork as well as modelling based on ethnomathematical considerations are given special notice. Aspects of theory and disciplinary history are also covered in this section which moreover includes findings obtained from actual fieldwork.

Contents: Systematic and Comparative Musicology: concepts, methodology, disciplinary history · Experimental and empirical research · Computational and modelling techniques · Neuromusicology · Music cognition · Acoustics and psychoacoustics · Comparative approaches and comparative methodology · Concepts of ethnomusicology · Data and Sound analyses in ethnomusicology

Frankfurt am Main · Berlin · Bern · Bruxelles · New York · Oxford · Wien
Distribution: Verlag Peter Lang AG
Moosstr. 1, CH-2542 Pieterlen
Telefax 00 41 (0) 32/376 17 27

*The €-price includes German tax rate
Prices are subject to change without notice
Homepage http://www.peterlang.de